Design Things

Design Thinking, Design Theory

Ken Friedman and Erik Stolterman, editors

Design Things, A. Telier (Thomas Binder, Giorgio De Michelis, Pelle Ehn, Giulio Jacucci, Per Linde, and Ina Wagner), 2011

Design Things

A. Telier
Thomas Binder, Giorgio De Michelis, Pelle Ehn, Giulio Jacucci, Per Linde,
and Ina Wagner

The MIT Press
Cambridge, Massachusetts
London, England

For information about special quantity discounts, please email special_sales@mitpress.mit.edu

This book was set in Stone Sans and Stone Serif by Toppan Best-set Premedia Limited. Printed and bound in the United States of America.

Library of Congress Cataloging-in-Publication Data

Design things / A. Telier . . . [et al.].
   p.   cm.—(Design thinking)
"Thomas Binder, Giorgio De Michelis, Pelle Ehn, Giulio Jacucci, Per Linde, and Ina Wagner."
Includes bibliographical references and index.
ISBN 978-0-262-01627-8 (hardcover : alk. paper)
1. Architecture and technology. 2. Design and technology. 3. Architecture—Psychological aspects. 4. Design—Study and teaching (Higher). I. ATELIER (Project).
NA2543.T43D47   2011
724'.7—dc22

2011004587

10   9   8   7   6   5   4   3   2

Contents

Series Foreword

As professions go, design is relatively young. The practice of design predates professions. In fact, the practice of design—making things to serve a useful goal, making tools—predates the human race. Making tools is one of the attributes that made us human in the first place.

Design, in the most generic sense of the word, began over 2.5 million years ago when *Homo habilis* manufactured the first tools. Human beings were designing well before we began to walk upright. Four hundred thousand years ago, we began to manufacture spears. By forty thousand years ago, we had moved up to specialized tools.

Urban design and architecture came along ten thousand years ago in Mesopotamia. Interior architecture and furniture design probably emerged with them. It was another five thousand years before graphic design and typography got their start in Sumeria with the development of cuneiform. After that, things picked up speed.

All goods and services are designed. The urge to design—to consider a situation, imagine a better situation, and act to create that improved situation—goes back to our prehuman ancestors. Making tools helped us to become what we are—design helped to make us human.

Today, the word "design" means many things. The common factor linking them is service, and designers are engaged in a service profession in which the results of their work meet human needs.

Design is first of all a process. The word "design" entered the English language in the 1500s as a verb, with the first written citation of the verb dated to the year 1548. *Merriam-Webster's Collegiate Dictionary* defines the verb "design" as "to conceive and plan out in the mind; to have as a specific purpose; to devise for a specific function or end." Related to these is the act of drawing, with an emphasis on the nature of the drawing as a plan or map, as well as "to draw plans for; to create, fashion, execute or construct according to plan."

Half a century later, the word began to be used as a noun, with the first cited use of the noun "design" occurring in 1588. *Merriam-Webster's* defines the noun as "a

particular purpose held in view by an individual or group; deliberate, purposive planning; a mental project or scheme in which means to an end are laid down." Here,
too, purpose and planning toward desired outcomes are central. Among these are "a
preliminary sketch or outline showing the main features of something to be executed;
an underlying scheme that governs functioning, developing or unfolding; a plan or
protocol for carrying out or accomplishing something; the arrangement of elements
or details in a product or work of art." Today, we design large, complex process,
systems, and services, and we design organizations and structures to produce them.
Design has changed considerably since our remote ancestors made the first stone tools.

At a highly abstract level, Herbert Simon's definition covers nearly all imaginable
instances of design. To design, Simon writes, is to "[devise] courses of action aimed at
changing existing situations into preferred ones" (Simon, *The Sciences of the Artificial*,
2nd ed., MIT Press, 1982, p. 129). Design, properly defined, is the entire process across
the full range of domains required for any given outcome.

But the design process is always more than a general, abstract way of working.
Design takes concrete form in the work of the service professions that meet human
needs, a broad range of making and planning disciplines. These include industrial
design, graphic design, textile design, furniture design, information design, process
design, product design, interaction design, transportation design, educational design,
systems design, urban design, design leadership, and design management, as well as
architecture, engineering, information technology, and computer science.

These fields focus on different subjects and objects. They have distinct traditions,
methods, and vocabularies, used and put into practice by distinct and often dissimilar
professional groups. Although the traditions dividing these groups are distinct,
common boundaries sometimes form a border. Where this happens, they serve as
meeting points where common concerns build bridges. Today, ten challenges uniting
the design professions form such a set of common concerns.

Three performance challenges, four substantive challenges, and three contextual
challenges bind the design disciplines and professions together as a common field.
The performance challenges arise because all design professions:

1. act on the physical world;
2. address human needs; and
3. generate the built environment.

In the past, these common attributes were not sufficient to transcend the boundaries
of tradition. Today, objective changes in the larger world give rise to four substantive
challenges that are driving convergence in design practice and research. These substantive challenges are:

1. increasingly ambiguous boundaries between artifacts, structure, and process;
2. increasingly large-scale social, economic, and industrial frames;

3. an increasingly complex environment of needs, requirements, and constraints; and
4. information content that often exceeds the value of physical substance.

These challenges require new frameworks of theory and research to address contemporary problem areas while solving specific cases and problems. In professional design practice, we often find that solving design problems requires interdisciplinary teams with a transdisciplinary focus. Fifty years ago, a sole practitioner and an assistant or two might have solved most design problems; today, we need groups of people with skills across several disciplines, and the additional skills that enable professionals to work with, listen to, and learn from each other as they solve problems.

Three contextual challenges define the nature of many design problems today. While many design problems function at a simpler level, these issues affect many of the major design problems that challenge us, and these challenges also affect simple design problems linked to complex social, mechanical, or technical systems. These issues are:

1. a complex environment in which many projects or products cross the boundaries of several organizations, stakeholder, producer, and user groups;
2. projects or products that must meet the expectations of many organizations, stakeholders, producers, and users; and
3. demands at every level of production, distribution, reception, and control.

These ten challenges require a qualitatively different approach to professional design practice than was the case in earlier times. Past environments were simpler. They made simpler demands. Individual experience and personal development were sufficient for depth and substance in professional practice. While experience and development are still necessary, they are no longer sufficient. Most of today's design challenges require analytic and synthetic planning skills that cannot be developed through practice alone.

Professional design practice today involves advanced knowledge. This knowledge is not solely a higher level of professional practice. It is also a qualitatively different form of professional practice that emerges in response to the demands of the information society and the knowledge economy to which it gives rise.

In a recent essay ("Why Design Education Must Change," *Core77*, November 26, 2010), Donald Norman challenges the premises and practices of the design profession. In the past, designers operated on the belief that talent and a willingness to jump into problems with both feet gives them an edge in solving problems. Norman writes:

In the early days of industrial design, the work was primarily focused upon physical products. Today, however, designers work on organizational structure and social problems, on interaction, service, and experience design. Many problems involve complex social and political issues. As a result, designers have become applied behavioral scientists, but they are woefully undereducated for the task. Designers often fail to understand the complexity of the issues and the depth of knowledge already known. They claim that fresh eyes can produce novel solutions, but then they wonder why these solutions are seldom implemented, or if implemented, why they fail. Fresh eyes can indeed produce insightful results, but the eyes must also be educated and knowledgeable. Designers often lack the requisite understanding. Design schools do not train students about these complex issues, about the interlocking complexities of human and social behavior, about the behavioral sciences, technology, and business. There is little or no training in science, the scientific method, and experimental design.

This is not industrial design in the sense of designing products, but industry-related design, design as thought and action for solving problems and imagining new futures. This new MIT Press series of books emphasizes strategic design to create value through innovative products and services, and it emphasizes design as service through rigorous creativity, critical inquiry, and an ethics of respectful design. This rests on a sense of understanding, empathy, and appreciation for people, for nature, and for the world we shape through design. Our goal as editors is to develop a series of vital conversations that help designers and researchers to serve business, industry, and the public sector for positive social and economic outcomes.

We will present books that bring a new sense of inquiry to the design, helping to shape a more reflective and stable design discipline able to support a stronger profession grounded in empirical research, generative concepts, and the solid theory that gives rise to what W. Edwards Deming described as profound knowledge (Deming, *The New Economics for Industry, Government, Education*, MIT, Center for Advanced Engineering Study, 1993). For Deming, a physicist, engineer, and designer, profound knowledge comprised systems thinking and the understanding of processes embedded in systems; an understanding of variation and the tools we need to understand variation; a theory of knowledge; and a foundation in human psychology. This is the beginning of "deep design"—the union of deep practice with robust intellectual inquiry.

A series on design thinking and theory faces the same challenges that we face as a profession. On one level, design is a general human process that we use to understand and to shape our world. Nevertheless, we cannot address this process or the world in its general, abstract form. Rather, we meet the challenges of design in specific challenges, addressing problems or ideas in a situated context. The challenges we face as designers today are as diverse as the problems clients bring us. We are involved in design for economic anchors, economic continuity, and economic growth. We design for urban needs and rural needs, for social development and creative communities. We are involved with environmental sustainability and economic policy, agriculture competitive crafts for export, competitive products and brands for micro-enterprises, developing new products for bottom-of-pyramid markets and redeveloping old products for mature or wealthy markets. Within the framework of design, we are also challenged to design for extreme situations, for biotech, nanotech, and new materials, and design for social business, as well as conceptual challenges for worlds that do not yet exist such as the world beyond the Kurzweil singularity—and for new visions of the world that does exist.

The Design Thinking, Design Theory series from the MIT Press will explore these issues and more—meeting them, examining them, and helping designers to address them.

Join us in this journey.

Ken Friedman   Erik Stolterman
Editors, Design Thinking, Design Theory Series

Author Biography

Even if "A. Telier" has been intensively doing research on interaction design and related areas for the last twenty years, his name is not known in the research community. Probably from a strong case of shyness, or some other form of psychological fragility, during these years he (or she) has hidden behind a large variety of pseudonyms. We know for certain that he has widely published and has frequently appeared in Aarhus and Malmö as Pelle Ehn; in Copenhagen he has also gone by the name of Thomas Binder. In Italy he is well known as Giorgio De Michelis, while in Wien he has adopted a feminine pseudonym: Ina Wagner. Moreover, in recent years he has augmented the confusion by creating new younger aliases: in Denmark and Sweden he has appeared as Per Linde, while between Finland and Italy he appears under the name of Giulio Jacucci. This list is not complete, but illustrates adequately a behavior whose deep reasons merit attention. It seems as if he or she needs a multiplicity of personalities to deal with a complex subject like design, investigating and practicing several aspects of it as well as proposing different viewpoints on it, without being able to take a consistently uniform point of view.

A turning point in his/her life has been the project *Atelier* (the name cannot be casual!) where, with all his/her different names he/she has played almost all the roles, multiplying him-/herself like a Fregoli of research. At the end of the *Atelier* project, A. Telier has spent some years reflecting on its outcomes, coming out finally with this book—*Design Things*—which he signs for the first time with his/her true name. From many viewpoints *Design Things* can be considered, therefore, the synthesis of this twenty-year research.

Acknowledgments

A book is a thing as it lies in front of the reader, as it enters the bookshelf of students, or becomes part of an argument. It is a thing to be appreciated, appropriated, contested, or rejected as it mingles with the aspirations, imaginations and experiences of the reader. We who have designed this thing feel both a thrill and anxiety for the moment when the object of our imagination, nurtured through several years of discussion and numerous rewritings, takes on a life of its own.

Many people have contributed to the work presented in this book. The *Atelier* project funded by the FET-program of the European Union gave us a unique opportunity to work together with colleagues and students across Europe on both conceptual projects and design experiments on the architecture and technologies for inspirational learning environments. This work forms the shared material from which we have developed what is presented in this book, and we are grateful to everyone who took part, most prominently, in Oulu: Kari Kuutti, Antti Juustila; in Malmö: Sofia Dahlgren, Håkan Edeholt, Janna Lindsjö, Simon Niedenthal, Bo Petterson, Peter Warren, Tomas Sokoler, Jörn Messeter, Mette Agger-Eriksen, Annika Nyström; in Vienna: Rüdiger Lainer, Andreas Rumpfhuber, Dieter Spath, Michael Gervautz, Kresimir Matkovic, Thomas Psik; and in Milan: Marco Loregian.

As the manuscript evolved, we where fortunate to discuss it with yet other colleagues who took time to comment on both our ideas and the way we presented them. We will especially like to thank Liam Bannon, Jacob Buur, Daniel Fällman, Jonas Löwgren, and Peter Ullmark, commentators on the first instantiation of this thing at a seminar in Malmö, January 2007. They helped us at a crucial point in a long process of discussing and writing to keep track of the audience we were addressing.

The writing of this book has been enriched by the useful comments of many reviewers and has been supported by the engagement of the series editors, Professor Ken

Friedman and Professor Erik Stolterman. The editorial team at the MIT Press, including Doug Sery, Judith Feldmann, and Katie Helke, has been essential in producing a book that meets ambitious standards of quality.

Many more should be mentioned for their contributions toward making A. Telier come into being as the author of *Design Things*. We appreciate everyone who helped turning this object of our imagination into the thing you now hold in your hands.

1 Introduction

Challenges to Design Practice

The etymology of the English word "thing" reveals a journey from meaning an *assembly*, which was decided on beforehand to take place at a certain time and at a certain place to deal with certain "matters of concern" to the community, to meaning an *object*, "an entity of matter." So, the term *thing* goes back originally to the governing assemblies in ancient Nordic and Germanic societies. These pre-Christian things were assemblies, rituals, and places where disputes were solved and political decisions made. It is a prerequisite for understanding this journey that if we live in total agreement, we do not need to gather to solve disputes, since there are none. Instead, the need for a neutral place, where conflicts can be negotiated, is motivated by a diversity of perspectives, concerns, and interests.

This shift in meaning of the word *thing* is also of interest when reflecting on the practice of design, and thus it forms a starting point for this book. We suggest that we revisit and partly reverse the etymological history of *things*. A major challenge for design today has to do with what is being designed—not just a thing (an object, an "entity of matter") but also a *thing* (a sociomaterial assembly that deals with matters of concern). How can we as designers work, live, and act in a public that permits a heterogeneity of perspectives and actors to engage in alignments of their conflicting objects of design? How can we gather and collaborate around *design things*? These *things* themselves modify the space of interactions and performance, and will be explored as sociomaterial frames for controversies, ready for unexpected use and opening up new ways of thinking and behaving.

If we try to conceptualize and expose a practice of designing as a mode of inquiry rather than as a professional competency or a particular domain of expertise, the focus of attention will be more on *designing* rather than on the designers or design. These are some of the issues that were addressed by Bruce Nussbaum, the curator of the conversation on innovation at *Business Week*, in his speech "Are Designers the Enemy of Design?" (given at Parsons, the New School for Design, in New York in March 2007).

The speech proposed some controversial issues on design that, when published in his blog that March (Nussbaum 2007), provoked a passionate discussion (see, e.g., *NextD Journal* 2007, which collects more than fifty comments on Nussbaum's talk).

Bringing Nussbaum's arguments to the point, we can say that he accused designers of being incapable of understanding that today they must design with people. At the same time, he expressed some irritation with the fact that today everyone is designing ("The process of design, the management of the design process, are changing radically. Egos and silos are coming down, participation is expanding, tools are widespread and everyone wants to play." . . . "The emerging question is therefore: how do [designers] . . . switch gears from designing for to designing with?").

Nussbaum's talk ends with this claim: "your design thing is a glorious thing that has the potential of changing our lives in a myriad of ways in a myriad of places." His major point here is that designers today have a great opportunity to increase their influence on society, if they enlarge their views on how to understand major changes in society and the environment.

Reactions from designers to Nussbaum's talk range from appreciation of the points it raises as an occasion to open a discussion on design from a broader point of view, to refusal to accept the critique (good designers are already taking users into account; good designers are concerned with ecological issues), as well as a call for more engagement (design is corrupting itself when it becomes a pervasive approach to business).

The debate following Nussbaum's talk is only one example of the discussion about design that has recently reopened, in fields like architecture, industrial design, and interaction design. Another prominent example is the "design thinking" debate as sparked by *Change by Design* (2009) by Tim Brown, CEO of successful design and innovation firm IDEO. The design community is challenged to think beyond both the omnipotent designer and the obsession with products, suggesting that designers should be more involved in the big picture of socially innovative design. The reasons for this renewed attention to the very nature of design are manifold, and a short survey of some of them may help to clarify some of the issues that have been raised.

First, many participants in the discussion observe a decrease in the quality of the social environment, in which human beings live, and see the poor performance of the *things* and spaces that are designed as one of the causes of this decline. On a large scale, cities, roads, airports, railways, waste management systems, and so forth contribute to impoverishing the space in which people live, homologating it irrespective of cultural, social, and geographical differences. On a small scale, offices and houses, while enriching their technological equipment, become increasingly more generic and less capable of reflecting the identity of their inhabitants; tools and artifacts clutter spaces and require ever more time for their maintenance and use.

Second, the boundaries between different types of design are disappearing: the need for increasingly more flexible spaces and tools embeds intelligence and servomechanisms in buildings and machines; computers are becoming more pervasive, and their locations must be designed as well as their functions and features; computer workstations today are universal tools that everyone uses during his or her everyday activities, and therefore their design focuses more on interaction and less on the functions of the machine.

Third, design practice is dramatically changing because, on the one hand, it increasingly involves multidisciplinary teams, where human scientists, engineers with different specializations, architects, and designers cooperate. On the other hand, technology plays a growing role in shaping the practice of designers as it provides them with tools that increase the efficiency of their actions and interactions, while introducing constraints to their fluidity. The hegemonic ambitions mentioned above, as well as the closure of the diverse disciplines, push each member of the design team to try to assume a leadership position, and this affects the quality of collaboration, often to the point of failure.

Fourth, the quality of design becomes difficult to define: Is it mainly to do with aesthetics or, conversely, with functions and features? This uncertainty about qualities and their relevance in relation to each other has a negative impact on design practice. What is missing is a clear statement about the relationships among functional and aesthetic qualities: Can we simply add aesthetics to functions and features? Can aesthetics affect performance? Who evaluates design: users and/or stakeholders directly with their feedback, users and/or stakeholders indirectly with how they use a design, marketing managers, or a peer jury as in public contests?

Finally, how strong should the link be between design and innovation? Is good design necessarily innovative? Most observers see a positive relationship between creativity and innovation, but how do we address the conflict that arises when users and stakeholders reject the outcome of a design practice even if it is innovative or, in the worst case, because it is (too) innovative? This last question is strongly connected with the role of users and stakeholders in the design process: Even when we assume the need for people-centered design, is direct participation of users necessary to good design practice, or is it sufficient that designers base their design on a deep knowledge of stakeholders' practices and needs?

We could continue our list of questions demonstrating the controversial nature of design and explaining why the debate is passionate and still alive. Most of the reactions to Nussbaum's provocation involve the claim that it does not take the increasing complexity of design into account, and that to meet this complexity not fewer designers but more skilled designers are required.

The Approach of This Book

This book does not intend to develop a new contribution to the debate, in which all the people behind A. Telier are legitimate and active participants. Rather, this book wants to seize the opportunity to take a step back and try to understand why the debate has been reopened today and which new features have emerged in it, shaking designers' conceptions of themselves and opening questions that go beyond the differences between various schools, cultures, and disciplines.

A. Telier's understanding of design practice is rooted in previous research and design experiences, and it has been shaped by common experiences from the *Atelier* project (2001–2004). In that project, we, in collaboration with students and teachers of architecture at the Academy of Fine Arts in Vienna and of interaction design at the School of Arts and Communication in Malmö, studied design education practice, developed prototypes to enhance such education, introduced prototypes in different real-use settings, and reflected on these interventions to learn about how to improve both architecture and technology and the learning situation. This was built on a participatory approach that involved students, teachers, and researchers as reflective codesigners and evolved from early explorations of practice and ideas in field trials with gradually more integrated scenarios and prototypes.

Although our empirical work within *Atelier* was with design schools and design students, our general reflections and suggestions on how to approach and support contemporary design practice cover a wide range of professional design practices. There are differences between professional designers and students of design, who engage in "legitimate peripheral," that is, not yet fully developed, participation. Students don't have to deal with all the constraints of a real-life project; hence they spend much less time on detailing their design in cooperation with engineering and other specialists. In our attempt to better understand the complexity of design work, of *things*, objects, space, place, information technology, and design itself, we mix stories from our work with design students and their teachers (masters) with case studies and examples from professional design work.

Atelier inspired us to look for ways to combine creative design practice with a participative approach to design, reaching out to and engaging stakeholders, eliciting their cooperation and creative contribution. This combination seems to be not so common. While participatory design emphasizes democratic values and the need to bring improvements to users, and greatly values and respects their active contributions to the design, the creative design process also seeks to achieve a certain level of aesthetic quality and experiential value. Participatory design projects have during recent years opened up to the creative disciplines, their ways of working and their uses of technologies. They look to art and design for inspiration and seek to engage users in creative-experimental processes. The focus, however, is more on envisioning and supporting use than on aesthetics and creativity. Designers, on the other hand, rarely take up participation as a major issue or concern. Architectural design and planning, for example, although embedded in large networks of engineering specialists and consultants, producers, builders, local authorities, and the client or investor, has remained a relatively closed process. This has something to do with the fact that relationships within this actor network are normally "punctuated," restricted to particular stages of the planning process and to specific tasks. This has also constrained the possibilities for architects and designers to engage with stakeholders.

Designers today have to deal with issues and interdependencies that previous generations did not face. For example, the ecology of materials and techniques is of growing importance, requiring designers to select, combine, and assemble different materials in innovative ways. The increasing cost-consciousness of clients and investors forces designers to consider maintenance costs, special services for users, and changing social uses from early stages. As a result, design work has to become intensely cooperative, involving a diversity of stakeholders. Increasingly, many designs are open by intention, as they build on wide participation on the one hand, and further enable such participation—in public debates, in projects of all kinds, in artistic events, in community building—on the other hand.

We can say that at the heart of design is the need to mobilize cooperation and imagination. The design process needs to be kept open to requirements that by necessity are evolving, as well as to be able to arrive at novel and sometimes unexpected solutions. Openness implies that decisions about possible design trajectories are not made too quickly, and requires that the various stakeholders involved present their work in a form that is open to the possibility of change. It puts emphasis on the dynamics of opening and expanding, fixing and constraining, and again reopening.

This short summary of our experience within the *Atelier* project shows that at its end we were rich with new or renewed questions, with diverse, sometimes not fully aligned conjectures. And in fact, the group of people behind A. Telier, while discussing what to do next, arrived quickly at the idea that instead of writing something to narrate, describe, and document the project, we were more interested in reflecting on those questions and conjectures. This book is not about, but after *Atelier*. However, throughout the chapters we frequently refer to the setting of the *Atelier* project and collaboration with students and teachers of design in both schools. We also recurrently make references to interventions, in the form of *things* that we designed. For this reason, in the appendix we provide descriptions of the prototypes we built as well as of those of students' experimentations that we refer to throughout the book.

Our specific approach in this book is to address the many open issues we briefly described above by developing a language for speaking about design work in a reflective way. This is mirrored in the different conceptual approaches each chapter takes on describing our design experience, from both a designer's and a design researcher's perspective. One perspective is on the design process, the dynamic "qualities" that describe its potential for transformation. Another focus is on the object of design, on the activities that promote the multiple transformations of this object, and on the *thing* that is finally "handed over." A third perspective is on a variety of strategies designers engage in, which we describe as *metamorphing, performing,* and *taking place.* A complementary perspective is on the relation between design and use. And finally, we touch on the design of controversial *things.*

We do not aim at developing a coherent and exhaustive theory of design. Our ambition is to open up fruitful avenues for talking about a practice that is being challenged and is changing, as it seeks to discover and make people experience something that does not yet quite exist, in increasingly complex contexts of use.

A. Telier is thus the writer of a book where the reflective designer (see Schön 1987) is reinventing him- or herself while he or she looks back on the practice of design and design learning. Whereas the focus of Donald Schön was on the relationship between knowledge and action, and the reflective designer was the professional aware of the complexity of his or her practice, here the focus is on the interaction between people with different backgrounds and competencies while sharing knowledge, and the reflective designer is the professional who is able to interact and collaborate with people with different backgrounds and expectations in the transformation of objects and *things.*

So what is suggested is a "deconstruction" of the individual designer and the object of design, an edifying approach for reflection and dialogue for, by, and with fellow designers and design researchers. This deconstruction begins, following Heidegger (1971), with the *things* themselves, or more specifically in our case with sociomaterial *design thing*s. Such *things,* or rather events of *"thinging"* (as Heidegger would put it), gather human beings; they are events in the life of a community and play a central role in community members' common experience. In this spirit, Bruno Latour has called for *"thing* philosophy" and "object-oriented politics" (Latour and Weibel 2005), and by doing so has also challenged designers to make public the object of design. *Things* are not carved out of human relations, but rather of sociomaterial, "collectives of humans and nonhumans," through which the objects of concern are handled. At the same time, a designed artifact is potentially a thing made public, since once it is delivered to its users, it becomes matters of concern to them with its new possibilities of interaction. A turn toward *things* can, as will be elaborated upon, be seen as a movement away from "projecting" and toward design processes and strategies of "infra-structuring" and *"thinging."* So as we approach design in the following chapters, our focus is not on the individual designer and the material object in isolation, nor is it on the user as such; rather it is on *things,* projects, objects, artifacts, devices, materials, places, infrastructures, designers, users, stakeholders, publics, and so on, in collectives of human and nonhumans performing and transforming the object of design. Rather than following Nussbaum's suggestion to design with people, and despite our own participatory design background, we will in the following more fundamentally explore designing for, by, and with such sociomaterial *things.* Hence the title of this book: *Design Things.*

Guide through the Book

This inquiry into designing sociomaterial *things* is detailed in the coming eight chapters. To orient our readers we provide a short guide through the chapters, suggesting dilemmas and questions and supplying a summary overview of the content of each chapter.

Chapter 2 How can we combine the perspectives of pragmatism and phenomenology with a view of design that reaches beyond the cognitivist approach? How can we integrate insights into and experiences with a mature professional design practice with accounts of an evolutionary and participative learning practice to move to a fuller understanding of creative design? What is the role of inspirational resources in design work? This chapter provides an introduction to our understanding of design practice, which emphasizes the involvement of the designer in practical action in the world, as well as the collective dimension of design. It exemplifies this understanding through illustrations of how professional designers handle multiplicity and openness in their work. It also addresses the notion of design as learning and the inspirational aspects in design work.

Chapter 3 What are key qualities of the design environment and of design practice? How can we describe their potential for dialogue (with people and materials) and transformation? How far do these qualities enable aesthetic experiences? In this chapter, we elaborate on a number of such qualities, based on "'bottom-up"' ethnographic observations. They include the richness of materials, techniques for creativity, and, not least, configurability. These design qualities, we suggest, can direct the designer's attention toward specific "aesthetic experiences" of a situation, and support her competence to recognize and evoke those experiences in future design situations.

Chapter 4 How can we conceptualize what is being designed? How is what is being designed accessible to designers? This chapter investigates *things*, devices and the object of design and the interplay between things and words. We propose a view of design as accessing, aligning, and navigating among the "constituents" of the object of design. People interact with the object of design through its constituents, be those constituents *things*, artifacts, or representations. In experiencing *things*, objects, and devices people are primarily involved not with different types of materials, but in different kinds of interaction.

Chapter 5 How do designers mobilize, manage, and transform artifacts and their interpretations? Our approach explores how the web of "constituents" is weaved around a drifting object of design as the designer engages in its transformations. Design work is looked on as an act of "metamorphing," where design concepts are envisioned and realized through objectifying and manipulating a variety of representations.

Chapter 6 How do designers express and experience design objects? The approach here is to describe and explain the evolution of the design through the designer's performance of it. This includes considering narrative temporalities, fictional spaces, and creative constraints as basic features of performing design, and looking at characteristics of staging design events. We suggest an interventionist, participative and experiential understanding of design as purposeful staging and accomplishing of events.

Chapter 7   In which space does design take place? In this chapter, we propose particular notions of place and landscape to explain how the design environment is performed in the work of designers and how a situational ground is enacted and transformed as design artifacts emerge. We suggest the concept of an "emerging landscape" as an alternative to the notion of an abstract design space, an experienced landscape in which the designer journeys and dwells.

Chapter 8   How does design relate to use? How can users participate in design? How can designers participate in use? In this chapter we elaborate on the notion of design projects as *things*, as potentially controversial assemblies of humans and artifacts, and the interplay between design and use. We suggest the concept of "design games," aligning design and use, and relate it to concepts like "boundary objects" and "infrastructuring." Using these concepts, we go on to explore strategies for designing use before use (participatory design) and for designing design after design (meta-design).

Chapter 9   Where will the design studio of the future be situated, who will participate, and what kind of "design games" will they play? Is there a new role for the professional designer to play that takes place "outside the box," by participating in controversial public events? In the final chapter we reflect on such issues of design "outside the box," extending design into political processes, public debates, and possibly even subversive but creative misuse. In doing so we reflect on values that guide such design and we look into a few controversial issues, such as: Are designers the enemy of design?

2 Design at Work

We start our conceptual journey by reflecting on our common theoretical groundings. Our approach to studying design is guided by an interest in design as involvement in practical action in the world, in "design practice" (in contrast to, e.g., "cognition") and is grounded in theories of situated activity. Instead of focusing on the individual designer, we focus on the collective dimension, paying attention to the material aspect of design practice in its ability to engage all our senses, to designers' interactions with the physical environment, and to the collective emergence of creativity in design. Apart from revisiting our own intellectual history as researchers and designers, we provide a reflective account of examples of professional design practice, based on several years of participatory observation in an architectural office, which illustrates the notion of "open planning" that has been formative in some of our thinking. The chapter ends with a reflection on learning as legitimate peripheral participation.

Common Grounds

Donald Schön, through his books on *the reflective practitioner* (Schön 1983, 1987), has probably offered the most influential account of design practice. Classical are his descriptions of how designers learn and conduct professional artistry through processes of *reflection-in-action*, in which knowing and doing are inseparable, and he delineates how these are carried out in *on-the-spot experiments* where the materials of the situation (models, sketches, drawings) at hand "talk back," often in surprising ways, and where the *naming* and *framing* of the specific problematic or puzzling design *situation* are important activities. In engaging in reflection-in-action the professional designer uses a broad repertoire of images, contexts, actions, and cases, sometimes also referred to as a *repertoire of exemplars*. Of special relevance to our context of creative design practice are his studies of the architectural studio as an educational model for this kind of reflection-in-action, and the observation of such a *reflective practicum* as characterized by learning-by-doing, coaching rather than teaching, and a dialogue of reciprocal reflection-in-action between teacher and student.

This perspective on design is heavily influenced by the pragmatist philosophy of John Dewey, a general epistemology of creative and investigative processes, where *experience*, seen as growing out of encounters with real-life situations, is taken to be fundamental to understanding. In his theory of inquiry, as expressed in his main work on research philosophy *Logic: The Theory of Inquiry* (1938) and his specific work on aesthetics, *Art as Experience* (1934/1980), creative processes include everyday practical reflections as well as artistic production and scientific research. According to Dewey, all creative activities show a pattern of controlled inquiry: framing situations, searching, experimenting, and experiencing, where both the development of hypothesis and the judgment of experienced aesthetic qualities are important aspects within this process. The main difference between doing scientific research and making art is that the former aims at the production of theories whereas the latter concerns inquiries into materials used in the production of artworks.

Hence, for Dewey, aesthetics is not limited to fine art theory, and the concept of *aesthetic experience* is not limited to art. Instead, aesthetics is a more general human predicament: every human is potentially able to acquire aesthetic judgmental skills and to participate in creative practices (cf. Aristotle on the intellectual virtue of *phronesis*, the faculty to make wise judgments). Östman (2005) has developed an interesting Deweyan-pragmatist theory of design (also inspired by later pragmatist philosophers such as Richard Buchanan, Richard Shusterman, Richard Rorty, and Frank Jackson). In this tradition, aesthetics is not a question of turning our attention to idealized, remote values of abstract beauty or the beauty in nature, but a matter of recognizing aesthetic experiences in everyday life situations. Experiences occur all the time in the creative and investigative process, but when reinforced by emotion and reflection, they can grow into aesthetic experiences. Aesthetic experiences, as opposed to ordinary experiences, are characterized by being unified and growing toward a state of fulfillment. This includes a kind of organizing energy and a human interaction with the situation, both of which render a degree of felt wholeness and *aesthetic quality*. An aesthetic quality is something we experience, it is bodily and anchored in the senses. Aesthetic experiences are not, however, instances of sheer pleasurable perception; rather, they develop in the creative process over time and are both intellectual and emotional. As for art-centered experiences, these do not differ fundamentally from other aesthetic experiences, but are more intense and provide us with the means to grasp the liberating energy of aesthetic experiences.

A fundamental aspect of a pragmatist view of design (and art) is the inseparability of doing and experiencing. Dewey writes:

It is not possible to divide in a vital experience the practical, emotional, and intellectual from one another and to set the properties of one over against the characteristics of the others. The emotional phase binds parts together into a single whole; "intellectual" simply names the fact that the experience has meaning; "practical" indicates that the organism is interacting with events and objects which surround it. (Dewey1934/1980, 55)

Jean Lave puts forward a similar view, arguing that whereas "traditional cognitive theory is 'distanced from experience' and divides the learning mind from the world, theories of situated activity do not separate action, thought, feeling, and value and their collective, cultural-historical forms of located, interested, conflictual, meaningful activity" (1993, 5). Practice in this perspective is situated doing: and people's undergoing experiences and expressing themselves as they engage in practical action, often together with others. An important characteristic of such situated doing, and of the knowing that is constructed and transformed in activity, is that it is open ended. Lave considers doing and knowing as "inventive" in the sense of that they are "open-ended processes of improvisation with the social, material, and experiential resources at hand" (ibid., 13).

This perspective resonates with the phenomenological tradition, which focuses on the phenomenon of *human perception* as construed in Merleau-Ponty's reading, as active, embodied, and always generative of meaning. This reasoning also forms the background of the concept of *embodied interaction*, which has been introduced by Paul Dourish (2001). The notion of embodied interaction addresses how a situation must be considered as a whole. Meaning is created in the use of shared objects, and social interaction is related to how we engage in spaces and with artifacts. In this interplay the body plays a central role; in many ways, the body can be seen as the necessary medium for "having a world." This notion has stimulated research on the relationship between the use of things and the role of our haptic and kinesthetic senses. Drawing on the phenomenology of Merleau-Ponty (1962), Larssen, Robertson, and Edwards (2007) explore how technologies might *feel* to use and provide a framework for conceptualizing body-thing relations: when we interact with artifacts, "sensing and motor skills are in constant dialogue, performing in concert" (2007, 272). "Attending to the thing" and acting on and through it is basic to design practice. A perspective on embodied interaction requires focusing on the "temporally fine-grained coordination between the mobilization of multimodal resources (talk, facial expressions, gestures, glances, bodily postures, objects manipulations, etc.), the timed use of artifacts and technologies, the constant rearrangement of participant frameworks and the changing foci of attention" (Mondada 2008, 30).

The ethnographic orientation in our own research has enabled us to build insights into the situated, embodied, and collective nature of design work. However, the kind of multimodal analysis required to arrive at a deeper understanding of how bodies come into dialogue with the people and things around them is still in its infancy. In a recent project on supporting participatory creativity in urban planning projects, supported by mixed-reality technologies and a tangible user interface housed in a tent on the site of the project, we have started analyzing the language of body, imagery, and sound, which participants use for creating and debating urban scenes. In this exploratory study we have seen that although talk and dialogue are essential elements of design work, the language of body posture, gestures, gaze, and movement, of

Figure 2.1
Participatory creativity: coconstructing and exploring audiovisual scenes in an urban project (source: IST-4-27571 IPCity).

(visual) artifacts and sound all interact together in intricate ways. It is their multiplicity and multimodality, together with a large freedom in how to make use of them, that foster participants' creativity (Wagner et al. 2009; figure 2.1).

Our perspective on design practice is guided by this attention to the body, artifacts, spatial relations, and their interplay as an aesthetic experience and a source of creativity.

A View on Collaboration in Design

Another perspective we bring to understanding design practice is our focus on collaboration in design. Traditionally, studies of design look at it as an act of individual creation, with a focus on the designer's underlying cognitive processes and on design representations as "cognitive artifacts" (e.g., Purcell and Gero 1998). Researchers in this tradition tend to look at visual design thinking as a rational mode of reasoning (Goldschmidt 1994); they often focus on its early stages and on the role of design representations in the concept-formation and problem-solving phases of a project (e.g., Suwa and Tversky 1997; McGown, Green, and Rodgers 1998). Although many of these studies are inspired by Schön's (1983) work, they are rooted in cognitive psychology and in the tradition of laboratory studies.

Research on computer-supported cooperative work (CSCW) has produced detailed studies of work in a diversity of domains, among them also design work. CSCW is concerned with how understanding of material practices can inform design (Schmidt and Bannon 1992; Randall, Harper, and Rouncefield 2007). Many researchers have addressed the crucial role of inscription and material artifacts in cooperative work. It is typical of cooperative work in modern work settings that multiple actors interact "through" a collection of artifacts of various kinds. In our own research, we have studied a plethora of representational and coordinative artifacts that can be found in architectural offices, arguing that

Architectural work proceeds through the architects' producing successive objectifications of the design and interacting with them in a variety of ways, inspecting them, comparing them, assessing them, etc. That is, the conspicuous display of representational artifacts can be seen as the fundamental means of making the not-yet-existing and in-the-process-of-becoming field of work immediately visible, at-hand, tangible. (Schmidt and Wagner 2004, 363)

We have also pointed at the multiplicity, multimediality, multimodality, and openness of many of these design artifacts, and at their "boundary qualities." The concept of "boundary objects" (Star 1989) is used to denote artifacts that, at the boundary between different local practices, facilitate loosely coupled collaboration between these communities. In the words of Bowker and Star:

Boundary objects are those objects that both inhabit several communities of practice and satisfy the informational requirements of each of them. Boundary objects are thus both plastic enough to adapt to local needs and constraints of the several parties employing them, yet robust enough to maintain a common identity across sites. They are weakly structured in common use and become strongly structured in individual-site use. (Bowker and Star 1999, 297–298)

The public availability of a "collaboratively organized world of artifacts and actions" (Suchman 1987, 50) is important, because it enables the "communicative potential of actions and artifacts within any shared environment" (Robertson 2002, 302).

This view on cooperation in design opens up another relevant connection with actor-network theory (ANT), with its focus on the object-in-design and the multiplicity of actors contributing to its emergence, but also with its interest in the semiotics of materiality (Law 1999, 4–14). ANT draws attention to the relational and nonsingular aspects of objects. Properties and forms of entities (things, objects) are acquired in relation to other entities, human as well as nonhuman. If objects are seen as an effect of an array of relations, it follows that they do not exist in and of themselves; rather, they are performed and emerging. Law (1999) proposes the notion of *fractional objects*, using the metaphor of the fractal to find a definition that is neither singular nor plural. *Translation* is the term Latour (1999) uses for describing a drift or mediation in our intentionality in the process of designing, a shift that affects both the actors and the object they act upon (Latour 1999, 175–215). This line of thinking, which defies the simplicity of the singular, helps deepen our understanding of the object-in-design, its trajectory through multiple representations and their translations. Cooperation in design is not just something we can study observing designers' interactions with each other but something we can "read off" the artifacts they produce, their evolving and relational aspects.

Studying the trajectory of an object-in-design also draws attention to the temporal structuring of the design process, which is an important feature of the work. Time is rooted in the historical, material, and discursive practices through which it is measured (Latour 2005). In this sense, it would be more felicitous to talk of "timing," rather than time, as a practice. Typical of complex activities, such as design work, is a certain degree of uncertainty about how long they will take. At the same time, they are structured by "given" or socially negotiated urgencies, deadlines, and rhythms. Timing is crucial to understanding the engagement of multiple actors with the design process. Aspects come to the fore such as rhythm, the alternation between slow-paced, contemplative work and fast-paced work, between tension and relaxation. Designers alternate between activities such as browsing through material, traveling to other places such as the site of a project or event, free-floating thinking, and doing concentrated work under the pressure of deadlines, all while additional actors and actants are entering and exiting the design process.

Finally, the designer must consider the relationship between time and place. Time has to be read from somewhere; process is embedded in place. What is present is located somewhere, and a trajectory in time is often one that connects different locales. Also, what is present (in a particular place at a particular time) is always mediated by what is absent, each temporal location "elucidating the dense, complex and multi-layered connections between people who are not copresent in time and/or space" (Gregory 1994, 117). Michel de Certeau includes the dimension of time in his definition of space:

A space exists when one takes into consideration vectors of direction, velocities, and time variables. Thus space is composed of intersections of mobile elements. It is in a sense actuated by the ensemble of movements within it. Space occurs as the effect produced by the operations that orient it, situate it, temporalize it, and make it function in a polyvalent unity of conflictual programs or contractual proximities. (de Certeau 1984, 117)

What we propose is to extend our view on design practice from the individual to the design team and their engagement with materials, and from understanding how this supports their "thinking the design" to understanding the rhythms and place-making activities, in which collectives of actors and actants contribute to the object-in-design. Place is constitutive of social practice, and, as we will see, designing involves traveling between places that are both present and absent, and thus envisioning the future.

A Glimpse at Professional Design Work

Most of our earlier research during more than twenty years has been concerned with actually doing design work and reflecting on the process and products of our own design activities, rather than studying other designers' work from a distance. For the most part this has been done as action research (Bjerknes, Ehn, and Kyng 1987) and in the tradition known as participatory or collaborative design (Greenbaum and Kyng 1991), with users as codesigners in multidisciplinary design teams. Many of these projects have been concerned with the computer in the workplace—with design at work. Apart from our engagement in design, we also have performed extensive ethnographic fieldwork studying design practice. Several years of such fieldwork in an architectural office helped us gain a deeper understanding of the creative aspects of design work but also of the coordinative effort that aligning the perspectives and knowledge of a large network of specialists and stakeholders requires (Wagner 2004; Schmidt and Wagner 2004). Case studies at several other studios as well as a series of interviews with Austrian and French architects complement these rich data.[1] They corroborate that, with some variation, the practices we observed are common. As part of this research we also engaged in joint creative writing about architectural projects, developing a conceptual approach to design practice. To paraphrase Schön, we have been working as "reflective practitioners."

One of the main insights from these studies was that design work consists of producing design representations in different modalities, scales, and materials, in a constantly transforming process of ongoing refinement and increased specificity. To be able to work in this way, designers typically have to mobilize resources from a diversity of disciplines and to enlist the cooperation of experts of all sorts. This view of "design as transforming," as well as multidisciplinary and cooperative, has led us to look at *multiplicity* and *openness* as main characteristics of design work (Lainer and Wagner 1998b). On the level of method, openness requires organizing work as an informal, fluent process. On the conceptual level, the focus is on fuzzy concepts, preliminary specifications, and working with contradictions and constraints. There are some good reasons for maintaining openness in a design project: the designers naturally want to expand the solution space so as to be able to see things differently, and to keep a design open to novel and surprising solutions; at its core, design work is about cooperating with others, and mobilizing one's and others' imaginations; and designs are often complex, which makes it difficult to define and fix the details of a design in a simple, linear process (Wagner and Lainer 2002).

Our emphasis on openness as a main characteristic of professional design work is anchored in detailed observations of several architectural design projects. The particular practice we describe here builds on mobilizing inspirational resources; working with analogies, metaphors, and themes; and taking an experimental approach, based on fuzzy concepts and placeholders. One of the projects whose genesis we observed was the planning of a movie theater. The basic design principles, as formulated by the chief architect in his first brief of the designer team, were: to create a large volume within a densely populated urban space that "barely touches" its surroundings (thereby creating a specific tension between autonomy and referentiality); to maintain the notion of a floating "skin" that uses light to produce an almost imperceptible metamorphosis, from hermetically shimmering in the morning to communicating the building's contents—projected cinematic images, people's movements—in the evening; and to construct one large container housing a stack of volumes (the movie theaters), thereby creating in-between spaces and vistas.

Within the design team, the design concept is present in the first few early sketches, as well as in the metaphorical language and imagery used by the chief architect in describing it (figure 2.1). It takes some effort to give it real presence in project meetings and in the actual process of drawing up plans. One of the team architects mentions different levels of grasping the design concept within the team, which gradually, in recurrent discussions of the design's details, is externalized and concretized in a growing number of sketches, an initial simple-scale model, and gradually turned into shared knowledge. The chief architect introduces metaphorical descriptions, such as "tissues as membrane," as well as reference examples. For example, in the notion of the buildings "barely touching," the play between closeness and distance can be seen in what Rowe and Koetter, using the example of Sant'Agnese on Piazza Navona, describe as "affected and untouched. The compressed space exerts pressure" (Rowe and Koetter 1978, 108).

Physical models of the design serve specific purposes in this early phase. One of the initial problems is how to pack eight movie theaters into the volume. Here the chief architect will emphasize the importance of openness and fuzziness, engaging in free-floating thinking and playful explorations. The team starts out with the ground plans of the theaters—2D rectangles or squares—to get a feeling for the dimensions. As a next step they use small blocks of foam to experiment with different ways of positioning them within the available volume, creating different combinations, perhaps realizing that the initial idea leads to spatial arrangements that are far too complex, "disturbing the influx of light and a certain generosity, that this is too complex and dense" (interview by I.W. with Rüdiger Lainer, January 6, 1999), and that there are additional problems of accessing, corners, edges, and so forth. The model (in white, without color to indicate material) can be presented for the competition by endoscope. This facilitates the presentation of the spatial situation within the building, in particular for those technical consultants who need a good understanding of the characteristics of the interior space.

In further work on the design concept, a series of *themes* emerges. Themes express the design concept in the language of images and metaphors. They define the basic points of view to be taken when working on specific tasks. Most design decisions have an element of ambiguity, as there is rarely one best solution. Themes serve as guidelines for considering different options, their advantages and disadvantages. As such, they simultaneously shape the structure of the object-to-be-built and structure project planning. One theme is the building's skin as supporting the floating character of the building and as a transformation layer that uses texture and light for mediating between interior and exterior spaces, with light seen as flooding and radiating; another theme is the notion of the interior as one monolithic space with stacks of containers; still another is the dramaturgy of space, produced by the combination of materials and light, on the one hand, and the design of foyers, staircases, and gangways as in-between spaces, on the other hand. One of the main problems here is to find an adequate language for communicating such qualities. Such a language differs from the one required for technical detail. It is rich with imagery and metaphors and grounded in (haptic as well as visual) experience and context. Qualities such as distance ("barely touching"), density and compactness (the interior space as "monolithic" and "hermetic"), and texture (the skin as a "fabric" rather than a smooth glass surface) require the construction of rich narratives if they are to be grasped by others who can then fill in their own particular ideas. Metaphors and visualizations (sketches, models, and images) play a large role here; often rather spontaneous forms of communicating are used.

At times, the architects' work is quite experimental, as can be seen in another project, where the architect systematically sought to widen the solution space for a building that is based on the idea of a "generously spacious" and flowing structure covered by a skin and containing an "organized labyrinth" of interior spaces. In this project, the architect worked with a large number of inspirational materials: images of landscapes (prints from books, memories from particular movies) and of landscape-like structures for dwelling; images of abstract structural systems and path systems, self-generating systems (linear, grid, net), as well as compositional strategies (labyrinth); examples of figure-ground plans; and so forth. Reconstructing how the design concept took shape, the image of Gaelic broths (ditches) together with some visualizations of path systems (direct or minimal) influenced the idea of the interior space as an organized labyrinth, with the path system forming its "spine" (figure 2.2). Combined with the image of earth-sheltered Tunisian houses, this gave some notion

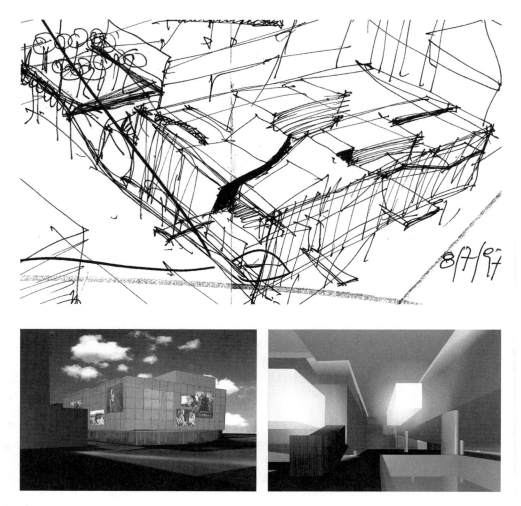

Figure 2.2
First expressions of a design concept (source: Project "Eurocity," Rüdiger Lainer).

of how to assemble volumes and voids (lecture halls and courtyards) in this interior space. Images of plaitings and wickerwork helped to disrupt thinking along obvious lines. Instead of using cast glass for the skin, which covers the whole structure, both walls and voids, the architect explored other possibilities such as plaited plastic hoses filled with water.

Another crucial aspect of design work is the ability to work with "fuzzy concepts" and to maintain projects at different stages of incompletion. It accounts for the fact that architects often work with preliminary specifications, which at any given moment

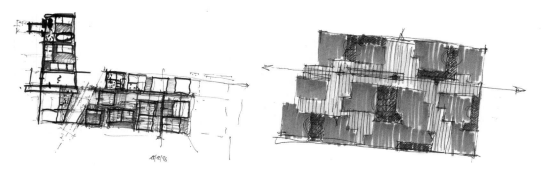

Figure 2.3
Exploring the notion of "organized labyrinth" (source: Rüdiger Lainer).

cannot be defined with precision. A placeholder stands for something that is still in the process of being formed. It underpins the passage from possibility to actuality, which is the work of design. Working with placeholders is a method for representing relatively complex systems before they have taken shape. Placeholders facilitate communicating about something that has not been specified in detail. They enable people to focus on the concept rather than on a particular material, product, or constructive solution. Placeholders may range from very small things (e.g., a missing parameter in a product specification) to large ones.

This is best illustrated by a small urban planning project in the area of the *Gasometers* in Vienna, in which the architects made systematic use of this technique. Their approach was to define spaces of different qualities rather than specific objects. Much time was spent within the team to clarify these concepts, which were "encircled" by using metaphors, producing sketches, and searching for associated images. The "Vitrine" (showcase) stands for one of these qualities, with several layers of meaning. As an "osmotic wall" it mediates between inside and outside, between public space and the world of consumerism and entertainment (figure 2.4). The Vitrine can be entered, walked through, or used as exhibition space: "Working with placeholders means to look at the specific space of 'Vitrine' or the preliminary specification of the 'principle façade' as an hypothesis" (Zschokke 1999).

Fitting these spaces with different qualities into the existing one of buildings and roads requires a high level of fuzziness. Details have to be ignored in order to highlight the main structural qualities of the design. Here the principal architect thinks aloud about how to use different representational techniques for the idea of creating layers of different heights, working with the concept of "Vitrine":

what you did with the layers, these "Vitrinen," . . . when we do this in virtual blocks, in 3D, here the question of the base (of the "Gasometer"), that we say, we have these basic blocks, and define, for this we use a dotted line, now I take this front part, this area we have done already,

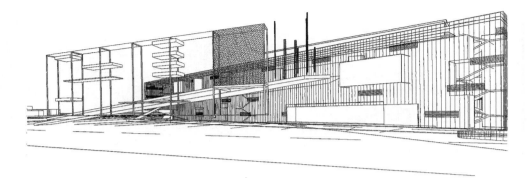

Figure 2.4
The "Vitrine": working with placeholders (source: Project "Austria Email," Rüdiger Lainer).

Figure 2.5
Fuzzy concepts: "diving in and cutting out" (source: Rüdiger Lainer).

there is the "Vitrine," this we have defined, where one can put something in, and then this part in the back, and there somewhere is this grid, it consists of these elements of diving in or cutting out, . . . one could do this symbolically, . . . a kind of simulation, to show the principle. (Observation, November 24, 1998)

The small sketch, a section from a series of "simulation drawings," visualizes the "diving in or cutting out" (figure 2.5).

Although quite specific, this architect's design practice reflects some common principles and strategies. One of our interview partners described the importance of inspirational material—not only images but also textual descriptions that invite multiple associations:

You have to use a diversity of methods that help you define the "essential" in a kind of allegory with the help of texts that have an imaginary quality. . . . James Joyce's *Ulysses* is such a text that defines the urban experience without working with drawings. (Interview by I.W. with Adolf Krischanitz, March 28, 2001)

The process this architect describes is one of working on layers, with the design concept being concentrated in each of these layers. A designer needs the "stranger's gaze," the creative gaze that simultaneously implies closeness and distance. He emphasizes the movement of closing and reopening the design concept in particular situations, to research, integrate additional resources, and so on: "You cannot design unremittingly but have to confront your design with almost its opposite—removing, reproducing, collecting, quantifying, qualifying, and so forth" (ibid).

These and other observations led us to think of creative design as:

• Systematically cultivating the "art of seeing": working with metaphors, analogies, and themes that help express, contrast, and intensify the design concept so as to create a common understanding, to evoke imaginations rather than prescribe, invite others into a dialogue, and the like.
• Engaging with a plethora of materials—inspirational resources as well as material conceptualizations of the design concept (text, diagrams, comics, video, sketches, rough "sketch" models, virtual 3D models, CAD drawings), with the diversity of design artifacts increasing the designer's possibilities of evaluating the design, as each representation helps make particular aspects of a design visible.
• Engaging in a movement of closing and opening, in a rhythm that is characterized by formulating "themes," searching for "facts," and experimenting with different solutions.
• Being able to work in a "meandering" way, with "floating concepts," while maintaining things at different stages of incompletion—architects use expressions such as "working with placeholders" (a method for representing relatively complex systems before their form is finalized) for their ability to keep a sense of things that are tentative and incomplete. They define bandwidths for development.

The Role of Inspirational Resources in Design Work

Inspirational and experiential resources play an important role in creative design work. Professional work, as well as legitimate peripheral participation in such work, is stimulated by resources that provide an element of surprise and discovery and may help the designer to see things in a new way (the chance finding of a perfectly suited material in an unexpected place, a strange combination of objects that provides a novel solution, etc.).

Inspiration has to do with particular qualities of objects, people, ambience, and places. It always emerges in a context. Such inspirational resources are ubiquitous:

My approach is, when you have formulated a question in your head, you just have to go on the street and quite often the answer passes you on the next T-shirt, you just have to read attentively, it is written on a T-shirt, there you have all the answers you need, a kind of urban I Jing one plays. . . . And from this perspective I think inspiration can come from anywhere. (Interview by I.W. with Gregor Eichinger, April 18, 2002)

However, designers may also engage actively in collecting and mobilizing inspirational and experiential resources in their work. We find examples of designers working with inspirations from different aesthetic and scientific discourses—from the fine arts and the theater to biology and mathematics. While some designers use pictorial material for generating and expressing their ideas, others prefer poetry and metaphorical text; others build their designs on (historical) research, the assembling of facts or "datascapes" (MVRDV 1999).

Inspirational objects occupy a special role in design work, as can be seen from designers' collections of artifacts (often images) that crystallize important concepts (e.g., the concept of simplicity in John Pawson's 1996 booklet *Minimum*). The same goes for examples or precedents of buildings, recent or historical, that stand for particular principles, solutions, or qualities (Lawson 2004); and similarly for materials, as, for example, in Toshiko Mori's exhibition *Immaterial/Ultramaterial*: "[T]these skins, gels, and fabrics—manufactured or improvised—aim to revolutionize not only how we design and build, but also how we think such terms, in confounding traditional categories of surface/depth, structure/enclosure, inside/outside, and nature/artifice" (Chi 2004, 5).

In our interviews with designer-architects we identified some of these objects that inspire their work. Objects or places are not necessarily inspirational in themselves but may be so in connection with a project, idea, or particular task:

What provides inspiration is not the object as such, the source, but what I can do with it, how I can manipulate it. If you work with a painting by Ernst Caramelle [fig. 2.6], it has nothing to do with urbanism, only if you start doing things. . . . Any object—for example a simple cup—may become inspirational, but only if you load it up with associations, additional meaning, put information into it. (Interview by I.W. with Rüdiger Lainer, August 30, 2002)

These objects are not to be taken literally; rather, they are *objets trouvés* that inspire the designer's thinking, help him or her to express and communicate ideas, and capture particular qualities of a design. Inspiration often arises from the transient and ephemeral ways in which objects, people, or an ambience are encountered, their "peripheral presence in the back of one's mind," as it was strongly expressed by

Figure 2.6
Painting by Ernst Caramelle (left); extremely fast-paced: fashion photography (right).

architect Gregor Eichinger, who has a large collection of fashion magazines in his office (figure 2.6). Short-lived events that are fast, quickly assembled, and ad hoc, such as film, video, and fashion photography, are important resources:

film tries to use images, sound and content for creating dense, shortened, intense moments. . . . it is not just film but where things are assembled and produce an atmosphere. . . . [Fashion photography] is also a short-time event. Some things need to coincide—fashion, the photographer, the styling, graphical aspects . . . extremely short-time, much faster than film. (Interview by I.W. with Gregor Eichinger, April 18, 2002).

In her examination of movies and their influence on us, Sobchack (2004) argues that we see, feel, and comprehend films with our entire body, in a physiological and sensual way. She quotes Shaviro, who also expresses this idea:

The important distinction is not the hierarchical, binary one between bodies and images, or between the real and its representations. It is rather a question of discerning multiple and continually varying interactions among what can be defined indifferently as bodies and images: degrees of stillness and motion, of action and passion, of clutter and emptiness, of light and lack. (Shaviro 1993, 255–256)

This means that the transient and ephemeral—watching a movie, or taking a nightly train ride and watching images passing by—affects our imagination in an embodied

Figure 2.7
3D Wunderkammer—a travel metaphor.

way. Watching the movie *The Piano*, Sobchack writes: "The film not only 'filled me up' and often 'suffocated' me with feelings that resonated in and constricted my chest and stomach, but it also 'sensitized' the very surfaces of my skin—as well as its own—to *touch*" (2004, 61). The (moving) images are absorbed by the body (and not necessarily processed intellectually), creating brief, intense moments of tactile sensation that stir the onlooker's imagination.

The design of the *3D Wunderkammer*, a visual archive for designers, was grounded in our observation of the transient and ephemeral character of how designers encounter inspirational material (figure 2.7). We used the metaphor of travel and "the world as exhibition" as stimulating ways of encountering materials. Clicking, browsing, and scrolling through websites with material is replaced by continuously moving— walking, flying—through a particular geography. The continuous movement has a zooming effect—images grow "into the screen" and disappear again. The "magical" aspects of the digital world, such as virtual floating, flying, teleportation, and moving through solid objects, was used for reinforcing the experiential character of traveling through visual worlds in search of inspiration (Wagner and Lainer 2002).

Learning as Legitimate Peripheral Participation

We also found these characteristics of creative design work when observing students of design. There are some obvious differences between how professional designers and design students work that stem mostly from the fact that a large part of professional design work consists in detailing a design so that it can be produced, a process that involves a myriad of technical problems and requires dense cooperation with specialists of all sorts, under tight budget and time constraints (for a description of coordinative artifacts and practices supporting this sort of work, see Schmidt and Wagner 2004). But when we look at the creative, conceptual aspect of design work (which in a professional project is not limited to a first "conceptual phase"), we find striking similarities.

This is not surprising, though, since in art schools students are socialized into the professional practice in a process of what Lave and Wenger (1991) call *legitimate peripheral participation*. For them this concept "provides a way to speak about the relations between newcomers and old-timers, and about activities, identities, artifacts, and communities of knowledge and practice. A person's intentions to learn are engaged and the meaning of learning is configured through the process of becoming a full participant in a socio-cultural practice. This social process, includes, indeed it subsumes, the learning of knowledgeable skills" (Lave and Wenger 1991, 29).

Our notion of learning to become a professional designer in a situation of legitimate peripheral participation was shaped by our ethnographic studies of students' work practices, studies that included the use of cultural probes.

Learning proceeds by students working with design representations in different media, gradually transforming them into a design through a process that is nonlinear, informal, and highly cooperative. The diversity of material and media is an important facilitator of learning. Students work with and produce text, diagrams, comics, video, sketches, sketch models, screenshots, virtual models, and prototypes—material of different degrees of abstraction, scale, and materiality.

Learning is highly interactive. Students constantly switch between individual and collaborative work. They share knowledge and design material, use collective displays, take turns in working on a specific task, and arrange spontaneous meetings. While switching mode and tasks, they modify their space, expanding and concentrating it according to their needs.

Other people, both copresent and distant, are a crucial part of an inspirational learning environment. Students receive regular feedback from peers, teachers, and external reviewers; they listen to guest lectures, and they meet and network with people while exploring the city, a particular context or site. And there is always the need to bring the impressions and the material they've collected back to the studio, to make it visible and share it with others.

Conclusion

This chapter has focused on design practice against a rich background of pragmatism, phenomenology, and CSCW, including an ethnographic account of a particular architectural practice. Our understanding of design unfolds through examining the material practices of "doing design," as well as the material features of design artifacts, their multimodality, and designer's performative interactions with and through these artifacts. This view of design explains why we do not seek to "model" the design process or to direct our attention to particular tasks, techniques, or design strategies (such as problem solving) but rather focus on particular "qualities" of the environment of space and artifacts in which design takes place that are supportive of a highly creative, mediated, and distributed process. It leads from *prescribing* particular patterns or workflows to *describing* and *enabling*. It allows moving from a rather general "theory" of design to concept-based accounts of observed practices, whereby the different concepts we develop and explore in this book help unravel the richness and diversity of design practice.

As a next step, we describe the design qualities we have identified through our work, inspired by the notion of aesthetic experience. They deal with questions such as: what are the characteristics of an environment that help designers capture, express, elaborate, and detail a design idea and let it grow into a concept of an object-to-be that can be communicated, understood, and analyzed? How do designers arrive at a different view of things so as to be able to come up with a creative/innovative design? If inspiration is an experience derived through practice, are there special features of the environment that can be termed "inspirational"?

3 Qualities of an Inspirational Design Environment

Aesthetic Experience and the "Qualities" of a Practice

We have introduced the term "inspirational learning" as a metaphor for talking about creative design work and inspirational environments—environments that support aesthetic experiences. Dewey saw aesthetic experience as a human faculty that can be trained and acquired. He looked at thinking as a process of inquiry, or of investigating, and he saw a strong connection between learning and aesthetic experience. Aesthetic experiences are embodied, and they are shaped by the "objective conditions" in which learning takes place. These conditions include "equipment, books, apparatus, toys, games played. It includes the materials with which an individual interacts, and, most important of all, the total *social* set-up of the situations in which a person is engaged" (Dewey 1938/1969, 45). The crucial point here is to support specific aesthetic experiences (through the use of design qualities and other inspirational materials) and to support the development of the competence to evoke those experiences or recognize them as aesthetic qualities in future design situations. It is this notion of aesthetic experience that has inspired our thinking about the "qualities" of inspirational design environments.

The notion of "qualities" is not new to design, and there has been research on "qualities-in-use" or use-qualities. The field of "Usability engineering," for example, tries to advance quantitatively specified planned for characteristics of devices, such as user performance, ease-of-use, and user satisfaction. Taken by themselves, however, no matter how well they are understood, these aspects say very little about how users experience qualities-in-use. More contextual approaches, which focus on the meaning of devices in use, typically consider the design of affordances, constraints, feedback, coherence, learnability, multisensory redundancy, variability, robustness, and so forth (Krippendorff 2006). We might add that these qualities of course have no meaning at the time of use until they are experienced in one way or another, or transformed from public things to objects of use.

There have, however, also been more specific attempts to work with qualities-in-use. One example is work by Jonas Löwgren and Erik Stolterman (2004). They see a language for use-qualities as something that can increase the ability to design, something that can help articulate a sense of quality, something that can help build a design repertoire; but they do not see qualities as something that can mechanically be built into a device at project time. For use-qualities of digital devices, they include anything that has to do with motivation (playability, seductivity, anticipation, relevance, usefulness), immediate experience (plasticity, control, immersion, fluency), broader social relevance (social action space, personal connectedness, identity), structural engineering qualities (transparency, efficiency, elegance), and creation of meaning (ambiguity, parafunctionality, surprise).

The qualities we have identified are similar, but they focus on the practice itself, on what designers do and how they make use of a diversity of resources:

• *Materiality and the diversity of representations, creative density*, and *connections—multiple travels* capture the richness of design materials as well as the idea of traveling that is present in the notion of the "world as exhibition."
• *Narrativity, reprogramming*, and *dimensionality and scaling* connect with the participatory design tradition; they focus on techniques designers (and users) employ for sparking creativity.
• *Configurability* is a quality of the place for design, but it is also what we will later describe as a quality of metadesign, using components and patterns, ontologies, and ecologies.

Looking back at the particular example of professional design practice (described in chapter 2), we can also think of these qualities as themes that emerge as part of this practice, shaping designers' thinking about both the process and the object of design. They describe characteristics of space, artifacts, materials, aesthetic experience, and process that are lived and can be recognized. They are dynamic, as they capture the potential for transformation from a design concept to a thing that can be used and enjoyed. If we take a view on aesthetic experiences inspired by Dewey, the design qualities may be seen as useful materials for intellectual and emotional experiences within an inspirational design environment. In the learning process characterized by what Dewey called *learning-by-doing*, the design qualities become materials for the development of specific aesthetic experiences. They potentially support the building up of aesthetic experiences and the ability to judge aesthetic qualities as part of a growing repertoire of (paradigmatic) exemplars of (aspects of) design situations.

We identified these qualities through observation of both professional design work and students' project work; the language for describing them reflects how the designers we observed think about their work. Some of them emerged early; others were perceived and articulated only at later stages. They were described and illustrated using fieldwork material—short textual descriptions together with images and video clips.

This material and the concepts it represents were discussed, resulting in more precise ideas about their implications for the design of inspirational environments. The conceptual work never stopped; we constantly reread, reinterpreted, and reillustrated the qualities with new examples, as our understanding of them getting more precise and more grounded. Some of the qualities were transformed into new design perspectives.

The Richness of Materials and Connections

Materiality and the Diversity of Representations

In design practice, materiality is seen as more than a technical property of the materials from which a building or designed artifact is made; "it is a precondition that promotes ideas, creativity, and pleasure in architecture, and it guides us to the loftiest aspirations of theory" (Jorge Silvetti, in Mori 2002, xvi). Materiality comprises physical properties such as texture (roughness or smoothness, details), geometry (size, shape, proportion, location in space, and arrangement in relation to other objects), material (weight, rigidity, plasticity), and energy (temperature, moisture), as well as dynamic properties; material artifacts engage with all our senses (Rodaway 1994). Our interactions with materials are not just physical but spur our thinking and help us communicate ideas that would be difficult to communicate through words alone, adding an experiential dimension to our action (Jacucci and Wagner 2007).

In the studio or classroom, material often is present in the form of random collections (leftovers from previous projects, samples, etc.). Finding specific material for a model may influence the choice of material for the building, as in this example where two students discuss the semiotics of various materials:

T: *(Stands up and starts looking into a paper bag filled with materials)* For wood we can use cardboard and for glass something transparent, and for the fabrics we should take something semitransparent.

V: Yes, I also thought that . . . no, actually it does work . . . The properties are that it is not solid and it does not stand. But I think that the fabric does not have to be opaque.

T: But there are also transparent fabrics . . .

V: It depends on what we want to differentiate in this model to represent what it is about . . .

It is crucial to explore the physical properties of material—to smell, feel, and manipulate it. In another episode one of the students is shaking a transparent plastic sheet (figure 3.1). At first she does this to try out the consistency, but soon the material starts making sounds, so she continues to explore the sound by playing the sheet as an instrument. This direct experience with real material helps the students develop new design ideas. Gore reports on student work with concrete vessels, where

Figure 3.1
Exploring materials.

in cycle 1, perhaps they come up with an "interesting" mix of concrete; in cycle 2, they might discover that the mix flows well into small cracks; in cycle 3, they might discover that the cracks sponsor a beautiful texture of ridges on the surface; in cycle 4, they might develop a way to optimize the mix for intensifying the texture; in cycle 5, they might discover that the addition of color intensifies the texture, and so forth. (Gore 2004, 42)

In general, we can say that the availability of different materials, media, and representational forms is necessary for conveying and exploring different (conceptual, technical, aesthetic) aspects of a design. Important design decisions occur in the transitions and translations between representational formats and scales. Iwamoto, for example, shows how "translations between rapid prototyping and full-scale mock-up, between seamless form and standard sheet material, and between computer model and spatial or phenomenological effect" helped design students to cope with the "later translation of the digital information to full scale" (Iwamoto 2004, 35).

We can see this diversity of materials and representations also in pieces of art, such as Robert Smithson's work *Mono Lake Non-Site*. Hogue points to the "Dialectic between Site and Nonsite" (i.e., the site of a project and the gallery, which is non-site) and the rich set of representations Smithson uses for letting both concrete experience and imagination merge: "the rocks indicate collecting and placing, the bins frame or establish boundaries, the photographs suggest walking or moving about the site, the maps indicate location, and so on" (Hogue 2004, 54).

But it is not just the diversity of representations that is fundamental for design work; their richness is also important. Lawson points to the fact that "design conversations are extraordinarily compact since they are full of references which in turn point to huge chunks of information." This is possible because "enormously complex and sophisticated sets of ideas can be referred to using simple diagrams, catchphrases (for example, 'round shapes in square containers') or even single words (for example 'belvedere')" (Lawson 2004, 445). We would add that it is possible because designers can point to sets of extraordinarily rich visualizations in these conversations.

The materiality of some of these representations plays a crucial role in envisioning particular aspects of a design. For example, architects work with a great diversity of models of different degrees of abstractness. These models help experiment with and develop aspects of a building, such as color or ability to interact with daylight. The qualities of the materials chosen for a model play an important role in these experimentations. The surface (texture, details) of a material, its tactile properties, its temperature, its dryness or wetness carry ideational, interpersonal, and textual meaning, with different materials (clay, cardboard, aluminum foil, plastics) conveying different aesthetic qualities and conceptual aspects (Ormerod and Ivanic 2002). The Russian designer Vladimir Tatlin held that design should "derive from exploring and exploiting a material's intrinsic qualities, and be considering how it might combine with other materials" (quoted in Fredrickson 1999, 53). He put emphasis on the physical, tactile, and dynamic properties of materials, rejecting a privileging of the visual.

This role of material features can be seen in an example of models students built to convey the idea of "something that flows out of a crack in the mountain." In the rough sketch model to the left, a piece of soft plastic material visualizes the "flowing," and the small cardboard model that has been inserted into a large clay model of the valley stresses the compactness of the flowing building (figure 3.2). As Rogan remarks,

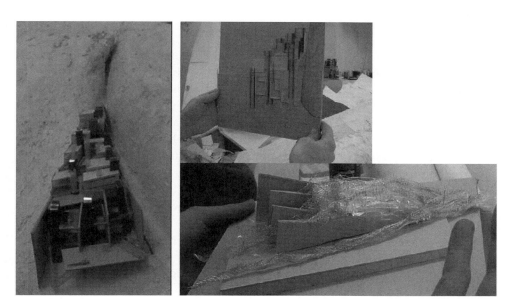

Figure 3.2
Something that flows out of a crack in the mountain.

Figure 3.3
The big shared model.

messages conveyed by a physical artifact are coded in a language that cannot be separated from the medium itself. The power of artifacts is that they communicate those messages "in a more subtle, elegant, discreet or economical way than a natural language is capable of" (Rogan 1992, 109).

For another example of messages embedded in material features, consider students making some of their design interventions publicly visible through placing materials on a large shared plaster model of a mountain valley, visualizing, for example, a path or a river (figure 3.3). These material traces, made from wool or modeling clay, convey the mutable and temporary status of their design ideas. They exploit what Brown and Duguid (1994) think of as the "border resources" for shared interpretation that physical artifacts present.

There is a temporal dimension to the diversity and richness inherent in the material aspect of designers' work (see also chapter 5). The models students built to convey the idea of something that flows out of a crack in the mountain (see figure 3.2) were developed over several months of work and are indicative of a shifting focus in the students' thinking. Although they were produced in a sequential order, they maintain their relevance as they communicate complementary aspects of the design project.

There is an additional temporal aspect to designers' transforming and translating, which is captured by the notion of simultaneity (Brose 2004). "Jumping" between formats, scales, and media is a movement that bridges the differences between acts, experiences, and events "before" and "after," thereby creating a sense of "extended present" or quasi-simultaneity. What appears sequential if we look at design activities step by step becomes simultaneous when we look at designers' transforming, jumping, and holding present the diversity of previous and more recent design materials.

Creative Density

Our fieldwork observations show how engaging in an immersive mass of material may support intensity in design situations. While some people want things to be messy and rough, such as in writer's Friederike Mayröcker's office, others may want to have things in order and cleaned up. Mayröcker prefers to be immersed in slips of paper, manuscripts, newspapers cuttings, brochures, folders, and books, in piles, hung up like laundry, on the piano, or the TV set (figure 3.4). Schmatz describes this "creative density" as constitutive of Mayröcker's work: "Her discoveries (in this chaos) are

Figure 3.4
Friederike Mayröcker's working space.

submitted to a poetic exercise, which—folded across the workspace—extends into the perceptive-sensual apparatus of the writer and reader" (Schmatz 1998, 197). It is not just the presence of a great diversity of texts but the physicality of the arrangement, with, for example, paper clipped onto a clothes line, which enables the chance encounters that stimulate Mayröcker's writing.

Creative density means space for odd, surprising, or useless objects in the studio and the chance to find something unexpected in surprising or interesting combinations of those objects. This accounts for the renewed interest of art historians in the historical *Wunderkammer* (cabinets of curiosity), collections of strange, unique, and often exotic objects. The artful and sometimes accidental arrangements of objects (according to color, size, material) or just the sheer pleasure of seeing them together did not suggest predefined relationships and interpretations between the seemingly disparate objects:

The metaphor of traveling among beautiful strangers is apt, because the compartmentalized organization makes even the familiar appear unfamiliar. And, in spite of insistent borders, the beholder senses that such extravagantly disparate objects must somehow also be connected. Reminiscent of a vast and perplexing database, the sight of so many conflicting wonders arouses the desire to enter the labyrinth to try to navigate the elegant maze. (Stafford 1996, 75)

This is also emphasized by one of the architects we interviewed: "how books are arranged (in a bookstore), how you may 'drift through' and how you encounter other books while searching for one, this is the surprising element in these spaces . . . things encountered by chance" (interview by I.W. with architect Dieter Spath, April 4, 2002). Moreover, he argues, a crowded or limited space may provide stimulating perspectives, with things and spaces layering over each other:

This provides a real possibility that you may rapidly switch between these worlds and are able to mix them together. . . . Often when we sit here and watch TV while on the table are these big scale models . . . watching TV and out of the corner of one's eye looking at the model and then all of a sudden [we will want] to change something. This state of not looking-at-directly, this second level, to look without focusing, is an interesting situation. . . . these are the chance happenings that are free gifts and which bring distraction and stimulation at the same time. (Interview by I.W. with architect Dieter Spath)

Furthermore, access to material from other similar or quite different projects can help one to assume different perspectives on one's own ideas and concepts. Browsing through this other material is a sort of cruising through ideas and inspiration. Designers pick up a lot of ideas and material during their daily back-and-forth between the home and the studio, as well as during outings to particular places. Preserving this material and making it available to ongoing work are crucial. The environment can in some sense be seen as a "sea" of design material. One of the architects articulated that the material he produces and analyzes has to reach a certain level of density before he can feel sufficiently confident and free to make decisions. Perhaps this feeling of having produced and considered nearly everything possible—this creative density of material that one can dive into—is important for making a "great decision" (interview by I.W. with architect Dieter Spath).

A crucial insight from our fieldwork is that creative density can only be partly designed or prepared, as it is the product of the particular organization of a particular design practice. It is important therefore to help practitioners *cultivate* the creative density of their environment. Again, we must consider a temporal dimension. When designers working on a concept for a particular project are going back and forth in their project timeline, they may want to have certain material constantly present, as reminders of design principles, earlier steps, and so forth, whereas access to other material may only be needed at specific moments. It is a fine balance between the presence and absence of design material, between memory that enriches and memory that gets in the way of a fresh look at the developing object-in-design.

Connections—Multiple Travels

People both copresent and distant are a crucial part of an inspirational design environment, as representatives of diverse cultural contexts and skills, of (controversial) viewpoints and emotions. Design students receive regular feedback from peers, their teachers, and external reviewers, spontaneously, or as part of more formal arrangements. They listen to guest lectures and they meet people when they are in the outside world, exploring the city, a particular context, or site. As we have seen, an essential part of design work consists in going back and forth between media and design representations as well as between the studio and places in the outside world. The designer needs to bring these impressions and collected material back to the studio, to make them visible and share them with others.

Design practice may benefit from this traveling back and forth between "realities," as in this next example, where "cultural probe" material (Gaver, Dunne, and Pacenti 1999) depicts places where interaction design students go to be alone, to think or daydream, before taking their ideas back to the studio (figure 3.5). In interaction design, exploring context and bringing the perspectives of different actors into the studio is important.

The metaphor of traveling captures this quality. In our observations of design work, we came across a story of an architect traveling home from a first jury meeting late at night, when the train passed a paper factory. The image of stacks of compressed paper shaped his idea of the arrangement of movie theaters as stacks in a large volume. The train ride (as a metaphor) stands for a flow of images that pass by, for the unconcentrated look of the (tired) traveler whose gaze is caught by an image. It also stands for the flow of random, transient impressions. A certain level of vagueness is conducive to ideas taking shape, while at the same time remaining floating.

Figure 3.5
Traveling between the studio and other places.

Designers may also draw inspiration from bringing an outside space into their studio—the site of a project, street life seen just in front of the door, a significant place in the city—as is the case in an architectural office with a large window that opens onto the street outside (figure 3.6):

We wanted . . . contact with the street outside . . . we have these Venetian blinds, they enable you to switch yourself off but you may also leave them open . . . this has a positive effect, this possibility of being in touch, this has something refreshing for me, when the traffic passes by, maybe because we rarely go outside, working so much . . . it is like a screen . . . with our heads a little above people passing and you overhear parts of their conversations. (Interview by I.W. with architect Anna Popelka, May 22, 2002)

Some architects and urban planners, such as Robert Mull, create their office at the site, turning the site into a planning space. The physical presence of the context—being exposed to the "genius loci," the spirit of the place—influences the planning process. Also, having to cope with the problems of setting up a temporary office may become part of the process, if the architect needs to reprogram the site for the requirements of his or her own work (figure 3.7).

There is also the need to forge and maintain connections between materials and places. These connections may be of varying nature and quality: chronological, narrative, driven by the desire to contrast or confront. One of the architecture students reported that on her trip to Ghana, after observing and recording a place, she would put up a red carpet and watch how this intervention changed the place and people's behavior (see also chapter 5). She mentioned that, although she took pictures, made notes, carried out interviews, and produced videos, it was hard to capture the richness of the experience in these materials. While you are there, your body subconsciously absorbs the place. Back home, you take a second journey through the collected material, remembering with your body even subtle things like the smell of a place. The notion of *multiple traveling* refers to the fact that a designer may repeat the journey through the material again and again, with new perspectives coming to the fore each

Figure 3.6
Bringing street life into the studio.

time. This resonates with Hogue's argument that the site of a project "could be seen as a specific set of locations, a variety of narratives, and therefore suggests many possibilities for action" (Hogue 2004, 55). Artists such as Gordon Matta-Clark and James Turrell, for example, have turned site selection into part of the creative process.

Techniques for Creativity

Narrativity

In our fieldwork, we identified strong narrative elements in the way a diversity of design representations melt into "assemblies" that tell a story, such as the story of the design concept or of a particular choice of material and product. Stories are created around images and sketches, which are often produced in intense conversations, while talking through a design problem. These "narrative sketches" consist of two closely interwoven types of material—the sketch, on (transparent) paper, of a plan, and the story (Wagner 2000; see also Tomes, Oates, and Armstrong 1998). Figure 3.8 shows an

Figure 3.7
Site office for Project "Start Down" (2001), Linz.

example of a narrative sketch created by an architect while talking, drawing, and using color, metaphorical text, and descriptive text for explaining his ideas of the interior space of a building. These types of visual-verbal relationships are crucial for many design disciplines. As Mitchell argues: "all arts are 'composite' art (both text and image); all media are mixed media, combining different codes, discursive connections, channels, sensory and cognitive modes" (1994, 95).

The narrative element can be explicit, such as in diagrammatic sketches for expressing stories of use or particular qualities of a space and other narrative visualizations. The card in figure 3.9 (left) tells the story of how convenient it may be to live above a street market: "you are in the midst of cooking and realize that you forgot something . . . then you just rush downstairs to get it." The drawing (right) communicates the idea of visitors leaning on and sitting in the facade of a building—the facade "as something that you can lean on [*belehnbar*], or that you can sit on [*besitzbar*], this idea of a lounge" (transcript, video observation). The model (left) has been augmented by

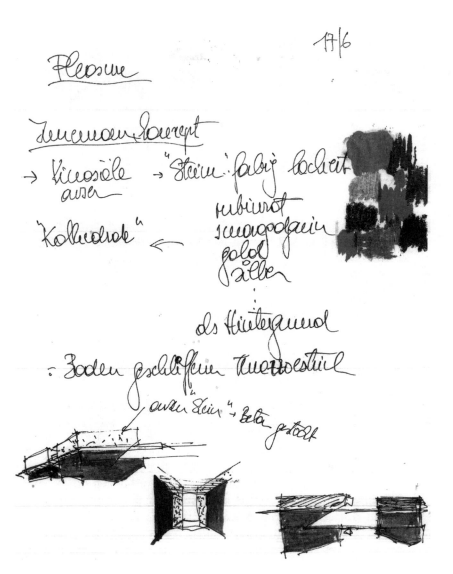

Figure 3.8
Narrative sketch (source: Rüdiger Lainer).

Figure 3.9
Narrative collage, sketch, augmented model, detail of model.

pictures illustrating use; the detail of the model (right) speaks of the attraction the students felt when seeing the crumbling wall of an old building's courtyard.

Creating narratives is an important part in the education of interaction designers. The examples illustrated in figure 3.10 are from students presenting their work using video cards and collages. The collage depicts situations where technology is troublesome. Students also use narrative techniques for enacting design, using a full-scale mock-up of the actual environment and placing a mock-up of the design artifact in the scene. In this way they reenact narratives that took place in physical space by combining stories and props. The easy configurability of the studio supports these narrative enactments of a design concept. Working with scenarios in this way is reflective, since it explicitly engages designers with the user's environment. At the same time it is experimental in the way it supports the visualization of future activities.

Artists and architects have found a great diversity of ways to introduce narrativity into their designs. Pablo Neruda designed his own houses. His designs reflect his poetry

Figure 3.10
Narrative collages with video cards and other objects.

as well as his biography. One story tells that, lacking a desk for his study, Neruda claimed that the sea would provide him with one. In fact, he later used a piece of wood that was washed ashore for constructing his desk. His houses are narratives turned into material.

Some architects use built architecture as a stage for narratives. Sound, light, video, and color projections create varying atmospheres and produce events. The layering and connecting of these different media allow differentiated ways of experiencing, walking through, listening to, and viewing the space (Lainer and Wagner 2000). Lozano-Hemmer's interactive light installations in cities, for example, introduce narrativity and memory into built architectures (Lozano-Hemmer 1998). Janet Cardiff equips visitors of a building or part of the city with a CD walkman or small video recorder. While following the artist's directions, they become involved in the stories they watch and listen to at the same time. Voices, footsteps, music, the sound of a car, or gunshots make up a fictional soundtrack overlaying the actual indoor or outdoor space (Biagiogli 2000).

These different types of narrativity are an integral part of design practice, and they sometimes become embedded in the design. Although we do not think that they need explicit encouragement, they can be stimulated as well as augmented through special technological and spatial interventions.

Reprogramming

Some designers contend that essential to design practice is the ability to develop a concept-based understanding of a design. The design idea, which may be represented in a first sketch, model, or textual description, needs to be mobilized, flexibilized, and extended, in a process that helps reprogram the "facts" of a site or context, and generate a different view. This different view rests on the designer's ability to perceive the novel within the familiar, to discover relations between seemingly incongruent objects and notions—"to relate the unrelatable." It requires the designer to transform and reprogram—to explore solutions and contexts, to shift perspectives, to carry out

Figure 3.11
Using light for transforming the atmosphere (left); filling up the gas tank of a car (right).

experiments, to present and perform, to have time and space for free play and day-dreaming, and to generate a different view (Lainer and Wagner 1998b).

Interaction designers reprogram by blending the perspectives of different actors or by disrupting social conventions of interacting. Figure 3.11 shows two examples of reprogramming activities that occurred in the interaction design studio. On the left, a scenario was changed by the use of light, that transformed the "warm and cozy living room into the cold sterile setting of the bathroom" and into an experience that was meant to influence the perception of the room's use. On the right, a "body mimicking" exercise is illustrated. By recording a situation of use and acting with the video as backdrop, students could, for example, experience just how much time for thinking you have while filling up the gas tank of a car (Jacucci, Linde, and Wagner 2005).

Encouraging students to "see things differently" is an explicit teaching principle in the architectural master's program. The juxtaposition of perspectives and questioning of concepts is supported in various ways. Students are encouraged to collect and mobilize inspirational objects, to experiment with atmosphere and context, and to learn to analyze contexts and spatial elements. They use different design situations, media, and materials as a means of seeing things differently. For example, one student, while working on a project about the beach, "started seeing beaches everywhere, also where the sunlight was reflected on the road" (interview by I.W. with Dieter Spath). The student's observing particular meanings of a beach within an urban context changed her perception and understanding of the city and her concept of a beach. A change in context helped her think differently about beaches.

Another example comes from a feedback session with a student who was working on an underground parking space in her project of revitalizing an area with immigrant workers (see chapter 4). Her teachers challenged her approach, asking her to transcend

Figure 3.12
How students express their seeing a place in a different way.

the traditional categories: for example, to work with contradictions—"the mosque, outside lively, inside an oasis of tranquility"; to let market and street reach into the park; to use empty shops for parking; to connect living with the car, for example by parking the car directly in front of the living room and using its sound machine. These suggestions were not meant literally; the teachers' intention was to make a space for creative thinking. In another design project, a table in a deserted courtyard was turned into an elegant dinner arrangement and an industrial skyline transformed into a ship (figure 3.12).

Artists such as Rafael Lozano-Hemmer and Janet Cardiff (Biagioli 2000) play with the notion of reprogramming, through transforming the master narrative of a specific building or place by creating layers of audiovisual elements that recontextualize it, suggest different readings, and turn a building or site into a repository for distant memories.

Dimensionality and Scaling

In his interviews with expert designers Lawson heard them describe how important it is for them "to see things encapsulated in one small image." Herman Hertzberger, for instance, told him: "It's a sort of imperative for me, you know. I insist upon having my concentration on quite a small area, like a chess player. I could not imagine playing chess in an open space with big chequers" (Lawson 2004, 447). The concentrated view helps the designer gloss over details and focus on the essential conceptual aspects of a design.

Designers also need to experience an object in different scales and from different angles. Specific codifications have been developed for technical design representations that indicate which elements are appropriate for different scales: for visualizing the impact of the urban situation at the territorial, town, or neighborhood scale, for

Figure 3.13
Sketching expressing issues of scale (source: Rüdiger Lainer).

Figure 3.14
Viewing a model in real size within an outdoor environment.

representing whole and detail from different perspectives. As general design strategies often have implications for concrete questions and design details, designers want to be able to zoom in and out but also to move from one scale to another. The coded representation of an element at a certain scale refers to complex realities and their perception. A simple sketch may express implicit but precise references common to most people (figure 3.13).

Designers use different techniques of exploring scale and dimensionality. They may walk through a model using an endoscope, such as in this example of architecture students who carried their models to the site, producing images of them in real size in the space, to explore how the environment would react to the model (figure 3.14). They may take close-up photographs of an object, exploding a small detail by projecting it onto the wall, thereby giving it an oversize spatial dimension. This possibility of blowing up small details or scaling down pictures of buildings to the size of a person lets objects and their environment mutate in surprising and inspiring ways (figure 3.15).

It is important to make the scale changeable. In some situations it may be instructive to expand the scale larger than normal, let's say 2:1. Another technique is to take

Figure 3.15
Scaling—blowing up a detail; collaging real people into a miniature scene.

Figure 3.16
Unusual views.

the unusual view on an object or scene that can be achieved by, for example, using the (web-)camera as an artificial eye. Sometimes it is important to be able to see a scene from both above and below, as in this example from the interaction design class (figure 3.16).

Configurability

For architects, configurability is closely connected to a space's properties. Whereas *flexibility* connotes the possibility of relatively simple changes to a design so as to adapt it to different or shifting social uses (e.g., moveable walls), *variability* means that a designed space or artifact, without elaborate transformations, can accommodate a

Figure 3.17
Personalized workspaces, growing over time.

variety of functions (Lainer and Wagner 1998a). The *backstage* and the *garage* are examples of spaces in which anything is possible. But there are also some quite elaborate examples of configurability, such as a building by Diller and Scofidio (the Center for Digital Culture in New York), which has been conceptualized as "a fundamentally updateable, technologically and profoundly re-arrangeable (physically)" building setup. The architects used the metaphor of open source code for modeling the building as a space "capable of being rewritten, upgraded, reprogrammed, reconfigured to accomplish previously unanticipated tasks" (Moreno 2002).

Configuring and reconfiguring is another important aspect of design practice. We observed how at the beginning of a project the architecture students set up their workspaces (figure 3.17). As the project would progress, these workspaces would become dense with design material, exhibited on the surrounding walls and on parts of the desk. Sketches, plans, model, a panorama print of a site, and the computer were all assembled in one desk space. One student put two desks on top of each other to make room for a desktop computer, turning the desk into a three-dimensional space. Students' configuring spatial elements and tools is very different from the predesigned mobile and flexible "individual workstations" that have become part of office design (Antonelli 2001). These are highly personalized workspaces, whose features and components grow over time, expressing students' identity as well as the progress of their work.

The concept of configuring also applies to the ways students arrange and rearrange design materials. In the process of conceptualizing and detailing, the design representations and their relationships change continuously. Arranging and rearranging material in the workspace is an essential part of this process, with the physical landscape of things on the walls and tables in constant movement. Personalizing one's workspace presents the opportunity to surround one's self with the things that matter and to exhibit one's work, to make it visible for others. Designers have played with specific ways of personalizing, such as leaving simple marks—the chair taking on the pattern of your clothes, the ceiling showing some image of relevance for you or your work

(Fukasawa, *Personal Skies*; Antonelli 2001)—or as, for example, in the MVRD building (Winy Maas), where the personal may take somewhat eccentric features, such as hanging up a Murano glass piece.

The need for configurability also arises as the intensity of the work makes it desirable to be able to use the space for multiple purposes, solitary work as well as group discussions and presentation, sketching as well as building models, having a nap, or eating lunch:

to remain in one space, this is what many of them do, to stay over night . . . a space that for a short time turns into this magic space which you don't want to leave . . . This is something essential for producing architecture, that you don't sit all the time, that you stand like at a work-bench, in clothes that may get dirty . . . to be able as the architect-planner to work on materials, hard materials such as steel or wood, to place a machine . . . that the space enables this . . . This is an important quality, to hang up samples of materials . . . to use the space in a much 'tougher' way, because it is a workshop and not a space for writing. . . . I also think that one's attitude is different, when you get up and manipulate things instead of being seated in a constrained space . . . this makes a difference from the perspective of your body, if . . . the scale of a model is of a size that you may place a doll's house in it, some effort is needed to move it . . . where you start simulating architecture in its materiality. (Interview by I.W. with architect Dieter Spath)

The changing spatial configurations of students' work environment also reflect the fact that students have to work out ideas in a group or individually and present them for critique and improvement, in a pattern that allocates work along the temporal axis of a semester program. These presentations range from frequent, sometimes weekly *Korrektur* sessions, round tables (at the studio, with students and teachers convening around a table), and informal "desk crits," to the more formal "midterm crits" and "end crits," with invited external reviewers—architects, urban planners, and so on. The meetings give an important rhythm to student activities, providing deadlines for improvement, and they have their physical expression in students' workspaces.

The *Zeichensaal* (drawing space) at TU Graz is a well-documented student project (Gstöttner et al. 2003); its idea to provide the architecture students with a multifunctional space that can be adapted to varying needs. Its main feature is its workshop character—students can work on anything, from sketching and drawing to building models. One architect remembers having used the regular floor pattern as a ruler for measuring. Another feature is the possibility for personalization. Some students brought in an aquarium. Installing a TV set and a kitchen made the boundaries between work and living quite fluent (Andreas Rumpfhuber, personal communication).

The mobile workplace is an expression of this desire to quickly configure and adapt one's workspace. Designers of a mobile workplace pose questions such as: how do nomadic workers move their culture and knowledge between the places they visit, set up camp for a longer or shorter period of time, find a place for contemplation, a shelter

Figure 3.18
Mobility—Hans Hollein (left); "Mobil träumen"—Eibert Draisma (right).

from the stressful surroundings, appropriate a place for themselves, even if only for a very short period of time? The number of mobile offices is growing (figure 3.18), one of the earliest being architect Hans Hollein's "bubble office." We see the nomad worker traveling the world with the Internet in his or her backpack, or daydreaming while on the move (NL architects; Antonelli 2001).

A central issue of inspirational design environments is to support and encourage designers or design students to experiment creatively with configuration, on different levels and across different aspects of the environment: spatial arrangement and furniture; the landscape of artifacts (which can be arranged and rearranged in different ways but also tagged, furnished with hidden sensors or visible barcodes); electronic components and devices (scanners, readers, input and output devices); and so forth (Binder et al. 2004).

Conclusion

Our descriptions of the qualities of an inspirational design environment are "bottom-up" conceptualizations of insights produced by ethnographic research. They also reflect the ways the designers we observed and interviewed talked about the creative part of their work. In this sense the set of qualities is "coinvented," with their descriptions becoming richer throughout the project, as our possibilities of expressing and interpreting them grew. Our key experience is that the set of qualities we identified did not lose its conceptual power. On the contrary, it remained stable over time as students discovered further materials for the development of technologies and underwent specific aesthetic experiences. The images representing fieldwork observations or examples from art and architecture, which map the field for contemporary design work, evoke certain of the qualities and continue to stand for them.

One of the results of this research is a better understanding of the desirable spatial properties of a design environment (see figure 3.19), which can be summed up as:

• Creative density, facilitating chance encounters of surprising combinations and layers of materials and, connected with this, the studio as exhibition space and memory.

Figure 3.19
Examples of spatial interventions and configurable elements enabling creative density, configurability, and connectivity.

• Configurability of space and materials for a diversity of purposes, activities, and identities, with configurable (modular) and partly mobile elements.
• The possibility to work on-site, being exposed to the "genius loci," where designing itself becomes an intervention in the site.
• Connectivity through real or medial windows.

A design environment of space, materials, devices, and people shaped by the qualities we have identified is a *pedagogical space* in Dewey's sense, as it reflects specific attitudes and enables aesthetic experiences.

At the same time, our description of qualities has stimulated conceptual development, supporting our reflection about the participatory design processes. They have in particular inspired our thinking about:

• Design work as proceeding through transformations of design representations in different materials, formats and scale—what we will call "metamorphosing."
• The object-of-design as being continuously transformed, hence at the same entangled in time, fractional, and a boundary object.
• How temporal and performative aspects—the fact that designers' artifacts have a history, emerge as part of *specific events in time* and become part of *performative action*—turn into important resources for action.
• Configuring as place-making—how the design environment is evolving and produced through the acts of designing, and how designing can be conceptualized as a traveling between places, present and absent, of the here-and-now and of future possibilities.

4 On the Objects of Design

The previous chapters have introduced, on the one hand, relevant aspects of the practice of design, and on the other, the qualities that characterize it. Where does that practice take place, and how are those qualities grounded? These questions become unavoidable with respect to our purpose of understanding design as a creative, participatory process, going beyond the different views of design that emerge from various design cultures.

To provide some order to our discourse, let us first pay attention to the artifact that is the outcome of the design process. With respect to this artifact, there are two main perspectives (the reader will forgive us for the sharp generalization we make here): the engineering and the architectural. For the engineering perspective, the outcome of the design process is a device that provides users easy access to some functions: a chair is a device for sitting; a cellular phone is a mobile device for making telephone calls, exchanging short messages, and for a growing number of other functions; a personal computer is a general-purpose tool for information processing and communication; and so on. From the architectural perspective, the outcome of the design process is a *thing* that modifies the space where people live: besides and beyond its functions (living for houses, hosting artworks for museums, sitting for chairs, etc.), the designed *thing* aims to change the experience of its users; it is rich in aesthetical and cultural values, opening new ways of thinking and behaving. In some sense, the outcome is open to unexpected uses and/or behavior, generated by the way its users appropriate it and by the breakdowns that might occur. As the reader has already understood from the previous chapters, this book adopts and discusses the architectural perspective.

From the architectural perspective, therefore, design is the process through which new *things* are created and delivered, changing the space of interaction of their users: the practices of designers as well as the qualities of the design process, which we have described in the previous chapters, play a crucial role in giving the *thing* to be designed the manifold facets that go beyond its mere functions, opening to its users new possibilities of action and interaction. It has to be emphasized that design is a peculiar process in which the focus is on a thing that does not yet exist (other experiences deal with the appropriation of the *things* that populate the space where human beings live). To better understand how designers shape it, we need to pay close attention to the way they deal with it before it comes into existence. Everything they create and import during the design process and the design space itself merit attention from this viewpoint, since the practice of designers consists of moving in that space, creating and manipulating those things, and the discourse they engage in, in the meantime. All the things that inhabit the design studio (we will concentrate on things in this chapter, leaving the design space to chapter 7) make places for assembling and sharing. As a special kind of emergence—contributing to give life to the not-yet-existing—they avoid characterizations of finality or enclosure. We need a conceptualization of these things, explaining their role in the design process and capturing their potential for openness, continuity, and performance.

On Things and Objects

As discussed in the introduction, Heidegger (1971, 174–182) recalls that a *"dinc"* (*thing*) was the governing assembly in ancient Germanic societies, made up of the free men of the community and presided over by speakers fluent in the law. At such *things*, disputes were solved and political decisions were made. The place for such things was also often the place for public religious rites and for commerce. This original *thing*, from the pre-Christian culture of Scandinavia and in North Germanic languages, was a way to assemble and share various matters of concern to the community. Even today, *things* contribute to creating the landscape we share with other human beings. As Heidegger again claims, *"thinging"* gathers human beings, and *things* are events in the life of a community and play a central role in their common experience.

This social grounding of things has been recently brought to the attention of philosophers and social scientists by Bruno Latour, who has widely written on this issue (see, e.g., Latour 2004 and the catalog of the exhibition "Making Things Public: Atmospheres of Democracy" in Karlsruhe: Latour and Weibel 2005), opposing *thing* to object. Using Heidegger's terminology, an object is any physical or virtual entity from the "present at hand" viewpoint, decorated with a specific sense with respect to human existence, whereas a *thing* is the very same entity per se, whose life unfolds far beyond any human perception and understanding of it. In other words, in Heidegger's and Latour's perspective, objects seem to be reducing entities to some predefined scope, reifying them, whereas *things* make them public, presenting them as matters of concern, irreducible to any specific function or role. We are not fully convinced by this opposition between complex things and simple, reified objects: design seems to us better characterized by the opposition between two distinct and distant complexities, namely, the new *thing* design creates and the object through which the latter is created.

The *things* around us constitute the everyday fabric for experiencing and making sense of the world. We develop our skills in language and embodied action by actively relating to and engaging with them. Philosophy, linguistics, semiotics, sociology, anthropology, and several other disciplines make use of different types of inquiries. Issues on how the social is ordered and structured through spatiality and materiality—what *things* do and the relation between them and representations, what *things* mean and their role in the creation of places—have received enormous attention in philosophy and the social sciences. Classical debates, such as realism versus constructivism or idealism versus materialism (among the most recent contributions reviewing the entire debate on this issue include de Certeau 1984; Appadurai 1986; Brown 2003, 2004a,b), were generated and influenced by that attention. The phenomenological tradition gives us tools to approach everyday life by returning to concrete *things* and occurrences rather than the abstractions describing them. Bread on a table is not just a meal; it is also the hands weary from a full day's work dropping the knife, the children telling stories from school, the remembrance of youth in tasting a familiar dish. Phenomenology as a theoretical backdrop has influenced computer scientists like Terry Winograd and Fernando Flores (1986) and Paul Dourish (2001), but it also bears a strong association with artistic work.

For example, Merleau-Ponty (1962) perceived the work of Cézanne as a phenomenological project. Rather than distancing meaning from *things* through imposing stylized affections, Cézanne tried to reduce the surface between consciousness and its intentional object. The French poet Francis Ponge in his "thing poems" expressed how presiding over the world deprives one of the experience of it: "Kings never touch a door. It is a joy unknown to them: pushing open whether rudely or kindly one of those great familiar panels, turning to put it back in place—holding a door in one's embrace" (Ponge 2000, 23). For Ponge, to describe the simple and concrete was a way out of the abstract generalizations imposed by a long philosophical tradition that constrained artistic expression. Leaving aside the emotions of the subject he turned toward the object, but the focus of attention was really the interplay between them. The blending of words and devices was of utmost importance and in contrast to the dominating dichotomy of subjects and objects. Even through this turn to materiality and things as devices, his strategy was to infuse signs, names, and letters into the things, without substituting those signs, names, and letters for things. This intertwining gave rise to a new object, the "*objeu,*" from *object* and the French *jeu* "to play" (Cornell 1993, 67). The *objeu* is not permanent and lacks the definitive character of the physical thing, capturing in an open, dynamic manner the interplay between the human beings inscribing the things with words and signs and the things themselves. Giving rise to new *objeus* is ephemeral, and it resembles sketching or drawing. Such a perspective resonates well with a culture that favors bricolage and performativity, and we have learned to cope with indeterminacies in constructive ways. From now on we will use the term "object" to name experienced things, embodying the deep relation with words and signs Ponge has richly characterized. An object is intrinsically plural since the words and signs, characterizing the interplay between human beings and a *thing* generating it, are embodied in other *things* that are therefore contributing to its constitution. The ephemeral nature of objects derives from the fact that the *things* constituting them can always reemerge in their being, by themselves, matters of concern.

As recalled in chapter 3, design practice, in fact, gathers and mobilizes a great quantity of materials in different formats, both physical and digital. This diversity of materials is highly inspirational, but its importance goes beyond mere inspiration. Design proceeds from the expressions of ideas, aims and opportunities for design. In many ways, envisioning and realizing concepts is carried out through the manipulation of a variety of representations, viewpoints, and embodiments. Design can thus be viewed as a kind of bricolage, where different materials are brought together, mixed, and configured in various iterations. Transforming representations and shifting between modalities, scales, and materials highlights different aspects of design and is carried out to widen the design space, communicating ideas and narrowing down concepts. It is a challenge for the designer to handle a multitude of different media and representations. The transference from one medium to another without losing essential qualities is often a crucial issue.

The possibility of integrating (inscribing: Ferraris 2005) digital content within things provides the opportunity to create new kinds of devices—mixed devices—that are both physical and digital, going beyond the simple decorations of things with words, which human beings perform while appropriating them. Creating and interacting with these mixed things can help to maintain and forge new connections between different representations. Hybrid forms of design representations provide a new approach to design work, inhabiting landscapes of mixed media expressions. From the designer's viewpoint, the object of design is constituted by things as devices that are taken as they are, for their capacity to recall some special quality of matter, by *artifacts* that are built to allow a rich interaction with the not yet existing *thing*, and finally by *representations* that allow us to view it. The distinction between *things*, devices, artifacts, and representations is used in these pages to characterize how the *things* constituting an object of design have different ways of playing their role: from giving sense directly to the object of design to being only a support for the words and signs giving it, from being taken as they are to being built to shape the object of design.

Objects and Experience

The object of design is, therefore, constituted by the *things* as devices, artifacts and representations that designers create or import during the design process, by their experience of *things*. While they are immersed in design, *things* disappear, contributing to the emergence of the object of design; but whenever they exit—even temporarily—

design, then *things* reappear to them as matters of concern. Let us recall and rephrase the most relevant features of objects, introduced in the literature we surveyed above.

First, Latour's (2004) distinction between *smooth, risk-free*, and *tangled* objects: on our view, it seems that *things* that are brought into human experience lose their smoothness and risk-free character when they are enriched and/or transformed by the experience of their users, ceasing to be only those *things*: if some architects take a sample of a material, say, a Carrara marble, and begin to make reference to it as the texture covering the facade of the building they are designing, then it is no longer merely a smooth and risk-free piece of marble. Or a washing machine that was bought as a standardized, smooth, risk-free tool, after several years is no longer as smooth and risk-free as it originally was, and its use requires knowledge and experience in order to correctly program it, to avoid malfunctioning, and to recognize any signs indicating that a breakdown is imminent. That is, the distinction between smooth, risk-free, and tangled is not of the devices per se, but depends on the experience of their users: an object's becoming tangled is sometimes intentional and sometimes accidental, but always social and experiential.

Second, Law's (2000) *fractional* objects: all objects of human social experience are fractional, in the sense that they are neither singular (as we will see, they are constituted by a collection of linked *things*, artifacts, and representations) nor plural (the collection is bounded by the *object* that constitutes it). The many *things*, devices, artifacts, and representations constituting, for example, the design of a new chair, are neither parts of a unique *thing* nor an arbitrary collection of loosely coupled items: confusion may result in trying to discuss them, but it is limited, since the designers are capable of situating them with respect to the chair they are building.

Third, Susan Leigh Star's *boundary* objects (Bowker and Star 1999): again, on our view, all objects of human social experience are boundary objects, since they are performed by participants in a common experience and help them to cooperate despite their different interests, cultures, and viewpoints, and despite their belonging to different social worlds, to different communities (even the members of a very tight community also belong to other communities, to other social worlds). In the design process, beyond the team of designers who are developing the product, there are always other stakeholders who participate in the process: at school, teachers, comrades, visitors; in professional life, customers, jury members, citizens. The multiplicity of the participants cannot be reduced to a dichotomy between actors and stakeholders, for even actors and stakeholders are different from each other in an irreducible way, so that the object of the design process, with the diverse *things*, devices and representations constituting it, is the boundary that couples all the actors, all the stakeholders, and all the levels between them.

From our perspective, the objects of human social experience are at the same time entangled, fractional, and boundary objects, since the three attributes characterize

three of these objects' different qualities. To summarize our view: during social experiences, human beings interact with and through the objects that populate and decorate
the place where they live, while also giving sense to these objects. These objects constitute the boundary separating and joining the actors of the process (boundary
objects); on the other hand they contribute to creating their shared memory, giving
sense to the actors' common experiences. Social experience and the interactions
articulating it continuously transform these objects without canceling the traces of
previous representations, of previous releases: they are entangled in such a way that
a paradoxical situation emerges where objects, while helping people to share an experience, also obscure the experience from them. The growing complexity of contemporary society has radicalized this paradoxical situation, so that today an experience is
as confused as it is rich.

To deepen our understanding of the objects of human social experience, let us
survey some of their features and our interactions with them.

Objects and Their Constituents

Let us imagine the architects of a studio presenting the design of a villa to their customers. First, they present an overview of the villa through various drawings that show
it from different views. Later, they show their customers the 3D models they have
built in polystyrene foam covered with different textures, the material they have
chosen for its walls (e.g., with a special stoneware clay), as well as those (marble, wood,
different types of paint) suggested by the customers. The customers move around each
of them, looking at the villa as a whole. Finally, answering the questions of the customers, the architects explain the features of the villa making reference to diverse
iconographic materials (the plan of the villa, showing the distribution of the rooms
and corridors; drawings of various relevant details—the staircase, the inner part of the
windows, the pillars sustaining the ceiling of the living room; photo-compositions
showing the villa in its environment; pages of catalogs showing the furniture they
suggest) and non-iconographic materials (samples of the textures that will be used in
different parts of the villa—wood essences, stone types, clay, bricks, etc., to be compared with the samples of the materials characterizing its environment—pieces of
stone, a small heap of sand, flowers and plants; the lamps they have chosen, which
are distributed in the studio). While in conversation with the customers, the architects
draw several new sketches to make note of the customers' indications and also to show
how they can be embedded in the design. As frequently happens today, if they use a
3D CAD system, many of the items they present to the customers are virtual, and the
customers see them through video projection from a PC. Others are physical, since
they convey physical qualities to the observers; and finally, some of them are mixed,
if they use special technologies like the texture brush *Atelier* built to cover a polystyrene foam 3D model with a virtual texture (figure 4.1).

Figure 4.1

From a different perspective, some of these objects are common items they have collected where the villa will be built (stones, plants, wood pieces, etc.); others are artifacts they have built or bought (models of the furniture, samples of texture, bricks, etc.); others are representations of the different features and views of the villa (plans, perspectives, frontal views, details, etc.).

Looking to the above scene, we can ask: What is the villa designed by our architects and discussed by their customers? The villa is the object of the activity of the architects and of their interaction with their customers, but people interact with it through different artifacts and representations. Let us call all of them *constituents* of the *villa design* object.[1]

Therefore, on the one hand, constituents are more than representations or views of an object; on the other hand, they are more than *things* reminding us of some of the features and qualities that we have created or imported to shape it. Each one of them offers a partial view of the object together with a set of possibilities for interaction. The students of Atelier offered us an unlimited number of examples of diverse constituents of the object they were designing: images of various types on the walls (figure 4.2); video projections on the walls and on special curtains (figure 4.3); and 3D models (figure 4.4), to name just a few.

For one project that aimed at developing novel concepts for stadiums, students explored a site close to Vienna. The project set the task of collecting information to construct a multifaceted mapping of the area. A grid map of the 4×4 km area was produced, and each student was assigned four "pixels" of the map to explore. Students were also assigned a set of parameters, from allergies and poverty to light, patterns, sounds, beaches, animals, and water. They returned with a lot of material, which they used to set up a large (4×4 m) operational model of the site that would help them visualize their data. The pixels were created using a variety of techniques that involved

Figure 4.2

Figure 4.3

Figure 4.4

Figure 4.5

assembling a diversity of materials from organic such as grass to more traditional materials. During the project they also built several other constituents, using them to discuss and share their views and the object they were designing: for example, students built large plans that hosted smaller 3D models, bar codes, colors, and lines (figure 4.5) to make their ideas standardized and sharable.

Constituents, then, are not the object the students are designing, but each of them allows them (and their teachers) to interact with the object and to discuss its different features. As this story clearly shows, objects do not exist per se; they exist only through their several, diverse constituents. Even when the object to be designed is something physical, such as a building, a chair, or a machine, its embodiment, when it comes to existence, remains just a constituent among others. The stadium designed by the Vienna students, like the Rialto bridge by Andrea Palladio, exists as a design object even if it has no embodiment.

The object, in fact, is not only the thing in itself, but also its enrichment through the inscriptions generated by the interactions people have or have had through and with it. The object of design is not its outcome, its embodiment: the latter may be less rich than the process of bringing it into existence; some of its constituents may light up its sense or evoke qualities that it in itself does not adequately embody.

Let us go back again to our villa design story, and imagine that after a period of time the villa has finally been built: the building is another constituent of the "villa design," the main reference over others, the one offering the most complete set of interactions to its users, the embodiment of the design. However, the other constituents do not cease to exist, but continue to contribute to the richness of the "villa design" object. In other words, all pictures, drawings, physical models, narratives, handbooks, and so on documenting an object at a certain moment increase the number of the object of design's constituents, making reference to previous, future, and/or alternative versions of it, while it is being designed. Historians of architecture pay a great deal of attention to all the available items architects built during the design process to interpret the building that was the outcome of that process: constituents of the object of design are in fact a primary source of knowledge about the way the final building took form and the intentions of its architects.

The high number and diversity of participants in an experience, as well as the growing number of constituents of an object of design while it is proceeding, may become problematic, as participants lose the ability to share the entire web of constituents that constitutes the object, and therefore the object itself. The creation of a service that collects and keeps track of all the constituents of an object (an archive) is only apparently a complete solution of this problem, since it cannot avoid the creation of new constituents (the next section will thoroughly discuss the evolution of objects) outside of the archive's control; its enforcement by means of rules imposed on the delivery of any constituent to the archive may also be ineffective, since the existence of a complete archive cannot guarantee that people will share all the constituents of the object it contains. The only way to constantly improve how we share an object is to increase the interactions among its participants: this itself cannot guarantee a complete sharing, but it can grant a continuous extension of sharing.

The "materiality and diversity of representations" that characterize design, which we spoke of earlier, reflect the multiplicity of constituents that make up an object in its specific context.

New Constituents

How do designers build the constituents of an object? This question is also relevant to the problem of sharing constituents, which we noted just above.

A constituent is either created (in our "villa design" example, some designers create, during the design sessions and during interactions with the customers, new constituents of the villa—sketches, precise drawings, various views, 2D and 3D models, written documents—using both physical and/or digital means) or imported from the outside (via samples of the textures, catalogs of furniture companies, pictures of villas already built, etc.).

In both cases, new constituents emerge from the interactions among their creators or importers and directly involve only some participants in the design process: the fact that a constituent is shared among all the participants cannot be taken for granted. Therefore, especially for those who did not contribute to their creation, sharing constituents is a central issue in the design process. Despite the efforts participants make in order to enforce sharing, each of them shares only some constituents with other participants and shares different subsets of them with different participants. Interactions among people, on one hand, augment the constituents those people share, and on the other hand, create and/or import new constituents or update existing ones, increasing those still to be shared by the other participants. Moreover, the memory of human beings has a limited capacity. Therefore, as the number of constituents grows, the number of those constituents that participants forget also grows, even if they are accessible somewhere, increasing the differences in their understanding.

We also observed that students produce a variety of scale models, using different materials and techniques. Whereas a small "sketch model," rapidly put together from crumbled foil and clay, may help them visualize the design concept, other more elaborate models my help them develop particular aspects of a building, such as spatial layout, color, or interaction with daylight; as in this example of the series of models students built to convey the idea of "something that flows out of a crack in the mountain" (also discussed earlier). While in the rough sketch model (figure 4.6) a piece of soft plastic material visualizes the "flowing," the small cardboard model that has been inserted into a large clay model of the valley (left) stresses the compactness of the

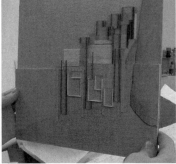

Figure 4.6
Three models of the same intervention of a construction in an alpine landscape.

flowing building, and the half relief (below right) conveys the rhythm of the spatial layout. Here each model has its own mode of expression, with the series seen together as forming a multimodal representation of the design concept. These were three different constituents introduced at different stages, but they also provided complementary access to the design.

Constituents are also distributed in space, which creates a further dimension in the sharing problem. Other participants may share newly created constituents, interacting with them or accessing them where they are located. They will remain unaware of a new constituent, unless they move to its location or bring it to where they are after being adequately informed of its creation. Digital constituents have weaker space and time constraints, since they are accessible from anyplace where there is a workstation or a connected display. Laptops and mobile networks extend accessibility potentially to anywhere.

If a person is not familiar with a newly created constituent, she should at least know that it exists and where it is: the knowledge of existing constituents and of their location is a necessary intermediate step in the process of sharing an object.

What matters here is that generally only a subgroup of the participants will be involved in the creation and/or importation of any new constituent: effective communication is necessary, making every participant aware of the existing constituents moment by moment, of their updating, or at least of other participants who know of it. Effective communication allows all the participants to share the knowledge about existing—both updated and new—constituents; otherwise every person will have a different idea of the object being designed (De Michelis 2006).

A map describing which constituents of an object exist and where, who knows of their existence and location, and their contribution to the object itself could not avoid a high degree of fuzziness, since it would change in a continuous and distributed way.

Special attention should be dedicated also to the destruction (cancelation) of constituents, a move that counterbalances the creation of new ones. Destroying constituents, in fact, helps to reduce the explosive growth of the constituents of an object that has a long history, which of course means more time for constituents to accumulate. However, doing so can also affect the object's integrity and inadvertently cancel relevant information about it. Destroying constituents is not like forgetting them: whereas the latter is in some sense a reversible phenomenon, since we can at least try to recall what we have forgotten; destruction is irreversible, except where participants are able to re-create the destroyed constituent. The difference between irreversible destruction and reversible oblivion recalls the irreducibility of *things* we briefly discussed at the beginning of this chapter.

To return to design, the dynamics of creation and destruction of constituents points to its social dimension: if design involves not only designers with different professional skills and different roles, but also several diverse stakeholders, then it is evident that any constituent contributes to a highly diverse boundary. Any actor in the design process needs to know the particular constituents that constitute the boundary between her and the other actors.

Context

Since, in accordance with what we have said above, there are objects that are not embodied (like the villa before construction) and we do not attribute a special status to the embodiment of an object when it exists, it should be clear that within an experience, an object cannot be reduced to any specific physical embodiment as the *thing* underlying it. The reduction of an object to the *thing* embodying it, when it is possible, in fact transforms it, detaching it from the people living that experience, from the place where it occurred, and makes it public. Designers live through this detachment experience when they deliver the outcome of their design; poets go through it as well, and so do novelists and essayists, when they publish their texts. A villa, as the object of a design experience, is not the (embodiment of the) villa that is ultimately delivered to the customers; and the outcome of the design process is not the villa where customers live. Although both the first and the third are objects of human experience, and they differ only because the experience of designing it is different from that of living in it, the second, the embodiment of the villa, is a (public) *thing*. Putting aside *things* and the questions they pose, at this point we cannot avoid a new question: What is an object? How does it emerge in human social experience?

Within their interactions, designers move about, converse, look at and touch devices, design and build artifacts, draw sketches and more precise drawings, write or annotate paper documents, use tools installed on a workstation to access, store, modify, and/or create virtual documents, and so on. While doing any of these actions, they converse, they talk to themselves, they associate words with what they touch and look at. Associating words with devices they perform, and eventually, they share distinctions and recognitions. They distinguish something from the background and from other devices that could be considered of the same type, and conversely they recognize that something belongs to a class they already know. The criteria for distinction and recognition may be of different types: on one hand, relational, functional, aesthetical, dimensional, and so on, and on the other hand, pragmatic (where, when, and who). It is impossible to foresee which criterion will play a relevant role in a particular case. In particular, designers distinguish a set of devices, artifacts, and representations from the other devices, artifacts, and representations that are left in the background, and they recognize the former as constituents of an object, while the other constituents belong to its *context*. The recognition of an object and its distinction from its background, its context, are not objective. Social interaction is what lets them emerge through the people's conversations and the shared knowledge they generate. One example of context can be seen in an urban planning project where

Figure 4.7

interventions had to be designed for a specific suburban area. Layers for each type of urban element (roads, rivers and lakes, railroads, settlements, industrial buildings, etc.) were made of transparent slides and collages of materials. Two stacks of layers were used, one corresponding to the current situation, the second one visualizing the proposed interventions, for example, populate an area or extend roads. The model was animated and presented dynamically, allowing users to explore the relationships between elements so that the element higher in the stack would be more visible. The grouping and ordering of the layers made it possible to visualize the impact of various interventions (figure 4.7).

Recognitions and distinctions are reflected by the names used for the object and its parts. Social interaction invests devices, artifacts, and representations with words, making them constituents of an object or part of its context. Pooling devices together as constituents of an object (through relationships of synonymy, part, variant, attribute, quality, performance, etc.) creates a web of words that characterizes the object, or, to use a terminology from computer science, its *ontology* (Fensel 2003). The ontology of an object is therefore a map of its constituents: the references to it, to its parts and components, to its qualities and performances (and to the qualities and performances of its parts and components). In fact, the ontology of an object links its constituents to each other. Besides typical ontologies, which reflect the rational approach to design practice—in architecture, the characterization of buildings through their parts: rooms, deck, walls, windows, doors, and so on—in the design experience, more sophisticated ontologies also emerge, based on metaphors and analogical thinking. The students of Atelier gave us some very interesting examples of metaphorical ontologies. For example, in one assignment students had to perform an exploration of working tools. They first made studies of tools by analyzing their form. They would then have to create 3D models based on the movement of the tools in use. One of the students, Tim, worked on saws. The assignment was such that Tim developed a large series of constituents (photographs, drawings, projected images, models) of his project, elaborating on saws and their attributes, parts, and qualities: a full ontology of saws emerged from the constituents he created (figures 4.8–4.11).

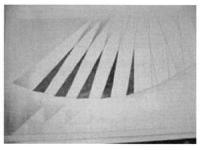

Figure 4.8
A photograph and a drawing elaborating the saw.

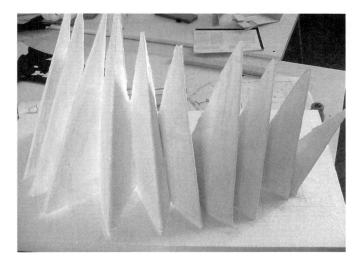

Figure 4.9
A 3D model derived from the saw.

As we said above, objects emerge through their constituents. Now we can elaborate on this assertion a bit further: the act of distinction (of the object with respect to its background, its context) is the same as the act of recognition (of the constituents of the object): the boundary between an object and its context emerges together with the web of the constituents characterizing the object.

Above we dwelled on the role played by words in transforming materials and devices into constituents of an object: it frequently happens that words inscribed into some sort of support material become themselves constituents of that object. The owner's manual for a machine, the document presenting an architectural

Figure 4.10
Projecting the model on the walls.

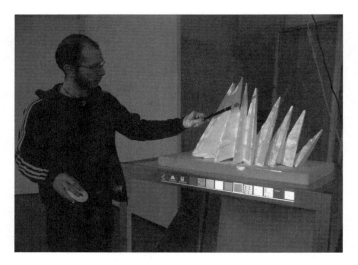

Figure 4.11
Painting 3D model of the saw with a texture brush.

Figure 4.12

project, and the "broken" warning sign attached to a water tap are all examples of written constituents. If we extend the transformation of words into constituents even further, then the stories we tell about an object may also become constituents of it: "narrativity" as a design quality, which we discussed briefly in the previous chapter, is strictly connected to the relationship between words and the constituents of an object. Again in the stadium project, a group of students reported on their excursion to London–Lille–Paris as well as on their emerging initial ideas for an "extreme stadium," by staging a "poetry game" with a multiple-projection installation (figure 4.12). Their narrative was based on contrasting the memories of those who had participated in the excursion with those who had remained in Vienna. The presentation consisted in the two groups associating short phrases with the pictures shown. This dialogue of experiences and concepts was embodied spatially with four projections: on a setup of double layers of transparent cloth facing each other, on the ground (projected from above), and on the wall. This spatial configuration expressed the contrasting positions of the groups. The double layers of cloth created interesting spatial effects, blurring and distorting the projected images. As it was filmed, the performance became a new narrative constituent of the stadium object of design.

In their study of famous buildings of modern architecture, the students of Vienna Academy built models of them, varying some of their features (see figure 4.1, above). The distinction of the building with respect to its environment presented students with the opportunity to understand both the influence of the context on the perception of the building and the qualities of the building per se, in some cases bringing a new and unexpected perception of it (figure 4.13).

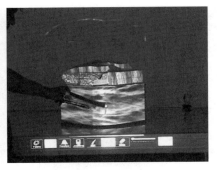

Figure 4.13
A house transforms into a cliff by changing its external coverage. The complex relationship between objects and their contexts creates a space where designers can practice patterns of design such as "creative density" and "ephemerality" (see chapter 2).

Alignment

As we said above, different people create different constituents of an object in different moments, in different places, by and with different materials. The constituents of an object are very diverse: they range from physical to virtual and/or mixed artifacts, from abstract written or 2D or 3D graphical representations to more realistic models, to the physical embodiment of the object; from artistic, expressive views to formalized, precise representations, sometimes enriched with computational power; and so on. Some of them are complementary (characterizing different parts or different aspects of the object), other are overlapping (characterizing different viewpoints and/or different scales of the same part of the object), and others are partially complementary and partially overlapping.

As part of his individual stadium project, one student projected images of two residential buildings on double layers of cloth, which he arranged in the curved shapes of the buildings, with the buildings facing each other, in order to re-create the site (figure 4.14). During the presentation the two buildings were undergoing changes. While the class watched, he visualized the transformation of the balconies into seating arrangements for viewing a soccer game in the space in between. The student held a barcode scanner in one hand, with which he scanned barcodes he had placed on diagrams and plans, and a switch in his other hand. This allowed him to direct the display of media onto the three different projection surfaces. A physical model representing his design of bathrooms and other spaces underneath the stadium was augmented with touch sensors. He used this arrangement for projecting detailed drawings of this space onto the wall in between the two buildings.

In this example, several constituents are used concurrently to communicate the project: the picture of facades and therein the interventions on the two large

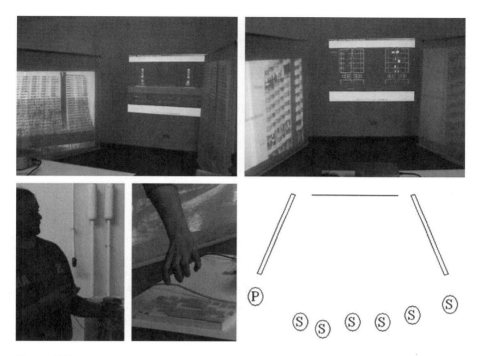

Figure 4.14

projections, the 2D plan in between, the physical model used as a navigation map, and finally the arrangements of the projection in space. All of these provide different views and communicate different aspects, all of which have been developed consistently.

Through the creation of new constituents the object evolves, augmenting the knowledge characterizing it. Its evolution's distribution in space and time is not a streamlined process, and therefore, inconsistent constituents may emerge. In reference to the design context, a prospect and a plan of a building may not offer views of the same building, even if they are constituents of the same object. Thus, there is a problem of alignment: can the constituents of an object be aligned? And if yes, how can this happen?

The CAD systems, widely used in all design fields, have apparently solved this problem, transforming the relationship between an object and its constituents into one between an artifact and its views. From a CAD perspective, the alignment problem does not exist, since there is a core model in the memory of the system that constitutes the object. Moreover, the CAD system is capable of automatically aligning all constituents once a change has been introduced in any of them. The system transfers the change in the core model and, through it, propagates it to all other constituents.

However, the CAD perspective assumes that the only legitimate constituents are those created through and in it. In the previous chapter we discussed the variety of representations and the relevance of materiality in design practice. This contradicts the above assumption: even when a design team widely and continuously uses a CAD system, designers create and/or import a large variety of constituents not based on that system. Because of this, the alignment problem still remains open and in fact with a higher criticality, since designers may rely too heavily on the automatic alignment of CAD-based constituents, disregarding the other ones. This should not be read as criticism of the utility of CAD systems; rather, it is a warning about the distorted view that proposes those systems as capable of simplifying the social complexity of design practice. Even with CAD systems, design still faces the alignment problem, since the practices of human beings cannot be fully restricted by any constraint.

However, within the design process participants feel that they are interacting through its constituents with the object itself. The devices and materials they interact with get sense from the object of which they are constituents. Their misalignment in most cases is not a problem: the misalignment of the constituents does not cause designers to feel a lack of integrity in what they are designing. If and when people view things as constituents, interacting with and through them, they align them with each other. The alignment problem is a complexity problem: when the experience becomes too complex, then alignment becomes critical. Alignment can be supported, helping people to manage complexity via automatic propagation of changes or by signaling new misalignments or, mainly, by increasing communication within the team.

Therefore, we can exclude two limit cases of perfectly aligned and of fully misaligned constituents: perfectly aligned constituents, which would refer unambiguously to the very same object, are in fact impossible in human experience. By contrast, fully misaligned constituents, referring to intrinsically different objects, are associated with the failure of the design process. Generally, the constituents of an object have a certain degree of alignment, but they are not fully aligned. Sometimes it is not even clear if they are aligned or not: the different viewpoints and the partiality of the representations they embody may create a certain degree of ambiguity with respect to the object they refer to. This is because each interaction involves a limited number of constituents and people in different moments and places. Therefore, the misalignment among the constituents of an object reflects the dynamics of the relationships among the people interacting through and with them, where every new interaction, to the extent it is innovative, modifies some constituents and/or creates some new ones.

As the number of constituents increases, the question of if and to what extent they are aligned may provoke great confusion in the participants, since the object then loses its ability to stand as a boundary among them: its status as a bridge between people with different cultures, languages, and experiences is contradicted by the controversial images they receive of it. But this is a very rare case, because people know how to manage a certain degree of misalignment. In fact, they have developed various techniques for aligning, at least relatively, the constituents of an object. First, the true absolute alignment can be performed, propagating a change to all the other constituents, making new versions of them and ordering the versions accordingly. Second, a relative alignment can be reached by contextualizing contradictory constituents, for example, naming them by author, date, and place of creation, so that people can see the different options created within their interactions without necessarily choosing a unique constituent among them.

To understand alignment thoroughly, we must shift from thinking of it as a quality the constituents of an object may or may not have to conceiving alignment as a process. Within human experience, there is a continuous intertwining of alignment and misalignment, generated respectively by propagating changes, contextualizing contradictory constituents, creating new constituents, or changing existing ones. As a result, misalignment does not disintegrate the object of design. Alignment and misalignment are strictly coupled in human social experience, since the socialization of innovation can only be grounded on a shared understanding of what is changing and has to be changed. Therefore, we can claim that within human social interaction the constituents of an object are never perfectly aligned and are also never misaligned beyond the limit, guaranteeing that the object maintains its identity.

In the design context, the intertwining between alignment and misalignment creates conditions where social creativity is effective, that is, where the qualities discussed in chapter 2—materiality and the diversity of representations, experience of dimensionality and scaling, narrativity, reprogramming, creative density, and the transient and ephemeral—couple with reliability, avoiding the risk of transforming design into a never-ending narrative where individual creativity does not take responsibility with respect to the design process.

Navigation

When interacting with and through an object, designers often need to move from one constituent to another, either to narrow their view of the object (for example, moving from a general view of the facade of a building to one of its windows), or to broaden it (moving from a window to the wall containing it), or to change the type of interaction with it (touching the texture covering the facade presented in a drawing, changing a detail in the door of the building shown in a 3D simulation, etc.). Whenever a person enters in an architecture studio, she will be surprised by the number of drawings, models, and materials covering all of its walls and all accessible vertical and horizontal surfaces and by how often designers move from one constituent to another.

Figure 4.15
Several constituents and their integration: projections, 2D representations with barcodes, physical models.

In preparing a project presentation, one of the architecture students plotted out her CAD plans with barcodes on them. In one of her printouts she integrated the barcodes into a diagrammatic representation (figure 4.15, right corner). She presented her work using multiple interactive artifacts that triggered the playing of sound and visual media on a projected screen (figure 4.15, upper right). Barcodes were integrated into posters that displayed plans and diagrams (figure 4.15, upper left). A physical model of the section of the stadium and surrounding environment was made interactive with touch sensors (figure 4.15, bottom; figure 4.16).

The growing number of constituents of an object of design reflects, on the one hand, the diversity of interactions designers and stakeholders have with it and the impossibility of performing all of them with only one constituent; on the other hand, it indicates the complex history of decisions, discussions, changes, uncertainties, afterthoughts, and reexaminations that generate changes in the design. In both cases people need to move from one constituent to another: to become able to interact in a certain way with the object in the first case, and to access the updated object in the

Figure 4.16
A full view of the spatial layout for the presentation.

second one. We provided the *Atelier* students with "The Tangible Archive," a support to store physical, virtual, and mixed constituents together, to help them to manage the complexity of navigating among diverse constituents (figure 4.17).

Sometimes a designer will want to move from the constituent she is interacting with to another one of which she knows when it was built, by whom, and where it is. Sometimes, though, she wants to move to a constituent that does not exist yet, or perhaps a version of it exists, but at another place not accessible to her, or perhaps it has not been created yet but she knows that it can be created. This second more complex situation suggests an interesting interrelationship between the diversity of interactions and changes in design (see above): any change, as we have said above, needs to be propagated into all the constituents of the object. This requires time, and frequently the designer will need to access the updated version of a particular constituent that does not yet exist. However, the desire to access nonexisting constituents can go much further than this limited case: people may want or need to access a constituent that they know could exist, even if though it does not exist yet. For example, a designer may need to access a 3D model that has not yet been built, or a perspective designed from a viewpoint not yet developed.

In other words, the number of constituents that people participating in an experience are dealing with is larger that that of the existing constituents. This is similar to the situation human beings experience with language: the space of possibility that language opens to them is larger than the number of phrases they have already used. Therefore, navigation is what allows people both to access and to create new constituents, so that both accessing and creating constituents appear as steps in living an experience and not as isolated actions. The idea of multiconstituent objects that we

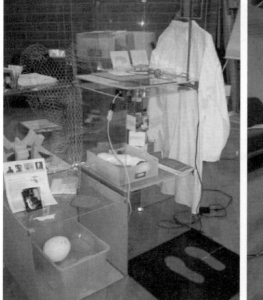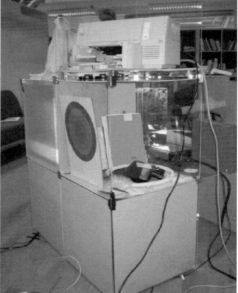

Figure 4.17
The "Tangible Archive" and organizing zone from Atelier was a place for informal storing, combining and presenting mixed materials.

are developing in these pages tries to emphasize experience as the main context of any human action or interaction.

Navigating among constituents is a major practice within design and thus needs to be adequately supported within it. Navigation is sometimes constrained by the fact that in many situations participants may access only a limited number of the media supporting the constituents, and therefore they need to access the most suitable of them in that moment. Recognizing this fact is important because many computer-based tools like CAD systems allow for an efficient navigation among the constituents they support, but they pay no attention to the other types of constituents. In other cases, navigation is constrained by simple lack of information; if people don't know about updated constituents, they cannot access them and so are forced to continue working with obsolete ones.

Of course, navigation among constituents is very important to inspiration, because it brings forth the creative density within which a diversity of representations can support designers in changing their views and their interpretations of what they are doing.

Expansion/Contraction

As we have said above, different participants in the design process concentrate their interests in and interact with different subsets of the constituents of the object being designed: for example, in the design of a machine, the technical engineers interact mainly with the drawings and models related to the functions of the machine, while industrial designers are mainly interested in the constituents that present the machine's external shape and its interfaces.

Moreover, breakdowns occurring in the design process may bring about a modification in the relationship of participants to its object. On the one hand, a radical change (e.g., the transformation of a window of a building into a French window) makes some constituents obsolete (e.g., the detailed view of the window) or irrelevant (e.g., the specification of its materials), while it requires that new constituents be created, substituting the former ones (all that regards the new French window) or to be absorbed in the design object (e.g., a description of the threshold the French window creates between the building and the outdoors). In particular, it is interesting that in making changes, designers experiment with the dependence of the object of design on their viewpoints, positions, and practices during the design process: in other words, a single object can have different instances (choosing a French window induces, for example, a shift from having only the building as the object of design to a different view, where the object of design is the building and its outdoors). When two instances are part of each other, we can see two movements from one to the other: expansion will augment the set of constituents constituting the object, and contraction will reduce it. Both these movements change the boundary between the object and its context: expansion transforms part of the context into constituents of the object, whereas contraction liberates some constituents, returning them to the context.

Expansion and contraction play a relevant role with respect to distinction and recognition, which we discussed briefly in the section above entitled "Context." Distinction and recognition, in fact, are based on the capability of participants to share the expansion and contraction of an object in accordance with the practice in which they are engaged. The expansion and contraction of objects with respect to context are intrinsically social phenomena. It could not be otherwise, since they are the outcomes of social interaction: the boundary between an object and its context (as well as the diverse webs of constituents characterizing diverse objects) reflects the way people interact.

Distinctions and recognitions are effective to the extent that they are shared by people participating in an experience: when sharing becomes difficult, this creates further problems, since participants may become unable to share the object itself that is the focus of their interaction at any moment. Expansion, in particular by augmenting the constituents that make up an object, may create some misalignment that participants are not aware of, while contraction may break some of the links that serve to guarantee the alignment.

Configurability, reprogramming, dimensionality, and scaling are some qualities of design made possible by expansion and contraction, since they depend on the capability of designers to modify their viewpoint, perspective, and objectives.

Conclusion

Analyzing the concept of the object of design in detail at an adequate level of granularity allows us to understand the practice of designers within their design experiences. The relationship between an object and its constituents, as well as the way people interact with constituents and through them with objects, accounts for how people interact and communicate with and about the objects of design. The interplays between things and words, distinction and recognition, sharing and innovating, alignment and misalignment, object and context, all appear as strictly related to each other as different aspects of human practice. Supporting design practice, from this viewpoint, requires the creation of a platform where participants can access, modify, align, and navigate the constituents of an object, and when needed, expand and contract it, sharing their knowledge about their actions and interactions.

From this viewpoint, ontologies are one of the most relevant research themes we need to investigate, since the web of constituents constituting an object is based on an ontology and reflects it (we could say it is an instantiation of an ontology). Ontologies are strictly coupled with languages (with language games) but they are not the same. Whereas language games define the space of possible communication of the people participating in an experience, ontologies define something more specific and concrete: the space of their possible interaction, where interaction refers to vested behavior, that is, to any behavior whose sense can be shared.

Objects of design can help account for many of the relevant and problematic aspects of design, in particular the fact that design is a practice where people deal with something (the *thing* to be designed) that does not yet exist. In fact, the designed *thing* emerges, if and when it emerges, primarily at the very end of the design process, when designers deliver the outcome of their work. Thus the object of design lives without being embodied into any special constituent until it reaches its end. But when it reaches its end, then designers deliver to customers the constituent embodying their object itself. It is important to emphasize this: what designers deliver is not the object, but just its embodiment—what they deliver is a *thing*, not an object. Customers who receive the *thing*, which is the outcome of design, can experience the *thing* again as an object, but as a different object: not the object of design, but the object of their experience.

The outcome of design is decontextualized with respect to the design experience, but good design delivers things that are rich in the sense that the design choices have given to them. As Latour (Latour and Weibel 2005) indicated, things are decontextualized but convey sense to the people interacting with them: things are matters of concern insofar as they are able to offer people new possibilities of experience. The quality of design transforms the richness of a design experience in the richness of its outcome, which itself constitutes the basis for a rich experience for the people interacting with it.

Things are not mere devices: a chair is not just a tool for sitting, a personal computer is not just a tool for information processing. During their lives, human beings experience objects, *things*, and devices; and in saying so we distinguish different types of *interactions*, not different types of materials.

5 Designing as Metamorphing

Design work is characterized by gathering and mobilizing a great quantity of materials in different formats, both material and digital. As expressed in chapter 3, this diversity of material being present in the design process is highly inspirational, but its importance goes beyond mere inspiration. Design proceeds by the expression of ideas, needs, and opportunities. What we can expect from the discussion in chapter 4 is that there is such a thing as an object of design, and it emerges and evolves through the successive becomings of constituents in a web of design. The web in itself constructs the design space in which the eventual design artifact evolves. This chapter will elaborate how this web of constituents is woven and how this weaving revolves around a shifting object of design. We will address how design takes place through the designer's engaging in the transformations of the objects of design. Design is described as an act of metamorphing; to create the metamorphoses of the objects of design and to reflect on the effects of the changes is the core of design work. In many ways, designers envision and realize concepts by objectifying and manipulating a variety of representations of design.

In *What's the Sound of Thunder?* (Asplund 2004), Swedish sociologist Johan Asplund attempts to widen the scope of current philosophy of science. The starting point is his fascination with an old theater machine used, at the Drottningholm Theater in Stockholm, for producing the sound of thunder. The machine consists of a wooden box lined with sheet metal and containing a number of stones of various sizes. It is operated manually by lowering or raising one end of the box, making the stones roll, their friction against the sheet metal producing a sound quite like thunder. Analyzing his fascination and the relationship between the machine-made sound and the sound of actual thunder, Asplund realizes that the sound is produced in a special way. It does not play a recording of the authentic sound, which could have easily been done. Neither is the sound an attempt to imitate the actual sound, like onomatopoetic sounds like "wrooar" or "boom," something all of us have tried at one time or another. Instead, the machine produces a miniaturized experience of the sound. The effect is a playful "performed imagination"; we can fully understand that this is not the sound of thunder but we have no problem accepting it as such. It is a fascination with the unfamiliar that can nevertheless be recognized, the transformed that has retained just enough of the original.

To explain his fascination, Asplund makes use of the concepts of *simulation* and *simulacrum*. Simulation would be the attempt to imitate the actual sound of thunder as realistically as possible. Simulacrum would imply that the sound produced is close enough to real thunder to recognize it as such, while preserving the difference between the illusionary and the real. Simulacrum can be said to be a process of transference between different entities through their commonalities. The difference between the entities forms a creative gap and is manifested as an act of transformation and metamorphoses, wherein the actor must engage his imagination to understand both the common and the unique aspects of the associated expressions. He is thus building a web of "thunder." The observed differences are actually more like variations on a common theme of thunder. Moving between the variations strengthens the perception of the theme in a playful way that resembles the idea of bricolage. Central aspects of design can be viewed as a kind of bricolage where different material, are brought together, mixed, and configured in various iterations. Transforming representations and shifting between modalities, scale, and material highlight different aspects of design and widen the design space, communicating ideas and narrowing down concepts. It is a challenge for the designer to handle a multitude of different media and representations. The transference from one media to another without losing any essential qualities is often a crucial issue.

Looking at such an evolving network of relations that eventually stabilizes itself in what can be considered a "factual" design proposal, we might ask ourselves what is there to begin with. We do not want to take a common understanding of ideas and concepts as starting points for the design process, which are successively narrowed down into a materialized design artifact. Instead the focus is on movements between different representations, as illustrated in figure 5.1. The perspective focuses foremost not on the individual act of the designer but rather on the changes readable in the representations and how those changes came about.

To the left in figure 5.1 is a printout of a book on sign language used as inspiration in a project about a tracking system for recognizing hand movements. To the right is a kind of representation that most often is made relative late during a project, a UML model illustrating the inheritance of classes. Though not from the same project in this case, these kinds of representations often coexist within the same project. As they are elaborated and discussed in different situations, representations and materials undergo many translations or metamorphoses. Tim Ingold analyzes the concept of skill while reflecting on the making of artifacts and the relationship between form and substance (Ingold 2000). His perspective, while defining certain points about the skill exhibited by a craftsperson as he uses different tools to make artifacts out of specific materials,

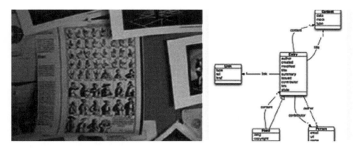

Figure 5.1
Two different kinds of design representations.

is similar to the more-often cited work of Donald Schön (1987) on the reflective practitioner:

Life is not contained within things, nor is it transported about. It is rather laid down along paths of movement, of action and perception. (Ingold 2000, 242)

This stance is grounded in a view where human action is situated in social and material contexts. What Ingold claims is that instead of thinking of making something as something that happens when two separate things are put together (the maker with a certain intentionality and plan and an instrument with a certain functionality to manipulate materials with certain properties), we can think of this situation as a foundational condition of involvement of the craftsperson, his tools, and the raw materials. Thus intentionality and functionality are not preexisting properties in the user and the used, but rather are immanent in the activity itself. Skill, then, is not just a question of applying mechanical force to exterior objects; it also includes care, judgment, and dexterity in a fine-tuning of movements that can reach a rhythmic fluency, which is the trademark of a skilled practitioner. From this perspective, materials, representations, and the agent are all parts of a force-field, where the interface between them is emerging rather than being constituted from inherent properties residing in the different parts.

Circulating References

A fruitful attempt to better understand the unfolding of these constituents that makes possible the "building of a web," in this case related to scientific work and knowledge production, can be found in the writings of French philosopher of science Bruno Latour. Latour uses the term "circulating references" to describe how matter gradually moves along a chain before eventually ending up as knowledge. The concept is an attempt to restructure the representational dilemma inherent in the relationship between words and things; what really happens when we move from referent to sign?

Space becomes a table chart, the table chart becomes a cabinet, the cabinet becomes a concept, and the concept becomes an institution. (Latour 1999, 36)

Latour gives a close and detailed analysis of his participation with a group of soil scientists on a field trip to Amazonas to explore whether the rain forest is advancing over the savannah, or vice versa. Sampling and classifying vast collections of soil and plants, taking meticulous notes on locations and circumstantial facts on the sampling, moving between sites, carrying equipment and samples from field sites or to hotels, the scientists use an array of scientific methods and instruments to transform pieces of the world into shareable facts. One example is the use of the pedocomparator, a box with rows of smaller boxes where clods of earth can be placed, classified, and transported. The instrument is a hybrid object, through which the world of things becomes a sign, and is eventually articulated as a collection of facts in a written article. The world is sampled in pieces and separated before it's reassembled by the scientists into more abstract entities, more suited for transportation and presentation. It is mobile rather than abstract, because the scientific graph, for example, is perhaps not necessarily more abstract than a piece of soil. Within scientific discourse the graph is just as concrete as any material artifact or entity. It simply works in another context. An especially mobile entity of importance for knowledge production is the written text.

The written text, in its turn, mobilizes its own internal references of charts, diagrams, and tables. All these references are a means of keeping something constant through the series of transformations. The different stages are not copied from the preceding one to the next, but rather are aligned with each other, so that at the final stage it is possible to return to the first. This is a constructionist perspective on knowledge production, where knowledge doesn't reflect external states or things by resemblance; instead, the correspondence of words and things is seen as a focus only on the outer extremes (language/nature) of a chain with many links. The term "reference" is what Latour uses for matter (nature), which gradually moves along the chain to form (knowledge representation). The transformations bear little resemblance to each other, and the coherence of the different stages, of what we call *things*, depends on how well the steps are articulated. The approach dissolves the representational dilemma between words and things.

It can be argued that the production of scientific facts and the design of objects follow the same patterns that we see in Latour's point of view, especially if we understand this pattern as one of unifying diverse components into a meaningful whole (artifact or fact). The seeds for a design gain material properties as they are expressed by the designer in the form of different design representations. As the changes are reflected, the ideas are subject to metamorphoses, conceptual change, and further materialization in new representations. They are developed in relation to the previous expressions and circulate like Latour's references, not only until the designers make a final decision, but afterward: they are also subject to change through the appropriation of users and integration with culture and everyday life. A major part of design representations concerns the objectification of ideas, gradually narrowing down the concept. But it is not just a question of the relationship between the signifier, the representation, and the signified, or the thing represented, but a complex network of expressions, not all of which concern the actual design idea. Just as in Latour's view, where one science hides another; the design process also holds a variety of other kinds of material. Some of them are representations of work or context, some relate to project organization, and some are inspirational artifacts that might seem to have no relationship at all to the design task at hand.

Numerous artifacts tend to be used in any given project, as can be seen in figure 5.2. During a project, designers develop their work in parallel sketches, showing forms of, for example, a building's facade, detailed plans, depictions of atmospheres and situations, 3D models, and collages of visual and tactile material. These heterogeneous

Figure 5.2
Design representations from an interaction design project: representations from work (upper left), storyboard scenario (upper right), brainstorm map (bottom left), and video sketch (bottom right).

representations are often manipulated simultaneously, and they often evolve into different versions.

While the reference to Latour constitutes a useful analogy, we can still observe differences in focus. What emerges in Latour's arguments is a problem of control. How can we validate the chain of circulating references as a truth—how well are the links in the chain connected? For Latour, institutions can be characterized by these orderings, and usually what is relevant is a process of ordering. Ensuring rigidity in the chain of translations is also performed to achieve reversibility in the whole chain of circulating references. What emerges in design, rather, is more an issue of successive giving form to the object of design. During this process, more is at stake than just the convergence of references. In many of our observations, we observed a reversed process of "disordering." Metamorphing is often outside of intentional acts. The interstice as such is the event; there is no goal, or the goal is of a second order to the experience of the in-between. Another similar articulation of metamorphing is the fact that this disordering is a reversed mediation. With that we address the resolving of an achieved structure, a liberating process of disordering such as reprogramming. Reprogramming refers to the ability to see something as quite different than it is. This is illustrated in several instances of design work, in a process that requires divergence rather than convergence in the interaction with artifacts. These aspects are at the core of Asplund's story of the sound of thunder. The differences observed are common enough for coherence, but still, different enough, to mobilize an imagination that would lead to unexpected experiences. This implies that metamorphing can include very marginal nodes in the building of a web. Furthermore, while Latour's description of scientific work illustrates a movement from matter to fact, this movement is less obvious in design. On the contrary, the movement can be said to be reversed, going from fact to matter in the sense that factual circumstances are indefinite starting points for design projects that move toward materialized forms. The need for reversibility is less pressing for the designer. Instead, the direction forward and toward the designed form is what drives the designer's inquiry and the unfolding web of design.

Transforming Representations

In chapter 2 we referred to both Dewey's notion of inquiry and Schön's theories on the reflective practitioner. Dewey's critical stance on empirical and rationally inspired epistemology emphasizes how knowledge production takes its starting point in active doing. Experience does not stem from passive observation, but is developed through creative investigations and interaction with the environment, which is continuously changing. These investigations are not performed as a random process, but inquiries can be said to be a controlled attempt to change an intermediate and vaguely understood situation. The inquiries and interactions produce consequences that have to be framed and integrated in our understanding as to be part of a provisional solution to situations that formed starting point for the inquiry. For Dewey, inquiry is the resolution of a puzzling situation; the goal is not a change in beliefs or confirmation of knowledge in the inquirer, but answers to problematic situations.

Dewey's ideas were, as stated in chapter 2, foundational for Schön's search for a structure in professional inquiry such as performed by a designer "reflecting in and on action." In *The Reflective Practitioner* (Schön 1987) he analyzes how a therapist and a supervisor of design students engage in their inquiries. Despite their occupational differences, both practitioners share several similarities. In both cases, the therapist controlling conversations with his patient and the supervisor directing the work of his students, the practitioner treats the situation as unique and acknowledges that no universal methods or techniques are applicable. This is not to say that they start from scratch, with no previous valuable experience. On the contrary, they use their professional experiences in artistic ways while still confronting a situation they consider not fully understood. Both can hold several ways of looking at the problematic situation at the same time without disrupting the flow of the inquiry. Both the student and the patient have tried to resolve their problematic situations but have failed. What both practitioners try to do is reframe the situations in order to understand them better. This process is highly experimental. The consequences of the reframing have to be investigated in on-the-spot experiments. As a result, unexpected and new situations arise that have to be further examined. The unintended changes infuse the situation with new and sometimes surprising meaning. In transforming representations and design as metamorphing, the interaction with materials shapes the situation and "talks back" to the designer's inquiries. This back talk is manifested both in communication with others and in individual inquiries into materials and situations. We will look at one example illustrating the necessity of not getting stuck in the "circulating references." This example is based on observations of an important collaborative design situation, the critique session.

Transformations in Dialogue

In a spiral of appreciating, reframing, experimenting, and reappreciating, the inquiry continues until the designer achieves a satisfactory coherence between artifact and idea. If the designer fails to reflect on the back talk, the changes required to drive the inquiry forward will not occur. In many cases, the transformations act as common ground for communicating with other actors. In learning environments for design these are, of course, very important situations. The various materials for design are used in different ways to align the many participants in the conversation.

In this example from the Verdichtete Gemeinschaft project in Vienna, a student, H, is having a critique session with her supervisor while she presents her project. She was working on an underground parking garage as part of project to revitalize an area with immigrant workers. Examining the translations, going back and forth, the supervisor wants to push the student forward, making her transcend conventional views on the unsolved design situation. The supervisor tries to challenge her conceptualization of the problem and tries to make her frame the problem differently, and to work with untraditional views of well-known problems such as heavy traffic being problematic for city life. Another issue is the nature of her metamorphing. The evolving nature of her models is condensed and many perspectives are contained in one model, instead of having several versions.

On the table are a large model, her laptop, several books, pictures, and a large map of the Brunnenmarkt area on which she places a much smaller sketch model. She mentions that she has read a lot of material since the last critique session. During the session, the focus changes on the different versions of the model. The dialogue is like a negotiation, wherein different props are highlighted, put aside, and then brought back again.

One of her topics is the street with its many parked cars and the question of space for children to run around and play. But first she points to the larger model, explaining that the main problem here is the ground floor—perhaps the building could reach across the street since during winter time it is quite cold. Placing shops there is not an option. The next issue is that she would like to open up the park, construct a second level so that people may park their cars underneath. They should have enough space there for doing the things they would do in the street, such as doing repair work on their cars. Her model shows a construction that leaves space for the trees. The supervisor argues that this second layer with the openings for the trees will be far too expensive—did she calculate how many cars would fit into the space?

The student then looks at her model, saying she no longer finds it useful. The supervisor alludes to internal strata and layers and the different territories that may be created—what combination of private-public, noisy-calm would work, since these are the parameters that define the structure. One might, for example, lead the street up to the living space (on the second level), thereby letting the public space come closer.

H listens while opening her computer. She is looking for material to back up her arguments.

Supervisor: Maybe you could plan for an underground garage, opening it to market and street and here you could add some terraces—[H hesitates].
Supervisor: You could let them enter the park easily—this is also a certain quality, those cars, with their windows pulled down and the music—
H: But it doesn't work like this [pointing to a picture with parking cars]—the cars block everything.

The supervisor argues against this "orderly garage culture"; one might see the car with its loud stereo as part of people's everyday life—the point is to question the separation of functions—look at Mies who tested his ideas rigorously (he refers to a project in

Figure 5.3
Backing up arguments by bringing forth specific material.

Figure 5.4
Shifting focus by addressing a certain aspect of the material at hand.

which Mies van der Rohe created "staples of one-family houses"). Here the supervisor is trying to reframe the problem and to see positive potentials in unintended effects, such as a blending of private and public. The student insists and refuses to reformulate her original problem of children not being able to play in heavily trafficked streets. The session continues with discussions on the park. The supervisors tries to explain that the overall situation might be too complex for her single model; perhaps she should build several models, one for each problem. For successful transformations, each metamorphosis has to be reflected. But the student is not open to change of the situation and sticks to her original problem framing.

H opens her computer again—a drawing shows parking for 77 cars between the trees. She insists:

H: I'd like to separate children's playing from the traffic so that there is no need to watch them.

Supervisor: Why not play in the street?

H: I read that most accidents happen with children who run between parking cars.

Supervisor: Do you have data?

H: In this book—look at this picture, and be honest, a street with parked cars, nothing ever happens there.

While this example tries to illustrate the necessity of reflecting on each step in the series of transformations inherent in design, it also reflects how supervisors try to use their experience from previous design cases to fit to the special situation at hand. In reflecting not only in but also on action, a repertoire is built for the designer that allows for applying experiences from previous situations to the situation at hand. This application will overlap with the new situation only partially, but in the tension between the situations, new and unique design knowledge can be formulated. It is a question of seeing the unfamiliar in a familiar way. But the unintended effects due to the differences must be observed. It is a "seeing as" that can change underlying presumptions.

Supervisors know that periods of profound engagement with materials and engaged dwelling with design representations have to be balanced with a certain amount of distancing. Performing the transformations of the currents that are at the heart of design requires fulfilling the metamorphing and letting go of earlier defining characteristics. It is true that heavy traffic must be taken into account in urban planning, and without judging this specific case, it can be stated that the act of metamorphing implies moving ahead and making decisions. It is a matter of not getting stuck in the evolved environment of design representations.

While this design situation was thoroughly analyzed by Schön in his "Educating the Reflective Practitioner" (in Schön 1987) in terms of the dialogical sequencing that takes place between student and teacher, we can also interpret the situation as one of the supervisor displaying his skill not only in the reframing of the problem but also in a specific sensitivity to the wholeness of the web of constituents for design. He knows that something is missing that will not allow the prospective leap forward. In one of Schön's examples the supervisor tells the student that she must "draw and draw" to calibrate her material. This does not imply an endless series of transformations, but rather a successive elaboration of the different domains of design, such as scale, siting, and structure. They are nodes in the web of constituents that must be explored and experienced to be understood not in isolation, but in relation to each other, together. The nodes can each be understood, described, and discussed separately, but a "designerly" way of thinking requires seeing their place in the whole process. Part of design knowledge rests on this ability to "see what is missing" in the web, knowing that parts of the web are like empty placeholders that can be filled in a successive weaving of the whole toward the design artifact. In the following example we will observe an architect student performing this weaving, successively filling the placeholders and observing.

Designers Circulating the References

An important aspect of design work is to gain a conceptual understanding of the design that is solid enough to carry work forward, but flexible enough to allow innovation. It is a matter of extending and opening up the design space in such a way that what exists can be imagined in a new way. The concept of reprogramming refers to how ideas are generated by the factual but recognized and transformed into something different. Transforming the representations is one way of reprogramming their underlying ideas. Experimenting with scale, dimensionality, colors, and social perspectives are all examples of reprogramming activities.

Following Tim, one of the architecture students, in an assignment, we can observe how he transforms different representations of an object, a saw, in order to eventually make a model of a shelter. This example does not concern a design solution to a problematic situation, but is more an exploration of materials and tools that eventually leads to a model for a shelter. This kind of project is common in many design schools, and it illustrates well the diversity of materials in design and how design can proceed through metamorphing, transforming the different representations in a way that results in constructive inquiry. The project was about making visual and material studies starting from a working tool. Each student chose a work tool, such as a hammer, sickle, chisel, or saw. They first made studies of the tool by analyzing its form. They would then have to create three-dimensional models from observations of movements of the tool in use. These studies produced a series of visual and material explorations on drawings and several models for each tool. The starting point of the exercise was to find a tool on which the students would work for the first semester.

Observation and Representation
The first exercise they had to perform was to take photos of the tool. Students had to take ten black-and-white pictures, following certain guidelines: showing the tool as an object; showing it caught by the eye of the camera; showing its identity; revealing a context of use and meaning; showing its geometrical structure and material quality; and displaying it in images twice the size of the object.

The importance lies in the search for the object's identity, which is for the most part not obvious but has to be revealed by the spectator, for example, through the photograph. Tim's choice was a saw as used for cutting down trees. In his photos he tried to capture the saw's shifting shadows according to its movement, as observed from different sides.

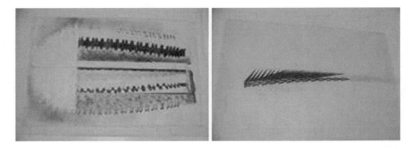

Figure 5.5
Freehand drawings of the saw.

Freehand Drawing

The next exercise was to draw the tool freehand, as can be seen in figure 5.5. The students had to work on their architectural view of the object, including all sides of it by rotating the object in space and drawing it in pencil on one A1 paper. Tim's first drawing focuses again on the saw's shadows. He draws the different appearances that occur when one moves and rotates the tool.

Certainly, all of the transformations mobilized in a design process might be difficult to experience. Encompassing artistic work, information analysis, social understanding, and technical experimentation, the process is iterative and lacks a clear center. Shifting perspectives and controlling the process, all while wanting to expand the boundaries to imagine the unexpected, requires being able to maintain connections. Nelson and Stolterman (2003) write on this interlinking of stability and creativity as beneficial for design and being at the core of design work. They refer to Csikszentmihali's concept of flow in terms of tension and how a designer's intuition depends on the ability to grasp the wholeness of the situation, including the ability to imagine change. The same representation can itself contain several interpretations and might occur in many versions. As pointed out by Akin (1986), this doesn't mean that the meanings they carry are contradictory, but that they enlighten different aspects. In many instances decision making is inherent in one of several twists of a representation and backtracking is of great importance. This means that the representations are subject to juxtaposition and superimposition in a manner akin to bricolage. Often they are presented dynamically; inventing hybrid forms of representation is common in the field of work.

Reading/Drawing and Analysis/Abstraction

Tim's next step in his exploration of the saw was to move on to a level of reflection and analyze his own drawings. First learned and trained as a technical skill, the architectural drawing should become a primary mode of thinking and observing objects through abstraction. Tim's tasks at this stage included: representation in plan, section, elevation, and drawing the movements of the tool and the body.

Figure 5.6
The drawings became part of an architectural way of thinking as they were analyzed.

Next, the geometry of the tool's movement was broken down and drawn on paper at a 1:1 or 1:2 scale. The drawings were to consider the following aspects: the spatial limits of the tool while in use; the rhythm of the tool's movement; repetition and the passage of time; geometry of the movement (horizontal, vertical, circular, etc.); and the space inscribed by the movement.

Tim described the drawings as going deeper into the tool's movement, a separation of fast and slow. He tried to capture the tool's complicated geometrical "fanning out" by creating different drawings.

This parting of methods and focus offers a nice view on how the styles and rhythm of the students differ, some not focusing on the original plan but rather following their own imagination, according to the either visual or mathematical talent. Although their working space is severely limited and they are close together in the classroom, their works are quite autonomous and do not follow the same concept, either temporarily or materially.

Translation from Drawing to Model
The next job was to use the drawings to create a three-dimensional model, physical and non-moving but representing the tool's movement in space, and its repetition in time and space. Some materials were suggested, such as metal wire, wood sticks, paper, and cardboard. The scale was supposed to be 1:1 or 1:2. The first small models tried

to follow the idea of the drawings, but there was always some point, some direction missing. Tim built different models, some connected with and some disconnected from each other, to find the most suitable form and the closest identity of the tool.

As different representations exhibit and clarify different particular aspects of the design, it is important to forge and maintain connections between them. In many instances, students configure and reconfigure design materials so as to read and reread the configuration from different points of view and to be able to return to a particular moment where some specific issue emerged. In this process of reconceptualizing and detailing, the design representations and their relationships change continuously. Arranging and rearranging material in the workspace is an essential part of this process, with the physical landscape of representations on the walls and tables in constant movement. The transformation of representations is not a static sequence; the relationship between them evolves over time, and an important part of their impact is how they are arranged and rearranged in relation to each other.

What emerges is that manipulating the presence and absence of materials and bringing them into dynamic spatial relations in which they can confront each other are not just a context or prerequisite for doing the work; rather, they are an integral part of accomplishing the work itself. To manipulate the context is to do the work. Typically, what is important is not just to create or change a document or other materials, but to do so in the presence of and in relation to others. (Büscher et al. 1999, 27)

In this way the design studio turns into a landscape with an ever-changing topography of design representations. While moving toward giving form to an integrated whole, the designer intentionally keeps open the ambiguity and complexity. He or she creates a design world, a narrative of the imagined artifact, in which to act. The expressions and representations precede the posing of problems that follow from them, and new interpretations create yet new design worlds. In this evolving landscape of design representations, the transformations of the representation constitute the core of the work. As each representation can contain a seed of the eventual design, they carry something that is growing but not yet existing in its full state. In a way they are "pre-presentations" rather than representations. Every one of them has material aspects that are of great importance; but they do not make sense until they are fully materialized. To transform them is to do the actual design work, and in the process, the distinction between material and context often gets blurred. Tim's journey with the saw continued with an exploration of how the saw behaved while being used.

Movement in Context

The next exercise was to make a video about the tool in use, or in movement in its own context. The video was supposed to show the working space and the situation there, the appearance of the tool, its handling, movement, and so on. The length of the video was not to be longer than one minute, and filters, transitions, and so on were not allowed.

The trip shown in the illustration here was to the "Reservegarten," a botanical and zoological garden at Vienna's periphery. Students first walked through the whole terrain, including the greenhouses with exotic plants and the outside-terrariums with snakes and tortoises, a bee house, fishponds, and a labyrinth. The students' workplaces there had been prepared in advance according to their wishes.

There they had to shoot a video entitled "Movement in Context." Creating a video for the first time produces a lot of problems: how to handle the camera, how to capture the subject's movement, and last but not least, how to present a tool's use in an interesting way in such a short time.

Models of a Shelter

The last exercise was to create another model, including the most important results that could be considered a "shelter," which can be seen in figure 5.8. All the steps just described are assumed to analyze the tool, producing different representations and bringing the idea of the model, fitting the abstraction, nearer. Compared to the others, Tim's model was quite big, but it was somewhat difficult to see inside it. As in the beginning he was still very interested in playing with light and shadow and in the possibility of changing the outer appearance.

Before looking further at how Tim achieved this metamorphing of the model, we should pause for a moment to introduce a way of enriching the possibilities for this shape-shifting of design representations. We can see how, even though these different

Figure 5.7
A still from the video showing the tool during actual use.

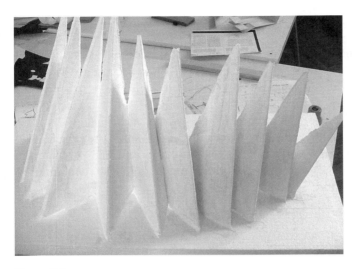

Figure 5.8
The model of the saw as a "shelter."

transformations are performed in a linear sequence in time, the evolving meaning of performing them is not inherent in the single list of transformations. The different transformations highlight different aspects of the work, and, as in Latour's case, they are circulating references of the saw as such and of the final artifact, in this case the model of a shelter. Taking photos and drawing the tool freehand are starting points, representations in different formats. Successively, then, the still-empty placeholders in the web of constituents are filled. Analysis and reflection are attached to the material representations; shooting video of the tool in use is yet another increment of the dimensions that underlie the final translation from drawing to model. Even if the drawings were one of the first tasks, the final translation from drawing to model couldn't have been performed, or it would have produced a very different result, without the other transformations. This is what enriches the "what-if" world built by the designer; the way he handles the whole network of relations is different from how he handles the singular transformations. Metamorphing refers to this managing of the whole web of circulating references. The saw universe acts as a scaffolding of placeholders for the object of design.

While we do find this building of a network for design, by engaging in transformations or metamorphing of representations, to be to some extent inherent in design work, we can also observe how particular strategies emerge in the work of different designers. As the relational aspects of the different representations or constituents are so important, it becomes an issue of how they might be connected and whether they are mobile or flexible enough. The Post-it note, for example, is a common form of

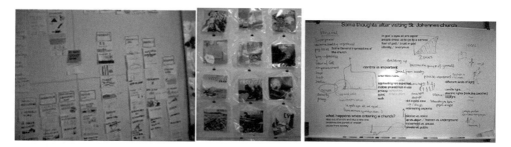

Figure 5.9
From let to right: Post-it notes, sealed plastic bags, and digital editing of the white board.

notation in many design studios in brainstorming or analytical work, because of the ease of putting it in another part of a mapping. Since, as already mentioned and illustrated, design is a movement forward toward the final artifact, it is also a matter of achieving a temporal closure in the metamorphing, so that we do not get stuck in an endless series of transformations. Figure 5.9 illustrates different strategies for this closing/opening up of representations. In one of the pictures, from a student project, this is done in a very explicit way. While attaching different keywords expressing value to different images and putting them together in plastic bags, the students felt that they had to make a decision and say "OK, this is how we will talk about them from now on." This was achieved by going to the local butcher shop and having the plastic bags vacuum sealed, making them stable objects no longer subject to change. In the final picture, a group of designers took a photo of a joint mapping annotated on a whiteboard. The photo was then edited on the computer, and yet further layers of text and imagery were superimposed.

It is an interesting issue how we might support these emerging strategies and how amalgamating digital media with material design representations makes for a rather specific platform. If we consider the example of the saw, which includes aspects of both circulation and transformations of the saw as a tool, a variety of "saw constituents" emerges as a web of heterogeneities. It becomes a matter of connecting the multiplicities and configuring them in relation to each other in a meaningful way. In the process, they "borrow" aspects from each other, or from yet other contexts. In the following section we look at some specific ways of metamorphing the architectural scale model.

Hybrid Design Representations and Materials

In our observations of designers use of material, it became evident that there is a divide between formats, on the one hand physical material and on the other hand digital media that reside mostly inside the desktop computer. Printing digital media, using these media as a material resource, and in the opposite direction, scanning images and transferring them to a digital format, of course occurs frequently. But it is time-consuming work, often absorbing people into individual work on the computer. Having material available only in digital format greatly diminishes the visibility of the work, which might let others participate in it directly, or at least be peripherally aware of it. Another drawback, just as significant, is how the time gap in the translations becomes immanent. As we go from one representation to the other, the chain between them gets weaker, as the transference is both time consuming and mentally absorbing. An open design space requires fluid movements between different representations, objects, and materials. One strategy for achieving that is blending the flexibility of digital media with the material qualities of physical objects.

Digital technologies have been concerned with the intertwining of the virtual and the physical for quite some time now. Canonical work by researchers like Weiser, Ullmer, Rekimoto, and others on tangible user interfaces has been foundational (see, e.g., Ishii and Ullmer 1997; Rekimoto 1997; and Weiser 1999), and a driving force for development has been the potential of computational resources to be integrated into everyday life and practices. It is no longer the case that computation remains inside the virtual world of the desktop computer. Instead, design materials for digital artifacts are recognized as both spatial and temporal. With digital technology we can build digital temporal structures. However, to design these temporal structures into artifacts that we can experience and interact with, almost any material can be of use in their spatial configuration. We have seen a huge variety of objects such as augmented paper, interactive toys, packaging with barcodes, all displaying the powerful potential to mix the digital and the physical. They are as such mixed objects, hybridizing the virtual and the material. It might also seem trivial that these kinds of hybrid objects are distinguished as primarily material or virtual. This identification can be through one property that actually is interesting, but these objects are also mixed and entangled in other ways; spatial/temporal, accessed from a variety of perspectives by different actors, both individually and collaboratively, and so on.

This idea of mixing the flexibility of digital media with the material qualities of physical objects was implemented in the Texture Painter, an application for "painting": virtual textures on physical models. The Texture Painter is not restricted to using only textures or still images; video loops can also be painted on surfaces. The digital media being "painted" can be scaled up or down, as well as rotated. It is possible to save states and then return to them later. Both professional architects and students have used this application to experiment with changing the properties of a model, by applying color, inserting movement and context, and varying its dimension in relation to other objects in physical space.

Figure 5.10
Mixed design artifacts: the CAD plan with barcodes, models augmented with touch sensors, and objects with embedded RFID tags, illustrating different aspects of a workplace, are all examples of mixed objects and provide ways to animate the environment through the use of dynamic media.

Figure 5.11
The saw/shelter model being "performed" by changing texture and light.

Many observations have been made on how digital media were applied directly to the model. The possibilities are quite numerous: create naturalistic textures that show the interior furnished with materials similar to the original; or the opposite: reinterpret the building, turning it into something completely different, as we can see in one model, transformed into something like a Las Vegas gas station by uploading neon signs and painting them in. In this example, which can be seen in figure 5.12, students used the Texture Brush for applying "accessories."

Again, very different strategies emerge among individual designers or groups. One group applied material to their model, aluminum paper and plastic wrap, to achieve another effect of projection by the Texture Brush. Another group painted people and cars together with a texture, which can be seen in figure 5.13, which looked like a collage, quite playful. What distinguishes them from most of the others is

Figure 5.12
Creating different aspects of the model.

Figure 5.13
Further ways of creating different versions of the model.

another style of using the Texture Brush: focusing on an idea or concept, rather than on a perfect architectural view. One student really appreciated the Texture Brush as a tool, calling it the perfect way to analyze proportions. He noted that every texture applied changed the visual proportions of a room or part of the building. Colors, geometrics, and so on, deceive the eye, opening up or closing a room, bringing comfort or the opposite. Every time the texture/video changes it creates a new view of the model.

These mutations of a model into something else can also be seen in another session with an architect who "painted" a variety of textures onto the model of a building for which a new attic had been planned, to explore the changing relationship between base and attic. It was interesting to observe how projections of different textures charged the building with meaning. One of the surprise elements was how painting a loop video showing waves onto the base transformed the model into a cliff with a bastion or a concrete socket with a spatial sculpture on top. Changing the context also changes the scale, from building to cliff. The projections helped erase preconceptions of the building, allowing the designer to see it differently.

Figure 5.14
Infusing movement in the model by working with video.

Another student group created their own video of movement, showing people on moving staircases, somebody walking, and camera drives on different kinds of staircases.

As this increases the entanglement of the model with other constituents we can also observe how the models blend with the surrounding space. The students also experimented with different backgrounds for their models, thereby changing their character.

As can be seen in the examples of design students experimenting with the Texture Brush, each instance of the models' expressions is dependent on more than just applying a texture to the model. A substantial quantity of different material is mobilized to construct the specific instances. Textures, videos, materials from books, collected images, optical markers, different projections, and the actual physical configuration are all applied to construct a unique situation—a situation that has to be interpreted and responded to. The outcomes of the experiments are not known in advance; they can be partially expected, but without continuous inquiries to the particular, there will be no growth for the whole.

The students captured these changes with a digital camera, as can be seen in figure 5.15, and it turned out that this double-digital-processing worked out fantastically—a Texture Painter layer, photographed by a digital camera—"even better than real-life paint."

In this series of explorations the architects used a 1:5 model of one of the furniture designs (the altar) by Andreas Rumpfhuber made from artificial stone in combination with virtual 3D models of the other pieces—ambo, legile, tabernacle, font—using optical markers for inserting them in different positions. The idea was to explore materiality, on the one hand, and to simulate the objects' relations in space, on the other hand. With different virtual paints, the white stone model

Figure 5.15
Documenting the temporal state of the model by taking a picture.

underwent a beautiful metamorphosis, even glowing at times. Accidentally turning the model upside down erased its original meaning and functionality. The altar became an undefined object, with the possibility of introducing completely different meanings. In combination with virtual models of the other furniture pieces it mutated from urban landscape, to entrance into the underground, to a megastructure of railway station and park, a seat for a coffee house, a children's playground, and a skateboard park. With these transformations, the designer started to see the model differently.

The reinterpretation of each transformation is of course important, as a new situation is the result of the metamorphing undertaken, and the accidental turning of the model makes it very clear how the new situations are often only partly known by the designer; in this case, the object of design is completely new. The example with Texture Painter clearly illustrates the act of interacting with a mixed object, transforming it in various ways, changing scales, backgrounds, and textures. But when is it transformed? When is representation X metamorphed into representation Y? Just as in Latour's case of circulating references, the current focus becomes a matter of *which* reference. In the example with Texture Painter you could save a state (a performed configuration of the model and used textures/images), and take a photograph of it; or when the model was unintentionally turned upside down, you could start to talk

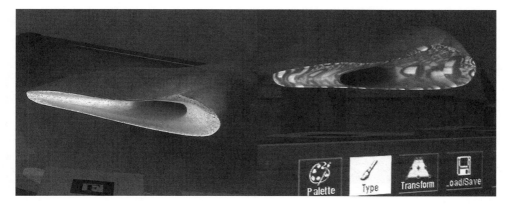

Figure 5.16
Creating different readings of an object.

Figure 5.17
When a still photograph of the model is taken and used instead of the model, or when students start to refer to the object in new ways, metamorphing has taken place.

Figure 5.18
The final presentation of the work on the saw/shelter model illustrates how objects and spaces
become intertwined.

about it not as an altar but as something completely different. When the designers
start to use the photograph as a focal point, they then start from those saved states
instead of starting from the beginning. Or when they talk about "the cliff" instead of
the model—then the metamorphing has taken place. It is no longer one of several
experimental transformations; its state is altered and the representation has gained a
new meaning, which then drives the work forward.

The designer has to detach himself from his activity and current engagement with
the design artifacts in order to reflect on them and their continuation. Transformations
cannot go on in endless iterations. The representations populate the design studio and
provide the necessary conditions for a true design engagement, but as Ingold puts it,
"to free up the qualities of objects themselves . . . is done by distancing ourselves from,
or stepping outside of the activities in which the usefulness these objects reside"
(Ingold 2000, 417). This is very similar to Schön's previously mentioned ideas of
reflection-on-action, where the acting subject takes a step back from reflection-in-
action, so that the two modes of activity can complement each other in producing
not only the object of design, but also the designer's knowledge of the artifact as well
as the process of developing it.

The studio becomes a space for embodied action, with the presenter as the focal
point in the performed narrative. Moving around the space, he is an active reference
to the interweaving of materials and place, changing the focus of materials positioned
differently in the space. Present in the space is also a multiplicity of perspectives of
fellow students, teachers or other visitors.

What the map cuts up, the story cuts across.
—de Certeau (1984), 129

We have seen how design proceeds through what we have called metamorphing. It is something different from the mere transformation of representations, inasmuch as it refers to a situation where the subject (designer) engages with the object (the object of design or design material) in such a way that transgresses the traditional view where a subjective agent acts on inert objects. It also refers to the entire chain of "circulating references," not just singular instances of transformations; and it includes the idea that manipulating objects also changes the surrounding space and the conditions for communicating within the space. In the cases described, the Texture Brush and the student transforming the representations of the saw, we can see how the representations are more like circulating references than abstracted metaphors. The argumentation has included views on objects, things, and representations as not being static or finalized. Instead, the concept of mixed objects or hybrid design artifacts endows them with the potential for being performed not only by the designers, but also in a joint enactment; they are mobile but still localized elements that compose an evolving story of design.

Another central part of our argumentation is how design proceeds through metamorphing different representations that are produced in the process. Latour's concept of circulating references stresses how coherence resides not within the different references, but in how well they are connected. This is perhaps at the very core of the idea of place making within a design context: that a space supports movement between different aspects of design, and the ability to explore them from different perspectives in a way that makes sense to other people not present. The example from the critique session illuminates how each of the performed translations must be reflected and how it is necessary to achieve temporary closure in order to move forward. We cannot get stuck in endless experimentation. The representations are also localized, which points to the important role of their material body and how it extends in space, transforming it through the interaction with the designers. They are references on a map of the intended design, but transforming and enacting them is a performed narrative that is carried out as a spatial practice. This practice is rich with material actors and augmented with the transformative potential of digital media. The concept of embodied interaction and the aspects of socially shared objects lead us to a theater metaphor and beyond. This issue of how performance concepts can enrich design will be explored further in the following chapter.

6 Designing as Performing

As we have seen, designing is about bringing forth something that does not exist through material transformations and communicative acts involving design artifacts. Artifacts can be seen as "multimodal texts," as they address different senses and modalities of communication. However, these do not operate as isolated texts or as artifacts in a passive exhibition. The role of these multimodal texts in experiencing design objects involves a processual activity, an action rooted in a social situation and discourse. According to the perspective of anthropology of experience and performance, "a ritual must be enacted, a myth recited, a narrative told, a novel read, a drama performed" (Bruner 1986, 7). And, following Clifford Geertz, these multimodal texts are also expressions in the form of objectifications, in our case, design artifacts. The perspective presented in this chapter explains how such expressions are constitutive and shaping, not as abstract texts but in the activity that actualizes the text, as the text must be performed to be experienced, and what is constitutive is its production in events.

Therefore, a performance perspective suggests a temporal analysis of the emergence and use of material features based on the notion of events (Jacucci 2004). Comparing different examples highlights different time frames of expressing and experiencing design (figure 6.1).

The creative density exhibited by Friedericke Mayröcker's office (introduced in chapter 3) is one that has accumulated over many years, in which the poet added layers and configurations of materials she wanted to be present in her work environment. There is no obvious (narrative, chronological, etc.) order. The three models visualizing "something that flows out of a crack in the mountain" exhibit a somewhat different time frame (see figure 6.1). These models have been developed over several months of work and they are indicative of a shifting focus in the students' thinking. Although they have been produced in a sequential order, they maintain their relevance as they communicate complementary aspects of the design project.

Let us look once more at the first-semester student who studied a saw and its movements, translating it into a physical model (figure 6.2). In a later session, using

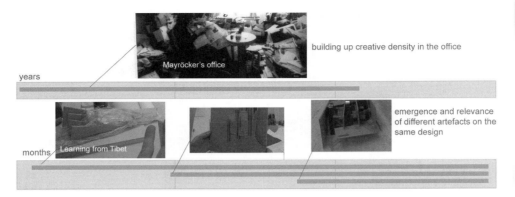

Figure 6.1
Temporal emergence of material features and artifacts in years and months.

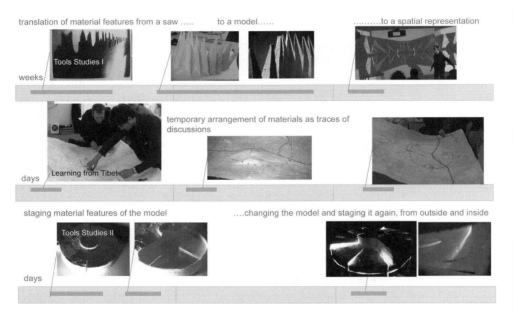

Figure 6.2
Temporal emergence of material features and artifacts in weeks and days.

different light sources, he highlights details of the model that exhibit distinctive material features, such as the dents in the saw. Using multiple projections, he transforms a collage of these details into a spatial installation. We can look at this as a particular material feature "circulating" through different representations, in a sequence, helping the student to explore its significance for creating an architectural space. Each transformation deepens the student's understanding of the material and makes the design concept more mature.

Figure 6.2 shows the example of the "Tools Studies" of the saw; a group working on "Learning from Tibet"; and another example of the "Tools Studies," showing the staging of modifications of a physical model. These students explore the properties of concrete step by step, with one discovery leading them to the next design intervention.

Another type of temporality can be identified in the ways in which the students make use of the large shared model in the project "Learning from Tibet" (see figure 6.2). Here we observed a more ephemeral apparition of material features, with students, from day to day, leaving material traces of their design thinking on the model or overwriting them in the next collaborative design session. These (temporary) traces serve as indices of planned or discussed interventions in the mountain valley. They change or disappear with the progress of students' discussions.

The last example in figure 6.2 from the "Tools Studies" (which was described earlier in more length) also has a temporal dimension. It shows how one model is transformed, over the course of a few days, to perform different visual effects through its changing shape and material features. A more general point is illustrated by these examples: a temporal framework is connected to the emergence of objects, which elucidates how these emerge in specific events. Hence our notion of *design events*. These events range from long-term activities, such as creating a material-dense work environment or design space, to creating design representations from different materials or exploring a specific material through circulating it through different representations— gradually transforming and translating the design concept, or even jumping between formats, scales, and media (all activities of medium duration), to brief communicative events (leaving temporary traces).

Narrative is often trivialized in approaches such as scenario-based design in HCI, which seems to have synthesized a compromise for software engineering, marketing, and design. In particular, each situation in design might require a different narrative strategy or style, and inspirational design requires more complex, metaphorical, and therefore more powerful approaches than simple scenarios.

Through the creation and manipulation of a variety of artifacts, designers communicate and experience the emergence of an object, be it a situation, an artifact, or a concept. The emergence can unfold as an interactional process involving many participants, where artifacts are used as resources to bring forth a shared design space.

Here artifacts and their features are used as constituents (see chapter 4) of the emerging object.

As we've noted, few researchers have looked at the cooperative nature of design work (see chapter 2), as design studies often analyze a designer carrying out a task from a cognitive perspective. However, both creating and maintaining a design space and constructing and transforming objects are experiential, expressive, and intersubjective processes.

Analyzing what design is, compared to other research-in-workplace studies, involves certain distinguishing issues. Even when the cooperative nature of design is acknowledged, there is a need to move beyond the focus on coordination and accountability. This means attempting to understand how objects and the design space emerge interactively in collective efforts that involve imagination, symbolizations, expression, and experience. We can engage in this enterprise armed with previous perspectives that address how, through social action, people express and experience culture, in particular the anthropology of performance and theater and performance studies (Jacucci 2004; Jacucci and Wagner 2005; Jacucci, Linde, and Wagner 2005). These perspectives make salient the structural relationship between experience and expression. This relationship has an eventlike and processual character and involves the collective manipulation of a fictional space. Further aspects will also be described, such as the energy and consciousness involved in performative acts that set them apart from everyday activities.

Like the previous ones, this chapter contains two sorts of contributions: descriptive, narrative stories of how objects were part of particular experiential and communicative events and came to be after purposeful sociomaterial configurations; and explanatory discussions that propose a performance perspective from which to capture the salient aspects of why and how such eventful manipulations of objects took place.

Anthropology of Performance

The concept of performance has been the object of a variety of studies and contrasting approaches across the social sciences, in anthropology, social psychology, linguistics, and so on. The term "performance" can be taken to address everyday life and can concern a variety of situations beyond theatrical performances and rituals. No relationship between performance theories and studies and design has yet been attempted, although anthropological works have already been applied to create new perspectives on design. One example is the notion of *bricolage* of French anthropologist Claude Lévi-Strauss (see Ciborra 2002), which has also been used to examine the consequences of the metaphor of "design as bricolage" for the relationship between design and science (Louridas 1999).

To formulate a performance perspective that is useful in furthering our understanding of how design is or can be accomplished, we will gather characteristics from the work of the anthropologist Victor Turner and from the philosophy of John Dewey and Wilhelm Dilthey, on which Turner based his work. Moreover, other anthropological works, such as those of Eugenio Barba (theater anthropology) and Schieffelin (performance ethnography) will contribute additional traits. We have also found it useful to integrate these traits with views from performance art, such as the writings and works of Vito Acconci, a pioneer in this area. We will start in the following section by describing the core relationship between expression and experience as proposed by Turner. A more detailed articulation of characteristics will follow, along with an analysis of specific design episodes.

Victor Turner, one of the founding fathers of performance studies, provided an explanation of how a performance perspective includes relating expressions to experience (drawing from the philosophy of Dewey and Dilthey). This explanation serves to address how experience, expression, and perception form an intricate relationship.

Turner studied the participation in and experience of performances in sociocultural communities. Design could often be characterized as a "meta-manipulation" of culture in that designers contribute to changing or reinterpreting culture. The fundamental mechanisms of expressing and experiencing are the same in their practical accomplishments, on the one hand, of devising a cultural performance or creating an artifact that produces and maintains a culture, and, on the other, of manipulating, acting toward, and interpreting artifacts to evoke the emergence of an object.

Turner and others proposed the anthropology of experience as an alternative approach in anthropology, where the experience of a culture is studied by analyzing its expressions. As Clifford Geertz comments in the epilogue of the book *The Anthropology of Experience* (Turner and Bruner 1986), expressions are "representations, objectifications, discourses, performances," like rituals and other performances, but also artifacts (Geertz 1986). Turner bases his approach on previous thinkers who addressed "experience": John Dewey, who saw an intrinsic connection between experience and aesthetic qualities, and Wilhelm Dilthey, who argued that experience urges us toward expression and communication with others (Turner 1986).

Following Dilthey, Turner explains how meaning, which is sealed up and inaccessible in daily life, is "squeezed out" (from the German *Ausdruck*) through expressions such as performances. In Turner's words, "an experience is itself a process which 'presses out' to an 'expression' which completes it" (Turner 1982, 13). According to this view, there is a processual structure of *Erlebnis* (experience or what is lived through); it has, first of all, a perceptual core. After perception, past experiences are then evoked, "but past events remain inert unless the feelings originally bound up with them can be fully revived" (ibid., 14). Meaning is considered emergent and not predetermined in the event; it "is generated by 'feelingly' thinking about interconnections between past and present events" (ibid.). Finally, it is not enough to achieve meaning for oneself, as an experience is never truly completed until it is communicated intelligibly to others or, in other words, it is expressed. As Turner puts it: "culture itself is the ensemble of such expressions—the experience of individuals made available to society and accessible to the sympathetic penetration of other 'minds'" (ibid.).

Considering the previous important characterizations of performance, it is interesting to question what kind of performance can be present in design. Most notably, performances have been considered in our civilized and technologically advanced societies by Victor Turner in terms of different characterizations, for example, the everyday,[1] the ritual, the drama, and liminality. While distinctions in nontechnologically advanced societies are clearer, as early as the 1980s Turner realized how complex, overlapping, and multifaceted phenomena were in industrialized societies and warned that the use of some of these typifications "must in the main be metaphorical." It is particularly interesting to discuss liminality for design.

The term *limen*, from the Latin for "threshold," originated from anthropological works such as Arnold van Gennep's (2004) *Rites of Passage*. Liminality is characterized by passing over a threshold to a new status or structure through separation, transition, and incorporation. Liminal phenomena have been explained to include rites of passage as social phenomena set apart from the order of the status quo, where performances are about the stripping of statuses, renunciations of roles, and demolishing of structures. New subjunctive, even ludic, structures are then generated with their own grammars and lexica of roles and relationships. While liminal phenomena are centrally integrated into the total social process, other phenomena that are similar but are set apart from the central processes are called "liminoid" by Turner (1982).[2] Liminoid phenomena are not only at the margins or in interstices but are fragmentary, plural, and experimental. Moreover, they are more idiosyncratic, quirky, and generated usually by specific, named individuals or particular schools and circles. Finally, while liminal phenomena are eufunctional (reinforcing social structure while apparently inversive), liminoid phenomena are critical and revolutionary in character. Turner uses liminoid phenomena to indicate not only particular cultural practices but also creative scientific and technical practices that are somehow set apart from the status quo.

We have explored above the relationship of expression and experience, which provides a core principle that is helpful in two ways: in framing the activity of accomplishing design in terms of events and in understanding the motivation behind the purposeful staging of such events. The inquiry in this chapter aims at characterizing design from a performance perspective, making salient three aspects: *liminality*, which illuminates the set-apartness and antistructural, protostructural endeavors of design; *drama*, which involves the reflexivity of experiencing and creating experiencing to "communicate about the communication system itself"; and the *performative aspects*, which include the expressive, experiential, processual, and structural aspects, along with the consciousness of the acts of design.

The Time and Space of Performing Design

Collective Emergence of a Fictional Space

The creation of a design space or field of work that does not exist is a characteristic of many design projects. Designers wander in search of a physical location, setting, or place that they do not interpret literally, but which will be used as a resource to create a "fictional" space. Performance has a lot to do with this process.

Culture viewed as speech, gesture, and action is performance; and performance not only requires but commands its own kind of space. (Tuan 1990, 236)

Spatial features may be functional, as in the case of the walls of a building, but they may also be symbolically charged, resulting in a specific perception of space during a performance. In a theatrical performance, for example, we are doing

An essentially interpretative act, translating real bodies, words and movements into the objects of another, hypothetical world; . . . everything within the defined spatial compass of the stage is to be read differently from the objects seen elsewhere. (Counsell and Wolf 2001, 155)

Although the creation of a fictional space can be seen as an exercise for a reader of a book (involving therefore a writer and a reader), in this context we refer to fictional space as something that emerges out of the ongoing interaction between participants in design, be it a short session or through a project. In theater we refer to fictional space, for example, as a representation of actions and human conflicts that participants create by performing and reacting to each other (Iacucci, Iacucci, and Kuutti 2002). It is fictional because it is not a substitute for reality. It is created by images that are free from the rules of reality and conventions. It has a perspective, and it is a space because one can be in it or out of it. There can be rules of being and behaving that come into play as one "takes part" and becomes involved in a fiction. Furthermore, from the inside one can look outside, and vice versa. "In some cases with performances we aim at such a space because in order to set the imagination free, we need to change some of the rules of reality. Hence we inevitably fall into fiction" (ibid., 174).

However, not everything that is put forward by participants can be fruitful for the performance. The collective emergence of the fictional space can be affected if it is interpreted by other participants and, even more importantly, if other participants are able to produce a reaction from it.

In improvisational performance, participants need to interpret performers' offerings (as actors and spectators do in theater) as they occur: actions, symbols, and props that are introduced into the scene are interpreted in the light of the unfolding action. This is necessary for the completion of the collective endeavor, which can lead to the construction of the fictional space. This completion is achieved by other actors reacting to offerings. In other words, interpretations are not only the product of the imaginative activity of a single participant. Rather, what makes them valuable during group improvisations is their interactional character or their collective emergence (see Sawyer 1999). This highly dynamic and interactive endeavor, which sustains a fictional representation, is what constitutes the imaginative ground on which participants contribute with their performance. Obviously, every contribution or reaction can potentially constitute an imaginative or creative achievement of some sort, and it can be produced by a variety of kinds of cognitive processes. Nevertheless, it is not free imagination. Every product of the participants' imagination that does not become part of the representation can be ignored or can constitute an obstacle to it.

The poetry game   A group of students reported on their excursion to London, Lille, and Paris, as well as on their emerging initial ideas for an "extreme stadium," by staging a "poetry game" with a multiprojection installation (figure 6.3). Their narrative was based on contrasting the memories of those who had participated in the excursion with those who had remained in Vienna. The presentation consisted of the two groups reading short phrases capturing their impressions and interpretations in a dialogue, while images were shown. This dialogue of experiences and concepts was embodied spatially with four projections: onto a setup of double layers of transparent cloth facing each other; onto the ground (projected from above), and onto the wall. The wall was used for projecting enlarged details of street signs (figure 6.3). This spatial configuration expressed the contrasting positions of the groups. The double layers of cloth created interesting spatial effects, blurring and distorting the projected images. Reviewers' feedback, which also included some criticism, pointed to important aspects of this conceptual performance. One comment was that "having these two layers of

Figure 6.3
The arrangement of four projections in space for the "poetry game."

fabric, with one and the same image appearing on two different scales, opens up opportunities for simulating a space." Another teacher saw in performances of this type a method for conceiving architecture by exploring the "simultaneity of oppositions or of things that seem unconnected." This is an example of how multimedia installations may become an integral part of design work.

This example shows how participants construct a fictional space participatively, in the designing, negotiating, and staging of the "poetry game." But during its performance, too, the spectators are part of the presentation and need to take part in the fictional space (as spectators of a theater performance) to be able to interpret the interactions of images, people, and words in the physical space.

From performance we learn what kind of contributions from participants can foster the collective emergence of a fictional space (Iacucci, Iacucci, and Kuutti 2002), for example: those that can be interpreted and "reacted to" by some other participant; those that can be part of the fictional space in which participants are performing (in that they can be interpreted as being part of it by other participants) as interpreted by some participant, and those that are inspired by the performance of physical actions, utterances, and significations by other participants. These conditions concern both the way those ideas are imagined (roughly speaking, by group performances instead of in isolation and all in the head), and how they can be embodied and interpreted (roughly speaking, through an enacted fictional space condensed in time, such as theater). This was just one phase of the larger project in which participants explored and elaborated a design space. They constructed an intersubjective interpretation of the problem, negotiating the use of language, symbols, and materials. The phase can be recounted as a story and considered as one of the events of which the project was made, with a beginning and an end. Moreover, the phase contained in itself a variety of events: the visit to the site, the collaborative construction of an installation model, and the performance of such an installation.

Learning from Turner's anthropology of performance, we can analyze the realization of performance, possibly linking the extent of realization to its effectiveness for design. For example, we can look at the liminality and dramatic structure of the event beyond a collective initiation and consummation of the experience and of the variety of expressions created observing the dramatic structure of breach (breach of structures, relations, roles), crises (role-taking, playing, conflict), or redressive or remedial procedures (mediation, resolution). From a liminality perspective there are other phases: separation, transition, and incorporation (reaggregation). While keeping in mind Turner's advice to use these concepts in a metaphorical sense, we can observe whether a redressive or reaggregation phase has taken place, for example, in the case of the above poetry game, the discussion with the tutor and professors and with other students to reflect on the experience. Design, as other cultural processes, includes these phases, which contribute to explain how design is collectively processed in time through events. These events in their redressive and reaggregative character help process group aspects such as identity, roles, and emotions. More importantly, they create the conditions for liminality where a phase of a project is concluded and its structure destroyed to create a new structure in a new phase of the project.

Performative Use of Constraints

In the traditional view of design that focuses on problem solving, constraints are seen as part of the definition of the problem, restricting what counts as an acceptable solution or as a requirement specification. However, practice shows that requirements emerge throughout the design process and that they are not always fixed restrictions but can be both helpful and flexible (see Gedenryd 1998). This flexibility of the constraints, it has been argued, is due to the incompleteness or poor structuring of problems. Design is a "wicked problem," to use the term suggested by Rittel and Webber: "In order to describe a wicked problem in sufficient detail, one has to develop an exhaustive inventory of all conceivable solutions ahead of time. The reason is that every question asking for additional information depends upon the understanding of the problem—and its resolution—at that time. Problem understanding and problem resolution are concomitant to each other. [. . . The] process of solving the problem is identical with the process of understanding its nature" (Rittel and Webber 1973, 162).

The designer may create constraints not because of a necessity inherent in the problem or one that is objectively valid, but for practical reasons. Gedenryd argues that constraints are useful because they reduce complexity and add structure. From this viewpoint a constraint is an instrument that is created for a purpose: "as an instrument it is actively formed to serve its purpose, by the person applying it toward this purpose" (Gedenryd 1998, 77). In this sense constraints are not objective and not even arbitrary, because they have a purpose.

From a performance perspective, constraints can do much more than simply reduce complexity and add structure. In the traditions of such theater directors as, for example, Jacques Lecoq, Philippe Gaulier, Keith Johnstone, Peter Brook, Augusto Boal, or John Wright, the main concern of a director is to avoid telling performers what to do, while at the same time driving the creative process in order to make them work creatively and make things happen. The problem of avoiding dictating outcomes is common to design, which aims at the collective emergence of objects that provide new insights by encapsulating unexpected features.

The problem is well known in most approaches to directing in the performing arts, where the major goal is to devise a performance by making it emerge with minimum control, and being ready to take advantage of the unexpected. As the theater director John Wright says, "this is a shifting and mercurial world where anything is possible and everything has yet to be found. This means that as a director or facilitator you've got to find strategies that are likely to make something happen rather than strategies for getting people to analyze what they think they might do" (quoted in Jacucci, Linde, and Wagner 2005, 24). A particularly relevant aspect for design activities is how the role of constraints can be developed within collective activities (ibid.).

It has been noted that the relationship between creativity and constraints is mysterious and symbiotic (Laurel 1993). "Creativity arises out of the tension between spontaneity and limitations, the latter (like river banks) forcing the spontaneity into the various forms which are essential to the work of art" (May, quoted in Laurel 1993, 101). Limitations are explained by Brenda Laurel as being constraints that focus creative efforts by reducing the number of possibilities open to us. In the case of how computer interfaces support engagement, Laurel distinguishes between explicit and implicit constraints on the one hand and between extrinsic and intrinsic on the other. Explicit constraints are undisguised and directly available as menus and commands. Implicit constraints may be indirectly inferred from the behavior of the system, for example, its not providing ways to draw in a text editor. "Extrinsic" and "intrinsic" refer to how constraints are related to "mimetic" action. In the case of a video game, extrinsic constraints refer to the context of the person as an operator of the system, while intrinsic constraints refer to the person as a player or protagonist in the story of the game. As remarked by Laurel (1993, 106), the "value of limitations in focusing creativity is recognized in the theory and practice of theatrical improvisation." In fact, her model of human–computer activity appreciates the role of improvisation within a matrix of constraints.

But there are fundamental differences between the way Laurel applies (implicit vs. explicit, extrinsic vs. intrinsic) constraints and the contribution of a performative use of constraints to design. Her design of software and computer interfaces addresses how to involve users in the theater of the electronic space and the action of its applications. Moreover, in Laurel's case, constraints can either depend on technical capabilities and the limitations of the system, or (preferably) be established through character and action in the interface. In our case, instead, constraints are not primarily researched as design features, be they desirable qualities or limitations on a human's engagement with interactive technology. We focus on the role of constraints as a resource that can be used when directing collective creative action during design, in the same way in which they can become resources in improvised performances following specific approaches, such as, for example, the practice of Keith Johnstone. So the designer or designers could be thought of as actors or directors utilizing constraints to make design happen. However, such constraints may also happen to become designed features in a later design stage. Or, conversely, design features of artifacts and practices they support may be used as effective constraints in some design trials, as long as they are made to work, as constraints, against a collective drive toward a form of action. But we research their quality during the exploration of different human relationships and activities with a given set of artifacts, infrastructures, and practices.

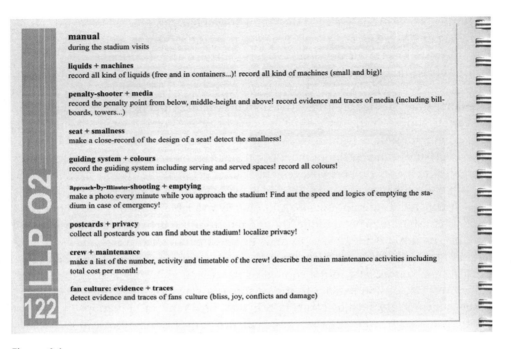

Figure 6.4
The "Manual" during the stadium visits, providing constraints.

Visiting stadiums One of the design projects at the Academy of Fine Arts in Vienna focused on developing novel concepts for stadiums. A warm-up phase in which the students worked on the "least expensive stadium in the world" was followed by an excursion to London, Lille, and Paris.

As part of their preparations for the visits, they had produced a guide with information about the nine stadiums and a handbook describing guidelines and different roles for different team members (figure 6.4). Each of them belonged to one of four groups—context, construction, hybrid, and conversion. They also assumed specific roles—from recording all kinds of liquids and machines to recording the guiding systems. That helped them focus on particular aspects of the stadiums and their environments. One of the instructions students received was to use a particular rhythm, such as taking a picture every thirty seconds from the moment they stepped out of the underground until they arrived at the stadium (figure 6.5).

There followed the "laboratory of hypotheses and prototypes," during which students worked on their own ideas of an "extreme stadium" in Vienna, exploring typologies. The result was a compendium of themes, hypotheses, and prototypes. The students returned from the London–Lille–Paris excursion with lots of material—videos,

Figure 6.5
Pictures and recorded sound were part of the documentation.

photos, *objets trouvés*, their personal diaries. Their task was to use this material to create a themed presentation. One of their teachers evoked the notion of "multiple traveling" (see chapter 3), which he described as

The first journey when a project starts is to the place of an intervention itself in order to experience the authenticity of the place. . . . It is your body that subconsciously absorbs the place. Back home you perform your second journey through the collected material, remembering with your body even subtle things like the smell of a place. This journey through the material has to be repeated again and again.

Like any design project, this example presents a variety of uses of constraints. The assigning of roles to different group members in the visits to the stadiums constitutes constraints that allowed an "embodied" and on-site analysis during the visit, as students were embodying specific aspects of analysis on the site. Whether it reduced the complexity by allowing the group members to concentrate on one aspect or, on the other hand, allowed the complexity of the stadium, which would otherwise be hidden if looked at in a more holistic manner, to be blown up, is arguable. The performance perspective points primarily to a different aspect, besides the complexity or structuring of a problem. It has to do with considering how the constraints are embodied in specific events. Assigning the roles was crucial during the visit to the stadium. It was crucial at a specific time and place as part of an event with a beginning and an end. In the second part of the example, the development of the "operational model" is made possible by particular choices of representation techniques and materials. From a performance perspective, techniques need to be invented anew to be able to provide a novel insight. The example above of the visits represents an attempt to organize techniques and constraints to ensure the effective collection of narratives. When considering many performers, writers, and composers, it is clear that the creative process comprises a small part of intuition and a large part of hard work applying well-mastered techniques and approaches. The question is, however, how much these techniques are reusable or how much they can be transferred from one person to another or from one group to another.

Purposeful Staging of Design Events

The etymology of the term "performance" shows that it "does not have the structuralist implication of manifesting form, but rather the processual sense of bringing to completion or accomplishing" (Turner 1982, 91). A performance is always something accomplished: it is an achievement or an intervention in the world (Schieffelin 1997). According to Turner, performances are not generally "amorphous or open-ended, they have diachronic structure, a beginning, a sequence of overlapping but isolable phases, and an end" (Turner 1987, 80). It includes an initiation and a consummation. "There was one way I loved to say the word 'performance,' one meaning of the word 'performance' that I was committed to: 'performance' in the sense of performing a contract—you promise you would do something, now you have to carry that promise out, bring that promise through to completion" (Acconci, in Acconci and Moure 2001).

The stadium in the city   A student had prepared a football field and two slide shows, with one screen displaying cultural aspects of soccer (images, sound, video) and the second screen displaying her design ideas in the making. The slide show was operated through a sensor that had been fixed underneath the soccer field (figure 6.6). The presentation itself was designed as a soccer game, with the building sites being the teams—stadium versus museums—explaining the design ideas being the team tactics, and herself as the referee, with a yellow card and a whistle signaling a "bad idea" and scoring a goal a "good idea." In the words of the performer, "the idea was to have soccer games or soccer tools such as the ball or the yellow card as sensor tools. The architectural project also used soccer terminology instead of common architectural words."

When the ball touched the goal, a sensor triggered off a reporter's voice shouting "goal, goal" and the cheering of the spectators (figure 6.7). The yellow card was also shown to members of the teaching staff who interrupted the presentation with questions and comments. Spectators were invited into an arrangement as in a stadium:

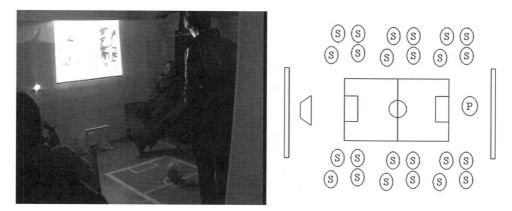

Figure 6.6
Arranging the spectators as in a noisy stadium.

Figure 6.7
A miniature soccer field as an interface to guide the presentation.

"In the presentation them sitting around me, like in a stadium, the whole atmosphere was like in a noisy stadium."

This presentation was understood as a first "emphatic" step in the design project. The roles of all the soccer-specific artifacts and symbols were part of an immersion into the "soccer world" with its language.

The design project focused on an "extreme stadium" in the area between Vienna's two large museums. The presentation of this concept included careful configurations

Figure 6.8
Arranging posters and projection so that they form an enclosed space.

of space, artifacts, and interactive media. First posters and projections were arranged so that they formed an enclosed space, thereby re-creating the trapezoid square in the city of Vienna, which the student had analyzed (figure 6.8). She later explained: "First I wanted to create a new space with those hanging posters, a space that can only be experienced when you walk through the room, change your seat. But the reviewers cannot do that, I mean they could, but you know, they are too lazy maybe. So I arranged the posters and everything so that they could see it from one perspective." The final arrangement is shown in figure 6.9.

In the final presentation artifacts augmented with sensors and tags were "scripted," associating images and sounds with different interactions. Interactive technology exploited the articulation in material qualities, spatiality (touch sensors in a solid section that becomes an interactive skyline), and affordances (turning the pages of a diary), rendering them more expressive. Artifacts acquire meaning through material qualities, their spatiality, and the way participants interact with them. This is evidence of how tangible interfaces can support performative conversations with mixed objects.

This project exemplifies how design proceeded by developing a multiplicity of affordances to the object of work. It showed the importance not of an ostensible product or specification (a model) but rather of accomplishing events. In each event we observe a change in what the object-in-design is and a change in the art and relevance of the techniques used to converse with design material. According to this view, accomplishing an event can complete or conclude a phase. After the completion of a phase there can be a translation of what the object of design is, in terms, for example, of a shift from an abstract concept to architecture. In other cases, the completion of a phase might mean a change in the techniques, instruments, or, more generally, the constituents that are used to manipulate the object.

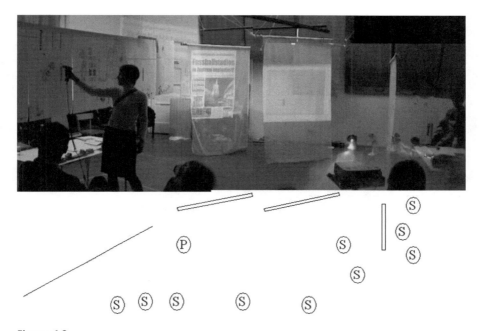

Figure 6.9
The final arrangement during the presentation.

Consciousness and Energy

Unlike other kinds of behavior, performance requires more effort in terms of the energy, skill, and consciousness (thinking) of the acts. Eugenio Barba's approach contributes additional traits and features, such as the skills, energy, and consciousness (thinking) of the performer. For example, Barba and Savarese (1999) distinguish between daily and extra-daily "techniques" (Barba and Savarese 1999, 9):

the way we use our bodies in daily life is substantially different from the way we use them in performance. We are not conscious of our daily techniques: we move, we sit, we carry things, we kiss, we agree and disagree with gestures which we believe to be natural but which are in fact culturally determined.

In daily techniques, we follow the principle of least effort, that is, obtaining the maximum result with the minimum expenditure of energy, but "extra-daily techniques are based, on the contrary, on wasting energy" (Barba 1995, 16). The principle might even be the opposite: "the principle of maximum commitment of energy for a minimal result" (ibid.).

Performing models of Viennese modernist architectures   The setup for this project was used in a trial with first-semester students whose assignment was to carry out an

Figure 6.10
Video walkthroughs in painted models.

analysis of one of the icons of modern architecture—Villa Tugendhat by Mies van der Rohe, Ville Savoye by Le Corbusier, Haus Müller by Adolf Loos, and so on. They were required to read texts reflecting original and contemporary views on these buildings. They had to build models on a scale of 1:50 and 1:20 (of an interesting spatial detail). They used the Interactive Stage and Texture Painter for exploring scale, materiality, and context.

In this design project students also performed camera walkthroughs in a painted model (figure 6.10) and the video was projected onto one of the large screens. Students also had to constantly change the lighting in the room to create the right conditions according to the situation; for example, using optical markers requires light, while some textures make a greater effect in darker conditions.

"Performance," in this case, refers to how these configurations can be seen as staging and performing the multiple constituents of the objects of design. These exist for a limited time; they are ephemeral, although they can be saved and reloaded (to some extent). As performances, they are recorded with pictures or through videos, or they have to be performed again. The shared understanding in the review after the presentations was that the processual aspect was more important than the final product. These performances present, for example, a process through which a model can acquire totally different meanings according to its costumes and stage designs. It is not one final form or one final structure that is important, but the process of seeing the same object change. We can, however, extend consciousness beyond the act to larger phenomena, including a social reflexivity in which a "group tries to scrutinize, portray, understand, and then act on itself" (Turner 1982, 75). "Consciousness" here refers more to the capacity, beyond the moment-by-moment acts, to consider larger situational aspects and systems of meanings such as the weaving of artifacts, references, utterances, and other expressions into constituents, and being able to reflect, negotiate, and collectively experience the emerging object of design.

Intervention and Experiential Knowledge

The etymology of the verb to "intervene" is from the Latin verb *intervenire*, which means "to come between." This has evolved into the contemporary sense of occurring, coming in between two events also by way of hindrance or modification, entering as an extraneous feature or circumstance. Performance is there to emphasize the opportunity of exploiting the features of our involved action in the world and also in the way our accomplishments produce changes in it and therefore new insights for us. Performance is expression, and "like construction, signifies both an action and its result" (Dewey 1980/1934, 82). Performance approaches to knowing insist on immediacy and involvement (see Denzin 2003) and favor an experiential, participative, and interventionist epistemology. Dewey argues against the separation of theory and praxis; this is relevant to our discussion, given how directed action and its results are central in generating knowledge:

all of the rivalries and connected problems grow from a single root. They stem from the assumption that the true and valid object of knowledge is that which has been prior to and independent of the operations of knowing. They spring from the doctrine that knowledge is a grasping or beholding of reality without anything been done to modify its antecedent state—the doctrine that is the source of the separation of knowledge from practical activity. If we see that knowing is not the act of an outside spectator but of a participator inside the natural and social scene, then the true object of knowledge resides in the consequences of directed action. (Dewey, as cited in Kuutti, Iacucci, and Iacucci 2002, 97)

Curving, cutting, and illuminating as artifact transformations   This design project was about making visual and material studies starting from a working tool (e.g., a saw). The architecture students first made studies of a tool by analyzing its form. They would then have to create three-dimensional models from observations of the tool's movements while in use. These studies produced a series of visual and material explorations through drawings and several models for each tool. One step included transforming the drawings to a three-dimensional physical model, representing the movement of the tool in space and its repetition in time and space. To reinforce the spiral movement by a new model, the student created a gyroscope, cut out of "styropor." He pointed out how the flakes of styropor that resulted from the cutting gave him a feeling for the space that got cut off.

The act of cutting was documented by photographing the model during this process, focusing on particular details, shooting close-ups, arranging the flakes, or

Figure 6.11
Representations created during the carving process.

Figure 6.12
Further representations resulted in cutting the hollow model in a subsequent phase.

changing the illumination setup, and photographing the model from different directions (figure 6.11).

In a subsequent step, the student created another model that, incorporating the most important results of the previous phases, can be considered a "shelter." The student wraps his gyroscopic model up in plaster. The result is a plaster cast to which he applies several interventions, staging and recording them. He cuts it open in one place to get an interior view (figure 6.12). Outside he changes the surface by adding rough material to show the destructive side of a saw. Additionally, he photographs the contrast of light and shadow on his model, creating an abstract picture series that contains views of the interior, where light is floating in through small fissures in the shell.

Carving out bits and pieces of a foam model becomes a performative project when these actions are staged, recorded, and used as a resource to narrate an emerging object. The student first carved out the shape of the model in figure 6.11 in several steps, carefully staging and recording them as happenings. Even the residue of materials may be significant, as the leftover flakes conveyed the space that was carved out of the model. These leftovers do not simply disappear (unless put into a bin); they witness some of the actions that has been taken and the design decisions that motivated it.

Figure 6.13
Left: the red carpet in one of the places visited. Right: the poster presentation of each place with a description and photograph.

The shape was used to create a hollow model that was transformed stepwise through several interventions that, appropriately staged and recorded, also became happenings (e.g., the model is cut into two pieces). The result of this design exploration is not the final state of the model but rather a collection of recorded "happenings" with the artifact.

Connecting remote communities and locations in Africa Another example is that of a master's student who did a field study in Africa for a programming project. She developed ideas for radio stations and distributed libraries. She visited several different places as locations or sites for a network of libraries and radio stations. After observing and recording the place, she would put a red carpet on the ground and take a picture (figure 6.13). The places were very different with and without the red carpet. Without the carpet the places were crowded and people were moving around the place in a lively fashion. The carpet influenced people in various ways, making them go away or gather around it, or even making the place deserted. The feedback from supervisors and architects valued her intervention more highly than her ideas about the radio and libraries. Professor Robert Mull told her: "You introduced a different type of space into the situation in a very brave way. You intervened in that situation." Part of the discussion was on the inspiring reflections that her interventions caused.

The simplest art of intervention is to modify an artifact. The way the modification is staged, recorded, performed, and recounted denotes a performative strategy. The intervention becomes a "happening" that generates new artifacts and new interpretations of what the emerging object is. We can draw an analogy with performance art, where the work may be accomplished anywhere, not always following a script.

Participants include not only the artist or the spectator but also strangers (Goldberg 2001). The artist might frame a particular aspect of everyday life. The work is created and lives on as a photograph and a textual account, sometimes also as a video. Allan Kaprow, a pioneer of performance art, used the word "happenings" instead of "theater piece or performance because he wanted this activity to be regarded as a spontaneous event something that just happens to happen" (Carlson 1996). As an example, Vito Acconci's "The Peoplemobile" (1979, in Acconci and Moure 2001) was a flatbed truck with a face-like mask that was driven into public places, where a crew off-loaded steel panels and configured them into a different arrangement each day: on the first day they formed a wall and a staircase, on the second day a three-part shelter, and on the final day a table with two benches, while a loudspeaker on top of the truck was used to address the public. Although some of these pieces were carefully prepared and rehearsed, performance art helps to explain how an intervention in an environment is recorded as a happening (even if carefully staged) and creates a new understanding through "anecdotal" records that often go beyond what was recorded.

As we mentioned earlier, the effectiveness of these interventions lies in the way people can make them part of larger performative structures, in the way, for example, that they construct narratives that are in themselves constituents of objects of design.

From Methods to Making Things Happen

Methodologically, performance implies the uniqueness and contingencies of "happen-ings" (Jacucci and Isomursu 2004). This contrasts with positivistic movements that strive toward repeatable methods and techniques. While these are desirable for some aspects of design, in some situations this is counterproductive. As artists and designers claim (Fellini, for example, in an interview), too explicit a consciousness of the method or technique is not always desirable because it disturbs the delicate balance in engaged action that some people might call improvisation (Ciborra 2002) and that always contains a good portion of surprise. This goes beyond the debate on design methods of the 1970s with famous quotes from Christopher Alexander like the following: "if you call it 'A Methodology,' I just do not want to talk about it" (Alexander 1971, 4). In particular, some situations call for not a step-by-step description of a technique but rather a set of principles. If one were to trivialize the way of doing as a technique and apply it as such, the result would be disappointing and predictable. An example is the famous success of the creative writing instructor Robert McKee (1997). Here the instructions are given not as a method or technique but as principles to be used or misused (inverted) and are effective just the same. This translates to performing design with the irreducibility of translating specific design techniques directly from, for example, theater practices (some problems are documented in Jacucci 2006). Several attempts have been made, especially in interaction design, to introduce new methods or techniques that would capture the effective aspects of performance in expressing and experiencing objects of design, such as staging and enacting scenarios (for reviews, see Iacucci, Kuutti, and Ranta 2000; Iacucci and Kuutti 2002). These are ill-framed attempts most of the time, as they result in trivial enactments that are predictable. They also fail to recognize how much performance is already included in design practice. For example, the attempts to mock the Forum Theater of Augusto Boal fail to use governing principles of performance, focusing instead on formal protocols of conduct: set up a stage, act out the scenario, and have the audience interact. On the contrary, performance signifies action, and its result and its approaches to knowing insist on immediacy and involvement. For this a certain level of "tacitness" (Polany 1983) is required.

Collective Creativity

Staged events can be the product of an interactional and negotiative process through which the emergence of objects can become a shared experience. Some practices in the performing arts help to understand how individuals have creative "independence," but at the same time are influenced by other participants and their manipulations of the environment. What we need to make clear is that such interpretations are not only the product of the imaginative activity of a single participant. Rather, what makes them valuable within group improvisations is their interactional character and collective emergence. An actor reacts to another actor's offer of a newly created symbol or utterance by imagining an interpretation and thereby creating a new offer. This emphasizes the point that what we are concerned with in supporting such performances is not the psychology of creativity, or the creativity of the product, which can be a solitary creation. Most of the studies on creativity tend to focus on creative activities that result in objective products (see Sawyer 1998). Moreover, studies have focused on individual behavior, personality, and cognitive processes (Ward, Finke, and Smith 1995; Koestler 1964/1990). Others, like Csikszentmihalyi (1997), have attempted also to consider contextual and cultural factors. However, when speaking about the creative surroundings, Csikszentmihalyi considers "being in the right place" or inspiring environments as "comfortable" places. In these studies, the interaction with material circumstances, artifacts, and also play and performance are not considered. By contrast, group improvisations make salient at least two aspects of creativity: the moment-by-moment process of creative activity and the collective emergence of a fictional space.

The Primacy of Sense Experience

The study of communication has been criticized recently for having a cognitive and linguistic bias. The anthropologist Ruth Finnegan (2002) argues that an anthropological approach challenges "the focus on 'meanings,' 'symbols,' and 'verbalized articulations'" and instead draws attention to "the role of human-made artifacts and their multi-sensory dimensions" (Finnegan 2002, 7). The result is a distancing from the written word and intellectual meaning toward a variety of ways of human interconnection—sounds, touch, sight, movement, material artifacts—and the "significance of shared experiences, dynamic interactions, and bodily engagements beyond the purely cognitive" (ibid., 8).

Objects of design increasingly combine artifacts, architectures, and interactive media. Designers and design researchers, beyond symbols and physical things, have turned to "action" and "environment" to "create new products and reflect on the value of design in our life" (Buchanan 2001, 11). To have value and significance, visual symbols and physical artifacts have to become part "of the living experience of human beings, sustaining them in the performance of their own actions and experiences" (ibid.). These are configured in space and artifacts, in the way these afford, invite, and oblige interactions. Performance may be considered in the creation of artifacts or architectures, especially in the ways these carry a performative potential that is unleashed through participants' interactions. Vito Acconci explains his performative architecture with these words:

The viewer activates (operates) an instrument (what the viewer has at hand) that in turn activates (builds) an architecture (what the viewer is in) that in turn activates (carries) a sign (what the viewer shows off): the viewer becomes the victim of a cultural sign which, however, stays in existence only as long as the viewer works to keep the instrument going. (Acconci 1981, 18)

The Role of Computational Media

Another implication of these perspectives for design work is to discuss a different epistemological role for information technology (IT) in design that contrasts with cognitive or "problem-solving" approaches. These have led to a focus on a particular kind of application of IT that addresses limited aspects of knowledge and experience. While information and communication technologies were originally applied to address linguistic and cognitive problems, anthropology can provide unexplored views that emphasize lived experience and the unspoken, the interactive and creative process of communication and its multimodality. This is, of course, supported by the recent advances in ubiquitous computing and multimedia, tangible interfaces, and other technologies that provide novel ways to augment the physical environment and create mixed realities. Combinations of media, spaces, and interactivity can take place in design artifacts. The emergence of tangible interfaces and mixed media can create multiple constituents of objects, as artful assemblages of digital media and physical artifacts. This provides distinctive opportunities for experiential, presentational, and representational interaction. In project-based learning about design, participants (students) stage spatial narratives with multiple projections, perform interactive artifacts, and exploit bodily movements in mixed representations. These cases show

how multiple and mixed affordances of objects acquire a spatial dimension and integrate physical artifacts and bodily movements and, more importantly, how they evolve and are situated in time. Several aspects of these new interactions have been explored by Dourish (2001), who, drawing from ethnomethodology and phenomenology, proposes a new model of human–computer interaction based on the notion of embodied interaction. This is defined as "the creation, manipulation, and sharing of meaning through engaged interaction with artifacts" (Dourish 2001, 126). We contribute by showing how design and a performance perspective put configurability in a different light if we compare it with the formulation of embodied interaction (ibid.). The episodes contained in this chapter propose a view of configuring as staging with the aim of constructing specific expressions and sensory experiences. Resources for this purpose involved not only "immediate tasks," the "improvised sequential organization of interaction," or affordances, but also how to make spatiality, artifacts, and digital media manipulable so as to privilege perception over recognition.

Conclusions

In this chapter we introduced perspectives that help achieve yet another characterization of how design takes place or can take place. Taking a performance perspective, we have explored the relationship of expression and experience framing the activity of accomplishing design in terms of events. Moreover, we can understand the motivation underpinning the purposeful staging of such events. We can move beyond the "moment-by-moment" of the sketching designer or the longer-term formation of objects. Performance contributes with an interventionist, participative, and experiential epistemology. Performance imposes the primacy of sensory experience. Ways of gaining knowledge that some might refer to as techniques need to be invented anew every time: they do not exist as entities independent from the individuals and groups of people who perform them. With this perspective, we answered such questions as: How do objects emerge? How do participants manipulate, express, and experience them? We distinguished different strategies or aims in the purposeful staging of design events: accomplishment, intervention, and processualization.

7 Emerging Landscapes of Design

In this chapter, we examine the context in which design unfolds. Some scholars talk about design as "navigating" a design space. In their view a search for generic opportunities in a space abstracted from the particular circumstances of the design problem represents an ideal worth pursuing. In this perspective, the practical environment is at best a general resource, providing the designer with the broadest possible array of designer options. We have already shown in previous chapters how the design environment has much more specific inspirational qualities than such a view would indicate. Here, we will further explore how design takes place and suggest that a landscape of design emerges through the designer's dialogical engagement with the environment. What we have in mind are very literal spatial practices through which the environment becomes entangled in the evolving design. The environment to us is neither just a simple constellation of material objects nor a generalized repository of professional tools and media. Instead we will argue that the environment becomes a "lived landscape" in which the designer journeys and dwells. There is congruence between this emerging landscape and the object of design, as it is through experiencing and transforming the design environment that the designer creates the things that constitute the object of design. The designer must make sense of the environment as an assemblage of particular places and eventually turn the emerging landscape of design into new places from which a landscape of use can be imagined.

We present our argument in five steps. We begin by reviewing examples of the spatial practice we have observed in our fieldwork with design students. Here we will point to the design environment as being actively engaged in the way designers work. We argue that keeping the environment "clean and empty" is as much a result of a particular spatial practice as the more visible manifestations of designers engaging with the environment to form an elaborate material backdrop to what is designed. We will then delve deeper into the notions of space and place and particularly the growing interest in reinstating place as the context of action. This provides a framework for understanding how design takes place as encompassing both the temporal and the spatial.

In the second part of the chapter, we focus on the tensions between grounding design in the place of designing and taking off into a space imagined. We do this by first going over the findings from a group of students struggling with the design of "an entrance to a world of their heroes." Here the students appeared reluctant to accept the space of the assignment. Rather than seeing their work as making a place in space, we discuss what they do in light of de Certeau's notion of space as practiced place (de Certeau 1984, 117). Without necessarily generalizing the strategies and tactics displayed by the students, we claim that the students respond to the ambivalence of place as both open for appropriation yet already ingrained with expectations and experiences, by enacting a lived landscape of design that reaches beyond the particularities of places.

We then take a step back to look more closely at what constitutes the practice of designing—the envisioning of *what could be* in other times and places. We discuss what designers do in relation to two competing conceptualizations: Simon's suggestion of a "generic design space" that is independent of the designer (Simon 1996, 133), and Schön's proposal of a virtual world enacted in the interactions between the designer and the design situation (Schön 1983, 157). These two competing conceptualizations both consider the relation between the particular "here-and-now" of the design work and the potential "elsewhere" of the design in use, and we argue that the virtual world of Schön can be seen as an emerging design space or landscape that may allow for an envisioning of *what can be* through the exercising of *what is*.

This leads us to a more detailed inquiry into different dwelling strategies of four student groups working on the same assignment in a confined studio. In another sidestep to a discussion of what kind of space keeps the design object in shape, we analyze the students' practice as the coemergence of landscape and place, in which both are plastic and drifting.

We conclude the chapter by relating the notion of the emerging landscape of design to the discussion in previous chapters. We will argue that just as the object of design can only be experienced through what is constituted by things, the landscape imagined can only be manifested through the particularity of places.

How Design Takes Place

For anyone who has visited an architectural design office or a traditional design school studio, it is evident that design in a very direct fashion manifests itself in the environment. The design office will often be crowded with cardboard models, posters, and drawings but also with material samples, tools, and sometimes also a variety of artifacts with a more opaque relation to the work of design. In larger offices, a visitor obtains an immediate sense of the intensity and mood of various projects, simply by tracing the way project materials get combined and how they sometimes form places of their own within the larger whole of the office (Cuff 1992, 155–156; Yaneva 2005). Observing the work of engineers, one may have to look closer to observe how space and design interact. In engineering offices, one will often have to enter the labs, the individual offices, or other "fox holes" to see projects growing out of whiteboard sketches, disassembled products, or small experimental setups, while the organization's front office might provide "cleaner" facilities for negotiating what Bucciarelli calls "bureaucratic politics" (Bucciarelli 1995, 19). Other design professionals, such as graphic or IT designers, may create a project space almost entirely housed within their computer workstations (see, e.g., Turkle 1997). Although different design professionals inhabit their work environment in different ways, we will claim that the environment is not just there for the designer to make use of. Designers must appropriate the environment in order to become productive as designers. This appropriation is never fully completed. It is ongoing and closely tied to the project at hand.

To better understand what we mean by this ongoing appropriation of the environment, let us return to the two students we followed in the Möbel Leiner project (the facade project). The two architectural students have been working together for some weeks on a project for a new facade for a Vienna warehouse. They have individual desks together with other students in a large studio/drawing room. Having divided the work so that one student works on a 3D model in cardboard and the other on drawings and photos on the computer, they are preparing for the next day's presentation shortly before handing in the final project. Around them they have printouts, photos from the visits to the site, and wooden pieces to be fitted into the model. A nearby worktable is being used for constructing the 3D model, and at times both of them move to other occasionally empty tables, to review the project materials together.

The drawing room does not display any obvious order. Several students are working there at the same time. Leftovers from previous activities such as empty bottles from last night's wine or scrap materials from other projects seem to be lying around with no concern for what should happen to them next. Occasionally the students scour the room for things that may be of use. During our field visit a sheet of transparent plastic is found and quickly examined by two students. It is put into a paper bag for possible later use.

If we expected the students to inhabit a particular location in the drawing hall as *their place*, this is hardly what we see. At times, the two students work at their own desks. Just as often, however, they may go to one of the temporarily incorporated adjacent tables or move things to each other's tables to combine views on models and drawings. Moreover, the drawing room is not the only place of work. They also move around in the Academy building, to work in the workshop, or to pass by other students in the café or in the working rooms of other project groups. One of them even takes a quick trip to the warehouse site to gather additional footage for the project presentation. From what we see, the students live the environment in a flow

Figure 7.1
The Vienna students often visit other students at their tables.

of interactions through which they make it their own. They are not arranging a well-confined place but energetically exercising the situation to be on stage for the presentation the next day.

In our everyday language, the question of where we are implies both a reference to the particular situational circumstances of whatever action we are engaged in and a reference to a larger space of maneuver within which these particularities may subsequently unfold. If we are on the phone and someone asks where we are, we will often answer by naming the activity we are engaged in: "at work," "shopping," "in the garden," or even explicitly address where we are heading: "on my way home," "in the middle of something," "close to the supermarket." Only rarely will we make accurate reference to a geographical location, as the activity we are engaged in would not be understood from the location alone. The students are obviously somewhere when they are sitting close together at a drawing table in Vienna, comparing models and sketches. This "somewhere" is not only together, and not only immersed in the stuff they have produced. It also refers to a particular context of previously seen models and to a situation of intimacy and commitment shielded from outside intrusion. This context forms a horizon that distinguishes this *somewhere* from, for example, an occasional chat among the same students at the same spot inspecting scrap material for later use.

Often this duality of locus and horizon is described with reference to place and space. The place of action is taken to mean the immediate and embodied surroundings of the activity, whereas the notion of space connotes a more fluid action space through which the students travel during the course of their work. Yet this way of distinguishing place from space does not capture the fluidity by which the students move and act. The two students gathering around the computer do not seem more in place than the student collecting footage at the building site. On the other hand, the studio and the academy building is not just inhabitable space. It is continuously "traveled" along particular paths that manifest themselves not through exclusive habitation but through ephemeral traces that, like the bag of scrap material, offer opportunities for future action.

In our search to discover how design takes place, we need to get closer to a framing that can hold the fluid movements we observe. As suggested by several authors, place and space are not just there, independently of how we act (see, e.g., Ciolfi and Bannon 2005). In our actions, we are present in the world in a lived engagement with the environment. This engagement *takes place* in the double sense that it brings in the environment as a place of action at the same time as it enacts this place in a particular way that makes it become meaningfully lived with respect to the action. Following Gaston Bachelard, we may conceive of place not merely as the situational *here and now* of human action but as the basic inner structuring of our being in the world. Bachelard suggests (discussed in Casey 1997, 285) that we perceive the environment as a journey through places simultaneously in the world and in our mind. The way we know of and remember the world around us is through reference to those places of the mind most strongly rooted in our childhood experience. Extending Bachelard's perspective, we may think of places as both imagined and enacted. If letting something take place—in Bachelard's terms—involves a sort of domestication of *what is* in relation to an accumulated yet personal mental topography, then it also points to this place-taking as an enactment of appropriation and dwelling that produce the "here-and-now" within a horizon of the familiar. This perspective views place as the context of action similar to Schutz's notion of everyday action as positioned within the horizon of a life-world, conceptualized in Schutz's (1982) terms as "the world within reach." Bachelard conceives of this horizon as imagined within the lived biographical experience, but via the link to Schutz, we may extend this scheme of imagination and enactment to the social interactions imaginable in the language of the everyday circumscribing the action. What these arguments point to is a concept of place that is not a place in space, but a place among places that are at the same time lived and imagined.

To get a sense of what such a strong concept of place may mean in our context, we will compare the work of the two architectural students in the Möbel Leiner project to the work of interaction design students from another sample of our fieldwork. Here we followed interaction design students in Malmö as they took part in a robot competition set up as a one-week workshop for master students. The students worked with the LEGO Mindstorm robot-building kit. They had to rework a robot design of another group and prepare it for a robot race on a racing field with unknown obstacles. The students worked in two competing groups, sharing a large studio where each group had a building kit and a computer.

Before going further into the work of the Malmö students, let us first recapitulate how design can be seen as taking place for the architectural students. We have emphasized how they move about and how they appear to feel equally at home as they visit other students, prepare cardboard models, or take a trip to the warehouse site. We have noted that they domesticate the environment not by exclusively appropriating their own territory but by "traveling" and leaving traces and repositories along several "pathways." If we had expected the architectural students to inhabit a confined place of work tables and drawing boards, we found them instead journeying between places familiarized within the common horizon of their project.

At first sight, the interaction design students in Malmö inhabit their studio in quite different ways. The studio itself resembles an open office environment with movable chairs and tables and groups of lounge-like soft chairs gathered around low tables. The students worked intensively all day in the studio, but, unlike the drawing room of the Vienna students, the studio in Malmö appeared somewhat barren. One student group quickly got together around a meeting table in a corner of the studio. They settled here sitting closely together with Mindstorm blocks on the table, and made no attempt to appropriate other parts of the studio. In the time we observed them the group acted almost as one person, going back and forth between tinkering with the Mindstorm blocks and discussing possible design principles. Filling the table with papers, LEGO blocks, and half-finished robots, the students passed materials around, and leaned over each other, intensely engaged with the project. Where we had difficulties delimiting where design took place for the Vienna students, the territorial boundaries of the place of design for this group of Malmö students were easy to identify. In terms of ongoing appropriation the Malmö students appeared to intensify their interactions at the common table, creating, as we will also return to shortly, a horizon of action enabling them to jump out from this restricted place to places elsewhere.

The other student group in Malmö displayed different spatial practices. They split up their tasks, with each student seeking out a comfortable place to do her work. Tables were moved casually and often to form new configurations, but none of these configurations obtained stability over time. What seemed most pronounced in the work of this group, however, was the accommodation of collaborative events. At a particular point in time, they brought together equipment and people to make a test ground for the robot they build. A computer to be used for the programming, the Mindstorm blocks, and the test racing field were all kept close together, as the students "camped out" in the studio to get ready for the competition. Work was intense and highly collaborative, new suggestions were made and tried out, and one could observe a flow through which tools, materials, and site were all closely knit. Yet as swiftly as they put

Figure 7.2
As design grew more intense, the group tightened the space.

up the test field, just as quickly did they tear it down, to proceed to something new. Nothing was left of their camp, and the students dispersed into other activities.

At first sight, the interaction design students engage their environment quite differently from the architectural students. The first group of Malmö students created a single intense spot in the studio almost as if to drill or dig out a place in the otherwise barren and empty studio. The second group of Malmö students was so much on the move that place became identical with event. The students did not leave obvious traces but rather erased all signs of their intense camp-out around the robots and fierce group discussion. At the same time, however, we observe how they literally "swarmed" the environment, alternating between spreading out and gathering closely together.

After the interaction design workshop in Malmö, we asked the students to offer reflections about the environment in which they work and to bring photos of places they found important in the course of their work. Despite the emphasis of the Malmö School to provide studios for the classes, both groups reported that they found the studio environment difficult to work in. They talked a lot about how difficult they found it to be in control of where they could be, and what would be acceptable to do in the studio, and also of the stability and accessibility of the computer network, which is essential to their work. When they presented their photos of places they found important, these were only rarely from the school, and to the extent that they were, they portrayed in-between areas such as the school cafeteria, some couches in the school hallway, or similar spots where the most remarkable common denominator was their indeterminacy as places of action. The majority of the photos, however, had quite a different mood, as they showed a view from a bedroom window, a snapshot from a walk in the woods, or the privacy of a bathroom. In light of Bachelard's notion of homeliness, these photos and the excursions to cafés and hallways give us a sense of the same kinds of personal journeying that came more directly to mind when following the architectural students. The pattern of movement, however, is still

Figure 7.3
Photos the Malmö students brought us of places they like to go to be alone, think, or daydream.

remarkably different. As already mentioned, the interaction design students seem to interact with the environment in a way that makes the present more pronounced, almost identifying place with event. The architectural students, on the other hand, work to build up potentials in an engagement with the environment where materials are rearranged and deposited for later use.

We will argue that both architectural students and interaction design students in these two vignettes are simultaneously imagining and enacting places of design. The obvious engagement of the material environment is equally pronounced for the two kinds of students, as the interaction design students enact their "empty studio" with similar energy as that of architectural students in maintaining the "messiness" of their drawing hall. The differences between the spatial practices have much to do with time and event and with the way the environments are already loaded with scripts and expectations. It is hardly a coincidence that what the interaction design students enact resembles a Cartesian grid of points in space, whereas the architectural students appear to clear an extended site for their work. In what follows, we will look further into how the way design takes place relates to what emerges as the object of design.

From Places to Landscapes

So far we have discussed design much like any other human activity, and our inquiry into how design takes place has not taken into consideration what makes designing particular and unique. There is a point to this, as we want to make sure that what we claim for design is compatible with what can be said about the situatedness of human action in general. When, for example, Harrison and Dourish (1996) claim, in a discussion of how to design technological environments for collaborative work, that these environments have to be appropriated by the users to become meaningful places, then we must assume that this is true for designers as well with regard to their environment.

When they further suggest that places cannot be designed but only provided for by the designer as a space for the user to appropriate, then we should ask how this can be accomplished through the engagement the designer performs with her own environment. We acknowledge that a salient characteristic of design is that what is enacted in the design environment does not only have to be meaningful in the here-and-now of the design situation but must also imply a potential for sense-making in other places. We are reluctant, however, to accept Harrison and Dourish's notions of space and place unconditionally, as they seem to imply an asymmetry between designer and user, where the former works from place to space and the latter from space to place. In the previous paragraph we made the claim that designers actively engage the environment through the enactment and imagining of places. We will now look into how other design students met an assignment that specifically urged them to work with notions of place and space.

As a three-day assignment, we asked mixed groups of interaction design students and architecture students to create an interactive spatial installation forming an entrance to the world of their own design heroes. The installation could be in any media and could be placed anywhere inside the school, but should be housed within the dimensions of 1.5 × 1.5 × 2 meters. In the terminology of Harrison and Dourish, we as teachers offered an open space (the school facility and the assignment) that they as students were to inhabit with a place for their heroes. What the students did, however, was to explore the framing we had given them. "Could the installation really be anywhere?" seemed to be the question for one group. They sought out a remote maintenance room in the school basement. Here they installed a series of looped video sequences of a setting sun to be contemplated by the visitor, while she could contemplate whether anyone could be a hero. Another group occupied itself with the idea of the hero as one who is truly able to appreciate reality. They filled a dark room with olfactory and tactile materials to be explored by the brave. Was this interactive? Or could the entrance just be the actual entrance to the school, only slightly modified with a dressing room, offering visitors the opportunity to enter the school as a hero undressed?

The students turning the school entrance into a (un-)dressing room wrote an accompanying text about what they called their "abc installation":

_A_ as in against the stream, _b_ as in blowing up and _c_ as in confrontation: the first aspects of this project. Three things that would happen in this entrance. We first talked about having some kind of question that people had to answer: are you against the stream? Well, what can you say. . . . Then my son asked me later that day: wouldn't it be disgusting to see a naked man in the street? And that is really the point in some way. One can then choose to be the disgusting naked man in the street, or one can choose to see the disgusting naked man in the street. If you choose to be the active part you take the door into the closet, the dressing room, where you can undress, or just think about it. You are then given a chance to be the hero, or at least consider it for a moment. So the entrance is then actually creating a hero. In that way, it will be very easy for anybody to be a hero—just taking on the challenge. Facing the danger, getting embarrassed. Stepping out naked on the red carpet.

The way we constructed the assignment put a demand on the students to bring in something of themselves—"the world of their heroes"—and to connect this, which could be rather personal, to the school environment. The assignment signaled that the "entrance" could be anywhere in the school, but in light of the unease displayed by the interaction design students in the robotics workshop in gaining control of the studios, this assignment may have been equally discomforting in its straightforward disclosing of personal heroes. We do not know what motivated the students to take on the assignment as they did, but it is striking how in their responses they all challenge the key elements of the assignment.

If we allow ourselves briefly to consider how the students might have approached the assignment had they followed a simple deductive approach, we could have expected something like the following. Step A: write down your heroes (everybody should be able to do that). Step B: think of a world the heroes can share and how it can be represented to a visitor (could be approached metaphorically: hall of fame, wax cabinet, zoo, etc.). Step C: consider what an entrance could be (some sort of transition zone that significantly alters what/how you perceive; examples could be putting on headphones, moving into an enclosed environment, or changing the visitors' own presence/appearance in the environment). Step D: find a good spot in the school to put up the entrance. We did not follow closely how the students worked through the assignment, so we cannot tell to what extent this kind of thinking played any role in what they did. From the variations they displayed, however, it is very likely that at some point they went through considerations similar to steps B and C. What interests us here though is the apparent complexity of steps A and D (even though we realize they may not have appeared as steps in the oversimplified way we have suggested here).

Let us first take what for the students turned out to be "good spots." This time, the students did not seek out the in-between spaces, as they did in the robotics workshop. Instead, they looked for locations that either already had or could be made to have a strong sense of particularity both in terms of the way they differentiated themselves from the school setting as such and through the particularity of the horizon of "movement" they were made to afford. Regarding the student group who chose to set up the installation in the basement maintenance room and show images of the sunset as seen from just outside the same building, it is difficult not to see this as a more or less direct commentary on the tensions between the "empty" studios and the vivid imagery of the photos the students brought us in the debriefing from the robotics workshop. But why did they choose the room in the basement to accomplish this; couldn't they just as well have set up the installation in a hallway or a studio? And, regarding the group who set up the school entrance as an (un-)dressing room, why were they drawn to such a well-defined place to create a new and twisted place of transformation? One could perhaps have expected that at least some of the students would have been drawn to locations that did not display such obvious preconfigurations. The one group that came closest to appropriate what may be considered an open space was the group that provided a sensory experience of taste, smell, and touch. Here, blocking of the sight of the visitor, together with the stimulation of those senses perhaps most neglected in the school environment, signaled a struggle with what was there (or was not there) rather than an appreciation of indeterminacy and openness.

We are aware that we are pushing a strong interpretation on a design assignment that in many ways specifically invites a poetic response from the students. And just as the students in the robotics workshop may mimic an abstract design space as they swarm and intensify a Cartesian grid of infinite points, so may the students of the hero assignment perform journeys and construct dwellings that interact directly with the work of Bachelard. Nevertheless, we see in the work of the students a deliberate search for what has structure and specificity in the environment. In our interpretation, they do not accept or appreciate the openness of the assignment. There are no "free spots" to choose for their endeavor, they seem to say. Instead, they appear to obtain openness in their own work by getting closer to and transforming what is already obviously structured.

But what then about the hypothetical step A: the choice of heroes to connect to in the installation? Here all three groups were hesitant to be explicit. If they wanted to nail down the structured places obscurely present in the claimed openness of the school setting, they reacted quite oppositely to the call for exposure of their personal heroes. They did not in any way dismiss the theme of heroism. On the contrary, their installations are fundamentally about inviting visitors to explore what it is to be a hero. In working on the experiential qualities of the chosen site, they are not working toward conveying or disseminating a particular perception of heroes and heroism. Instead, they are working to create an evocative environment that affords an experience but leaves it open what this experience might be.

Returning to Harrison and Dourish's notion of space as what is provided and place as what is lived, the work of the students' points, in our view, to what is missing in this equation. Harrison and Dourish write, as we will return to later, on how the design of technology determines subsequent activity. In this discussion they argue convincingly that designers must leave room for appropriation. When generalizing this point, as in the assignment discussed above, we can, however, get easily trapped in the implicit sequentiality of design and use (or more generally, provision and appropriation). When the students in the assignment search for structure, this can be seen as an exploration of what is already there. They can only get to the openness of the assignment through discovering what is fixed. What this means become more obvious if we think of them as arriving not at an "empty space" but at an unknown "land-scape." As Ingold discusses, we are always in landscapes and places formed not only by our own past and present but also by our appreciation of traces of what has already taken place (Ingold 2000, 172). So there is no "before" being in place, and there is no place without a sense of landscape. What this place is, and to what extent it allows us a viewpoint on landscapes of other places, can only be determined from within our engagement with the environment; and, as Ingold also argues, we have to conceive of both place and landscape as associated as much with task and activity as with tools and sensory appreciation of the material environment. (Ingold [ibid., 189] talks about taskscapes as a more appropriate notion than landscapes. We find, however, that the notion of landscapes as the imaginary horizon of our actions is more in line with our everyday language.) In this light, we can interpret what the students do as a search for places to make sense of that offer them a viewpoint on the landscape of the assign-ment. Even though the place and landscape they experience cannot be separated from the process of experiencing that is unique to their engagement, they look for places already imbued with meaning by others, and they develop their own landscape in dialogue and dispute with the landscape of their teachers, which they sense in the assignment. They inquire into this landscape of others through searching for and transforming the richness of places found, and they seem to offer a replication of this process in the installations they create, as they invite their visitors to experience a richness of the places appropriated and transformed.

What does this mean to the notion of space? Harrison and Dourish use the notion of space to capture how something is prepared while much is yet left open. The students surely also prepare something for the visitors in their installations while leaving the outcome of what is experienced largely untouched. What they not do, however, is "underdesign" the installations. Just as they explore the richness of places to inhabit in preparing the installation, similarly they strive for a richness and particu-larity of the finished installation as a place to experience. With a slight simplification we may say that where the space of Harrison and Dourish is in the world of our mate-rial environment and the place in the mind of the "dweller," the space of the students installations are in their mind and imagination, as will also be the case for the (differ-ent) space (or rather spaces) experienced by the visitors. Such a notion of space as experienced or lived is what de Certeau (1984) suggests in an analysis of the everyday of the modern city. He is interested in how people live in an urban environment inscribed with history and expectations. He sees the city as dense with scripts of dis-cipline and control, but also with heterogeneity and glitches. As people live in the city they, as he puts it, practice the places of the urban environment in order to establish a livable space. We will not go deeper into his analysis, but only note that by suggest-ing that "space is practiced place" (ibid., 117), de Certeau offers an interesting alterna-tive to the concept of space used by Harrison and Dourish. Instead of the formula:

space + experience= place, we have: place (of someone else) + experiencing = place (of one self) + space/landscape experienced. This is particularly significant when we want to capture how, as in the hero assignment, designers not only practice the school setting to make it livable, but furthermore through this engagement strive to facilitate further experiencing, this time of the visitors as they experience the installation. The space or landscape experienced by the designer can never be identical to the space or landscape experienced by the visitor; but in acknowledging that we meet the world in places and that what is experienced in practicing place is a landscape of possible movement, we rescue a concept of space or landscape that may connect to the hypothetical realm of design space and as-if-worlds, which we discuss in more detail in the following section.

Design Space and Virtual Worlds

Using the examples of design students' work, we have emphasized the direct and explicit engagement with the environment that informs the students' interactions. In our description, we have also sensitized ourselves to signs of porosity and flux of the "elsewhere," regardless of whether this takes the form of the photos of the everyday that students brought us, or whether it has the sense of other places invoked by the students' struggle with, for example, the Möbel Leiner assignment.

Within the broader discussion of design as a problem-solving activity, Simon and others position the designer as a navigator of a generic design space or solution space that holds every particular instance of problem solving to be an infinite point in this space (Simon 1996, 133). The designer must be able to decompose and generalize the problem in order to position the problem in the generalized design space. From here, solutions may be derived as instantiations of a particular set of generalized designs. This way of thinking about design has been very influential in the design of technological systems, where the system as such is supposed to be an ideally generic compounding of the design space. From this perspective, the system in actual use is just one among several appearances that the designed system may take. In terms of space and place, this could imply that a fundamental cycle of designing is a dissolving of the placeness of the problem into an area of infinite points in the abstracted design space, followed by a systemic combination of these points into a system from which new places may be instantiated. Many authors have criticized this approach, but it has nevertheless maintained a popularity particularly within technically oriented design, with its emphasis on generality. Recall the interaction design students at Malmö, who alternate between working in the studio and occasionally swarming and "camping out" around joint experiments, only to wrap up quickly after and disperse. This we may see as an acting-out of a design space of the kind proposed by Simon. Such a practice of design, however, both is localized and produces its own locale in order to work as shown by Fitzpatrick (2002). Schön's critique of the idealized design space can help us understand these practices.

Schön has criticized Simon for neglecting what Schön called "problem setting." According to Schön, the designer cannot approach a design task without actively framing the situation so that a problem evolves. As discussed earlier in chapter 2, this type of framing is not external to solving the problem. Rather, it is integral to the practice of designing. It is through imposing suggestions—what Schön calls "design moves"—that the design situation reveals itself to the designer. By alternating between these design moves and assessments of how these moves affect the situation, the designer enacts a virtual world in which problem and solution are simultaneously created (Schön 1983, 157). In contrast to Simon's idea of abstracting the problem from its particular context, Schön's virtual world originates in a conversation with the situation. Simon's "design space" concept is external to the designer and inherent in the generalized realm of the problem, whereas the virtual world of Schön emerges together with the designer's engagement with the situation.

"World" and "situation" resemble "space" and "place," but world and situation also imply a temporality of sense-making and action. Schön describes the designer as being in a dialogue with the materials of the "design situation." The "situation" is not what surrounds the conversation but, rather, the conversation itself in all its engagements. This conversation allows "moves" to emerge. The moves are assessed and then projected onto the situation in a nested shifting of framing, evoking, and enacting of what gradually stabilizes as a world imagined. For Schön, the nested character of the conversational situations forms the essential condition for the making of as-if worlds. We will see this conversation with the material of the design situation as not only a living of place/event but also as an emerging landscape in an attempt to grasp the double nature of designing as both a particular situated practice and a hypothetical practicing of a place imagined. Schön provides us with some important elements of such a conception by showing how the nesting of engagement, appreciation, and enactment may allow for an envisioning of *what can be* through the exercising of *what is*.

The Coemergence of Landscape and Place

In a five-week assignment, four groups of interaction design students were asked to work with the theme of *augmenting places* in relation to different groups of users: firemen, divers, power supply electricians, and emergency ward staff. The students were given a well-defined studio area in what we called the "concept lab"—a studio equipped with a grid installation in the ceiling and a toolbox of technologies for linking physical material to digital media. The concept lab studio formed a large cube, six meters by six meters by three meters, and each of the four groups had precisely one-fourth of the cube as designated area for its work. The assignment was structured in a number of fixed steps. The students had to carry out a short video-ethnographic study of the users for whom they were to design augmented places. Throughout the assignment, the students were provided installation-type formats for displaying their work. They were asked to stage and act out full-scale scenarios and to make use of a technological toolbox provided for them. Despite the strong preformatting of the assignment and the studio, the groups developed remarkably different spatial strategies to accommodate their work.

Tutoring and presentations were frequently carried out in the studio, and all students seemed concerned with defining the territory of their group in relation to these outside intrusions. Two groups were very restrictive in what they staged in the studio cube. They worked with certain installation elements that they wanted to make use of, often in a fragmented way that left it open how they would become part of the evolving whole. One group worked for days to master a particular projection technique demonstrated to them in a lecture. This condensed into the idea of conveying a visual imprint of the pain or relief of a severely injured patient. Their studio became the scene for the mastery of this particular expressive element. The overall conception of the design seemed to grow in the shadow of the focused experiment with form.

The other group, working with a similarly constrained transparency, obtained control through maintaining a distanced and conceptual gaze at what they designed. Where the first group immersed themselves in the mastering of possible expressive visualizations of pain, the second group explored concepts such as uncertainty and risk, which they identified in their field work with firemen. They created nested stages

Figure 7.4
On the left, a picture of the "concept-studio" taken on the first day of the Augmented Places project. On the right, a picture taken from the same spot three weeks later, showing how the students have appropriated the studio.

where these concepts became directive elements in microworlds for themselves and for the tutors to grasp through board games and tabletop installations.

As evolving places of design, the two student groups acted as if the studio was basically empty, becoming only gradually and tentatively filled with their work, as their experiments increased their confidence that something would start to mature. Their strategies, however, were radically different. The group studying the emergency ward searched for an amorphous design space of pain, relief, and caring through an almost totally contracted point of entry in the exploration of facial expressions. The group studying the firemen, by contrast, appeared to avoid the determinacy of the particular. They were engineering places that made the spectator envision a design that instead of highlighting the here-and-now of pain and relief nurtured the possibilities of escape and transport from place to place.

While these students controlled and constricted the final staging of the design and guarded the lack of specificity of the space available to them, two other groups of

Figure 7.5
The student group who turned their part of the studio cube into a homely environment also worked with homeliness in their final presentation.

students in the Augmenting Places assignment turned such strategies inside out. These two groups made the assigned studio into their primary workspace by conducting almost all of their joint work within the cube. The group working with divers made the studio into a workshop. Within the space, they moved around pieces of technology and field materials, and they put up screens and flip charts to make all of what they worked with visible and graspable. They built up and tested the stage for their presentations on the spot, and through the weeks, the space became a divers' workplace, where every new element had to be directly fitted into this hybrid place, as if it were an actual construction site. The place for designing became the place for the design, and every piece of the students' workshop material had to be made sense of in this transformation.

The fourth student group, working with power supply electricians, made their cube into a kind of designers' living room. Like the divers group, they basically lived in their cube for the weeks of the assignment. However, they turned it not into a construction site but rather into a lounge-like discussion area. With cushions on the floor and several display experiments to convey the atmosphere of the often-isolated work of electricians, they digested both the world of the electricians and the world of the design school. A domesticated place of reflection and visionary imagery became the basic mode for their design as they prototyped a sharable media space that could bring electricians together.

Space Constancy and Drifting Artifacts

Whereas Schön addressed the complexities of the coevolution of problem setting and problem solving in the process of design, others have taken up the question of how a designed artifact relates to the wider landscape imagined by a designer. For example, scholars working in actor-network theory (ANT) (such as Latour, discussed in previous chapters) have pointed out that scientists and engineers rely on the coproduction of contextual practices in order to make sense of particular artifacts.

Law and Mol have discussed the issue of context in terms of a space in which a particular arrangement of artifacts is operable (Law 1986; Law and Mol 2001). They take a map used by fifteenth-century Portuguese navigators as their starting point as they reiterate an actor-network-oriented analysis, demonstrating that it is not the particular features of the visual representation of the map of the seas but, rather, the full system of merchant stations, navigator schools, and political and economic negotiations that surround the sea trade that make the maps operable. According to Law and Mol, the actual maps did not differ significantly from those that Asian seafarers were able to draw in the sand. It was through the transportation and handing over of the maps that a landscape for travel was established. This example is in many ways seminal for the ANT tradition, but Law and Mol criticize the conceptual generality of the notion of space implicit in the example. The context/space of the map, they argue, makes simply too neat a coupling of social space and geographical space. From the perspective of ANT, the map as an artifact is an immutable mobile in the sense that it maintains its shape as it moves. The immutability depends on the particular configuration of the network in which it takes part. With the map example, this configuration is fixed in the network although the map moves in Euclidian space. The invariance of the artifact to the movements in network space defines the stability of the artifact (i.e., the fact that we can recognize the artifact as the same through its travels in Euclidian space). For Law and Mol, however, this stability becomes overdetermined if we can only conceive of this space as the overlaying of a Euclidian space of full mobility and a network space of completely still configurations.

Law and Mol suggest other possible notions of space, such as "fluid space" and "fire space," both of which introduce the concept of temporality. They discuss the Zimbabwean bush pump as an example of an artifact that has plasticity which can only be accounted for with reference to fluid space. According to Law and Mol the particular constellation of the pump's physical parts, its operation, and the purposes for which the pump is used all vary significantly from place to place. Rather than securing stable configurations of networks, the designers of the pump have apparently actively promoted this plasticity. Nevertheless Law and Mol insist that we must talk about the shape of the pump as invariant so as to account for how it is recognized and elaborated upon as a distinct artifact. In contrast to the rigidity of the landscape of the Portuguese navigator, who carved out secure routings in the "wilderness" facing the European merchants, the bush pump travels a space of continuity and flow in which configurations as well as the pump itself undergo gradual transformations. Law and Mol see in the sameness of this evolving artifact in fluid space a shift from static landscape to time-scapes, as the substrate through which artifacts like the pump perform.

Where fluid space is an attempt to come to terms with gradual change and adaptivity, Law and Mol address another difficulty of immutability in accounting for the otherness of that which is made stable. Invoking Bachelard, they talk about fire space as the field in which stability of shape is established in a flickering between what Simon calls preferred states and their often silenced counterparts: the states of turbulence and disorder. As an example of an artifact operating in fire space, they discuss an engineering formula used to calculate critical safety levels of airplane turbulence as used for designing military fighter-bombers. They argue that such a formula can only be made sense of through a constant shifting of focus between the optimality of safe and efficient flying and a patchwork of envisioned threats ranging from pilot illness due to turbulence to the potential destruction of the aircraft by possible enemy attacks. The three attributes of fire space that Law and Mol partly derive from Bachelard are first, that shape constancy is produced by discontinuity rather than gradual change; second, that the artifact achieves its shape through an oscillation between what is present and what is absent; and third, that this space has what they call a "star pattern," where the singular presence relates to a multitude of absent others.

With the ANT tradition and particularly Law and Mol's work we have stepping stones for understanding a design space as the landscape that gives the (designed) artifact its shape. This landscape is no longer a generalized space of problem solving, but a space that may be of fluidity or fire, as it provides positions and configurations for shaping the artifact. The design space is not only the realm of the designer but also the imagined landscape that makes the artifact make sense in use. What these contributions do not offer, however, are insights into how this sense-making is situated and experienced in the living practice of designers and users. To this end, we will follow a second stream of authors who have discussed precisely this enactment in use.

Enactment, Place, and Situation

If an artifact has to be positioned in a particular network to make sense and realize the intent that the designer has sought to embed in it, how then do the processes of sense-making and networking unfold as someone engages with pumps, formulas, or maps prepared by others? When considering artifacts that are defined mainly by a purpose of use, many scholars in the tradition of Simon have seen artifacts as embodying a particular cognitive model that the user must adopt. Researchers such as Akrich (1992), who is close to the ANT tradition, have favored the idea that the artifact is scripted with a particular user behavior. From this perspective, the interaction between user and technology can be seen as the unfolding of a script, where user action and artifact response follow a program already embedded in the technology. This perspective has been seriously challenged, however, by studies of technology in use.

Suchman questions the translation of even very deliberate "scripting," proposing instead that interaction with artifacts must be understood within the frame of the actors' everyday courses of action. Her microsociological studies of the interaction between mundane everyday artifacts, such as photocopiers, and people seeking to accomplish their work, show that even though such artifacts bear clear imprints of preconceived plans for action, these plans enter human work as resources to be appropriated and accommodated in the course of action, not as fixations of how work must be done (Suchman 1987). Underlying Suchman's analysis is the assertion that every human action involves the active coconstruction and enactment of the circumstances that make this action meaningful and legitimate. Suchman's perspective does not neglect the role of things and their compositional configuration as important elements in the context of work, but her view suggests that these must be seen as dispositions that must be invoked and made sense of.

With her notion of situated action, Suchman is primarily concerned with showing the contingencies of technology in use and their dependence on the deliberate "investment" of purposeful action on the side of the users. As we have already discussed, Dourish (2001) and others have sought to determine how we conceptualize what is enacted in a particular situation. Dourish is interested in the relation between, on the one hand, what is designed and made available to the user, and on the other hand, what is accomplished in use. Based on studies of computer-mediated communication, particularly video-links, he suggests, together with Harrison, that use context must be understood as a place made meaningful through the users' interactions (Harrison and Dourish 1996). Where the situated action of Suchman's users casually interacting with photocopiers points to the occasional and improvised linking of people and artifacts, Dourish shows that from a wider perspective, people are always in embodied interaction with the environment. Like Suchman, Dourish finds that this embodied interaction is what makes sense of the environment, but the slight shift in emphasis from action to interaction and from situation to place makes the user's engagement with the environment more profound. When Dourish then turns to what is designed or provided for the user, he calls this a "space," and takes this to be literally the provision of a spatial configuration of material objects. He claims that this space can only become meaningful as the users interact with it, and what the designer can accomplish is to make such sense-making possible.

Thus, for both Suchman and Dourish, there appears to remain a distinction between action (as individual human engagement) and environment (as what is available to any individual in a particular setting) and also a reluctance to involve any notion of individual agency or subjectivity. One may see the analyses of Suchman and Dourish as reactions to the idea that the designer can push agency onto the user (through the embedding of schemata or scripts in the designed artifact). But in this reaction, it is as if both the subjectivity of the user and the subjectivity of the designer are canceled out, leaving us with a somewhat probabilistic gap between design and use. Ciborra (2001) addresses this issue in a discussion of mood and attunement of action. Like Suchman, Ciborra takes action to be situated, but invoking Heidegger, Ciborra extends the notion of situation to encompass what he calls the mood of the actor (from Heidegger's discussion of *Befindlichkeit*). He describes moods such as panic, boredom, and improvisation that differ fundamentally in their appropriation of time. Where the person in a state of panic experiences a shortage of time that makes it impossible to act out any personal project, the person who is bored is occupied with killing time. As opposed to these two moods, the mood of improvisation allows a person to act outside of time (*ex tempora*), disclosing the matter of the world quite differently. In the mood of improvisation, we are disposed in such a way so as to open up to "the moment of vision and self-revelation where all possibilities linked to the being-in-the-situation emerge out of the fog of boredom" (Ciborra 2001). What Ciborra is after in his discussion with Suchman and others is to get beyond the situated as merely an intuitive accomplishment of plans. For Ciborra, improvisation is not the opposite of what is planned, but the opposite of boredom. In terms of interaction with technology, which is also his concern, he suggests that it is only through an examination of the moods engaged by the user in these interactions that we can come to understand what is accomplished when technology is used (Ciborra 1999; Ciborra and Willcocks 2006).

Let us return to our initial question of how landscape and place are engaged, enacted, and imagined by designers and users. How can we connect what is designed with what is made sense of in use? Here we will draw on this brief discussion of Suchman, Dourish, and Ciborra to complement our critique of the notion of design space as proposed by Simon. First, we read Suchman's work as a strong argument for disconnecting the intentions of the designer that figure so prominently in the design rationale proposed in the tradition of Simon from the intentionality of the user guided, as Suchman shows, by the particularities of whatever project he or she is engaged in. In this context, the strongest impact of Suchman's work is that it challenges the idea that the intentional scripting of artifacts carries over in any direct sense to the user through programmed interactions. Dourish adds to this opacity of the translation from design to use by making the embodied interaction with artifacts the primary locus in which the artifact can at all become meaningful. He thus rejects the idea that any kind of generic system or object instantiates itself in the context of use. In so doing, however, he also creates a mystery: how indeed does the coevolution of space and artifact as described above in the discussion of maps, pumps, and formulas take place? As we have noted, Dourish seems to cancel out the investment of intentional subjectivity on the side of the designer, in a response to the neglect of the subjectivity of the user in the systems design tradition with which he is arguing. This leads him to propose that what the designer provides is space, not place, a suggestion that appears to be at odds with the delicate engagements with place that we have seen pursued by design students. Ciborra helps us at this point, as he reinstates the subjective appraisal of the artifact environment as indispensable to any conception of the situated action. For Ciborra, there is no situation without a mood of those perceiving it, and in our view, this can take us directly to an appreciation of the designed artifact as symmetrically invested with meaning on the side of designer and user. Thus the situation in which the designed artifact makes sense must precisely be conceived as both manifested place and imagined landscape.

From Abstract Space to Landscapes Imagined

To sum up, we have discussed the shortcomings of the idea of an abstracted design space, and we have attempted to salvage a concept of space that can capture the traveling and the imagined landscape as it evolves in the process of designing. Schön provided us with the notion of a nestedness between the design situation and the places envisioned and imagined in the virtual world of design. Replacing the movement from the particular to the abstract with a conversational coevolution of appreciation and expansion of the situation of the design work, Schön enables us to see designing as a journey to and among places.

The detour to the studies of designed artifacts as immutable mobiles kept in place in a grid of network configurations reintroduced the concept of space as the structured field in which the artifacts can travel and maintain their shape. It takes work and continuous practice to establish and maintain this space. However, as Law and Mol's work shows us, the notions of shape and space must be developed beyond Euclidian geometry to accommodate fluidity and the presence of that which is made absent in the design.

Finally, the quick sweep through studies of technological artifacts in use reveals the tensions between the openness of appropriation and the scripting of interaction inherent in those artifacts. In the discussion of the work of Suchman, Dourish, and Ciborra, we have balanced the contingency of design and use with an appreciation of the unique and particular engagement of both designers and users as inconceivable without reference to what Ciborra calls the subjective mood or what Dewey (in the discussion taken up in chapter 2) calls experience. Taken together with what has already been said about designing as traveling among places, and the conception of design space as the imagined landscape of these travels, we return to examples of how design students work.

What kind of fabric is woven by designers as they set out to engage with a new design? We have seen architectural design students coming back from field trips with photos of foreign places in which students use such prosaic instruments as a red carpet to create a "home away from home." We have seen students turning the drawing hall into an subway ride by showing video footage to an audience lined up with their arms in metrolike straps so as to provide for a bodily presence in the experiential space of subway riding. These tentative dwellings are ephemeral, yet they are also attempts to probe for a ground from which the new may grow. It would be all too simple to think of them as discrete practices of *being there* or *being here*. If the students had brought the red carpet to the foreign place but not included it in the photos brought home, it would not have contributed to the fabric of design. Similarly, a joint excursion to the Metro for everyone to experience firsthand the sensations of a train ride may have been interesting, but it would have provided nothing like the experience of turning the studio into a sampled hybrid of subway and drawing hall. In a very practical way, the students are here weaving the first threads for the landscape in which the artifacts yet to come may acquire and maintain their shape.

This movement and connection between familiarizing what is unfamiliar in the field and putting distance between oneself and what is familiar in the studio can also be seen in the way interaction design students inhabited the studio in the Augmenting

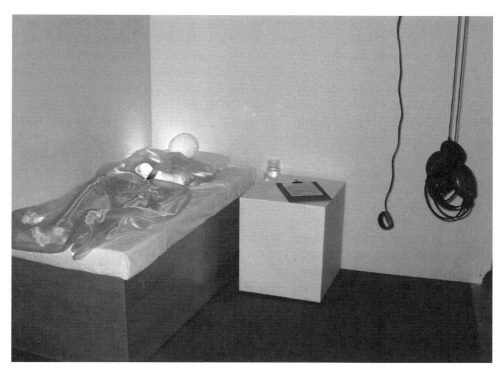

Figure 7.6
A landscape of pain and relief is evoked in the work of the design students proposing a set of wristbands to connect the emergency ward patient and her relatives.

Places assignment. The student group working with augmentation in the emergency ward made their first presentation of video material from a hospital by preparing a floor plan of the emergency ward placed on a table in the studio. The video could be played, while boardgame-like pieces were moved to premarked spots on the floor plan. This enabled the spectator to simulate a presence in the ward. The video was projected on an adjacent wall. To see the projection, the spectator had to turn away from the floor plan table and stand in front of the display screen. The presentation was considered unsuccessful by both the students and the tutors.

Although it contained provocative ideas for condensing and staging the presence in the field in the simulated world of the floor plan, the actual exploration showed that the experience disintegrated, as the bodily posture of the spectator had to break with the confines of the table-world. The "here-and-there" of studio and ward had not been transcended. It had only been reproduced in the *here* of the floor plan and the *there* of the video projection. In the days that followed the group concentrated on projecting a video image of a person onto a puppet's face. Putting aside the video material from the field trips, they went on to experiment with techniques of visually conveying a sense of pain and relief of the puppet patient. The students had not seen patients in pain during the field visits. They had been following nurses and doctors, but they were not allowed to make videos of the patients. In their experiments with video projections, they mimicked pain and relief. Using their own faces, they sought to find for themselves facial expressions that gave a sense of presence in the ward. The puppet head stayed with the students during the rest of the design work, becoming a centerpiece in a staged wardroom that students and tutors could visit.

The group also worked on a pair of wristbands that the patient and his relatives could wear. The wristbands made it possible to virtually pat and caress the wearer of the other band, and the band could display the wearer's sense of well-being. What the students proposed bore a strong resemblance to a number of other innovative designs that had been presented in lectures. The idea of two-way ambient and low-bandwidth "emotional" communication was well known to the students, but rather than seeing the wristbands of the students as a design outcome, heavily relying on these previous designs, we can see them as appropriations that—like the work on video projections on the puppet's face—provide scaffolding for the emergent landscape of suffering and care that is the true design contribution of the students. The move from the early attempts to represent the world of the ward to the evocative staging of pain and relief follows a path of appropriation and re-collection similar to Bachelard's places simultaneously imagined and enacted. This movement, however, is not only one of domestication. The students do not eradicate the *elsewhere*. They transform the *here-and-there* of studio and ward into a flickering pattern of pain and relief mutually defining the landscape envisioned, much as Law and Mol describe a star space. The students staged a demonstration where the spectator interacted with a wristband while watching a typical wardroom with a puppet patient, reacting to both the interactions and the cycles of pain and relief originating in an imagined world of illness. To appreciate the design, the students thus invited the spectator to dwell not only in the situated circumstances of the distant relative but also in the imagined landscape of the patient.

Conclusions

We conclude by relating what has been presented in this chapter to the discussion in previous chapters. We have sought out concepts of place and landscape that enable us to understand how the design environment is performed in the work of designers and how a situational ground is enacted and transformed as design artifacts emerge.

We have argued that we always act in places, and that these places are practiced in action in ways that allow them to unfold a plastic and drifting landscape. There is always place, yet this place must be engaged and appropriated by both our mind and our bodies. If we recall the initial examples of the spatial practices of architecture and interaction design students, we can think again of the places that the students enacted, reevaluating the way the environment affects the work of the students. We pictured the architecture students' environment as vivid and full of traces of their actions, as opposed to the interaction design students' barren studio. From the perspective on place we have developed, we can now see that the studio of the interaction design students is energetically exercised as an idealized "empty space" counterbalanced by less exposed "elsewheres" of solitude or café gatherings. And the architectural drawing hall, with its many casual leftovers, now appears—paradoxically—more undetermined and empty.

But emptiness is not necessarily a sought-for quality. Where the interaction design students in our example have inherited the "empty space" as a conventional approximation of the generic design space proposed by Simon, the architecture students in chapter 6 provided us with several examples of a strong sense of the event/space with their drawing hall presentation. This sheds light on what we saw when the students of the "entrance"-assignment put so much effort into defining the placeness of the school building. With an unconventional format of presentation—a 3D installation and a seemingly invasive assignment: an entrance to the world of *your* heroes—the students' effort to establish and transform the place of their teachers appeared to be just what the teachers asked for. From this elaboration on place and dwelling, we claimed that there is no "point zero" for place-making and no space to act in. Space cannot be lived; we can only live in places.

We attempt to avoid an asymmetrical interpretation of designer and user by revising the notion of design space in the tradition of Simon. We view the design space as an emerging landscape: as a virtual world, the landscape renders the places of design meaningful and evocative to the designers. In line with Simon, we do not see this space as confined to the places by which it is constituted. However, we depart decisively from Simon in suggesting that this landscape does not live with a design problem independent of the designer. Building on Schön, we have proposed that the landscape emerges in the designer's interactions with place. The landscape is not just there to be arrived at by any designer. It is intrinsically connected to the engaged conversation with the situation that is shaped by the circumstances and strategies of the designer. Furthermore, the landscape is not stable. It evolves and shifts as the designers work. Compared to the discussion in chapter 5, we can say that the circulation of references and the *metamorphing* of representations weave the spatial web in which the artifacts take shape. In this chapter, the example of the students working on pain and relief for patients in an emergency ward perhaps provides the best sense of such an emerging yet ephemeral landscape.

To maintain the symmetry of designing and everyday action, we have utilized de Certeau's notion of space as practiced place. We can now see this social space of *what is* and *what could be* as emanating from both use and design. However, there is no route around place and things to connect the landscapes of design and use. The work of Law and Mol on space that makes artifacts immutable mobiles adds conceptual and practical depth to this view. Conceptually, Law and Mol adhere to a geometric metaphor in relating artifacts to space. As they work from the observation that artifacts have shape and can be moved, they define space as the system of reference from which this can be observed. With mundane examples, they show that what they call "shape constancy" is obtained through a coevolution of both artifacts and space, be this in a movement of flow or in momentary flickering. Such a process of mutual becoming resonates with the movements of the design students, as they juxtapose and bridge *here* and *there*, for example in the Metro ride of the Stadium assignment, or the *now* and *then* of contemplation in the electrician-group of the Augmenting Places assignment.

In chapter 4 we discussed the difference between the object of design as what is uniquely experienced (though differently) as designers or users engage with things designed, and the assembly of things made public that constitutes such objects. There is an obvious parallel between the concepts of objects and things and the conception of landscape and place proposed in this chapter. The lack of fit between what is imagined by the designer and what is experienced by the user may be seen as a regrettable deficit, one that the designer has to minimize. By tracing how designers live a landscape of places in order to make new places livable, and understanding how these lived landscapes are exercised in what we with Ciborra call a mood of improvisation, we may see the contours of a more appropriate ambition for designers to invite yet new improvisations with a contestable parliament of things, rather than seeking to narrow the gap between objects and things by invoking a mood of boredom. To fulfill such an ambition the designer will have to invest intentions, agency, and imagined landscapes of use as intensely as ever, while acknowledging that all that is passed on are things in place. What this entails is the subject of the following chapter.

8 Participation in Design Things

Introduction

Things, Design Games, Participatory Design, and Metadesign

A thread throughout this book has been the nature of *things*—not least, the origin of *things* going back to the ancient governing assemblies and places in Nordic and Germanic societies, where disputes were solved and political decisions made. This is also the case in this chapter, where we will continue to explore the object of design and its constituents, the design of *things* as matters of concern and possibilities of experiences, and as well as how design takes place. But where the former chapters focused on the ontology of the object of design and its constituents, on artifacts as *things*, transformations, performance, and places, this one will rather focus on *the design thing*—on the ecology of the assembly or *thing*, traditionally referred to as a *design project*, and its networks and relations. Rather than the qualities of an environment, we here focus on the "agency" of designers, users, objects, artifacts, design devices, and other "actants"—the very *thing* of design itself, rather than the design of *things* only seen as objects. How does a *design thing* align human and nonhuman resources to move the object of design forward, to support the emergence, translation, and performance of this object? The perspective is one of participation, intervention, and performance in this sociomaterial *thing*. How is design and use related? Whom do we design for, and with? Where, when, and with what means do we design?

We will, with reference to *Atelier* and other design projects, reflect on how designers position themselves in these "collectives of humans and non-humans" (Latour 1999), on their strategies and tactics, and on their participation in these *things*. As the chapter evolves, we will explore two complementary positions and strategies: *participatory design* and *metadesign*. Participatory design is considered as an approach that tries to involve users in design, and, in this way, to encounter in the design process what Johan Redström (2008) has characterized as "use before use." Participatory design becomes a way to meet the unattainable design challenge of fully anticipating or envisioning use before actual use takes place in people's *life-worlds*. The latter, meta-design, has to do with how to defer some aspects of design until after the design project is completed, and opens up the approach of use as design, or "design after design." Metadesign becomes a way to meet the equally unattainable design challenge of all-encompassing anticipation or envisioning the potential design as it will occur in use after completion of the project design.

To deal with these *design thing* challenges we will discuss a more general understanding of design processes as entangled sociomaterial *design games*. This design game concept for exploring design processes will be elaborated on the basis of concepts of participation, communication, community, language, and artifacts (in the philosophical traditions of Dewey and Wittgenstein). We will focus on the constituents of the design object in the material form of prototypes and models, acting as boundary objects and conscription devices (cf. chapters 2, 4, and 5), and aligning participants in synchronous design games of designers and users (participatory design), as well as on infrastructures and the process of *infrastructuring*, binding together the design games of designers and future designers/users (metadesign). In both design approaches, we will explore sociomaterial *things* that modify the space of interaction (e.g., boundary objects in participatory design and infrastructures in metadesign) as frames for controversies that open up new ways of thinking and behaving. But first a note on the idea of a *project*, the kind of *thing* that is the major form of alignment of design activities and design games.

Atelier Project as *Design Thing*

"Project" is the common form for aligning resources (people and technology) in all larger design achievements. Projects have objectives, time lines, deliverables, and the like. In the *Atelier* project, for example, the resources to be aligned included the project brief, prototypes, cultural probes and sketches, ethnographies and other field material, project reports, engineers, architects, interaction designers, researchers, teachers, students and other stakeholders, buildings, devices, and artifacts.

The outcome of a design project is, as argued in chapter 4, both a device and a *thing*. It can be seen as a device, the embodiment of the object of design, providing users with access to some function such as the *Atelier tangible archive* for storing and retrieving mixed materials. But the *tangible archive* as outcome of the design process is also a *thing*, modifying the space of interaction for the students using it, ready for unexpected use, and opening up new ways of thinking and behaving.

Often a project is designed to go through a number of stages of gradual refinement, for example, analysis, design, construction, and implementation. However, the shortcomings of such an approach are numerous and well known: its top-down structure hindering adaptation to changing conditions, its hierarchical strategy hindering legitimate participation, the rigidity of its specifications, and so on. These are just some of the justifications for user involvement and participatory design approaches, as was also the case with the *Atelier* project.

Given our tradition of Scandinavian "participatory design" (see chapter 2), the project focused on design interventions, user participation and systematic reflection (for overviews, see, e.g., Greenbaum and Kyng 1991), and ethnographically inspired fieldwork (see, e.g., Suchman 1987). We applied a design-oriented approach that ultimately aimed to produce knowledge rather than specific devices (Fällman 2004). We studied design education practice, developed prototypes to enhance such education, introduced prototypes to various real-use settings, and thus also encountered unintended or unexpected appropriation by the students (the designing users), and, partly in collaboration with them and their teachers, reflected on the interventions to learn both about how to improve architecture and technology and the studio design environment. This design-oriented research process was built on a user-collaborative approach that involved users and researchers as reflective codesigners and evolved from early explorations of practice and ideas through experiments with, and appropriation of, gradually more integrated scenarios and prototypes. As a participatory design project, *iterative design* was a significant aspect of these interventions and reflections, shifting between provisions of technological possibilities, and probing for the relevance of these possibilities in interventions into the students' practice. The iterative design process for refinement of the studio as a place for design learning went through three design cycles, which we named *envisioning*, *prototyping*, and *experiencing*. Each design cycle was based on interventions in the everyday practices at the two design education sites in Vienna and Malmö. (For further details, see the Appendix.)

Rather than thinking of a project like *Atelier* as a *design thing* in terms of phases of analysis, design, construction, and implementation, a participatory approach to this collective of humans and nonhumans might rather look for the performative "staging" of it. Inspired by Pedersen (2007), we could then ask:

How should we *construct the initial object of design* for a project, that is, how should we align the participants around a shared but potentially controversial object of concern? In *Atelier*, for example, how should we align students and teachers in Vienna and Malmö, architects and interaction designers, with technical researchers and social scientists in Austria, Italy, Finland, and Sweden, as well as with European Union research officials, around architecture and technology for design learning environments as an object of design?

Furthermore, as work proceeds, how can the studied practices be made *reportable*? Examples from *Atelier* include fieldwork reports and ethnographies from the sites in Malmö and Vienna, and reports of direct participation by students and teachers in workshops and experiments.

How can the object of design be made *manipulatable*, that is, how are the constituents of this object given a form that can be experienced? Examples from *Atelier* include sketches and scenarios of future studio environments, models and prototypes of potential new design and learning tools, and collaborative development in design games.

How is the object of design made into a sociomaterial public *thing* that is open to controversies among participants in the project as well as those outside? Typically this may take the form of evaluative workshops or exhibitions. In the *Atelier* project, exhibitions of demonstrators and workshops envisioning the project object of design, with professional participants who were outside the student design setting, was important for the assessment of quality of concepts and technologies. In fact, the occasional opportunities to exhibit integrated demonstrators of the *Atelier* design learning environment to designers and researchers outside the project at three international conferences/exhibitions/workshops turned out to be the primary alignment mechanism for the concurrent and interdisciplinary design work in the project, bringing one design iteration to an end and opening up a new cycle of design work (the Gothenburg wall, the Ivrea wall, and the Vienna workshop). More specifically, the first alignment "wall" as we called it (the alignment of the first design cycle) was designed for the DC Jamboree, October 2002, in Gothenburg, Sweden (a conference on and meeting of international projects focusing on the "disappearing computer" research agenda). This wall was made from blocks of colored polystyrene, with niches cut out for the different devices. It had a strong physical presence, inviting people to walk around it and investigate. It was more a mock-up than a functioning piece of architecture, and it hinted at integration, long before we were able to actually demonstrate it. The second "wall" (the alignment of the second design cycle) was assembled for the DC Jamboree, November 2003, in Ivrea, Italy. It was much more elegant and functional than its predecessor, and it achieved a de facto integration of technical and spatial components. The alignment of the third design cycle took the form of a workshop around an assemblage staged at the CHI human–computer interaction conference in Vienna, Austria, April 2004 (figure 8.1). In fact, this book itself may be seen as a continuation

Figure 8.1
The Gothenburg Wall (left); the Ivrea Wall (middle); and the Vienna demonstrator (right).

of what began with the "walls" in Gothenburg, Ivrea, and Vienna; it is yet another attempt to transform and open up the *Atelier* project into public, potentially controversial *things*.

Projects, as Krippendorff (2006) has pointed out, are, however, only part of, or a specific form of, alignments in the life cycle of devices, and every object of design eventually has to become part of already existing ecologies of devices as objects of concern (in people's already ongoing life-worlds), be they digital like computer applications and databases, or physical like buildings, furniture, doors, books, tools, and vehicles. Hence, the beginning and end of a designed device is open and hardly ever constrained to the limits of the project. This is principally interesting because it indicates the importance of understanding how design in a project is related to users'/stakeholders' appreciation and appropriation, whether in the form of adoption or redesign, and how users make these devices into objects of concern and part of their *life-worlds* and evolving ecologies of devices, of their emerging landscapes. Design might be thought of as constrained to a specific project with given objects of design, resources, timelines, and specified outcomes, but since the embodiment of the object of design is a *thing*, this *thing* opens itself up for unforeseen appropriation in use in already existing and evolving ecologies of devices.

Hence, strategies and tactics of design for use must also be open for appropriation or appreciation in use, after a project is finished, and we may consider this appropriation as a specific potential kind of design. In fact, Krippendorff's notion also implies that we, in design for use, should also focus on the "before" the project, the "procurement" process of aligning actants in a design project and how the object of design becomes this specific object of design. This includes making explicit the often hidden performative "protocols of design." These are specific practices performing the often implicit and tacit rules according to which the project negotiations are carried out and take place, initially setting the stage for *design games* that establish the object of design (Clark 2007; Pedersen 2007). How did the *Atelier* project come about? For example, which "protocols" had to be acknowledged and followed, to deal with the EU Framework program for Emerging Technologies (FET), university administration policies in Sweden, Austria, Italy, and Finland, and teaching programs in architecture and interaction design at specific art and design schools in different countries?

For now, however, we narrow the focus to design project *things*, to the relation between design and use in these *things* as participatory design and as metadesign. First we elaborate the notion of (participatory) design as *intertwined design games* across design and use. We pay special attention to nonhuman constituencies of the object of design, their participation in *design things*, and the role of devices and artifacts as *boundary objects* and *conscription devices* binding these design games together. Second, we elaborate the notion of metadesign, the dilemma of not knowing your user, and having to design for "design after design." Here we elaborate *infrastructuring* as a perspective on the process of binding together design games (at project time) and design in use.

Participatory Design: Design for Use before Use

Early Participatory Design and an Emerging Theoretical Position

Designers' approach to *use* has dramatically changed over the years, from a total focus on the artifacts designed and their functions, on usability, via different ways of testing users, to studying use and involving potential users in the design process. Examples of approaches range from *user-centered design* focusing on use and usability (e.g., Norman and Draper 1986), *contextual design* focusing on the situatedness of use (e.g., Beyer and Holtzblatt 1998), to contemporary approaches of *experience design* focusing on creating an experience for the user (e.g., Sanders and Dandavate 1999; Sanders 2001). *Participatory design*, which will be our focus here, places special emphasis on people participating in the design process as codesigners. We could say that all these approaches try to meet the challenge of anticipating, or at least envisioning, and designing for use before use actually has taken place—*design for use before use* (Redström 2008). However, as Redström has stressed, the very concept of use is complicated, and, in a way, a somewhat patronizing perspective, dividing people into users and designers. People appreciate and appropriate artifacts into their life-worlds, but they do this in ongoing activities, whether as architects, interaction designers, journalists, nurses, or kids playing with their toys. But as mere users? This must be kept in mind when for the sake of convenience we refer to *use* and *users*. In fact, as we shall see, the origination of participatory design as a design approach is not primarily designers engaging in use, but people (as collectives) engaging designers in their practice.

As we mentioned earlier, participatory design has its roots in movements toward democratization at work in the Scandinavian countries. In the 1970s, participation and joint decision making became important factors at workplaces and in the introduction of new technology. Participatory design started from the simple standpoint that those affected by a design should have a say in the design process. This reflects the (at that time) controversial political conviction that we should not expect consensus, but potential controversies, around an emerging object of design. In this situation participatory design sided with resource-weak stakeholders (typically local trade unions) and developed project strategies for their effective and legitimate participation in *design things*. Hence, in these early *design things*, use and users existed before design and designers.

A less controversial complementary motive for participatory design, and, in the long run, probably the strongest reason for its acceptance in many organizations, was the potential to ensure that existing skills could be made a resource in the design process.

Hence, one might say that two types of values strategically guide participatory design (Ehn 1988). One is the social and rational idea of democracy as a value that leads to considerations of conditions for proper and legitimate user participation—*the very making of design things*. The other value might be described as the idea of the importance of making participants' "tacit knowledge" come into play in the design process, not only their formal and explicit competences—*skills as fundamental to the making of things as objects*. We could also think about this as the value of being able to express and share "aesthetic experience" in the pragmatic sense of embodied experience enforced by emotion and reflection, as discussed in chapter 2.

In previous chapters, we argued for an understanding of design grounded in pragmatism, especially with inspiration from John Dewey and the understanding that we "live in communication" with each other. This is also, as will be demonstrated, fundamental to our understanding of the practices of participatory design and design games. But we will begin our arguments with a discussion of how the conceptual foundation for design and participation was originally framed in a pragmatic interpretation of the linguistic turn in philosophy, and especially with reference to Ludwig Wittgenstein's famous (1953) aphorisms in *Philosophical Investigations* (see Ehn 1988). The attempt here is to unite these sources of inspiration in an understanding of (participatory) *design as activities of intertwined design games with a special focus on participation and the emergence and performance of the object of design*.

Wittgenstein directs us to think of the meaning of a word as its *use*, not as a picture of something else that is "out there" in the world. In this perspective, use or *practice* becomes the foundation for design. Wittgenstein suggests that the way we use language is through participation in multiple and intertwined *language games*. We learn to participate in a specific language game because it has a *family resemblance* with other language games in which we already have been participating.

Since this participation in a language game is a practice that goes beyond words, it also makes it possible to express or rather enact or perform experience beyond words. By your skillful participation you show what the words mean (which you may enact with reference to what Michael Polanyi often has been labeled "tacit knowledge").

Furthermore, according to Wittgenstein, participation in a language game is a kind of rule-following behavior, where these are not *a priori* formulated explicit rules, but simply rules that participants obey in practice as skilled performance, demonstrating their mastery of them. Some rules we even make up and alter as we play along. Creativity relies in particular on this human ability, in a language game, to follow a rule in a completely unforeseen yet still appropriate way; and this provides the opening for design.

On this view, the participatory design suggestion was to conceive of the design process as a set of such intertwined language games of design. From this followed the specific design challenge to set the stage for specific, shared design language games with a family resemblance to (professional) language games of different stakeholders, especially users (lay-designers) and (professional) designers. To put it in the language of this book, the challenge was to construct a sociomaterial *design thing*, a potentially controversial assembly, for and with the participants in a project, making this *design thing* an early assembly of the constituencies of the object of design.

Second, the proposition that the meaning of a word is determined in use was extended to all devices in the design process, not only words. Hence, in the language of this book, constituents of the object of design, such as systems' descriptions, specification documents, models, sketches, maps, mock-ups, and prototypes, were all seen as receiving their enacted meaning in their actual use, as performed, and, consequently, not primarily seen as detached descriptions of a design object. The quality of these design devices became a question of how well they supported skillful participation, and, thereby how well they supported communication in a specific design language game, for example, how well they supported the performance of "tacit knowledge."

This led to recommendations and practices where the basis for the design process became the (work) practices of legitimate but resource-weak stakeholders (actual or potential "end-users"). Work ethnographies and other ways to focus on the users' understanding became basic. So did engaging and participative design activities like participative *future workshops* (Junk and Müllert 1981). But most significant was the replacement of "systems' descriptions" with engaging "hands on" design devices like mock-ups and prototypes, and organizational games that helped maintain a family resemblance with the users' everyday practice and supported creative skillful participation and performance in the design process. There was a decisive shift in design methods toward user participation in "design-by-doing" and "design-by-playing" (Ehn and Kyng 1991; Ehn and Sjögren 1991).

The design challenge was, however, not only a question of creating family resemblance with users' everyday language games (at work), but also to support creative "moves" in the shared design language games. Maintaining family resemblance is not a question of obeying tradition, but of making a creative leap possible by enacting the rules in unforeseen ways.

Paradoxical as it sounds, users and designers do not really have to understand each other to play design language games together. Participation in a language game of design and the use of design devices can make different but constructive sense to users and designers. Wittgenstein notes that "when children play at trains their game is connected with their knowledge of trains. It would nevertheless be possible for the children of a tribe unacquainted with trains to learn this game from others, and to play it without knowing that it was copied from anything. One might say that the game did not make the same *sense* as to us" (Wittgenstein 1953, § 282). As long as the language game of design is not a nonsense activity to any participant, but a shared

Figure 8.2
Design games and mock-ups from early days of participatory design. The UTOPIA project (1982) on skill-based technology in the printing industry.

activity for better understanding and good design, mutual understanding is desired but not really required. The requirement for a good design device and good moves in a design game is not a shared understanding among all participants, but just that those moves make sense (though in different ways) to all participants (see Ehn 1988).

Design Games and Design Things—A Pragmatic View

This early understanding of participatory design and its recommendations still appear to be valid. Here we go beyond this view to rethink these practices in the perspectives of pragmatism and actor networks as developed in earlier chapters. At the same time, we broaden the scope to a more general view of sociomaterial *design things* as entangled design games, and of the interplay of human and nonhuman participants and constituencies. Given our earlier argument for an understanding of design grounded in the Deweyan tradition of pragmatism, we find interesting connections between

• notions of participation in language games and how "communication is to take part in a community";
• how "design-by-doing" and "design-by-playing" relate to "learning-by-doing" as a fundamental form of inquiry;
• how meaning as use relates to the proposition that in all vital experience "the practical, the emotional, and the intellectual are inseparable"; and
• how the sharing of embodied tacit knowledge that defies formalization relates to how aesthetic experience may be acquired and communicated.

One specific conceptual framework in this pragmatic tradition is the focus on collective, cultural-historical forms of located, interested, conflictual activities in "communities-of-practice" as developed by Jean Lave and Etienne Wenger (Lave and Wenger 1991; Wenger 1998; see chapter 2). Communities-of-practice resemble language-games as elaborated above, but the concept is broader and has its point of departure in the everyday practices of professional communities. We may say that the design practices of communities-of-practice are performed as language games. In communities-of-practice there is a strong focus on learning as the process of becoming a legitimate participant, establishing relations to other "older" participants and learning to master tools and other material devices (reifications or materializations of constituents of the object of design). Compared to language games, the focus is not on *language* as *practice*, but on *practice* in itself, and with *participation* as the fundamental epistemology, where participation is understood as the "complex process that combines doing, talking, thinking, feeling, and belonging. It involves our whole person including our bodies, minds, emotions, and social relations" (Wenger 1998, 56).

Thinking in terms of communities-of-practice in a framework for design and participation reveals a dimension of an internal power struggle, in attempts by participants to appropriate devices and social relations. Hence, the understanding of *things* as sociomaterial controversial events in the life of a community-of-practice (or across different communities-of-practice) is underlined, as is their central role in creating alignment (as in the actor-network technoscience framework).

Furthermore, the view emphasizes the foundational understanding that human action and participation is "stretched over, not divided among" the physical, social, and cultural contexts in which it emerges (Lave 1988).

Another important gain of this approach is the attention it draws to the practice of appropriation of design devices (and their agency), rather than just "languaging." Fundamentally, as Wenger (1998) has underlined, there is an important dialectic and close relations in communities-of-practice between participation and materialization (reification). Participation and reification constitute a shared repertoire: they reciprocally form each other. Through participation in the process of reification, we are "giving form to our experience by producing objects that congeal this experience into thingness" (Wenger 1998, 58). As reifications, design devices (and future objects of use) are, as Wenger argues, always incomplete, ongoing, potentially enriching, and potentially misleading. Hence, participation overcomes some of the limitations of reification. Reification in the design process may be seen as "temporarily hardening or solidifying of experience" through practices organized around an emerging sociomaterial *thing*, and use may conversely be seen as practices "defrosting" these reifications through participation in future appropriations (Björgvinsson 2007).

Hence, we can conceptualize participatory design and design project *things*, in a way parallel to language games, as overlapping communities-of-practice (users as legitimate peripheral participants in design, and vice versa, designers as legitimate peripheral participants in use; see Ehn 1995). This is also in line with Gerhard Fischer's (2001) suggestion for how we should understand the design process as the meeting between communities-of-interest.

    As a notion of design practices and *design things* that recognizes both these concepts, both the semantic and the pragmatic aspect, we suggest seeing these practices as performances of *participative entangled design games* (with a conceptual family resemblance to both intertwined language games and overlapping communities-of-practice).

    Hence, participatory design and design projects in general can be seen as processes of entanglement of at least three kinds of different design games:

The numerous everyday professional (design) games of both users and designers (*participants in everyday practice in a design project understood as design games*).

The constructed, specific design games that bear a family resemblance to these everyday design games and which designers help establish (*the staged design process as design thing*).

Specific performative "design-by-doing" and "design-by-playing" design games. Some of these design games include participatory organizational games, "concept design

Figure 8.3
Design games played in the *Atelier* project demonstrating several dimensions of "playing" in a design thing: as a professional design activity; as a staged activity in the design process linking use practice to design practice; as using a "performative" design game, playing out scenarios; and as playing a "video as design material game."

games" (Habraken and Gross 1987) or "video as design material" (Buur, Binder, and Brandt 2000) (*design methods and devices understood as design games, and the use of specific game-like design devices understood as design games*).

Nonhuman Design Participants and Constituencies

Before leaving the conceptual foundation for design project *things*, participatory design, and design for use, we will expand on the dialectic of participation and reification in sociomaterial *design things*. We do this with a focus on the role of design devices and artifacts (e.g., prototypes, mock-ups, design games, models, sketches, and other materials) in intertwined design games in a participatory design project, as we also return to some concepts discussed in earlier chapters.

Project work involves a strong focus on "representations" as constituents of the object of design. Traditionally they are thought of as gradually more refined "descriptions" of the object to be designed. In our understanding of *design things* and design games, the focus should instead be on these devices as on the one hand material constituents of the evolving object of design, and, at the same time, public *things*, supporting communication or participation across design games in the design process. They are potentially binding different stakeholders together, and there is clearly also a performative dimension of the evolving object. The different materializations or reifications of the constituents of the object of design have to be "translated" or "moved" by the participants. They have to be enacted by stakeholders of the object of design, and this is not a representative but performative act (cf. chapter 6).

We may also view design devices (simultaneous constituents of the design object and public *things*) as *boundary objects*, with a conceptualization borrowed from Susan Leigh Star (1989) (as discussed in chapter 4). The experience inscribed in design devices, for example, a model, make them useful in different intertwined design games. At the same time, they may be invested with lots of experience, for professional designers and users respectively, experience that is not shared across their respective professional design games (cf. the discussion above about how good design devices and good design moves are not necessarily based on a shared understanding among all participants, but participation that makes sense [though in different ways] in a shared design game). As mentioned in an earlier chapter, boundary objects might be weakly structured as to achieve flexibility and allow transference and commonality between design games, but strong enough to be used internally in specific design games. Boundary objects are, as discussed, reifications intrinsically bound to overlapping design games, hardened to stabilize experience, but also potentially available to be defrosted in subsequent use.

Hence, in any design process, it seems important, when establishing *design things* as shared design games, to consider how such boundary objects can be identified or developed, and, at the same time, to be aware of the diverse (and, to the designer, often unknown) experiences that may be associated with them within the other different but related design games at play.

We can also, as Kathryn Henderson (1999) does in her study of engineers' use of "visualizations" in the design process, regard these design devices as *conscription devices*, focusing on their use in overlapping design games as pointing to other devices to be designed. Hence, their role becomes not only one of making sense to all participants, but also one of aligning appropriations of the evolving object of design by suggesting directions for further manifestations and constituents, and for signifying potential transformations as next moves in ongoing design games. Or, more generally, as we argued with reference to Schön in the previous chapter, the "conversation with the material of the situation" is both a particular situated practice and a hypostatical practicing of an imagined place.

Furthermore, as we discussed earlier, the evolution of the object of design during a design process does not occur through the "mapping" of one description onto another. Instead, the design interventions are transformations characterized by a creative "metamorphing" of the object, increasing its variability, adding to the richness of the object rather than reducing it. Again, as a creative move, the metamorphosis makes this possible, but the success of the move is determined in use by participants in different design games, by their "enactment" and performance of these devices, simultaneously being constituents of the object of design and public *things* for structuring controversies across design games.

Maybe one could think of the different design devices within a project, adding to the evolving object of design and its final embodiment as outcome or *thing*, as part of the project ecology itself, where every new device has to find (or rather be given) its place in the ecology (competing and cooperating with already existing constituents of the object of design).

With such conceptualizations, the mixed-media devices, in the form of augmented models and design games that mix digital and physical embodiment, become especially interesting as design devices. As boundary objects they may embody many different perspectives and possible interpretations joined together by a shared "placeholder"—the boundary object. As conscription devices they blur the borders between different design devices, pointing toward the openness of an evolving design object rather than a specific device, eventually suggesting that the process of making and maintaining the web of transformations and metamorphoses of the object of design and its constituents is the object of design itself.

Figure 8.4 shows the Tangible Archive from the *Atelier* project, in which physical materials are associated with digital materials (as well as with other physical materials). This is an example of a design device for creating mixed-media boundary devices with the possibility for participants in different design games to add their experiences to the object of design, expanding and contracting its boundaries as they play.

Figure 8.4
The Tangible Archive from the *Atelier* project.

Bearing in mind this view of design things, participatory design, and design for use as participative performance of and in entangled design games, and design devices as vehicles for the evolving object of design, and, at the same time, public *things* for binding together these design games, we will now look into challenges to this participative design approach.

Metadesign: Design for Design after Design

Metadesign and Infrastructuring

One limitation of participatory design as conceptualized here is the focus on projects supporting identifiable users. The design process described is laid out to support such users' interests, and the products or services designed to be supportive of these as well. As critics have pointed out, and as has also become obvious with the *Atelier* project, immediate users are not the only stakeholders. Both immediate users and future users will appreciate and appropriate designed devices in totally unforeseen ways. Envisioned use is hardly the same as actual use, no matter how much participation has taken place in the design process. Does this mean that the idea of participatory design and the envisioning of "use before use" has to be given up altogether?

The most common reply to this challenge to participatory design has been to emphasize ideas of flexibility in use or open systems, designing tailorable devices, and making it possible for users to appropriate devices in use, by customizing and extending them according to their varying skills and needs (Nardi 1993). A similar approach has been to explore the idea of continuing design-in-use (Henderson and Kyng 1991). In a broader design perspective, this also corresponds to notions like "continuous design and redesign" (Jones 1984) and "unfinished design" (Tonkinwise 2005). Such approaches focus on how users appropriate a given technology. In this chapter, however, we are particularly interested in what designers do and how this relate to unforeseen users' appreciation and appropriation of the object of design into their life-worlds.

Whereas the fashionable use of "cultural probes," like disposal cameras and postcards in design, has essentially been a new way to allow designers to share specific situated user experiences as inspiration (Gaver, Dunne, and Pacenti 1999), what we are looking for here is in a way the opposite. How can users in their design games be inspired by and enact the traces, obstacles, objects, and potentially *things* produced by the professional designers? What we are searching for is a kind of *design-after-design*: design games different from those played by professional designers working on a project, but nevertheless design games (in use). This is not to suggest that all appropriations in use can or should be understood as design games, but only to open up for design approaches supporting this kind of appropriation.

One general approach in this direction is *metadesign*. Here both professional designers and potential users are seen as designers, much as in participatory design, but they participate not in synchronous entangled design games, but rather in design games that are separated in time and space. Such a metadesign approach has been described by Fischer and Scharff (2000) and Fisher and Giaccardi (2005), with reference to earlier work both in art (e.g., by Gene Youngblood and Derrick de Kerchove) and in theory of knowledge (e.g., by Umberto Maturana and Paul Virilio). Rather than focusing on involving users in the design process, this perspective shifts toward seeing every use situation as a potential design situation. So design takes place during a project ("at project time"), but also while the object of design is in use ("at use time"). In other words, there is design (in use) after design (during the project). Since there are many different approaches to metadesign, it should be clear that the "meta" in metadesign, as we use it here, is not an abstraction of design, but rather suggests design that takes place "after," "beyond," or "with" the design work at project time.

This view has a number of strategic consequences in relation to design for use in general, and not least participatory design. In design games carried out at project time, it has to be acknowledged that some design games continue on as users act on the designed *thing* during use, eventually also design games with entirely new stakeholders. As a consequence, it is crucial in the design game at project time to support design-in-use, design games at use time. Hence, the focus shifts from design games aiming at useful products and services to design games aiming to create good environments for design games at use time. Typically this will lead at project time to an occupation with identifying, designing, and supporting social, technical, and spatial infrastructures that are configurable and potentially supportive of future design games in everyday use.

In this shift from design for use to design for design, we seem confronted not only with intertwined design games, but also with a chain of one design game after another. As in participatory design, the designed devices are both constituencies of the objects of design and, as boundary objects, public *things*, but the objects of design in design projects and those in use are different. At project time, the purpose of design is to produce a potential *thing* that will be open for controversies from which new objects of design can emerge in use.

Susan Leigh Star has called this mediation *infrastructuring*, and it is more a "when" than a "what" (Star and Ruhleder 1996; Star and Bowker 2002). An infrastructure, like railroad tracks, cables, or the Internet, on the one hand reaches beyond the single event (temporal) and any one particular site (spatial); it is not reinvented every time, and is embedded in other sociomaterial structures. But on the other hand it is only accessible by membership in specific communities-of-practice. Infrastructure or rather *infrastructuring* is a sociomaterial *thing*; it is relational and becomes infrastructure in relation to design games at project time and during (multiple, potentially controversial) design games in use. Hence, this infrastructure is shaped over extended timeframes, not only by professional designers, but also by users as mediators and designers "infrastructuring" in ways never envisioned at project time. Infrastructuring entangles and intertwines activities at project time such as selection, design, development, deployment, and enactment with everyday professional activities at use time of mediation, interpretation, and articulation, as well as further design in use such as adaptation, appropriation, tailoring, redesign, and maintenance (Karasti and Baker 2008; Twidale and Floyd 2008; Pipek and Wulf 2009). Referring back to the previous chapter and the discussion inspired by Ciborra on improvisation as the "mood" of design, we can say that the infrastructuring mood of design is one that prioritizes *improvisation* not only at project time, but also at use time. Infrastructuring strategies have to do with conditions for how designers live or experience a landscape of places in order to make new places livable, and how these lived landscapes at use time are potentially exercised in moods of improvisation (as opposed to *panic* and *boredom*).

The challenge and object of design for professional design at project time is the design of such potential public *things* that through infrastructuring can become objects of design in use. But who the participants in this *thing* will be, and the way they may appropriate it, must be left partly open. As architect Stan Allen has put it:

an infrastructuring strategy must not only pay attention to how existing infrastructures condition use, but, in doing so, at the same time also deliberately design indeterminacy and incompleteness into the infrastructure with unoccupied slots and space left free for unanticipated events and performances yet to be (Allen, Agrest, and Ostrow. 2000). Years ago, Bernard Tschumi suggested such strategies for opening up controversial *things* as a kind of "event architecture" where the focus is on designing "architecture-events" rather than "architecture-objects" (Tschumi 1994). Here the infrastructure supports multiple and heterogeneous, often controversial, design games in use (rather than homogeneous and unitary ones). This infrastructuring may, for example, be achieved by explicit programming tactics exploring disjunctions between expected form and expected use, as in cross-programming (e.g., suggesting using a church for a bowling alley).

More generally, the "design for design" challenges also apply to more traditional design of urban spaces, buildings, or workplaces, and of technologies in support of work. Here the difficulty is that designing for these purposes requires on the one hand what Schmidt and Wagner (2004) call "orderings systems"—clusters of templates, standards, libraries, and so forth that regulate, standardize, synchronize, and connect local practices so as to take care of logical, functional, spatial, social, and other interdependencies in complex, often distributed settings: an urban space, a large building, collaborative work, and so forth. On the other hand, designers of such complex products (and the associated services) need to find ways of benefiting from the perspectives of multiple stakeholders. They also need to engage in the type of infrastructuring we've described to allow users to configure and reconfigure, to adapt to changing constraints, and so forth.

In another project, some of us have been facing some of these very challenges. Here the aim is to support groups of designers (architects, urban specialists, politicians, and "ordinary citizens") in collaboratively envisioning an urban project. We provide users with tools that allow them to create and manipulate visual and auditory scenes and join these scenes with the real environment of an urban planning site as an integral part of expressing and experiencing an evolving project. We have created a tangible user interface that supports users in producing and discussing these mixed reality configurations (Maquil et al. 2007).

One of the difficulties we face in this is that planners and architects, who master the techniques of graphical representation, often produce seductive images that aim to convince developers rather than support stakeholders' understanding and invite them into a dialogue. This is why we are experimenting with novel representational forms that help convey and experience the ambience of a place—urban rhythms, flows and movement (of people, traffic), temporal rhythms such as day and night, but also content that expresses experiences, such as isolation, sociability, fear, comfort, playfulness, and so forth.

A second challenge has to do with creating forms of participation that are not part of urban planning practices today: How do we give participating stakeholders the chance to contribute to the concept-formation process of an urban project, where certain qualities of a site are defined? Should they also be involved in questions of design? Or should only architect-planners get new tools for visualizing their concepts with carefully prepared scenarios, confining stakeholders to "just" playing with very small details? Although the use of the technologies we are designing can go both ways, we know that they are not neutral but "participate" in their own use. We make deliberate design decisions that strengthen the collaborative aspects of the tools and improve their potential in creating "boundary negotiation artifacts" that may help stakeholders to negotiate existing boundaries of expertise and responsibility (Lee 2007).

The design of infrastructures that are open to unexpected changes in potentially controversial design games in use stands out as a fundamental challenge for metadesign. It is precisely the design of such *things* that must be its object of design.

Infrastructuring Strategies

Let us now explore a few potential metadesign strategies to be enacted at project time, supporting flexibility, openness, and configurability of infrastructures as sociomaterial *things* in design games at use time.

From a technical point of view, such infrastructuring strategies could focus on the design and negotiation of "protocols" and "formats," or rather on "protocoling" and "formatting." Think, for example, of Internet communication protocols like TCP/IP, HTTP, and FTP, which have been essential to the success of the Internet. But this "protocoling" could also be understood more socially and developed as it is in diplomacy situations, for governing relations in the making of procedural agreements. From the digital domain one could also think of the making of file format conventions like ASCII, HTML, JPEG, and MPEG4. But perhaps more interesting is the making and use of "formats" in architecture. Here formats are principal solutions with clear characteristics, such as the "basilica." But the format also has some elasticity that makes it open to context, change, and adaptability, to deliberate transcendence without necessarily being distorted. The "basilica," for example, has not only been used in churches, but also in more secular buildings such as market halls (Ullmark, private communication, 2007).

More general strategies to create infrastructures that are flexible and open to design after design and unforeseen appropriation have to do with providing means for *configuring* (see chapter 3). There are at least two types of configuring design games that are played in use: *adapting a space* to a diversity of uses and identities, and *configurations of devices* within the physical space.

One quality of design learning environments emerged as particularly important in the *Atelier* project: the capability of being reconfigured dynamically and radically. The configurability of a space depends on its layout, the design of the infrastructure, and the design of the devices that populate it.

The examples we provided explore different aspects of configurability of design learning environments: associations of inputs, media, and outputs; spatiality and integration with devices; configuring furniture and work zones (*tangible archive*); and real-time configuration of mixed devices (*mixed objects table*). In all these examples, configurability includes interventions in the physical landscape of space and devices. The complex activity of configuring unfolds, and therefore has to be supported, on different levels and across different aspects of the environment: spatial arrangement (e.g., a *grid* for fixing projection surfaces); furniture (the *tangible archive* with its modules, the table); the landscape of devices, which can be tagged, furnished with sensors or barcodes, electronic components, and various devices (scanners, readers, connecting input and output devices); and digital components and their interactions (software infrastructure, associations of inputs, outputs, and media content in the database).

Hence our approach of designing architectural components that could be assembled and configured for specific purposes on the one hand, our notion of the *Atelier* architecture as augmenting existing places on the other hand. Our architectural interventions consisted in providing students with a kit of elements that they could configure and add to the environment. This infrastructure supported their need to configure and personalize their individual workspaces and to perform many different design games, inhabiting and transforming their environment, traveling through their emerging landscapes of design (see chapter 7). The possibilities in a specific practice for the configurations of space, appropriated in *configuring design games*, are, however, not *a priori* given. Designers might, when forming the infrastructure at project time, have certain games in mind, but which ones are really played is determined by actual use, and they might be very different from the design games that were envisioned.

In figure 8.5, the infrastructure of the studio is continually used to transform, appropriate, and personalize the studio for new design games and a diversity of uses and identities such as solitary work, group discussions, performing and presenting, and building models. The students reconfigured their studio environment for "one game after another." Below we explore four more specific configuring infrastructuring strategies based on *components, patterns, ontologies, and ecologies*.

Component strategies   A *component* strategy is a specific strategy for connecting design games at project time with design games at use time, based on the idea of building a configurable infrastructure. In the *Atelier* project, for example, we worked with general building blocks, components, and component assemblies. This is a kind of engineering or "LEGO block" approach, where especially exemplary prototypes may

Figure 8.5
One design game after another.

be seen as boundary objects between the design games of a design team and those of the "designing users"—boundary objects to be configured and appropriated by the users.

This configurability may be directly supported by software platforms, and over the years such component-based software engineering approaches have been developed to enable degrees of end-user tailorability (Wulf, Pipek, and Won 2008). A good example is the open source PALCOM architecture, which supports "assemblability" (of components) and "inspectability" (of assemblies of infrastructure and components). But infrastructuring can never be reduced to the technical platform (Büscher et al. 2007). Infrastructuring can never be decontextualized, even if the context is unclear from the beginning.

Rather than designing a technical platform ("thin infrastructure"), design at project time as infrastructuring may, as argued by Baker, be concerned with "thick infrastructure" (Baker et al. 2005), that is, with the mutual constitution of the social and the technical and the heterogeneity of potential design games.

And even when focusing "thin infrastructure," that is, on technical platforms and middleware software, supporting appropriation and use of different devices, it seems that involving users in design and evaluation is a fundamental strategy for success (Edwards, Belotti, and Newman 2003).

Pattern strategies   Another infrastructuring strategy is the development of *design patterns*, an idea that originates from the work of architect Christopher Alexander in the 1970s on a pattern language. It may be seen as an alternative configuring approach, more architectural than engineering in its orientation. Alexander and his colleagues aimed at identifying and articulating certain spatial configurations in buildings and towns. Such configurations they called *patterns* (Alexander, Ishikawa, and Silverstein 1977). Patterns are documented in terms of context of use, problematic situations, and proposed solutions. Design patterns are, in the pattern language developed by Alexander, systematically related to one another. More important for our context of metadesign and entangled design games is the suggestion that the work of articulating and refining patterns should be understood as a way to reconnect to traditions of local planning, supporting user participation in planning, and users' appropriation of their own environment.

Patterns and pattern languages have been adopted by, for example, both the *software engineering community* and by *human–computer interaction* researchers and practitioners (see, e.g., Borchers et al. 2001). Other patterns include those based on ethnographic observations supporting *interactive design in domestic settings* (Crabtree, Hemmings, and Rodden 2002), the *inspirational design patterns for embodied interaction* developed by Löwgren (2005), and the *generative design abstractions for pervasive computing products* developed by McCullough (2004). An important aspect of patterns seen as aspects of an infrastructuring strategy is the focus on their support for appropriation in use, as vehicles for design in use.

Ontology strategies   Yet another perspective on the infrastructure as a relation between design at project time and design at use time is that of domain-specific languages or environments. *Ontologies* have for some time attracted attention, especially in relation to the design of knowledge-based systems and in relation to specific domains. Typically an ontology is like a dictionary or glossary, but with a structure that enables a computer to process its content. An ontology consists of concepts and relations that describe a certain domain within, for example, architecture or engineering. (See, e.g., Fensel 2003.) As we suggested earlier, the totality of constituents of an object may be seen as its ontology (see chapter 4).

Ontologies are helpful for exploring complex domains, so, in a sense, it seems a reasonable infrastructuring design strategy to develop them at project time, at least if they are open and potentially evolving during use. But where do they come from, and how do they become appropriated in design games at use time? Any attempt to build a universal ontology comes in conflict with the evolution of the object of design in specific localized design games.

The ontology is not a conceptual map of the world as it is, but a boundary object among many in an infrastructure, perhaps even a *thing* intertwining design games at project time with those played in use. Ontologies, it seems, have to be not only situated, but also continuously negotiated as we play along. They must be open, controversial *things*. This brings us to a reverse infrastructuring strategy focusing on ecologies.

Ecology strategies   What would an infrastructure be like that is not total or universal, but that takes into account all kinds of existing, modified, and future artifacts and devices in a specific domain? The idea of an *ecology of devices* as suggested by Klaus Krippendorff (2006) (based on notions by Gregory Bateson and Kenneth Boulding) is one such approach. Generally, ecologies involve large numbers of plants and animals interacting by feeding on each other, reproducing, finding a niche (or becoming extinct), and so forth. Typically ecologists study ecosystems in specific and particular domains such as lakes or forests.

Though most people know more "species" of devices and artifacts than species of living organisms, less attention has been paid to ecologies of devices where, for example, windows, tables, chairs, lamps, doors, computers, displays, books, images, models, bags, tools, shirts, and shoes interact in an environment. Of course, a main difference between ecologies of living organisms and ecologies of devices is that whereas biological species interact on their own terms, the interaction of devices is performed by people using those devices.

What Krippendorff proposes is that in an ecology of devices the meaning of a device, or could we say its *affordance*, consists of its possible interaction with other devices, and that no device can be realized within an ecology without being appropriated by those actors who can "enroll" it. Hence the proposition is, in analogy with biological ecologies, but with a focus on appropriation, to explore *cooperation, competition, interdependence, reproduction,* and *retirement* (*death*) of devices in specific cultures, or we might say communities-of-practice or even design games. With such an approach to infrastructuring and the coupling of design games at project time and design games at use time, a design team would pay considerable attention to understanding the ecology of devices in the practice they are trying to design towards. This would not be very different from the kind of ethnographic and historical accounts made in many design projects today, but the focus would be different, since the ecological preunderstanding of the devices in play, for good and for bad, would dominate. But perhaps more important, protocols, formats, components, patterns, and ontologies, or other suggested boundary objects, conscription devices or infrastructures, would have to be seen in light of their contribution to the design games played in already existing ecologies of devices. How will users make these devices compete and cooperate today and tomorrow? Will they find a proper place and role for the new suggested constituencies of the object of design in their design games?

Design answers to such questions must by necessity be humble. Perhaps we can say that in this strategy one must at project time try to develop the very object of design as a *thing* that potentially, by the appropriation and enactment of its users, can make its way into their life-worlds and already existing ecology of devices. But these are not questions of design from nowhere. The answers are also a matter of how designers engage in strategies to make their designs advantageous among stakeholders who give meaning to specific ecologies of devices.

Hence, the strategies of participatory design and engaging potential future users are not contrary to metadesign and infrastructuring, but may, despite the uncertainties of who the future users will be and how they will appropriate infrastructures and new devices, be a most advantageous strategy even when infrastructuring. For example, after *Atelier*, some of us have joined forces with colleagues in the city of Malmö who have begun to explore participatory infrastructuring ground (<http://www.malmolivinglab.se>; Björgvinsson 2007; Hillgren 2006), focusing on so-called *Living Labs*. By definition, "a Living Lab is about experimentation and co-creation with real users in real life environments, where users together with researchers, firms and public institutions look together for new solutions, new products, new services or new business models" (see <http://www.openlivinglabs.eu>). In relation to *Atelier*, our Living Labs may be characterized as venues for open-ended prototypical practices or arenas for communication and negotiation, rather than places for appropriation of open-ended and configurable technology and architecture, and there is an even stronger focus on exchangeable mixed-media bricolage of "ready-mades" The first attempt was a lab where new media services and products are cocreated with a particular focus on audience participation and user-generated content. The lab was run by design researchers and students at the School of Arts and Communication at Malmö University in collaboration with the cultural media and performance center INKONST, the hip-hop movement RGRA (aka The Face and Voice of the Street), and a number of associated new media companies. New media experiences and practices were developed that focus on engaging grassroots enthusiasts, building on their needs and trying out concepts developed in a real-life setting.

Examples of collaborative projects growing out of this Living Lab as an arena for communication and negotiation include Barcode Beats and Hip-Hop Bluetooth Bus. Barcode Beats, a bricolage of ready-mades, is a musical instrument that converts barcodes into unique sound loops that can be combined to create music. The instrument was developed by interaction design students in collaboration with young people from RGRA. The instrument was tried out by RGRA at Malmö's biggest grocery

Figure 8.6
Living Lab participation and infrastructuring. The RGRA Street Lab team in action.

store, resulting in a remarkable live performance. RGRA has a strong focus on developing new ways for producing, spreading, and consuming grassroots productions. In the Living Lab, participants carried out collaborative experiments with spreading RGRA's music on local buses via Bluetooth. Experiments have also been conducted on how RGRA can produce mobile street news for mobile consumption.

Over recent years it has been possible to scale up this engagement with Living Labs design things (Björgvinsson, Ehn, and Hillgren 2010, <http://medea.mah.se>). To be able to maintain close working relations and trust we decided to grow three small collaborating labs in different parts of the city, rather than one large lab. "The Stage" is situated in the vibrant club, music, theater and subculture district in the city and focuses on cultural production and cross-media, in continuation of the first lab. "The Neighborhood" lab is located in the multiethnic suburb of Rosnegård and focuses on urban development, collaborative services, and social media. Finally, "The Factory" is a lab housed in a new cultural meeting place in the heart of the new media cluster in the city and functions as a full-fledged fabrication and prototyping lab. Though different in orientation and geographic location these three labs are all founded on shared ideas and values. They are all based on user-driven design and innovation activities, growing out of social movements. At the same time they are planned as open innovation social and technical platforms and integrated with the overall innovation system in the city. As such they invite collaboration between people, companies, public agencies, cultural organizations, and NGOs, opening the boarders and aligning potentially conflicting matters of concerns between users driving innovation, business incubators, new business models, research, and education.

Emerging design things range from a multiethnic group of women with a broad range of language skills organizing a collaborative service where they provide meals for a large group of arriving refugee orphans, to new tools and participative hands-on processes engaging citizens in urban planning, to the implementation of a Creative Commons business model supporting independent movie makers in financing and distributing their productions.

Though so far limited in scope, such Living Lab experiences point toward challenging ways of uniting participation and infrastructuring beyond the studio and the design project, in new kinds of *design things* over time that are "outside the box."

Design Games Revisited

In this chapter we have been reflecting on *design projects* as design things and entangled design games. The perspective has been strategic and conceptual. We have focused on two approaches: participatory design (designing for use before use) and metadesign (designing for design after design). Throughout our discussion we've developed a concept of design as staged and performed entangled controversial design games. These are design games in which design devices and artifacts act as vehicles for the emerging object of design, and at the same time, as *things* for binding these design games together. We elaborated on the concept of entangled design games both in relation to participatory design and metadesign. In participatory design, the focus is on the establishment of new, shared design games, as well as the emergence of shared objects of design. In metadesign, where, through greater heterogeneity and distance in time and space, users and designers are more loosely connected, the focus is rather on how design objectives from a project through infrastructuring may become *things* and eventually not only devices (objects of use), but also new objects of design. Configuring and design and use of materialized design patterns were seen as one promising approach for this, and so were design approaches that follow a meaning-making ecological understanding of *things*, objects, and devices.

In the early development of the perspective of participatory design, a new role was envisioned for the designer at project time in setting the stage for shared design games, of shaping a *design thing*. In this chapter, we have further elaborated on the role of the designer in supporting future appreciation and appropriation as a kind of design at use time, on infrastructuring public *things*. However, there may also be a new role for the professional designer and future design games that take place "outside the box." In the final chapter, we will open up this box, speculating about where future design games will take place and who the participants may be, extending design into political processes, public debates, and possibly even subversive but creative misuse.

9 Outside the Box

Out of the Homely Design Studio and . . .

All activities were performed in the studio. It was the room that was our heart. So the activities were carried out in a core. One becomes so affected by the fact of being involved in an environment that is so intense, so condensed. But if we had been thrown out in another environment. . . . Sometimes one should get out from the environment, and by doing so obtain distance and bring new things in.

—Comment from one of the interaction design students in Malmö

We opened this book by quoting Nussbaum's call for a reorientation of designers and design. Nussbaum sees a demand for design thinking applied to a broad array of societal challenges and a responsibility for designers to take up these challenges in a more open and egalitarian exchange with other societal stakeholders. Designers are necessary according to Nussbaum to ensure quality in our environment, but designers also have to let go of any elitist attitude that would make them hostile to the inclusion of other voices in the design process.

But it is not just the old-style designer who is being challenged to do new things or the well-known business of design that needs to be pursued in new ways. It is actually both, or perhaps more accurately, what is required is a new approach to design that reaches beyond the well-known designer professionalism as well as the established genres of design. We share with Nussbaum the view that designing as a particular way of engaging with change in our environment is what is in demand, and throughout this book we have pursued ways to conceptualize and expose a practice of designing as a mode of inquiry rather than as a professional competency or a particular domain of expertise. Unlike Nussbaum, we have not done this to promote a certain route toward innovation or business renewal and other design thinking gospels. Rather, our writing is based in our commitment to this particular mode of inquiry and an ambition to develop an edifying perspective that would support reflection and exploration among fellow designers and design researchers.

In this closing chapter we take a look at how we imagine that designing as a mode of inquiry may contribute to the enrollment of new stakeholders and new controversies on the road to a more engaging and sustainable human environment.

As indicated in the epigraph at the start of this chapter, the design studio of the future may become a highly saturated place where the many problems of the world are consumed and digested. The particular studio was very well equipped and quite supportive, with a highly configurable infrastructure, a place where the students found satisfaction and contentment. Spending time there became so convenient and sheltered that they eventually were submerged in this confined place. When they returned from their initial field studies, they stayed in the studio for the duration of the whole project. As a result the users never got involved until they were invited to the final exhibition at the studio—the studio became an augmented box detached from the rest of the world.

In one way, by augmenting the studio in this way, the students perform what is at risk in traditional design. On this traditional view, design should take place within the Heideggerian notion of dwelling and place, an ideal of homely, peaceful, and authentic existence. Design then becomes the ritualized resolution and healing of the heterogeneous and controversial everyday, sanctioned and guarded by the distinct landscape of design that is nurtured within the studio walls. On this view, the particular practice of designing as performed by the students involves design games that negate or rather bracket any conflicts of interests, both at project time and at use time.

In the *Atelier* project we concluded that design infrastructure and devices had to be able to support a much more mobile and flexible *taking place* of *design things*, which necessitated a shift in the object of design from augmenting a particular dedicated space to augmenting whatever place is available as a potential site for design and as a *design thing*.

In figure 9.1, students are shown leaving the studio and taking the design material to a public site (upper left). The public site is transformed into an emerging landscape of design (upper right); components from the studio as infrastructure and devices in design games are taken to a railway station (below). Hence, the use of the studio became more a place for building and exploring augmented models of the use of a public site (a railway station) and for experimenting with prototypes, which were strongly related to on-site experiments with the use of the actual space and interactions with the people occupying that space. For the design students, this move was certainly an important step out of the box of the design studio, understood both as outside the design studio and as beyond the boundaries of an elitist attitude of hostility to other voices participating in a *design thing*.

This led us to envision design as participation in controversial *things* far from the homely design studio. To elaborate on what this entails, it is worth recapitulating the design position developed throughout the preceding chapters. Chapter 2 depicted

Figure 9.1
Out of the box and into the site.

design practice and the designer as reflective practitioner against a rich background of pragmatism and phenomenology. No "model" of the design process was presented. Instead, we explored the notions of aesthetic experience, inspirational resources, and the qualities of a creative design environment as concepts for understanding design practice. In chapter 3 we elaborated a number of such qualities, based on bottom-up ethnographic observations. These had to do with the richness of materials, techniques for creativity, and especially configurability. These design qualities, we suggested, can direct the designer's attention toward specific "aesthetic experiences" of a situation, and support her competence to recognize and evoke those experiences in future design situations.

If these first chapters can be said to focus on the designer and her environment, on design practice and the qualities of a design environment that is supportive of (collective) creativity, chapter 4 starts from the other end by investigating *things*, devices, and the object of design, and the interplay between *things* and words. Returning to the *things*, the ancient governing assembly and place in Nordic and Germanic societies where disputes were solved and political decisions made, we suggested a view of design as accessing, aligning, and navigating among the "constituents" of the object of design. People interact with the object of design through its constituents, whether these are *things*, artifacts, or representations. In experiencing *things*, objects, and devices, people are involved primarily not with different types of materials, but rather in different kinds of interaction. In chapter 5, we explored this view on design and representations in relation to how the web of constituents is weaved around an evolving object of design as the designer engages in its transformations. Design work is looked on as an act of "metamorphing," where design concepts are envisioned and realized through objectifying and manipulating a variety of representations. Chapter 6 added a performance perspective to design and explored the relations between expression and experience. Here we suggested an interventionist, participative, and experiential understanding of design as purposeful staging and accomplishing of events. In chapter 7, we returned to the design studio seen as the place for design. We suggested a concept of a design space as an "emerging landscape" as an alternative to the notion of an abstract design space. The suggestion in many ways parallels the discussion of the object of design, but now focuses on the designer's interaction with place and the spatial practices through which the environment becomes entangled in the evolving design, an experienced landscape which the designer inhabits and journeys through. Finally, in the previous chapter, we once more explored the object of design, but now from the perspective of design as participation in public events and *things*. We elaborated upon the notion of design projects as potentially controversial assemblies of humans and artifacts, and the interplay between design and use. We also suggested a concept of design games that aligns design and use and is related to the concepts of boundary objects and infrastructuring. Using these concepts, we investigated strategies for designing use before use (participatory design) and for designing design after design (metadesign). As we have progressed through the chapters, the activities of the designer have become more and more comprehensive, but at the same time the borders of the design activity, and not least the design studio, have become more and more open. So the last few pages of this book will be dedicated to design and controversial *things* going on "outside the box."

Where will the design studio of the future be situated, who will participate, and what kind of design games will they play? These are questions of objectives, of the meaning of the object of design. They are political questions. In closing this chapter we will regard them as potential public controversial issues and *things*. Given the paradoxical situation that design thinking and massive user-participation in creative production seem to be not only an alternative, more "democratic" mode of production but also a major feature in the self-image of the contemporary business world we will reflect on the values guiding such design, and will point toward design tendencies and challenges in the fields of social media and social innovation.

. . . Into Controversial Design Things

The participatory approach to *design things* that we have been advocating throughout this book grew out of a concern for how design could support resource-weak groups when information technology was introduced to the workplace. It also meant a clear positioning of the designer in controversies regarding how design was to be implemented in use.

Democracy as the guiding value for participatory design leads to an interest in supporting participation and possibilities for users to express and communicate "tacit knowledge" skills, or as we would say within the framework of this book, the living of "aesthetic experience."

Continuing the ideal of participatory design outside the box of the studio and into use, the same guiding values, once advocated to counter a hierarchical and formalistic design process characterized by dominance, may prove useful. Dominance, hierarchy, and formalisms certainly characterize many participatory social, technical, and spatial infrastructures. Hence the rational idea of democracy and legitimate participation in design for design may lead to a focus on infrastructuring in support for communication and community-building that is free of coercion at the time of use. But we must, then, as Star and Ruhleder (1996) point out, pay special attention to those "marginalized by standardized networks" or infrastructures. This cannot be performed in any universal sense as "design from nowhere," but only, as expressed by Haraway (1988, 195) as "politics and epistemologies of location, positioning and situating, where partiality and not universality is the condition of being heard to make rational knowledge claims," and, as suggested by Suchman (2002), as "located accountability." On this perspective, design as democratic innovation becomes a question not so much about the "new" or about patents, but more about everyday practice at particular sites and locations committed to the work of envisioning emerging landscapes of design where social and material transformations take place by raising questions and possibilities (Barry 2001).

A possible frame of reference for such more democratic *design things* is the "agonistic" approach by Chantal Mouffe in *The Democratic Paradox* (2000). For Mouffe, "agonistic struggle" is at the core of a vibrant democracy. Agonistic democracy does not presuppose the possibility of consensus and rational conflict resolution, but proposes a polyphony of voices and mutually vigorous but tolerant disputes among groups united by passionate engagement. These are political acts and always take place in a background of potentially challenged hegemony. In this view, *design things* are always plural public spaces where different projects confront each other and the world. As such they are always striated and hegemonically structured. The goal of democratic politics and design becomes a question of empowering a multiplicity of voices in the struggle of hegemony and at the same time find "constitutions" that help transform antagonism into agonism, from conflict between enemies to constructive controversies among "adversaries" who have opposing matters of concern but also accept other views as "legitimate." These are, according to Mouffe, activities full of passion, imagination, and engagement. As such, they are more like creative innovations than rational decision-making processes.

It may be noticed that this "agonistic" view on democracy is very much in line with the early model of participatory design (Bjerknes et al. 1987; Ehn 1988) and struggles for "democracy at work." Hegemony within companies was at stake and "constitutions" or "negotiation models" to transform antagonistic struggles within the companies into passionate "agonistic" design and innovation strategies were tried out with special focus on workers and their local trade unions, on their empowerment and skills. Hence, it may be argued that an "agonistic" perspective on "democratizing" design and producing *design things* as "agonistic" enabling platforms is just a continuation of early approaches to participatory design.

With these reflections on values and accountability in mind, let's turn now to social media and social innovation and examples of how *design things* may be made public.

Social Media

President Obama's mobilization during his election campaign, citizen journalists reporting on the fatal shooting of an Iranian woman during protests against the government, critical bloggers in Sri Lanka, a public equipped with mobile phones as in the Philippines and Egypt, and the countermoves by threatened authorities like the shutting down of cell phones and critical Internet sites, and not least WikiLeaks making public classified media on, for example, the wars in Afghanistan and Iraq—all are recent events demonstrating the power of new media in more or less controversial public issues and situations. Social or participatory media and social networking are at the core of the sociomaterial *things* through which the politics of our contemporary societies are framed. Participatory media and Web 2.0 infrastructures like YouTube, Facebook, and Twitter have already for some years been extremely successful as platforms for massive participation in creating and sharing popular cultural material, and for engagement in more or less public issues, across both small and large, homogeneous and heterogeneous communities and places. In a discussion about *design things*, such participatory media cannot be ignored. What role could and should professional design play in creating and making public platforms like blogs, wikis, RSS, tagging, social bookmarking, music-photo-video sharing, mashups, podcasts, and video comments?

Exemplary participatory media infrastructures that blur any sharp distinction between form and content and directly challenge the issues of design and participation are open applications, infrastructures, and communities like open source, Wikipedia, and the Creative Commons. Wikipedia is growing as a gigantic participative open resource for creating, sharing, and negotiating knowledge. The creative commons as infrastructure supports the open sharing of creative content and intellectual property across design games rather than privatizing creativity and locking it into patents. The open source movement is in many ways the generic pattern for such communities and their design games (though it faces the risk of turning into an infrastructure too rigid for really creative design).

As pointed out earlier, participatory media have the potential to be turned into platforms for public controversial *things*. An early example is how Facebook in 2007 was appropriated for a kind of "open source politics." Amateur activists and major political nonprofit groups appropriated it as a powerful infrastructure for organizing worldwide protests against Myanmar's violent attack on a monk's pro-democracy demonstrations. Since then we have seen many such appropriations of standard media platforms turned into public controversial *things* as cross-media utilizing not only the Internet, but also mobile phone networks and more traditional mass media.

A more far-reaching example in terms of finding ways to redesign existing technology and turn it into a controversial *thing* is "the French Democracy" as analyzed by Lowood (2008). The background was the riots in a largely African and Arab Parisian suburb in November 2005, triggered by the electrocution of two teenagers fleeing from the police and incendiary remarks by the Interior minister. At about the same time, a computer game, The Movies, a Hollywood studio simulation and a toolbox for making animated movies for that studio, was released. The game play community, however, quickly found ways to tweak the game into a production tool for making independent animated movies. One of them was a freelance industrial designer with no experience in making movies. Under the name of Koulamata he in a few weeks produced and made public *The French Democracy* (Koulamata 2005), a filmic series of short stories commenting on the victimization of French minority groups through harassment and job discrimination and the state of French historical ideals of liberty and fraternity. *The French Democracy* was massively downloaded from the Internet and discussed in several online forums and soon also was taken up in the public debate in a broad spectrum of mainstream media like *USA Today*, the *Washington Post, Liberation, Business Week*, and MTV, as well as at art and film festivals.

This DIY (do-it-yourself) approach of finding technology and by creative "misuse" transforming it into a new design device for public discourse on public events is certainly also a challenge for professional design. What role should designers play in such controversial *things*, extending design into political processes, public debates, and subversive but creative misuse?

Social Innovation

Strategies for massive participation in design and design in use are also developed in other fields. Participatory design strategies that turn design into controversial events and *things* are in no way restricted to participatory media or the digital realm.

Returning to Nussbaum, it is interesting how he in a later blog links design and innovation to the current "transformational crisis" as discussed at the World Economic Forum summit in Davos in 2009, arguing that if we have a transformational crisis we need designers, innovators, and design thinkers who can transform the situation (Nussbaum 2009). He points in particular at the design for social innovation work that has been carried out in Great Britain, initiated by social entrepreneur Hillary Cottam, designer of the year in Great Britain in 2005 though not a professional designer, and Charles Leadbeater, innovation expert and government adviser suggesting "pro-am" and "we-think" for engaged professional amateurism outside the established economies in developing platforms for social change, participative public services, and so on (Leadbeater 2007). "Transformation design" projects, carried out with support from the British Design Council between 2004 and 2006, explored design interventions for better public service, tackling social and economic problems in areas like health, energy, the elderly, democracy, and citizenship. Substantial results in health care, for example, were reached by involving patients and caretakers in participatory design processes, and focusing on services and activities that correspond to their needs and interests, rather than on the efficiency of the health care system as such. Examples include self-support systems for individuals with diabetes and support for exercise and training to prevent chronic diseases. This kind of design for social innovation is now carried on not only by the British Design Council, but also by "service design" companies like Participle, live/work, and Engine. The think tank Young Foundation has been a major player in developing this social innovation perspective in theory and practice (Murray et al. 2010).

These European design experiences are also echoed on the American continent in manifestos such as *Massive Change* (2004) by Bruce Mau (2004), placing design as a major participative practice shaping our world, and in socially responsible design as practiced for the last decades by successful design companies like IDEO.

A parallel development in design for social innovation is the design orientation and international network that is growing out of the sustainable design movement. Whereas social entrepreneurship, service design and design thinking are defining factors of the British and American initiatives, this initiative has a stronger focus on self-generated, bottom-up collaborative services. In the view of Italian designer and researcher Ezio Manzini, who has been a main driver in establishing the field of "design for social innovation and sustainability," social innovation may be seen as a process of change in which new ideas emerge from a variety of actors directly involved in the problem to be solved: end users, grass roots designers, technicians, entrepreneurs, local institutions, and civil society organizations. Social innovation mobilizes diffuse social resources (in terms of creativity, skills, knowledge, and entrepreneurship). For this reason, it is a major driver of change. And it could be a powerful promoter of sustainable ways of living and producing (Jégou and Manzini 2008). In this perspective, design is no longer just a tool for the development of functional innovative consumer products, but is increasingly seen as a process for radical change, designing services, systems, and environments that support more sustainable lifestyles and consumption habits. A main concept for Manzini and his colleagues is that of *collaborative services*. These services are created by "creative communities" and are designed through local collaboration, reciprocal support, and sharing of resources. The role of the designer is initially to support the development of new concepts and later to make them attainable so they can result in "social" enterprises. These enterprises in turn can become core elements in the development of an active civil society with better quality of life and enhanced possibilities for sustainable economic development. Examples of collaborative services range from co-housing projects, where resources are shared in new ways across generations, and workshops, where unemployed can work on upgrading obsolescent products, to shared sewing studios, "home restaurants," and car pools.

However, there are also challenging examples of design for social innovation in the revival of the DIY tradition emanating from the "punk" generation and various "pro-am" collaborations. Such design practices are not limited to new media design, as in the example above where communities of young game players, in the "machinima" tradition, turned off-the-shelf games into their own advanced amateur media production tools. Similar inspiring social innovation examples can be found in more traditional design fields, for example, in the new roles for professional designers and user participation in fashion design. In *Fashion-able*, designer and design researcher Otto von Busch (2008) reports on a series of such inspiring projects where fashion design has been reverse-engineered, hacked like a computer program, and shared among participants as a form of engaged social activism, often in the DIY form of recycling clothes through "open source" fashion "cookbooks." What is the role of the professional designer in this kind of design after design and design in use as an application of the readymade strategy of recontextualization and reappropriation, once practiced by Duchamp in the artistic field, but now deliberately and skillfully practiced as an everyday design strategy?

One example takes us out of the design studio and back to the shop floor where participatory design first began. The shoe factory, Dale Sko, in the small town of Dale in the Norwegian countryside was once the main employer and pride of the borough.

In 2006, downsized from the peak of 250 employees to a dozen workers, the factory was in crisis and totally dependent on steady orders from governmental departments. That year six Norwegian designers were invited to a workshop. All the experimentation during the workshop was firmly based on collaboration on the factory floor. However, the project as a *design thing* and the shared design games were not carried out through master–apprentice relationships, but rather as challenges to the production assembly line by probing "nonlinear" means of action and codesign. Using machines "wrongly"— for example, at the wrong moment, using the wrong size of tools, assembling materials in wrong order—opened up new action spaces and challenged the need for technical investment and reinvestment. In this process the skill and creativity of both professional designers and workers helped change both the flow of production and the products designed. Dale shoes have since then been shown at fashion weeks in London, Paris, and Tokyo and are on sale in stores in London and other major cities. The design approach even won a special prize in fashion theory at the European Fashion Awards in 2008. The active relation to media and how the experiences were made public in this case is worth noticing. In national and local media, a spotlight was shone on the collaborative design process and on fashion photography to encourage others to match these values and the Norwegian atmosphere, all contributing to the image of Dale Sko and the small town of Dale as an innovative, progressive local player with global fashion connections.

The other example of fashion design for social innovation that we will briefly mention takes us from rural Dale in Norway to the vibrant city of Istanbul, Turkey. "Modified by me—Don't Commodify—Modify!" the predesigned labels read at the public clothes-swap and redesign event in Istanbul in autumn 2007. Such "Swap-O-Rama-Ramas" are organized around the world based on a Creative Commons license. Swap-O-Rama-Ramas are huge public events and DIY workshops where hundreds or even thousands of participants come to swap and modify clothes with support from professional designers and other participants. Participants gain entry by bringing a bag of clothes that is added to the pool of shared garment resources. The infrastructure on-site includes, besides the garment pool, sewing stations and specific workshops on sewing, embroidering, printing, repairing, knitting, and so on. In DIY sessions professional designers help participants get started. Participants even prepare for a catwalk; the event mimics a big fashion studio, but here every participant is a fashion designer. The social innovation here is perhaps not so much in the redesign and recycling of clothes, but rather in the new pro-am design practices, the sharing of aesthetic skills, and in the ways in which a new scene is created where fashion design is made into a public controversial *thing*.

In this book, the philosophical pragmatism of John Dewey has been a cornerstone for reflecting on participation as well as aesthetic experience in design. As a final note we will turn to his position on controversial issues and the public. Dewey argued

(Dewey 1927; Marres 2005) that in fact the public is characterized by heterogeneity and conflict. It may be challenging enough to design for, by, and with communities-of-practice in entangled design games where common social objectives are already established, institutionalized, or at least within reasonable reach. These are social communities supported by relatively stable infrastructures. But the really demanding challenge is to design where no such consensus seems to be within immediate reach, where no social community exists. In short, the challenge is to design a platform or infrastructure, for and with a political community, a public characterized by heterogeneity and difference with no shared object of design, not necessarily to solve conflicts, but to constructively deal with disagreements—public controversial *things* where heterogeneous design games can unfold and actors can engage in alignments of their conflicting interests and objects of design. *Res publica*, making *things* public (Latour and Weibel 2005), stands out as the ultimate challenge when we gather and collaborate in and around participatory media and *design things*.

Appendix: *Atelier* Experiments and Prototypes

The *Atelier* project was carried out by a multidisciplinary consortium of social scientists and ethnographers, computer scientists and systems designers, and practitioners and users from the field of architecture and interaction design. The School of Arts and Communication, Malmö University (coordinator), the Institute for Technology Design and Assessment, Vienna University of Technology, the Institute for Art and Architecture, Academy of Fine Arts in Vienna, Imagination Computer Services GesmbH, Vienna, Consorzio Milano Ricerche, CMR.DISCO, Milano, the Department of Information Processing Science, University of Oulu, and the Interactive Institute: Space & Virtuality Studio, Malmö, all participated in the *Atelier* project.

The two practical settings of inspirational learning environments that formed the basis for observations, design, and evaluation were chosen to be complementary. One was a "traditional" master's program in architecture. It was complemented and contrasted by the setting of a new-media-oriented master's studio program in interaction design.

The Academy of Fine Arts is Vienna's main university of arts; its history goes back to 1692. In 1876 the new academy building on today's Schillerplatz was opened, and in 1998 the Academy of Fine Arts received its official status as a university. The education of architects at the academy is based on the idea of "project-oriented studies." Led by a professor, the master's class organizes student projects, bringing together students from different years. The studio-like learning environment brings together a diversity of resources—disciplines, people, materials, and technologies. These resources include "hard facts" about context and requirements, images and metaphorical descriptions of qualities, such as atmosphere, movement, and spatial configurations, knowledge about construction, material, detail, and so on. The resources are multimedial—they range from physical objects like CAD plans, sketches, and scale models to samples, product catalogs, art books, and everyday objects, as well as immaterial resources, such as conversations and emotional reactions. The aim is to help students combine these resources in a movement of concentration and expansion, develop novel interpretations, and experiment with different methods, strategies, and ways of thinking.

The School of Arts and Communication at Malmö University, is by contrast, very young. It opened in the autumn of 1998 and now has about 800 students in a 5,000-square-meter open building. At the school students attend bachelor's programs ranging from graphic design and interaction design to performing arts technology and media and communication studies; master's programs in interaction design and media and culture studies; and doctorate program in interaction design and media studies. These programs are integrated with team-based research studios, where critical, experimental, artistic, and creative new-media design-oriented research is carried out.

The interaction design program at the master's level is a two-year full-time studio-based program with the goal of developing abilities for designing user-friendly interactive digital systems and media. About fifteen students are admitted each year. The program applies a broad perspective on the interaction design field. Examples of applications range from conventional task-oriented interaction and Web applications to computer games and interactive art installations. Interaction design is a multidisciplinary subject and students have a mixed background including computer science, design, art, and music. Besides the computer, they typically work with a mixture of video clips, mock-ups, and other physical representations, such as scale models, prototypes, and so on. The design studio is their permanent base, but they also have access to a craft workshop for designing physical devices, a "black box" where they can create full-scale mock-ups of scenarios, and a well-equipped music studio to record sound and music.

The two learning environments were very different. In the architectural master's class the emphasis was on working in an environment rich with materials and media. Students used computers for making CAD drawings and 3D visualizations, but particularly in the creative phases of their work, most of the materials they work with are physical, haptic things. Studying their work has exposed us to materiality in a way, which few other areas of work offer. In design practice, materiality is seen as more than merely a technical property of the materials from which a building or designed artifact is made. It is a source of creativity and inspiration. Designers work out, evaluate, extend ideas through intimate contact with all kinds of materials. Our work with the architecture students and the way we conceived technological intervention were also influenced by the fact that scale and dimensionality play a large role in their work and that it requires a level of precision that sometimes could only be achieved by carefully configuring space and technology relations.

At Malmö there is a complementary focus on portability and supporting an inspirational learning environment outside the design studio. This has to do with the nature of students' work, some of which needs to be portable and/or is designed for public spaces. Interaction design students focus more on people than on materials; hence they are often more participative in their approaches. This is also reflected in the studio's pedagogy, which uses a diversity of creative-experimental design methods, from "cultural probes" to "design games." Also, design students' work is closer to computers, and it was easier to integrate the technologies into their work practices than in the architecture class.

During our initial interventions, we noticed that the architecture students enriched their tradition of working with space by enhancing it with digital media. By contrast, the interaction design students used space as a resource in the process by giving physicality to digital material. The use of a diversity of materials and representations in the design process was typical for both sites, but there were also differences in the kind of representations used. One example we observed was the use of sketching and videos.

The interaction design students envisioned use situations to produce a short video of, for example, an idea about human interaction with artifacts. There were rules for capturing an enacted scenario, which ensured the roughness and openness of the video sketch. Part of the sketching took place while the students were acting out a scenario with materials and props. Here we see a similarity to architects' working with sketch models—quick 3D representations of a design idea. Architects' sketching is, however, more immediate; they often sketch while thinking and explaining an idea to others. Another difference is that their sketches are more abstract—with video one can easily get very concrete.

At neither site did learning take place in a traditional classroom setting. Typically based on project work, the education engages the students in processes that span a variety of settings, both the physical environment and the social and organizational setting. Ways of using the actual space differ a lot, not only between the two sites but also from project to project. One difference between the sites is that whereas the students have individual workspaces at the academy in Vienna, with rooms assigned to different projects, the students at Malmö do not have any dedicated workspaces.

The *Atelier* project studied design education practice, developed prototypes to enhance such education, introduced prototypes to different real-world settings (design and architecture classes), and, partly in collaboration with the students, reflected on the interventions to learn about how to improve both architecture and technology and the learning situation. This "pro-searching" is built on a user-collaborative approach involving users and researchers as reflective codesigners and evolves from early explorations of practice and visions through field trials with gradually more integrated scenarios and prototypes for inspirational learning.

Iteration is a significant aspect of these interventions and reflections. The iterative research and design process for the refinement of architecture and technology for inspirational learning environments went through three ten-month design cycles: envisioning, prototyping, and experiencing. The project took the somewhat unusual approach of "concurrent" development of technological infrastructure and components, with conceptual development of architecture and technology for inspirational learning environments, and investigations of design practice for architecture and interaction design students. The successful combination of early probings with technology, the rapid and flexible development of technological infrastructure, and successive hard-edged integrative development efforts resulting in working prototypes managed to stay closely connected with the overall framework of concurrent concept development and participatory pro-searching of practice.

In the field trials, we explored approaches to mixing physical and digital artifacts, experimented with ways of integrating the physical space into the students' learning activities, and investigated the possibilities of configuring the environment. The strategy for these field trials was not to create new and dedicated artifacts and spaces but to motivate students to integrate the prototypes into ongoing project work. This was enabled by what we see as the "open-ended" nature of the prototypes.

While technology development was carried out by several partners collaboratively, field trials took place in Malmö University and the Academy of Fine Arts in Vienna.

Interventions

The *Atelier* project worked with four kinds of interventions:

Pedagogical interventions   As part of the iterative design process, field trials were conducted in which students were encouraged to work with the *Atelier* technologies as part of their design projects. Both at Malmö and Vienna, specific project assignments were developed to facilitate students' explorations of the technologies.

Methodological interventions   While ethnographic field work was conducted to develop a deeper understanding of design and learning practices in both places, we also used creative-experimental methods, such as design games, cultural probes, and performative techniques, and took inspiration from art and architecture.

Spatial interventions   Throughout the project we introduced a number of spatial interventions or material for configuring a space in combination with the technological components: grids, displays, light, and modules, as well as physical materials.

Technological interventions   Eight "open-ended" prototypes or demonstrators were developed—Texture Painter, Mixed Objects Table, Interactive Stage, Physical Building Blocks, Tangible Archive, Tangible Image Query and Ontology Service, eDiary, and Tracking Table.

What We Built

Texture Painter

The Texture Painter uses a physical-digital brush to enable design students to "paint" various computer-generated visual overlays as textures on physical 3D models in real time. Using a brush, which is tracked, this application allows "painting" on objects such as models or parts of the physical space, applying textures, images, or video, scaling and rotating them.

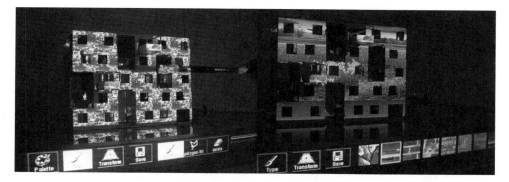

Figure A.1
Texture Painter.

This prototype, which was developed by Imagination, was used by the architecture students in Vienna who worked with real architectural models, transforming them by painting textures on the surfaces. It provides a fast and highly interactive way of experimenting with scale, color, background, and social use of an object or space. It helps create "mixed objects," where integration of the physical and the digital happens within one single object.

The Mixed Objects Table

The Mixed Objects Table included The Texture Painter and other tools and interaction modes for visual overlays on and around physical models. The Mixed Objects Table is an artifact that allows students to combine real objects such as architectural models with virtual parts. It consists of a tabletop construed as a back projection screen. Outlets for USB-cameras, RFID-tag readers, and barcode readers are integrated into the table frame. With a video camera and special markers, virtual 3D objects can be added to the physical model on the table.

The architecture students positioned their physical models on the table, for example, onto a projected plan, and used the Texture Painter for painting the model by selecting textures from a palette. They also used optical markers for placing virtual objects close to the model, capturing the whole arrangement with a webcam. What they get in real time, projected on a display, is the movie of the composed scene with the 3D objects popping out of the markers.

The Interactive Stage

The Interactive Stage combines elements of a theatrical space with technological augmentations that are used to input, manipulate, and output design representations, media, and events in the learning environment. The participant in the learning space is thus made a bodily part of the design representation.

Figure A.2
Mixed Objects Table.

At the Academy of Fine Arts, the stage consisted of a combination of Mixed Objects Table and Cave Corner. The Cave Corner was a low-tech immersive environment produced by a simple arrangement of a grid, three large projection screens that can be fixed at different angles, and numerous beamers. The grid provides an infrastructure for fixing lightweight, movable projection screens (easy-to-change projection material) and lighting equipment. The architecture students mainly used the interactive stage for presentations, for example painting a physical model and viewing it against different projected backgrounds.

The interaction design students at Malmö used the space to enact use scenarios and engage in design improvisations.

The Tangible Archive
The Tangible Archive and organizing zone is a place for informal storing, combining, and presenting mixed materials. It consists of a "physical database" containing different design artifacts, tagged to carry links to digital media. It is a place for physical

CAVE CORNER, TURM 3
BASIC CONFIGURATIONS

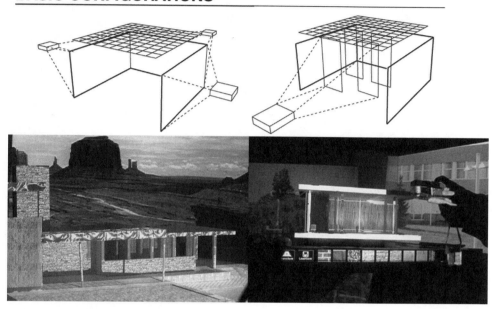

Figure A.3
The *Interactive Stage* at the Academy of Fine Arts.

exploration and knowledge sharing within an environment of project-based work and learning. The main interaction point is the Organizing Zone. Technically the Organizing Zone is connected to the hypermedia database, a projector, loudspeakers, and a printer. It also has a barcode reader and two RFID tag readers. It offers the possibility to view and easily manipulate entered media as well as to create a personal collection of digital media and real things.

The Physical Building Blocks
The Physical Building Blocks enable the students to customize their own environment. They consist of a system of Plexiglas modules that was developed to facilitate the configuration of the physical environment. The modules can be combined to form cubes, shelves, and vertical or horizontal working or projection areas, in a 1:1 scale. Modules are fitted together manually by readymade joints. The furniture can be used as a surface for doing work (with work zones being reserved for particular activities), as shelves for storing materials, or for projections.

Figure A.4
The *Interactive Stage* in Malmö.

The Tangible Image Query and Ontology Service

With the Tangible Image Query and the Ontology Service students had a set of tools for browsing and searching the Hypermedia Database: The small, colored objects invite students to "sketch" images in a fluid and ad hoc way. These "sketches" can be used for browsing the database. A parallel but different search method was provided through the Ontology Service, which operates on the basis of keywords. The search results can be displayed on three large projection surfaces that have been installed in the studio. One could either display query results in a 3 × 3 matrix on the central screen, or as a row of nine images on the bottom row of all three screens. The combination of Tangible Image Query, Ontology Service, and configurable display space provided students with an easy and imaginative way of browsing and searching. It also gave them a tangible way of setting keywords, thereby connecting the services in interesting ways.

Figure A.5
The Tangible Archive.

Figure A.6
The Physical Building Blocks.

Figure A.7
Tangible Image Query and Ontology Service.

The eDiary

The eDiary is a mobile application that supports students who visit a remote site to collect material for a design project. One or more visitors walk along a particular route. The path taken is recorded using a time and GPS (Global Positioning System) trace. These are created by the eDiary while visitors take pictures, videos, sounds, and text notes along the path. Back in the work environment, the media files and the GPS log can then easily be stored with an application (PathCreator) in a hypermedia database, creating a navigable and editable media path (a HyperDocument of the visit). Visitors can upload a picture as a map on which the path is visualized. Using multiple projections and physical interfaces, the visitors can reexperience the visit, linking the media material to other physical artifacts (posters, models, objects, etc.).

The components of these demonstrators were integrated via a shared, platform-independent infrastructure and a hypermedia database.

The Tracking Game Table

The Tracking Game Table is a tracking system that allows the manipulation of projected frames, in which images and videos are displayed. A specially designed wireless mouse communicates with the tracking system by a reflector. The frames can be moved around and scaled to different sizes, and videos can be started and paused. Playing

Figure A.8
The eDiary.

cards augmented with RFID tags carry links to media files, and when a selected card is held above a tag reader, the media is displayed in a new frame.

The Stories

Throughout the book we use examples from our fieldwork observations in Malmö and Vienna.

In addition to the anecdotes, listed in table A.1, references are made throughout the book to different versions of the *Atelier* demonstrators, called the "walls." The walls integrated the technology developed in the project through the software infrastructure

Figure A.9
The Tracking Game Table.

and had more or less uniform physical expressions. The different versions of the walls (the Gothenburg wall, the Ivrea wall and the Vienna workshop) were related to the progressively iterated design cycles in the project. They were presented at three international conferences and turned out to be the primary alignment mechanism for the concurrent and interdisciplinary design work in the project, bringing one design iteration to an end and opening a new cycle of design work.

More specifically, the first alignment "wall" as we called it (alignment of the first design cycle) was designed for the DC Jamboree, October 2002, in Gothenburg (a conference on and meeting of international projects focusing on the disappearing

Table A.1

The stories/events/sites, description, chapter, story aspect, and meaning of each project.

Story/event/site	Description	Chapter	Story Aspect	Meaning
Facade—furniture house Observation—AKA Vienna	The furniture house is located in three adjacent buildings. Students' task in this sponsored competition was to integrate the lean facade of one of the buildings with the other two.	3	Finding specific material for a model	Diversity and materiality
		3	Narrative representation explaining "leaning on" the facade	Narrativity
		7	Description of the place of design and its use	The place of design
Learning from Tibet Observation—AKA Vienna	A group of eight students worked on a project in the Alps near the Italian-Swiss border. Their task was "to learn from Tibet" (the destination of a field visit) for their designs. A general concept was developed within the group. Then individual students chose particular interventions like buildings or paths in the valley.	3	Something that flows out of a crack in the mountain	Diversity and materiality
		3	Large shared plaster model of a mountain valley	Diversity and materiality
		4	Something that flows out of a crack in the mountain	Diversity of constituents
		6	Emergence and relationship of different models as developed over time	Narrative temporalities of design events

Table A.1
continued

Story/event/site	Description	Chapter	Story Aspect	Meaning
	Focuses on a particular area in Vienna's 16th district with a particularly high density of immigrant workers. The students were free in their approach—to design an object, do an urban plan, create an intervention, etc.	3	Picture in a drawing living on top of a street market, depicted as the market in the drawer	Narrativity
	The students at the Academy learned how to experience and interpret a city in a different way.	3	How students express seeing a place in different ways	Reprogramming
Verdichtete Gemeinschaft Observation—AKA Vienna		5	Critique session on an underground parking space	Nature of metamorphing
	A series of workshops on methods of participatory inquiry. Further material in the form of pictures, collages and a game were produced, all concerning the process and the environment of the interaction designer.	3	Students presenting their work using video cards and collages	Narrativity
	Resulted in a very rich collection of material, varying from transcripts of videos, inspired by conversation analysis, to narrative accounts from the students coming from the probes.	5	Post-it notes, sealed plastic bags, and digital editing of the white board	Achieving a temporal closure
Participatory inquiry Observation—Malmö		7	Pictures and notions of inspirational place	Imagining and enacting places of design

Table A.1
continued

Story/event/site	Description	Chapter	Story Aspect	Meaning
Amuse Observation—Vienna AKA	Started with the analysis of design methods in architecture and arts, then to design machinery, a wish machine that would improve the design process of an architect. (1) The mind flash—inspirational moments. (2) The common room—cards and games. (3) Scaling workshop.	3	Viewing a model as in real size within an outdoor environment	Dimensionality and scaling
		3	Collaging real people into a miniature scene	Dimensionality and scaling
Augmenting Places Intervention 1—Malmö	Material and virtual rooms with a focus on "augmenting places for collaboration." Students worked in four groups and developed proposed interactive artifacts and services for four different use contexts: Emergency room in the Malmö General Hospital, Fire station, Construction diving, and Electrical power maintenance. The assignment took as its starting point the possibilities of augmenting the environment of the user, with the condition that this augmentation is not static but dynamic.	3	Using light for transforming the atmosphere	Reprogramming
		3	Filling up the gas tank of a car	Reprogramming
		3	Unusual views from ceiling or pavement	Dimensionality and scaling
		5	Design representations from a design project	Artifacts used in a project are numerous
		7	Showing how the students have appropriated the studio	The co-emergence of landscape and place
		7	Familiarizing unfamiliar in the field, distance to what is familiar in the studio	From abstract space to landscapes imagined

Table A.1
continued

Story/event/site	Description	Chapter	Story Aspect	Meaning
Interactive Stage (modernist architecture) Intervention 2—Vienna AKA	Each student group (2 students) was asked to carry out an analysis of one of the "icons" of modernist architecture. They had to build models in scale 1:50 and 1:20 (of an interesting spatial detail) and use Interactive Stage and Texture Painter for analyzing scale and materiality. They worked with textures expressing the original ideas of the architects as well as with material of their own choice, exploring how materiality and context change the meaning of the building.	4	Using the texture brush to stage differently modernist villas	Constituents of design object
		5	Observe how projections of different textures charged the building with meaning.	The entanglement of the model with other constituents
		6	Performing models of Viennese modernist architectures	Consciousness and energy
Stadium Project Visits Intervention 1—Vienna AKA	As part of this project the architecture students at the Academy went on an excursion to London to Lille to Paris from which they returned with lots of materials in their bags—videos, photos, *objets trouvés*, their personal diaries, etc. Their task was to use this material for creating a themed presentation. Visits: (1) Pixeling—in a visit creating pixels out of a remote place (2) Visits to Stadium using constraints and different roles (3) Poetry game—dialoging in space two separate experiences	6	The field visit is to organize techniques and constraints to ensure the effective collection of narratives	Performative use of constraints
		4	Poetry game dialogue of experiences and concepts was embodied spatially with four projections	Stories we tell about an object, may become constituents of it
		6	Fictional space in the designing, negotiating, and staging of the "poetry game"	Fictional space

Table A.1
continued

Story/event/site	Description	Chapter	Story Aspect	Meaning
	Students' next assignment was to design an "extreme stadium." We followed the work of three students on their individual stadium projects.	4	Multiple projection create a 3D spatial layout and the presentation is guided by the sensor augmented plan	Constituents are concurrently used to communicate
Stadium Project	Students experimented with the technological and spatial possibilities provided by Atelier, e.g., by exploring multiple projections in space.	5	Design representations from an project	Mixed design artifacts
Stadium in the city	Stories:	6	Showing the proceeding of the project through design events, importance not of an ostensible product or specification (a model) but rather of accomplishing events	Importance of accomplishing events
Intervention 1—Vienna AKA	A student prepared a presentation of her idea of the stadium between two large museums using the metaphors of soccer stadium. A soccer field and two slide shows, with cultural aspects of soccer (images, sound, video) and the second screen displaying her design ideas "in the making." Operated through a sensor that had been fixed underneath the soccer field.			
	In the final presentations plotted students used multiple projections, posters, barcodes and sensors integrated into models.			

Table A.1
continued

Story/event/site	Description	Chapter	Story Aspect	Meaning
 Tools Studies Intervention 2—AKA Vienna	Students were asked to choose a working tool, to conduct a set of observations with it, to document these in various representational formats—pictures, freehand drawings, diagrams, models—and to use this material for reflecting upon construction, movement in space and use of space. Finally presented using the Interactive Stage and the Texture Painter. In the "analysis and abstraction" part of this exercise they were asked to draw the movement of the tool and the body and to break down the geometry of the movement. They were drawing on paper in scale 1:1 or 1:2, considering issues such as spatial limits of the tool while at work, the rhythm of the movement, repetition and the passage of time, the geometry of the movement, and the space inscribed by it. Finally, they were asked to produce a video of the tool in movement.	4 5 6 6	Developed a large series of constituents, a full ontology of saws emerged from the constituents he created The story of the study of the saw to the creation of a mixed media model From pictures, to drawings, to models to mixed and spatial representations performed Curving, cutting, and illuminating as artifact transformations	Metaphor-ical ontologies Reprogramming activities Narrative temporalities of design events Intervention and experiential knowledge

Table A.1
continued

Story/event/site	Description	Chapter	Story Aspect	Meaning
	As a three-day assignment, we asked mixed groups of interaction design students and architecture students to create an interactive spatial installation forming an entrance to the world of their own design heroes. The installation could be in any media, could be placed anywhere inside the school but should be housed within the dimensions of 1.5 × 1.5 × 2 meters.	7	Exploring the given problem framing	Reprogramming activities
			Searching for the proper place	Enacting a lived landscape of design
Entrance project Observation—Malmö		7	Responding to the ambivalence of place as open for appropriation	Integrating sensory experience of taste, smell and feel in space
	A design assignment for the interaction design students called Process Communication. The assignment had the form of a robot competition. The students worked with the LEGO Mindstorm robot building kit. They had to rework a robot design of another group and prepare it for a robot race on a racing field with unknown obstacles. The students worked in two competing groups, sharing a large studio where each group had a building kit and a computer.	7	Setting up a workplace	Configuring the accommodation of collaborative events
		7	How the students have appropriated the studio	Adaptability to a diversity of uses and identities
LEGO Mindstorm robot building workshop. Observation—Malmö		7	Students different patterns of movement	Identifying place with event

Figure A.10
The walls. From left to right: The Gothenburg wall; the Ivrea wall; and the Vienna workshop.

computer as a research agenda). It was made of blocks of colored polyester, with niches being cut out for the different devices. It had a strong physical presence, inviting people to walk around and examine it. It was more a mock-up than a functioning piece of architecture, and it indicated an integration, long before we were able to actually demonstrate it. The second wall (alignment of the second design cycle) was assembled for the DC Jamboree, November 2003, in Ivrea. It was much more elegant and functional than its predecessor and it achieved a de facto integration of technical and spatial components. Finally, there was the alignment of third design cycle in the form of a workshop around an assemblage staged at the CHI human–computer interaction conference in Vienna, April 2004.

Notes

2 Design at Work

1. Our fieldwork was carried out at Architekturbüro Rüdiger Lainer in Vienna in the context of several research projects, in particular ESPRIT-LTR Project no. 31.870 Desarte, as well as two national projects—"FLEXSTAND—Flexible Standardization," and "Cooperative Planning." Also, the DFG project "Women in Innovative Companies" (Wagner and Birbaumer 2007) included extensive fieldwork in two architectural offices.

4 On the Objects of Design

1. The constituents of an object can be considered as its *affordances*. James J. Gibson, who introduced the term "affordance" in 1966, explored it more fully in his book *The Ecological Approach to Visual Perception* (1979). He defined affordances as referring to all "action possibilities" latent in the environment for an actor. These action possibilities are objectively measurable, independent of the individual's ability to recognize them but dependent on the capabilities of the actor. Gibson's affordances were appreciated for their relational nature, but they appeared to many scholars as contradictory in joining fuzziness (how can we handle something latent in the environment?) with an objective measure. Donald Norman redefined "affordance" in the domain of interaction design (Norman 1988): "the term *affordance* refers to the perceived and actual properties of the thing, primarily those fundamental properties that determine just how the thing could possibly be used. . . . Affordances provide strong clues to the operations of things. Plates are for pushing. Knobs are for turning. Slots are for inserting things into. Balls are for throwing or bouncing. When affordances are taken advantage of, the user knows what to do just by looking: no picture, label, or instruction needed" (Norman 1988, 9). Norman's definition has also been criticized because in order to overcome the fuzziness of Gibson's definition, it loses any reference to the relational nature of the concept. In this context, we extend the term to deal with the complex, long-lasting (and therefore changing) objects of our experience. We cannot have objects without subjects: the constituents of an object are in fact things considered by the designers as such. A constituent of an object is, therefore, not only a reference to some of the fundamental properties of a thing that determine how people can interact with it (like Norman's affordance), but also a distinct embodiment of possibilities for interacting with the object. Constituents

assume the form of and/or they are supported by a thing, but they are at the same time more or less that thing: more, because the object of which they are constituents gives them a richer sense; less, because it constrains their openness, their irreducibility.

6   Designing as Performing

1. This refers to the Goffmanian view of our performative acting in everyday situations.
2. *Liminoid* derives from the Greek *eidos* and means "like, resembling."

References

Acconci, V. 2001. Some grounds for art as a political model. In *Vito Acconci: Acts of Architectures*, ed. D. Sobel, M. Andrea, S. Kwinter, and V. Acconci, 19. Milwaukee, WI: Milwaukee Art Museum. Originally published 1981.

Acconci, V., and G. Moure. 2001. *Vito Acconci: Writings, Works, Projects*. Barcelona: Polígrafa.

Akin, Ö. 1986. *Psychology of Architectural Design*. London: Pion.

Akrich, M. 1992. The description of technical objects. In *Shaping Technology/Building Society—Studies in Sociotechnical Change*, ed. W. E. Bijker and J. Law, 259–265. Cambridge, MA: MIT Press.

Alexander, C. 1971. The state of the art in design methods. *DMG Newsletter* 5 (3):3–7.

Alexander, C., S. Ishikawa, and M. Silverstein. 1977. *A Pattern Language: Towns, Buildings, Construction*. Oxford: Oxford University Press.

Allen, S., D. Agrest, and S. Ostrow. 2000. *Practice: Architecture, Technology, and Representation*. London: Routledge.

Antonelli, P., ed. 2001. *Workspheres: Design and Contemporary Work Styles*. New York: The Museum of Modern Art.

Appadurai, A., ed. 1986. *The Social Life of Things: Commodities in Cultural Perspective*. Cambridge: Cambridge University Press.

Asplund, J. 2004. *Hur låter åskan?* [What's the sound of thunder?] Göteborg: Bokförlaget Korpen.

Baker, K., D. Ribes, F. Millerand, and G. C. Bowker. 2005. *Interoperability Strategies for Scientific Cyberinfrastructure: Research and Practice*. American Society for Information Systems and Technology Proceedings, ASIST 2005.

Barba, E. [1995] 2002. *The Paper Canoe: A Guide to Theatre Anthropology*. London: Routledge.

Barba, E., and N. Savarese. 1999. *The Secret Art of the Performer: A Dictionary of Theatre Anthropology*. London: Routledge.

Barry, A. 2001. *Political Machines: Governing a Technological society*. London: Athlone.

Beautiful Diversion. 2007. *NextD Journal* 10 (special issue).

Beyer, H., and K. Holzblatt. 1998. *Contextual Design: Defining Customer-Centered Systems*. San Francisco: Morgan Kaufmann.

Biagioli, M. 2000. Janet Cardiff—The missing voice. *Artfocus* 68:12–14.

Binder, T., G. De Michelis, M. Gervautz, G. Iacucci, K. Matkowitc, T. Psik, I. Wagner. 2004. Supporting configurability in a tangible computing environment. *Personal and Ubiquitous Computing Journal* 8 (5):310–325.

Bjerknes, G., P. Ehn, and M. Kyng, eds. 1987. *Computers and Democracy—A Scandinavian Challenge*. Brookville, VT: Avebury.

Björgvinsson, E. 2007. Socio-material mediations: Learning, knowing and self-produced media within healthcare, Doctoral Dissertation Series 2007-03. Karlskrona: Blekinge Institute of Technology.

Björgvinsson, E., P. Ehn, and P.-A. Hillgren. 2010. Participatory design and "democratizing innovation." In *PDC'10: Proceedings of the 11th Biennial Participatory Design Conference*, 41–50. New York: ACM Press.

Borchers, J., S. Fincher, R. Griffiths, L. Pemberton, and E. Siemon. 2001. Usability pattern language: Creating a community. *AI & Society* 15 (4):377–385.

Borgman, A. 1984. *Technology and the Character of Contemporary Life*. Chicago: University of Chicago Press.

Bowker, G. C., and S. L. Star. 2000. *Sorting Things Out: Classification and Its Consequences*. Cambridge, MA: MIT Press.

Brose, H.-G. 2004. An introduction towards a culture of non-simultaneity? *Time & Society* 13 (1):5–26.

Brown, B. 2003. *A Sense of Things*. Chicago: University of Chicago Press.

Brown, B., ed. 2004a. *Things*. Chicago: University of Chicago Press.

Brown, B. 2004b. Thing theory. In *Things*, ed. Bill Brown, 1–22. Chicago: University of Chicago Press.

Brown, J. S., and P. Duguid. 1994. Borderline resources: Social and material aspects of design. *Human–Computer Interaction* 9 (1):3–36.

Brown, T. 2009. *Change by Design: How Design Thinking Transforms Organizations and Inspires Innovation*. New York: HarperCollins.

Bruner, J. S. 1986. *Actual Minds, Possible Worlds*. Cambridge, MA: Harvard University Press.

Bucciarelli, L. L. 1995. *Designing Engineers*. Cambridge, MA: MIT Press.

Buchanan, R. 2001. Design research and the new learning. *Design Issues* 17 (4):3–23.

Büscher, M., M. Christensen, K. M. Hansen, P. Mogensen, and D. Shapiro. 2007. Bottom-up, top-down? Connecting software architecture design with use. In *Configuring User–Designer Relations: Interdisciplinary Perspectives*, ed. A. Voß, M. Hartswood, R. Procter, M. Rouncefield, R. Slack, and M. Büscher. Berlin: Springer Verlag.

Büscher, M., P. Mogensen, D. Shapiro, and I. Wagner. 1999. The Manufaktur: Supporting practice in (landscape) architecture. In Proceedings of the Sixth European Conference on Computer Supported Cooperative Work. Kluwer Academic.

Buur, J., T. Binder, and E. Brandt. 2000. Taking video beyond "hard data" in user centered design. In *Proceedings of Participatory Design Conference*, ed. T. Cherkasky, J. Greenbaum, and P. Mambrey. Palo Alto, CA: Computer Professionals for Social Responsibility (CPSR).

Carlson, M. 1996. *Performance—A Critical Introduction*. London: Routledge.

Casey, E. S. 1997. *The Fate of Place—A Philosophical History*. Berkeley: University of California Press.

Chi, L. 2004. Introduction. *Journal of Architectural Education* 57 (1):5–6.

Ciborra, C. 1999. Notes on improvisation and time in organizations in accounting. *Management and Information Technologies* 9 (2):77–94.

Ciborra, C. 2001. In the mood for knowledge. LSE Department of Information Systems Working Paper 94.

Ciborra, C. 2002. *The Labyrinths of Information: Challenging the Wisdom of Systems*. Oxford: Oxford University Press.

Ciborra, C., and L. Willcocks. 2006. The mind or the heart? It depends on the (definition of) situation. *Journal of Information Technology* 21 (3):129–139.

Ciolfi, L., and L. J. Bannon. 2005. Space, place, and the design of technologically enhanced physical environments. In *Space, Spatiality, and Technology*, ed. P. Turner and E. Davenport. London: Springer.

Clark, B. 2007. Design as Sociopolitical Navigation. Ph.D. thesis. Odense: University of Southern Denmark.

Cornell, P. 1993. *Saker. Om tingens synlighet*. [Quotes translated by Per Linde.] Hedemora: Gidlunds Förlag.

Counsell, C., and L. Wolf. 2001. *Performance Analysis: An Introductory Coursebook*. London: Routledge.

Crabtree, A., T. Hemmings, and T. Rodden. 2002. Pattern-based support for interactive design in domestic settings. In *Proceedings of the 4th Conference on Designing Interactive Systems: Processes, Practices, Methods, and Techniques (DIS 2002)*, 265–276. New York: ACM Press.

Csikszentmihalyi, M. 1997. *Creativity: Flow and the Psychology of Discovery and Invention*. New York: HarperCollins.

Cuff, D. 1992. *Architecture the Story of Practice*. Cambridge, MA: MIT Press.

de Certeau, M. 1984. *The Practice of Everyday Life*. Berkeley: University of California Press.

De Michelis, G. 2006. Community memory as a process: Reflections and indications for design. In *Theories and Practice of Interaction Design*, ed. S. Bagnara and G. Crampton-Smith, 235–247. Mahwah: Erlbaum.

Denzin, N. K. 2003. The call to performance. *Symbolic Interaction* 26 (1):187–207.

Dewey, J. 1927. *The Public and Its Problems*. New York: Henry Holt.

Dewey, J. [1938] 1969. *Logic: The Theory of Inquiry*. New York: Henry Holt.

Dewey, J. [1934] 1980. *Art as Experience*. New York: Berkeley Publishing Group.

Dourish, P. 2001. *Where the Action Is: The Foundations of Embodied Interaction*. Cambridge, MA: MIT Press.

Edwards, K., V. Belotti, and M. W. Newman. 2003. Stuck in the middle: The challenges of user-centered design and evaluation of infrastructure. In *Proceedings Conference on Human Factors in Computing Systems (CHI 2003)*, 297–304. New York: ACM Press.

Ehn, P. 1988. *Work-Oriented Design of Computer Artifacts*. Hillsdale, NJ: Lawrence Erlbaum.

Ehn, P. 1995. Informatics—Design for usability. In *The Infological Equation*, Gothenburg Studies in Information Systems 6, ed. B. Dahlbom. Gothenburg: Gothenburg University.

Ehn, P., and M. Kyng. 1991. Cardboard computers. In *Design at Work: Cooperative Design of Computer Work*, ed. J. Greenbaum and M. Kyng, 169–196. Hillsdale, NJ: Lawrence Erlbaum Associates.

Ehn, P., and D. Sjögren. 1991. From system description to script for action in design at work: Cooperative design of computer systems. In *Design at Work: Cooperative Design of Computer Work*, ed. J. Greenbaum and M. Kyng, 241–268. Hillsdale, NJ: Lawrence Erlbaum.

Fällman, D. 2004. Design-oriented research versus research-oriented design. Workshop Paper, CHI 2004 Workshop on Design and HCI, Conference on Human Factors in Computing Systems, CHI 2004, April 24–29, Vienna, Austria.

Fensel, D. 2003. *Ontologies: A Silver Bullet for Knowledge Management and Electronic Commerce*. 2nd ed. Berlin: Springer Verlag. First published 2001.

Ferraris, M. 2005. *Dove sei? Ontologia del telefonino* [Where are you? Ontology of the cellular phone.] Milano: Bompiani.

Finnegan, R. 2002. *Communicating: The Multiple Modes of Human Interconnection*. London: Routledge.

Fischer, G. 2001. Communities of Interest (CoIs): Learning through the interaction of multiple knowledge systems. In *IRIS (24th Annual Information Systems Research Seminar in Scandinavia)*, 1–14. Bergen: Department of Information Sciences.

Fischer, G., and E. Giaccardi. 2005. Metadesign: A framework for end-user development. In *End User Development: Empowering People to Flexibly Employ Advanced Information and Communication Technology*, ed. H. Lieberman, F. Paternò, and V. Wulf, 427–457. Dordrecht: Kluwer.

Fischer, G., and E. Scharff. 2000. Meta-design—Design for designers. In *Proceedings of the 3rd Conference on Designing Interactive Systems (DIS 2000)*, 396–405. New York: ACM Press.

Fitzpatrick, G. 2002. The locales framework: Making social thinking accessible for software practitioners? In *Social Thinking, Software Practice*, ed. Y. Dittrich, C. Floyd, and R. Klischewski, 141–160. Cambridge, MA: MIT Press.

Fredrickson, L. 1999. Vision and material practice: Vladimir Tatlin and the design of everyday objects. *Design Issues* 15 (1):49–74.

Gaver, B., T. Dunne, and E. Pacenti. 1999. Cultural probes. *Interaction* 6 (1):21–29.

Gedenryd, H. 1998. *How Designers Work—Making Sense of Authentic Cognitive Activities*. Lund University Cognitive Studies 75. Lund: Lund University.

Geertz, C. 1986. Making experiences authoring selves. In *The Anthropology of Experience*, ed. V. W. Turner and E. M. Bruner, 373–380. Urbana: University of Illinois Press.

Gibson, J. J. 1979. *The Ecological Approach to Visual Perception*. Boston: Houghton Mifflin.

Goldberg, R. 2001. *Performance Art from Futurism to the Present*. London: Thames & Hudson.

Goldschmidt, G. 1994. On visual design thinking: The Vis Kids of architecture. *Design Studies* 15 (2):158–174.

Gore, N. 2004. Craft and innovation: Serious play and the direct experience of the real. *Journal of Architectural Education* 58 (1):39–44.

Greenbaum, J., and M. Kyng, eds. 1991. *Design at Work: Cooperative Design of Computer Work*. Hillsdale, NJ: Lawrence Erlbaum.

Gregory, D. 1994. *Geographical Imaginations*. Cambridge, MA: Blackwell.

Gross, M., S. Ervin, J. Anderson, and A. Fleisher. 1988. Constraints: knowledge representation in design. *Design Studies* 9 (3):133–143.

Gstöttner, A., and C. Kappl, et al. 2003. *Open: 24h. Workground—Playground*. Vienna: Edition Selene.

Gurvitch, G. 1964. *The Spectrum of Social Time*. Dordrecht: Reidel.

Habraken, N. J., and M. Gross. 1987. *Concept Design Games (Book One: Developing, Book Two: Playing)*. Report submitted to the National Science Foundation Engineering Directorate. Cambridge, MA: MIT, Department of Architecture.

Haraway, D. 1988. Situated knowledges: The science question in feminism and the privilege of partial perspective. *Feminist Studies* 14 (3):575–599.

Harrison, S., and P. Dourish. 1996. Re-place-ing space: The role of place and space in collaborative systems. In *Proceedings of the 1996 ACM Conference on Computer Supported Cooperative Work*, 67–76. New York: ACM Press.

Heidegger, M. 1971. *Poetry, Language, Thought*. Trans. Albert Hofstadter. New York: Harper & Row.

Henderson, K. 1999. *On Line and On Paper: Visual Representations, Visual Culture, and Computer Graphics in Design Engineering*. Cambridge, MA: MIT Press.

Henderson, A., and M. Kyng. 1991. There is no place like home—continuing design in use. In *Design at Work: Cooperative Design of Computer Work*, ed. J. Greenbaum and M. Kyng, 219–240. Hillsdale, NJ: Lawrence Erlbaum.

Hillgren, P.-A. 2006. *Ready-Made-Media-Actions: Lokal produktion och användning av audiovisuella medier inom hälso-och sjukvården*. Blekinge Institute of Technology.

Hogue, M. 2004. The site as project: Lessons from land art and conceptual art. *Journal of Architectural Education* 58 (1):54–61.

Iacucci, G., K. Kuutti, and M. Ranta. 2000. On the move with a magic thing: Role playing in concept design of mobile services and devices. In *Proceeding of DIS2000, Designing Interactive Systems*, 193–202. New York: ACM Press.

Iacucci, G., C. Iacucci, and K. Kuutti. 2002. Imagining and experiencing in design, the role of performances. In *Proceedings of the Second Nordic Conference on Human–Computer Interaction*, 167–176. New York: ACM Press.

Iacucci, G., and K. Kuutti. 2002. Everyday life as a stage in creating and performing scenarios for wireless devices. *Personal and Ubiquitous Computing* 6 (4):299–306.

Ingold, T. 2000. *The Perception of the Environment: Essays on Livelihood, Dwelling, and Skill*. London: Routledge.

Ishii, H., and B. Ullmer. 1997. Tangible bits: Towards seamless interfaces between people, bits, and atoms. In *Proceedings of the SIGCHI Conference on Human Factors in Computing Systems*, 234–241. New York: ACM Press.

Iwamoto, L. 2004. Translations: Fabricating space. *Journal of Architectural Education* 58 (1):35–38.

Jacucci, C. 2006. Guiding design with approaches to masked performance. *Interacting with Computers* 18 (5):1032–1054.

Jacucci, C., G. Jacucci, et al. 2005. A manifesto for the performative development of ubiquitous media. In *Proceedings of the 4th Decennial Converence on Critical Computing: Between Sense and Sensibility*, 19–28. New York: ACM Press.

Jacucci, G. 2004. Interaction as Performance: Cases of configuring physical interfaces in mixed media. Doctoral Thesis, University of Oulu, Acta Universitatis Ouluensis.

Jacucci, G., and M. Isomursu. 2004. Facilitated and performed "Happenings" as resources in ubiquitous computing design. *Digital Creativity* 15 (4):223–231.

Jacucci, G., P. Linde, and I. Wagner. 2005. Exploring relationships between learning, artifacts, physical space, and computing. *Digital Creativity* 16 (1):19–30.

Jacucci, G., and I. Wagner. 2005. Performative uses of space in mixed media environments. In *Spaces, Spatiality, and Technologies*, ed. E. Davenport and P. Turner. London: Springer.

Jacucci, G., and I. Wagner. 2007. Performative roles of materiality for collective creativity. In *Proceedings of the Sixth ACM SIGCHI Conference on Creativity & Cognition 2007*, 73–82. New York: ACM Press.

Jégou, F., and E. Manzini. 2008. *Collaborative Services: Social Innovation and Design for Sustainability*. Milan: Poli Design.

Jones, J. C. 1984. Continuous design and redesign. In J. C. Jones, *Essays in Design*. New York: John Wiley.

Junk, R., and N. R. Müllert. 1981. *Zukunjfrtwerkstätten—Wege zur Wiederbelebung der Demokratie*.

Karasti, H., and K. Baker. 2004. Infrastructuring for the long-term: Ecological information management. Hawaii International Conference on System Sciences, January 5–8, 2004, Hawaii.

Karasti, H., and K. Baker. 2008. Community design: Growing one's own information infrastructure. In *Proceedings of the Tenth Conference on Participatory Design*. October 1–4, 2008, Bloomington, Indiana, CPSR. New York: ACM Press.

Koestler, A. [1964] 1990. *The Act of Creation*. New York: Macmillan.

Koulamata (A. Chan). 2005. *The French Democracy* (film). Available at <http://www.archive.org/details/thefrenchdemocracy>.

Kourik, R. 1998. *The Lavender Garden: Beautiful Varieties to Grow and Gather*. San Francisco: Chronicle Books.

Krippendorf, K. 1995. Redesigning design: An invitation to a responsible future. In *Design—Pleasure or Responsibility?* ed. P. Tahkokaido and S. Vihms, 138–162. Helsinki: University of Art and Design.

Krippendorf, K. 2006. *The Semantic Turn: A New Foundation for Design*. Boca Raton, FL: Taylor & Francis Group.

Kuutti, K., G. Iacucci, and C. Iacucci. 2002. Acting to know: Improving creativity in the design of mobile services by using performances. In Proceedings of the Fourth Conference on Creativity & Cognition, 95–102. New York: ACM Press.

Lainer, R., and I. Wagner. 1998a. Connecting qualities of social use with spatial qualities: Cooperative buildings—integrating information, organization, and architecture. In *Proceedings of the First International Workshop on Cooperative Buildings (CoBuild'98)*, ed. Norbert Streitz et al., 191–203. Heidelberg: Springer.

Lainer, R., and I. Wagner. 1998b. Offenes Planen: Erweiterung der Lösungsräume für architektonisches Entwerfen. *Architektur & BauForum* 196:327–336.

Lainer, R., and I. Wagner. 2000. Silent architecture—Narrative technology. *Digital Creativity* 11 (3):144–155.

Larssen, A. T., T. Robertson, and J. Edwards. 2007. The feel dimension of technology interaction: Exploring tangibles through movement and touch. In *Proceedings of TEI'07*, 271–278. New York: ACM Press.

Latour, B. 1999. *Pandora's Hope: Essays on the Reality of Science Studies*. Cambridge, MA: Harvard University Press.

Latour, B. 2004. *Politics of Nature*. Cambridge, MA: Harvard University Press.

Latour, B. 2005. Trains of thought: The fifth dimension of time and its fabrication. In *Thinking Time: A Multidisciplinary Perspective on Time*, ed. A.-N. Perret-Clermont, 173–187. Göttingen: Hogrefe & Huber.

Latour, B., and P. Weibel, eds. 2005. *Making Things Public: Atmospheres of Democracy* (Catalog of the Exhibition at ZKM—Center for Art and Media—Karlsruhe, March 20–October 30, 2005). Cambridge, MA: MIT Press.

Laurel, B. 1993. *Computers as Theatre*. Boston: Addison-Wesley.

Lave, J. 1988. *Cognition in Practice: Mind, Mathematics, and Culture in Everyday Life*. Cambridge: Cambridge University Press.

Lave, J. 1993. The practice of learning. In *Understanding Practice: Perspectives on Activity and Context*, ed. S. Chaiklin and J. Lave, 3–32. Cambridge: Cambridge University Press.

Lave, J., and E. Wenger. 1991. *Situated Learning and Legitimate Peripheral Participation*. Cambridge: Cambridge University Press.

Law, J. 1986. On the methods of long distance control: Vessels, navigation, and the Portuguese route to India. In *Power, Action, and Belief: A New Sociology of Knowledge?* ed. J. Law, 23–63. London: Routledge.

Law, J. 1999. After ANT: Complexity, naming, and topology. In *Actor Network Theory and After*, ed. J. Law and J. Hassard, 1–14. Oxford: Blackwell.

Law, J. 2000. Notes on the theory of the actor-network: Ordering, strategy and heterogeneity. In *Organisational Studies: Critical Perspectives*, vol. 2: *Objectivity and Its Other*, ed. Warwick Organisational Behaviour Staff, 853–868. London: Routledge.

Law, J., and A. Mol. 2001. Situating technoscience: An inquiry into spatialities. *Environment and Planning. D, Society & Space* 19 (5):609–621.

Lawson, B. 2004. Schemata, gambits, and precedent: Some factors in design expertise. *Design Studies* 25 (5):443–457.

Leadbeater, C. 2007. *We-Think*. London: Profile Books.

Lee, C. 2007. Boundary negotiating artifacts: Unbinding the routine of boundary objects and embracing chaos. *Computer Supported Cooperative Work* 16 (3):307–339.

Louridas, P. 1999. Design as bricolage: Anthropology meets design thinking. *Design Studies* 20 (6):517–535.

Löwgren, J. 2005. Inspirational patterns for embodied interaction. knowledge. *Technology and Policy.* 20 (3):165–177.

Löwgren, J., and E. Stolterman. 2004. *Thoughtful Interaction: A Design Perspective on Information Technology.* Cambridge, MA: MIT Press.

Lowood, H. 2008. Found technology: Players as innovators in the making of Machinima. In *Digital Youth, Innovation, and the Unexpected,* ed. T. McPherson, 165–196. The John D. and Catherine T. MacArthur Foundation Series on Digital Media and Learning. Cambridge, MA: MIT Press.

Lozano-Hemmer, R. 1997. *Displaced Emperors, Relational Architecture 2.* Linz: Ars Electronica.

Maquil, V., T. Psik, I. Wagner, and M. Wagner. 2007. Expressive interactions supporting collaboration in urban design. In *Proceedings of the 2007 International ACM Conference on Supporting Group Work, GROUP 2007,* 69–78. New York: ACM Press.

Marres, N. 2005. Issues spark a public into being. In *Making Things Public: Atmospheres of Democracy* (Catalog of the Exhibition at ZKM—Center for Art and Media—Karlsruhe, March 20–October 30, 2005), ed. B. Latour and P. Weibel, 208–217. Cambridge, MA: MIT Press.

Mau, B. 2004. *Massive Change: A Manifesto on the Future of Design Culture.* London: Phaidon, Institute Without Boundaries.

McCullough, M. 2004. *Digital Ground: Architecture, Pervasive Computing and Environmental Knowing.* Cambridge, MA: MIT Press.

McGown, A., G. Green, and P. A. Rodgers. 1998. Visible ideas: Information patterns of conceptual sketch activity. *Design Studies* 19 (4):431–453.

McKee, R. 1997. *Story: Substance, Structure, Style, and the Principles of Screenwriting.* New York: HarperCollins.

Merleau-Ponty, M. 1962. *Phenomenology of Perception.* London: Routledge.

Mitchell, W. J. T. 1994. *Picture Theory: Essays on Verbal and Visual Representation.* Chicago: University of Chicago Press.

Mondada, L. 2008. Using video for a sequential and multimodal analysis of social interaction: Videotaping institutional telephone calls. *Forum Qualitative Sozial Forschung* 9 (3):39. <http://nbn-resolving.de/urn:nbn:de:0114-fqs0803390>.

Moreno, S. 2002. Rewriting the museum. *Frame Magazine* 24:116–127.

Mori, T. 2002. *Immaterial/Ultramaterial: Architecture, Design, and Materials.* New York: Harvard Design School/George Braziller.

Mouffe, C. 2000. *The Democratic Paradox*. London: Verso.

Murray, R., J. Caulier-Grice, and G. Mulgan. 2010. *The Open Book of Social Innovation*. London: The Young Foundation.

MVRDV. 1999. *Metacity/Datatown*. Amsterdam: 01 Publishers.

Nardi, B. A. 1993. *A Small Matter of Programming. Perspectives on End User Computing*. Cambridge, MA: MIT Press.

Nelson, H. G., and E. Stolterman. 2003. *The Design Way—Intentional Change in an Unpredictable World*. Englewood Cliffs, NJ: Educational Technology Publications.

Norman, D. A. 1988. *The Psychology of Everyday Things*. New York: Basic Books.

Norman, D. A., and S. W. Draper, eds. 1986. *User Centered System Design: New Perspectives on Human–Computer Interaction*. Hillsdale, NJ: Lawrence Erlbaum.

Nussbaum, B. 2007. Are designers the enemy of design?—The reaction. <http://www.business-week.com/innovate/NussbaumOnDesign/archives/2007/03/are_designers_t.html#trackback>.

Nussbaum, B. 2009. The World Economic Forum: Lost ina fog. A design manifesto for Davos. <http://www.businessweek.com/innovate/NussbaumOnDesign/archives/2009/01/a_design_manife .html>.

Ormerud, F., and R. Ivanic. 2002. Materiality in children's meaning-making practices. *Visual Communication* 1 (1):69–91.

Östman, L. E. 2005. *A Pragmatist Theory of Design*. Stockholm: School of Architecture, Royal Institute of Technology.

Pawson, J. 1996. *Minimum*. New York: Phaidon.

Pedersen, J. 2007. Protocols of research and design. Ph.D. thesis. Copenhagen: IT University.

Pipek, V., and V. Wulf. 2009. Infrastructuring: Toward an integrated perspective on the design and use of information technology. *Journal of the Association for Information Systems* 10 (5).

Ponge, F. 1972. *The Voice of Things*. New York: McGraw-Hill.

Ponge, F. 2000. *The Nature of Things*. New York: Red Dust.

Polany, M. 1983. *The Tacit Dimension*. Gloucester, MA: Peter Smith.

Projekt ≥Multi Mind. 2000. *Kunst+Technik, Berlin 1999*. ARCH+ 152/153.

Purcell, T., and J. Gero. 1998. Drawings and the design process. *Design Studies* 19 (4):389–430.

Randall, D. W., R. Harper, and M. Rouncefield. 2007. *Fieldwork for Design: Theory and Practice*. London: Springer.

Redström, J. 2001. Designing everyday computational things. Gothenburg Studies in Informatics, no. 20.

Redström, J. 2008. Re:definitions of use. *Design Studies* 29 (4):410–423.

Rekimoto, J. 1997. Pick-and-drop: A direct manipulation technique for multiple computer environments. In *Proceedings of the 10th annual ACM Symposium on User Interface Software and Technology*. New York: ACM Press.

Rittel, H., and M. Webber. 1973. Dilemmas in a general theory of planning. *Policy Sciences* 4:155–169.

Robertson, T. 2002. The public availability of actions and artefacts. *Computer Supported Cooperative Work* 11 (3–4):299–316.

Rodaway, P. 1994. *Sensuous Geographies: Body, Sense, and Place*. New York: Routledge.

Rogan, B. 1992. Artefacts—Source material or research objects in contemporary ethnology? *Ethnologia Scandinavica* 22:105–117.

Rowe, C., and F. Koetter. 1978. *Collage City*. Cambridge, MA: MIT Press.

Sanders, E. 2001. Virtuosos of the experience domain. In *Proceedings of the 2001 IDSA Education Conference*, <http://www.sonicrim.com/red/us/pub.html>.

Sanders, E., and U. Dandavate. 1999. Designing for experiencing: New tools. In *Proceedings of the First International Conference on Design & Emotion*, ed. Kees Overbeeke and Paul Hekkert, 87–92. Delft: Department of Industrial Design.

Sawyer, K. R. 1998. The interdisciplinary study of creativity in performance. *Creativity Research Journal* 11 (1):11–19.

Sawyer, K. R. 1999. The emergence of creativity. *Philosophical Psychology* 12 (4):447–469.

Schieffelin, E. 1997. Problematizing performance. In *Ritual, Performance, Media*, ed. F. Hughes-Freeland, 194–207. London: Routledge.

Schmatz, F. 1998. Büro exemplarisch, verdichtet. In *Work and Culture—Büro. Eine Inszenierung von Arbeit*, ed. H. Lachmayer and E. Louis, 191–198. Klagenfurt: Ritter Verlag.

Schmidt, K., and L. Bannon. 1992. Taking CSCW seriously: Supporting articulation work. *Computer Supported Cooperative Work: The Journal of Collaborative Computing* 1 (1):7–40.

Schmidt, K., and I. Wagner. 2004. Ordering systems: Coordinative practices and artefacts in architectural design and planning. *Computer Supported Cooperative Work* 13 (5/6):349–408.

Schön, D. A. 1983. *The Reflective Practitioner*. New York: Basic Books.

Schön, D. A. 1987. *Educating the Reflective Practitioner*. San Francisco: Jossey-Bass.

Schutz, A. 1982. *Life Forms and Meaning Structure*. London: Routledge.

Shaviro, S. 1993. *The Cinematic Body*. Minneapolis: University of Minneapolis Press.

Simon, H. A. 1976. *The Sciences of the Artificial*. Cambridge, MA: MIT Press.

Simon, H. A. 1996. *The Sciences of the Artificial*, 3rd. ed. Cambridge, MA: MIT Press.

Sobchack, V. 2004. What my fingers knew: The cinesthetic subject, or Vision in the flesh: Carnal thoughts. In *Embodiment and Moving Image Culture*, ed. V. Sobchack, 53–84. Berkeley: University of California Press.

Stafford, B. 1996. *Good Looking*. Cambridge, MA: MIT Press.

Star, S. L. 1989. The structure of ill-structured solutions: Boundary objects and heterogeneous distributed problem solving. In *Distributed Artificial Intelligence*, vol. 2, ed. L. Gasser and M. Huhns, 37–54. San Francisco: Morgan Kaufmann.

Star, S. L., and G. C. Bowker. 2002. How to infrastructure. In *The Handbook of New Media*, ed. L. A. Lievrouw and S. M. Livingstone, 151–162. London: Sage.

Star, S. L., and K. Ruhleder. 1996. Steps toward an ecology of infrastructure: Design and access for large information spaces. *Information Systems Research* 7 (1):111–134.

Suchman, L. 1987. *Plans and Situated Actions: The Problem of Human–Machine Communication*. Cambridge: Cambridge University Press.

Suchman, L. 2002. Located accountabilities in technology production. *Scandinavian Journal of Information Systems* 14 (2):91–105.

Suwa, M., and B. Tversky. 1997. What do architects and students perceive in their design sketches? A protocol analysis. *Design Studies* 18 (4):385–403.

Tomes, A., C. Oates, and P. Armstrong. 1998. Talking design: Negotiating the verbal-visual translation. *Design Studies* 19 (2):127–142.

Tonkinwise, C. 2005. Is design finished? Dematerialisation and changing things. In *Design Philosophy Papers*, ed. AnneMarie Willis, 2/2005: 20–30.

Tschumi, B. 1994. *Event Cities (Praxis)*. Cambridge, MA: MIT Press.

Tuan, Y.-F. 1990. Space and context. In *By Means of Performance, Intercultural Studies of Theater and Ritual*, ed. R. Schechner and W. Appel, 236–244. Cambridge: Cambridge University Press.

Turkle, S. 1997. *Life on the Screen: Identity in the Age of the Internet*. New York: Simon & Schuster.

Turner, V. W. 1982. *From Ritual to Theatre: The Human Seriousness of Play*. New York: PAJ Publications.

Turner, V. W. 1986. Dewey, Dilthey, and drama: An essay in the anthropology of experience. In *The Anthropology of Experience*, ed. V. W. Turner and E. M. Bruner, 33–42. Urbana: University of Illinois Press.

Turner, V. W. 1987. *The Anthropology of Performance*. New York: PAJ Publications.

Turner, V. W., and E. M. Bruner, eds. 1986. *The Anthropology of Experience*. Urbana: University of Illinois Press.

Twidale, M., and I. Floyd. 2008. Infrastructures from the bottom-up and the top-down: Can they meet in the middle? In *Proceedings of the 11th Participatory Design Conference*, October 1–4, 2008. New York: ACM Press.

van Gennep, A. 2004. The Rites of Passage. London: Routledge.

von Busch, O. 2008. *Fashion-able: Hacktivism and Engaged Fashion Design.* University of Gothenburg.

Wagner, I. 2000. Persuasive artefacts in architectural design and planning. In *Proceedings of CoDesigning*, 379–390. Nottingham, September 2000.

Wagner, I. 2004. "Open Planning"—A reflection on methods and innovative work practices in architecture. In *Managing as Designing*, ed. F. Collopy and R. J. Boland, Jr., 153–163. Stanford: Stanford University Press.

Wagner, I., and M. Basile, et al. 2009. Supporting Community Engagement in the City: Urban Planning in the MR-Tent. In *Proceedings of the Fourth international Conference on Communities and Technologies*, C&T 2009, 185–194. New York: ACM Press.

Wagner, I., and A. Birbaumer. 2007. Les femmes cadres dans les entreprises innovantes. *Travail, Genre et Sociétés* 17:49–77.

Wagner, I., and R. Lainer. 2002. Designing a visual 3D interface—A reflection on methods. *Interaction* IX (6):12–19.

Ward, T., R. Finke, and S. M. Smith. 1995. *Creativity and the Mind.* New York: Plenum.

Weiser, M. 1999. The computer for the 21st century. *ACM SIGMOBILE Mobile Computing and Communications Review* 3 (3):3–11.

Wenger, E. 1998. *Communities of Practice: Learning, Meaning, and Identity.* Cambridge: Cambridge University Press.

Winograd, T., and F. Flores. 1986. *Understanding Computers and Cognition—A New Foundation for Design.* Norwood, NJ: Ablex.

Wittgenstein, L. 1953. *Philosophical Investigations.* Oxford: Blackwell.

Wulf, V., V. Pipek, and M. Won. 2008. Component-based tailorability: Enabling highly flexible software applications. *International Journal of Human–Computer Studies* 66 (1):1–22.

Yaneva, A. 2005. Scaling up and down: Extraction rrials in architectural design. *Social Studies of Science* 35 (6):867–894.

Zschokke, W. 1999. *Rüdiger Lainer: Urbanism, Buildings, Projects, 1984–1999.* Basel: Birkhäuser.

Index

ROCK N ROLL WILL ONLY BREAK YOUR HEART

Kenward Cooper

Here's my disclaimer. This is a work of nonfiction. This shit happened. It is not intended to cause harm to anyone. Detailed herein are events and experiences truthfully remembered by the author to the best of his abilities. Some dialogue may have been supplemented. If your ass has been called out in these pages, own it. If you choose to deny it, take a good look in the mirror and ask why you're lying to yourself. Some names have been changed and the surnames of some individuals have been omitted to respect their privacy.:

Cover by Rick Caballo
Cover photography © Safi Alia Shabaik
Interior design by KUHN Design Group

ISBN-13: 979-8-9862343-0-4 (hardcover)
ISBN-13: 979-8-9862343-1-1 (paperback)
ISBN-13: 979-8-9862343-2-8 (e-book)

In a Big Country
Words and Music by Stuart Adamson, Mark Brzezicki, Tony Butler, and Bruce Watson Copyright © 1983 Big Country Music Ltd.
All Rights Administered by BMG Rights Management (US) LLC
All Rights Reserved, Used by Permission
Reprinted by permission of Hal Leonard LLC

For LC

CONTENTS

❖

PREFACE

I've been told I choose my words carefully. In my youth, shyness could get the best of me, though. Music gave me a voice box. Something to talk about with my friends, something to identify with and immerse myself in. Being a fan of bands led me to want to interview bands and to pick up a guitar and make songs of my own. How much easier it was to speak through lyrics. I've been at fault in conversations where I have zoned out, preoccupied with thoughts of music. Girlfriends have hated me for this.

My life has been a song and dance of chasing dreams.

There have been countless times when I've told stories to someone about certain events I've lived, and what typically follows is the same reply, "You should write a book." In theory it sounds good. I've read a library full of rock n roll autobiographies to know how it's done. Every book on my shelf is rock n roll related, with the exception of Taschen's *The Big Book of Pussy*, but I'm not about to defend that one. I've always had the feeling, though, that a memoir is something one writes at the height or at the end of their career. I'm not in either of those brackets, but I'm all for breaking the rules and making one of my own.

INTRODUCTION

My ex-wife called. I didn't answer. A text came through an hour later, *I hope you're well and that I have the right number.* It's been three years since we last spoke. Nineteen since getting divorced. Too much bullshit came between us. Talking about the past and what might've been and should've been is not what I want to do right now. A discussion that undoubtedly will circle back to the days of playing and writing music together, and why we didn't get signed.

It's the middle of a pandemic, the coronavirus has everyone everywhere on lockdown. Maybe I should tell her I'm still alive. The phone rings again. I pick up. It's my friend Jimmy (Thrill) Quill. He's a fellow musician who knows about close calls and missed opportunities but always finds a way to stay creative. We relate to each other. He's a successful realtor, instrumental in nudging me to choose the same pathway in selling residential properties. When he asks what else I've been up to during this time, I divulge a music project I was working on and how it just fell apart. I say how I was trying to motivate the other members, that if we couldn't be in the same room together, we could still be active, build up our web presence, social media.

It backfired. Jimmy summed it up easily. "It's a broken system. Musicians don't know how they're going to do what they once did anymore. And you're still the guy who believes."

This is true. I've been a believer since I was a kid that I'd be doing all the things I ever imagined. No one gave me the instructions on how to start a magazine, but I launched one anyway. When you're twelve years old, anything seems possible. A few years later I had my first band and we were sitting in front of A&R people at Atlantic and Geffen. There were chance encounters with respected artists who offered contracts of their own. A marriage that ended because of an affair, which stung even more when that guy went on to hit the big time. Copyright infringement lawsuits. But it doesn't stop there.

Some people would have given up. If life is a test, I've been tested. If it's a game, I'm still playing. When passionate about something, keep it going. I don't know of a switch for turning on and off desire. There have been moments where perhaps the cover page changed, yet the narrative has stayed the same. As I get closer to my golden jubilee milestone, I know there will be other challenges, but I'm ready to keep furthering this adventure along.

1

SELL THE HOUSE

It was 1987, I was fourteen and had the bug in me about living in LA. What fueled it was having this obsession with music and being aware of all the bands and the scene that was happening on the Sunset Strip. I was buying every rock magazine on the planet. Most of what I was reading about and listening to at the time had one thing in common—Hollywood. It seemed if you wanted to do something, make your mark, that was the place to be.

A family vacation driving from our home in Las Vegas to Los Angeles was an easy trip, and one we would usually take once a year. This particular time, instead of just being content with the swimming pool at the Comstock Hotel, I was on a mission. It involved going to a shop on Hollywood Boulevard called British Imports. They specialized in rock n roll paraphernalia, concert T-shirts, posters, photographs, buttons, stage wear. I got myself a shiny zebra-patterned blazer. What happened next as I was about to exit the store was amazing. I noticed stacks of newspaper print magazines that were entirely dedicated to the local music scene. Best of all, they were FREE! Alongside that was a sea of flyers for bands promoting their upcoming gigs. Every single band, from one to the next, looked beyond cool, like they were already stars. I swooped it all up and learned about bands like Guns N' Roses, Jane's Addiction, Faster Pussycat, well before their debut records hit the shelves. The excitement of finding new music is something I can only describe as being comparable to when you're a kid walking into a candy store and you discover all the colorful boxes of treats. You just want to devour it all. For me, music is that, just another kind of sugar high.

The beauty of this newfound glory was all the unsigned bands listed their phone numbers in free music magazines. They called it a hotline back then. *BAM Magazine* was one of those free papers. Half of it, I'm not kidding, was filled with advertisements for clubs and tons more bands promoting their shows. Like the yellow pages for rock n roll.

I devised a plan right then and there that I would call every hotline number and request that they send me their demo. I wanted to hear all this stuff, and I wanted others to know about it. I named my publication *Rockstar Magazine*.

The phone call would start with a simple introduction; I stated my name, company, followed by how I'd like to review the band in our next issue and possibly do a future interview. I made it seem like the magazine was already established or in circulation. Some would question it or say, "Never heard of it," though most of them didn't. If the band was driven, they'd go for it. If they had a manager, they'd have them send a press kit. There was no shortage of submissions.

I'd started another magazine two years earlier, after subscribing to an international rock mag, which had a classified section in the back pages that featured other fans who made their own zines, appropriately called fanzines. I purchased a couple to see what it was all about. When I saw how basic, yet cool, these fanzines were, I put plans in motion to do my own. I wrote letters to the same bands that were interviewed in these other rags, received their demo tapes, and I was on my way. I called it *Raging Death*. Specializing in thrash/speed metal/punk.

One of the bands I featured was Righteous Pigs, from my hometown. The guitar player, Mitch Harris, would call me and sometimes ask to come over. I found this odd. I didn't let him. He would say, "Why, would your parents freak out?" I said, "Yeah, probably." He was only three years older than me, but with crazy long-ass hair down to his waist, I was convinced he looked like a criminal and would be trouble. Not long after, Mitch joined the band Napalm Death and continues to be a master of his genre.

Thrash metal was a moment for me. I don't like to use the word *phase* because that sounds temporary with no chance of cycling back again. And music isn't a phase. It's a mood. Just because you haven't listened to something in X amount of years doesn't mean you won't enjoy it again next time around.

I went to the last Slayer show ever, at the LA Forum on November 30, 2019. It felt full circle. But when you grow up on AM/FM radio and loving Top 40 hits, that part of you never leaves you. Even during my *Raging Death* days, I was listening to pop and rock records. I just couldn't tell Mitch, or my door might've been knocked down and met with a grindcore ass whooping. So as I was discovering new bands with more melodic sensibility, *Rockstar Magazine* began to take shape.

The phone bill was enormous. I remember telling my dad that I was going to make some long-distance calls to record companies and bands to request promo materials. He was okay with this. After the first month, he came to me with bill in hand and said with a puzzled look, "Ken, two hundred dollars?" I think him seeing the work in front of me and that I was banging away on this beat-up typewriter reassured him that what I was doing was legit. Any time after that when he would see me on the phone he would just say, "I hope it's not long distance." I'd put my hand over the receiver, shake my head, mouthing the word *no*. Eventually I outdid myself, racking up bills that would double the amount of that first bill. I was interviewing bands now and these calls could last an hour or longer.

I began planting the seed in my parents' ears about how we needed to move to LA. My brother, Scott, also added his weight. He was interested in acting so of course this move made sense to him as well. At the rate I was going, I'm sure the thought of my long-distance calls becoming local free calls was appealing to Mom and Dad. Being the supportive parents they were and wanting the best for their children, they gave in. I believe it was only several months from first talking about it until the house went up for sale and sold.

2

BACK WHEN

Vegas was a cool city to grow up in. We lived a few blocks away from Wayne Newton's Casa de Shenandoah. At that time the area was underdeveloped. Green Valley was mostly desert. I would cut through the dirt to get to my friend Cole's house. He always had junk food. It wasn't to be found in my house. My mom, Lissa, brought us up on health foods. She would make everything from scratch. Her own ice cream, which was delicious when it just came out of the maker, but leave it in the freezer after that and it would turn into a block of ice. Breads, muffins, carrot cakes. The best was when she got a dehydrator and would make us natural beef jerky using flank steak. She didn't believe in preservatives and nitrates and all the ingredients you'd find in store-bought packages. Her recipe was salt, paprika, and red pepper. It was a hit with everyone who tried it.

Mom was a stay-at-home mother. Packing lunches, driving my brother and me to and from school and any activities that followed afterwards. It was a pleasure for her. Not always for me if I opened the brown paper sack only to find a plain cheese sandwich, just a couple slices of cheddar on dry bread. To her credit she didn't want it to get soggy, knowing it would be sitting in my locker for hours before consumption. If I wasn't hungry, my friend Jerry would eat it. He was happy to have anything. Usually I'd see him dipping someone's leftover fries into whatever ranch dressing was still on the table.

He told me I was lucky to get a packed lunch. I understood where he was coming from. I knew I was fortunate.

On one occasion, my fifth-grade teacher, Ms. Kaufman, organized a Bring Your Parent to School day, which one student would participate in each week. At lunchtime, my mom came to join me in the classroom, while the other kids were on break in the cafeteria. Mom was wearing a faux-fur coat and holding a bag full of home-baked goods as she waited outside the doorway for the students to make their exit. One girl gushed, "Is your mom wearing a mink?! She looks like a celebrity!" I chuckled, how right she was.

Both my parents had a certain sophistication. Dad always looked handsome and wore tailored suits. What's more amazing is I have some of his old threads, and to this day they fit me like a glove.

When my mom met my dad, Lenn, in New York City, they were both involved in the arts. She was a singer and a dancer, while he was a singer and a graphic designer. They found each other at the train station. Lissa had put a coin in a gumball machine, but it got stuck. After she walked away, Lenn put another coin in to retrieve the gumball and went to give it to her. My mom joked that he got her for a penny.

My father designed the logo for the Folklore Center in Manhattan. The owner, Izzy Young, also gave him the work task of designing flyers to promote an upcoming show in the early 1960s for a singer by the name of Bob Dylan, who was working on his songs in the back room.

Dad could've been a recording star. He had a voice that was so smooth and wonderful. He took rejection too personal, though. One vocal coach told him that the world didn't need another Tony Bennett. A lame remark, considering Bennett's voice was gravely, Dad's was like butter. Someone else told him to just get a guitar and do what Trini Lopez was doing. In the sixties when one could walk into a record company without an appointment, he did just that. Meeting with John Hammond, the A&R man who signed Dylan to CBS/Columbia Records. Hammond listened to the demo, providing his feedback that my dad should ditch the country style and come back when he had something that represented his true sound. He never went back.

Mom was performing at the Taft Hotel in New York City as a belly dancer; her stage name was Zahara. When a columnist for the *New York Post* named Earl Wilson spotted her, he became an immediate fan and supporter. Every day he would write up something about Zahara. When he introduced himself, he grabbed her around the back, cupping his hands over her breasts, and asked if he could hold them.

"No you may not," she replied, and quickly his hands dropped. He said, "Zahara, I have a lot of respect for you. I know a producer in Hollywood I'm going to call, but you may not get anything because you're not the type to do what they expect you to do."

After that incident, my dad was given the title of manager, and he represented her, booking Zahara in other hotels throughout New York City, as well as the Catskills. In 1966 she would get hired on various photo shoots, one of them was an album cover for The Cosmopolitan Chorale's *Armenian Songs*.

When I found the record in the collection as a kid, I was in wonderment. *How's it possible my mom is on the cover, is she a singer, she made a record?* A similar occurrence happened when I discovered a 45 my dad had recorded of a song called "Mimi." It was a catchy, upbeat tune that I loved to play. When Mom told me it was Dad singing, I played it even more, often a few times back to back, every day, until it was completely scratched up.

In '68, Mom became pregnant for the first time. Her doctor gave her the referral to have the baby at a Catholic hospital that was two blocks away from where my parents lived. My dad's sister, Jeanie, had thoughts of her own, and maybe her being the older sibling, he listened. She suggested Mount Sinai based on the fact that Barbra Streisand had had her son there. My dad thought that was a great idea.

On the date of delivery, in the evening hours, the nurse announced that my father would have to leave because the baby wouldn't come until the morning. Without him there, my mom felt frightened. A nurse informed her that she would strap her down to prevent her from getting up at night or risking falling and inadvertently hurting herself and the baby. The ward she was in was filled up with other expecting mothers, all with their curtains drawn, but they left hers uncovered.

She was in the stirrups all night, with her arms tied above her head. Frightened by this occurrence, she couldn't scream at first as her labor pains increased. When her voice finally projected a sound, a patient next to her heard this and yelled out, "This lady's in trouble, help her!" The nurse hurried to untie her, instructing her not to push. In the delivery room, she could hear them saying the umbilical cord was wrapped around the baby's neck. The baby girl did not survive. Despite the claims of trauma my mom went through, my dad didn't believe holding the hospital liable would do them any good.

With this heartbreaking experience, NYC was not where they wanted to be anymore. My father resented his sister for having suggested Mount Sinai. He complained that he couldn't breathe from all the anxiety. An article in a newspaper spurred their decision to go West. Apparently it alleged that Howard Hughes was giving away free money to anyone who came to Las Vegas.

My mom went along with this gullible notion. By the time they drove cross–country, she was pregnant again. Lenn had in mind that he would take another shot at singing. He was still receiving royalty checks from Headliners, a company he'd designed typefaces for. Therefore, he could afford to focus on a music career without worrying about income, eventually securing a gig at the Las Vegas Country Club. In attendance one day was Ed Sullivan, the television personality who'd introduced the Beatles to America. Before my dad went into his next song, Sullivan requested that he repeat the same one again, and then once more after that. Dad sang the song "It's Impossible" three times in a row because the man liked it so much. It's a shame the legendary host no longer had his TV show at the time. He did, however, write about Lenn Cooper in a newspaper column when he returned to New York.

Performing at the Country Club lasted for a year. Dad recognized there was a lack of advertising and graphic art studios in Vegas, so he formed his own. The business grew quickly and soon acquired a clientele ranging from

TV stations to politicians to hotels and casinos. This gave him an opportunity to produce his own show at the Marina Hotel.

Lenn Cooper's New Faces featured up-and-comers, one of whom was the comedian Gallagher.

The perks of having accounts with hotels seemed like a treat in those younger years. Dad would take the family on the weekends so we could use the swimming pools. The choices of restaurants to have lunch at were plenty, and he would just sign for whatever we ordered. What a luxury, I thought. Back then it felt like an event just to go to the hotels. People would dress up. It seemed there was a sense of class. I'm pretty sure this is why to this day I love staying in hotels.

It was cool to see Dad's work everywhere. Logos he'd designed, posters and billboards. A particular favorite is still being used today, one he did when he first started out in New York. It's for Joyva, the caricature of a man wearing a turban. It had already been started when Dad stepped in to refine the image and lettering and oversee the vision. Go to any deli or specialty market, and it's likely there on halvah bars, tahini, and everything else Joyva makes.

NINETEEN SEVENTY-THREE

I was born Kenward Flanagan Cooper on September 28, 1973, in Las Vegas, Nevada. My mom chose my middle name based on the Gary Cooper character he played in *Love in the Afternoon*. It also happened to be the name of the doctor who delivered me, Dr. Flanagan. It was by cesarean I came into this world. My dad chose my first name. The origins of it are English. I read that it means "brave guardian." What he liked most was the consonance, and how it rolled off the tongue together with its surname. I love it, but it took nearly twenty years for me to fully embrace it. When you're a kid you do anything you can to not seem different.

There's a very early photo of me still in diapers playing a record on a phonograph. Music was always in the house. My parents would constantly be singing out loud. Mom had an operatic voice, although it was the popular songs she'd sing that grabbed my attention. "Strawberry Fields Forever" was my favorite of her repertoire.

It's well-documented that 1973 was a defining year for rock music. New York Dolls released their debut. Alice Cooper scored a No.1 record with "Billion Dollar Babies." Debbie Harry and Chris Stein became romantically involved. KISS formed. I like to think there's something in the air that ensured all this would have an influence on me in the years to come.

My brother and I started taking piano lessons at a young age. We had an upright, and the teacher would come to the house. I never practiced, neither of us did. When I had to recite the lesson from the week before, I could play it no problem. The teacher would congratulate me and I would grin, thinking I'd pulled a fast one on her.

I was raised Jewish, but I can remember a time when we celebrated both Christmas and Hanukkah one year, probably to give us the full-season experience. It stands out in my memory because Scott and I were each gifted record players and a couple of LPs.

I remember both of mine, a children's Superman record and one that featured the *Rocky* theme on it. Not long after, on a visit to Woolworths, in passing the Music Department, two album covers jumped out at me. Both looked like creatures with their face painted. One was Gene Simmons, the other was Peter Criss, from the KISS solo records. My brother grabbed Gene, so I was left with Peter as the only option. When we got home to play them, we both thought the intro to Gene's was the coolest thing ever—the part with his demonic laughter turning into a symphony before he kicks into "Radioactive" was just the greatest. The only song I ever found myself playing off the Peter record was "I Can't Stop the Rain." Even at five years old I could recognize a good song.

KISS would inspire us to want to start playing guitar. Piano lessons were no longer, so getting a cheap acoustic to learn on wasn't met with any resistance from our parents. Seeing all the cool shapes and colors of electric guitars at the shop we took lessons at immediately had my brother throwing a fit. He didn't want to play if it wasn't one of those. I think he made it through the first lesson, but it was a tantrum every time after. I lasted a little longer than him, though sooner than later the lessons stopped altogether. I didn't like the teacher, nor the lessons themselves.

We didn't have any interest in sports at that age. One summer, Mom thought it'd be a good idea to enroll us in soccer. She even went as far as buying us these great-looking Nikes, black with white swoosh and cleats. On the first day of tryouts, we were there for ten minutes before the coach announced to my mother, "Yeah, your boys aren't cut out for this."

In school I was always last to be picked for a team. Never fazed me though, because it just wasn't an interest. Until several years later when tennis hit me. I had a friend named Aric, who was in my class as well as in Hebrew school. He lived in a gated community where there was access to tennis courts. We played once in awhile, and when he mentioned he'd joined a tennis camp for the summer and how much fun it was, I decided to do the same.

We had a sense of friendly competition between us, not only with racquets. There was a time at school when something called a "slam book" was going around. Basically it was a list of random questions you had to fill out. One of the questions was "Who do you like?" This meant of the opposite sex, of your classmates. I read Aric's answer: Corrie. This was the cutest blond girl in our class, whom I also had a crush on. It so happened that Aric was out sick that day. I seized the opportunity and asked Corrie to be my girlfriend right then and there. She said yes. Insert smiley face.

Tennis camp was at a racquet club called Cambridge. Just fifteen minutes away from our house. It was great to spend the day there, learning how to serve, hit a forehand and backhand, and properly play the game. I could see and feel my improvements. My skills were sharpening. I had a wicked forehand. The coach even commented on it to my father. On a particular day there was extra excitement in the building, people were making a commotion over a kid named Andre who'd dropped in to use the courts. Only three years older than me, he was already making noise. You don't need to follow the game to know that Andre Agassi became one of the legends in the history of the sport. Every match he played I always rooted for my hometown hero. When he won his first major at Wimbledon against Goran Ivanisevic in a nail-biting five setter, I cried right along with him.

Once tennis camp came to an end, I was encouraged to continue playing. I should have insisted. I think my dad felt it was just going to be a summer thing, and it came with a price tag I'm sure he was happy to not cough up. At that time I thought I had to choose. I reasoned I could play air guitar on the racquet or I could play the real thing. Music won. To this day though, I watch all the Grand Slam tournaments and occasionally play for the fun of it. Still convinced I would've grown up to become one of the greats.

I took music very seriously at this age. Once I devoted myself to it completely, I wouldn't allow for any distractions. So much to the point that when Aric called me to go to the movies with him to see *Spinal Tap*, I asked first what it was about. He described it in certain words as a comedy about heavy metal. *No thanks.* I was not going to watch something that made fun of the music I loved.

Instead, I went to the store to browse the magazine racks. In the car my dad asked why I didn't want to go to the movies. I said it sounded stupid and that I wanted to pick up a new issue. He looked over and said, "Good." I could tell he was pleased I'd made my own decision based on what was important to me.

It was KISS that further fueled my interest in music after seeing them live. Posters were everywhere advertising their concert at the Aladdin Theater. I was ten years old and begged my parents to get tickets. The whole family went. None of us had any clue what to expect. I certainly didn't know the concept of an opening act. When the lights went out and four guys took the stage, I was puzzled why they didn't have the makeup on. I was looking at the bass player and justifying it in my head, *Okay, that's Gene Simmons, now who's the blond guy?* Whoever he was, he was a firecracker that couldn't stop running around the stage. It was exciting to watch. But halfway through their set, my parents wanted to leave. We were all holding our ears because it was so loud. When we got up from our seats, my mom asked an usher, "Why did they take the makeup off?" He replied, "This is the opening band, Mötley Crüe." If she hadn't asked, we would have left without seeing KISS. Dad took this as an intermission to grab some tissue from the restroom. We reclaimed our seats and plugged our ears.

KISS were amazing. They had a tank on stage that would fire explosives. It was a spectacle, completely entertaining. No wonder kids were hooked. After that night I was full on with music. My love affair with buying records began.

I had already amassed a collection of 45s from the year before, hits of the day from Hall & Oates, Duran Duran, Culture Club, Prince. Anytime we'd go somewhere that had a jukebox, "Little Red Corvette" always got my money.

It was time for a new guitar and my sights were set on a Mini Flying V. A full-scale neck was just too much guitar for me at the time. Now with an electric in hand, I was craving loud rock n roll. Def Leppard's *Pyromania* was a must. When Crüe's *Shout at the Devil* was released, my brother reminded me they were the band we'd seen open for KISS. He bought the cassette, and I hijacked it. One of the cool things about having an older sibling is they usually get turned on to something before you.

Some records he bought ended up in my collection. He didn't care for the harder stuff like I did. When I'd hear him play Bowie or the Blue Nile, it definitely caught my interest. His direction would ultimately shift to movies; once he got a camcorder, the fun began. Cole would come over and we would make our own films with my brother directing. Scott came up with this idea about a jade gemstone that was stolen. The dialogue was totally impromptu. Since Scott was older, fifteen, my parents felt there was no need for a sitter anymore if they were going out for an evening. Perfect time to make movies. We did some crazy shit and certainly didn't want any supervision. Climb up on the roof, all right, we'd shoot a scene from there.

One of the funniest things filmed was when our other friend from school, Joe, found out we had gotten our hands on an actual porn video starring seventies adult film star Seka. He asked if I could make him a copy since we had both a VHS and Beta player. "Sure, no problem." My brother told Cole to just take his shirt off and filmed him from the waist up making all these faces and pelvic motions. Then he edited it together with the Seka video to make it look like Cole was getting some serious action. When I gave the tape to Joe, he called up later all disturbed, agonizingly yelling at me, "WHAT IS THIS?! I'm getting ready and there's Cole on my screen, YOU RUINED IT!"

The original porn had come courtesy of a relative who had gifted it to my parents. When you find this material on the top shelf of your parents' closet, it's like striking gold. He had his own video distribution company. We visited him in California, where he was living the life. Nice house by the beach, sexpot wife, Porsche in the driveway. Not sure what else he was into, but a year or two after that visit, we found out him and his wife had been murdered.

My parents didn't shelter us from this kind of news. They did, however, worry a lot. No one can forget in the early eighties there was a big headline story about Adam Walsh, the young boy who was abducted and found dead.

It was the first time something like that became widely known. Right around the same time, there was an incident that happened at the supermarket. As my parents were paying for groceries, Scott and I wandered off to the candy machines at the entrance of the store. An adult woman approached us and asked, "Do you boys want to earn a quarter? All you have to do is help me carry these bags to that car right out there." She pointed to a vehicle where there was an older man waiting. Why wasn't he the one helping her then? My brother was quick to answer, "No, we're okay, our parents are right there." The woman disappeared. There's no doubt she had bad motives.

We had a sense of being fearless, though. There was a time when Mom and Dad went out for the evening. My brother didn't have a license yet. Still, he took the keys to the old Mark IV Lincoln. We picked up Cole and cruised around town, making a stop along the way at the airport, just to roam around. On another occasion, there was a party happening down the block from us that our parents were at, thrown by new people who'd moved to the neighborhood and had built this huge estate. It looked majestic. In the middle of the night I walked over there, let myself in, and had my own self-guided tour. No one questioned me, nor seemed to care that there was a kid hanging around.

When I ran into my parents, my dad greeted me like a long-lost friend, "Hey, what are you doing here?!" Mom asked, "Where's your brother?" Then my dad said there was something I had to see and whisked me away to check out this cave that had a secret slide that dropped into the swimming pool. The house was awesome, and the night was epic.

Parties would become a thing when junior high came around. The first big one was thrown by Corrie. She was now dating someone in high school, some dude that had a punk band called FSP, which stood for Fuck Shit Piss. Her parents were out of town and there was a concert in her backyard with FSP playing. My friend Jerry and I went. There must've been hundreds of people there. Beer cans everywhere. Jerry would pick them up off the ground and drink whatever was left unfinished. We went into Corrie's room afterwards, she was sitting on her bed like a kingpin who'd just pulled off the unspeakable.

My brother's antics rubbed off on Cole, who, without a license, was now sneaking out his mom's BMW and picking me up. We had a classmate, John, who had invited some friends over one night. When we got there, John was completely out of his mind, obliterated. It was the first time I saw someone our age completely wasted, and I didn't like it. It seemed like a different personality came out. The personality of an asshole. He came running out from his room shouting, "My girlfriend's naked, I'm getting ready to fuck her, you all get out of here!" We were there less than ten minutes before we bounced.

I started to get into trouble in school. Particularly after getting ahold of faculty phone numbers. Along with my friends Jerry and Joe, I started a crank call campaign that would spare no one. We were the Jerky Boys before they existed. If only we'd tape-recorded it. Three-way calls had become a thing and we took full advantage of this. Best was our singing telegram—I'd strum the guitar in the background, something similar to the "Bad to the Bone" riff, and make up an insulting rhyme using their name. "Hey Chris," strum, strum, strum, "you smell like piss." Sometimes we'd get a laugh or we'd be cursed out, or hung up on.

Another masterpiece was when one of us would pretend we were the father of the boy making the prank call. "Dad" would pick up the phone and raise hell at his son, "BILLY, GET OFF THE DAMN PHONE! I'M COMING UPSTAIRS WITH MY BELT TO TEACH YOU A LESSON!"

It was too much fun to just keep to ourselves. I think it was Jerry who invited another friend, Brandon, into the mix. That was a mistake. One of our teachers eventually recognized our voices. One day in class we heard an announcement over the loudspeaker. Three of our names were called, we were being summoned to the principal's office. That was odd, we hadn't heard Brandon's name being called. His voice had been the one that was recognized, he'd gotten caught and ratted us out. Instead of expelling us, the principal gave us all one week of in-house detention. This meant we had to attend school, but all our classes would be held in one small little room that just seated the four of us in cubicles. No PE and lunch would also be held in the same room. There were no windows. We didn't see outside until the end of the day. They would rotate teachers, one of whom we'd cranked. He found it amusing, though, he was a great guy and didn't deserve our stupidity. I'd always see him at every rock concert, because he had a second job as security. Usually after a concert, the next day at school he'd say to me, "How'd you like the show?" Later on, when all the boxing matches would be televised from Vegas, he would always be the main security guy ushering the champion into the ring.

Cutting classes became a thing, and then it turned into ditching school altogether. I had a few partners in crime. Usually it was Kenny, my ditch buddy, who rode his bike to school and would convince one of his friends to let me borrow their bike for the day. We'd ride all over town, go to record stores, grab fast food, or crash at someone's house to watch MTV all day. We'd allow ourselves an hour to get back to school just in time, since I always got picked up. Mom would be waiting. No clue that I just spent the day out 'n' about.

When seeking out a new guitar teacher, Vesley's Music was the place to go. An instrument store whose owner, Jerry Vesley, was a friend of the family. A young twenty-one–year-old with rocker hair had just started working there and I couldn't wait to take lessons from him. Mark Slaughter was a great instructor and I became his favorite student. Unlike the teacher I'd had before, Mark made it fun, teaching me how to play songs, rather than having me learn theory and how to read music. He'd balance the lessons with charting out chords and scales, always starting off with whatever song I wanted to learn for the week. This was so fundamental in training my ear as well as teaching me to recognize song structure. In a sense these lessons were my building blocks for songwriting.

Mark was just cool. He would joke around, talk about girls, sometimes a cutie of his own would show up with other friends. He had the vibe. There was a moment when he approached my dad about managing his band, Xcursion. Mark even went to his office for a meeting. I'm not sure why it didn't happen, though it's for the best that it didn't. Months later he formed a new band called Roz Parade, which was more radio ready than Xcursion and would propel him to his next opportunity.

Fast forward thirty-something years later, I had Mark on the phone and told him how he should think about rerecording a fantastic ballad he'd demoed, "Low & Lonely," which had never been released. That's how good a song can be, when three decades pass and it still leaves an impression. In 1986, when

Mark got the gig as a singer to join the Vinnie Vincent Invasion, he made it a point to tell me the news during one of our lessons. I was sad that he'd be leaving but totally happy that he was on his way to making it, and soon I'd have a friend who was a rock star.

I had been coming up with my own pieces of music and putting songs together, attempting to sing and recording it all on a tape recorder. I soon discovered I could record my guitar part first, put that cassette in the stereo tape deck, then pop another cassette in the tape recorder to add a second part. The cheap version of multitracking that every musician figures out.

It seems I was coming up with stuff since the moment I got an electric guitar. When you don't know how to play anything, you suddenly make it up. The germ of songwriting really clicked for me when a replacement teacher for Mark filled in. He was only there for one lesson, but it made a lasting impact. He wasn't a rocker like Mark, it was obvious his style was different. He asked what I was into, then started talking about punk. He demonstrated by playing on his guitar the riff to Poison's "Talk Dirty to Me" and then playing the Sex Pistols, making a clear-cut connection. Then he talked about himself and said he wrote songs of his own. He played me one called "Suicide." Singing it at the same time with all his might. The lyrics sang, "Suicide, suicide, how do you spell relief?" It was fantastic. That was the only time I heard this song, and I can still remember the melody so vividly. I don't know who this guy was, can't even remember his name. But I remember his song. I think the connector for me was here was someone playing his song right in front of me, as opposed to just hearing it on tape or record. It was more tangible. Once I hit the age of fifteen, I really felt I had the knack for writing songs. It made sense to me.

4

SWIMMING POOLS, MOVIE STARS

North Hollywood is where we settled when we made the move to California. It was strange to go from a five-bedroom/three-bathroom house on an acre and a half of land to a two-bedroom apartment. My brother got the second room to himself. I slept on a pull-out couch. The walk-in closets were big enough for me to make one my work station. I did the next few *Rockstar* issues from there. I didn't mind the apartment itself, I was too excited to be in LA and get started on the things I was pursuing. But why they didn't buy a house instead is a real shame.

In the building's garage, I recognized a long-haired musician getting out of his black Mustang. Doug Aldrich had a band at the time called Lion. Their record was already in my collection. New guitar teacher, problem solved. I took lessons from him for the six months we lived there. Learned more about lead playing from Doug than I had known before. After Doug, I stopped taking lessons, feeling I had the tools I needed. I wasn't setting out to be the next Eddie Van Halen, I was more into the idea of being a singer/songwriter who could play his own songs.

Doug had a friend, Denise, who would occasionally drop by. The type of rock vixen who could easily be the knockout from any MTV video of the era. I ran into her at a concert sometime after and we exchanged numbers. I called and invited her to go see Winger at Santa Monica Civic Auditorium, having gotten tickets from the label. How cool, I thought, to be fifteen and hanging out with a sexy girl who was older than me. A taste of things to come.

My magazine was finding its way into the hands of labels, PR firms, managers, and the like, just from my efforts sending it out. In the first month of my being in LA, MCA Records called to inquire the cost for a full-page ad. I immediately turned the phone over to my dad. As he'd had his own agency, it was right in his wheelhouse to know what the price should be. MCA purchased the back page to promote the release of their new band, Jetboy. A week later another label called to buy ad space. At this point my parents felt we'd made the right move in coming to LA.

With these ads in place, my dad decided we needed to up the ante and give the magazine a new look. He designed a great logo for it. He then drove back to Vegas to use the contacts he had there for typesetting and printing. My bedroom magazine went from being xeroxed and stapled together to now being printed professionally. It was on its way to becoming a prominent publication on the LA scene.

I enrolled at North Hollywood High for my first semester as a sophomore. I pretty much kept to myself, a bit shy to make new friends. I would take my brown-sack lunch and walk over to the backstops on the field, basically eating alone. Once in a while there'd be some other students there. One particular day there were two girls, they didn't know me, though I guess they'd seen me around. One asked if I was a musician. "Yes," I answered. She said, "I knew it! You're going to be so famous." It made me smile. She brightened my day, and I was sure she'd said it because she felt it to be the truth.

In one of my classes there were some music freaks like me that I started to talk to. I noticed a girl sitting in front of me who had flyers of bands in her binder. Bands that I'd featured in *Rockstar*. I was quick to say, "Oh I'm going to that show too," and sure enough I'd see her and a couple friends at the Whisky. On another night they wanted to take me up to the old Errol Flynn house. I can't remember if this was before or after it set on fire that year. I declined the invite. I wasn't big on hanging out when I had other interests keeping me busy.

As the semester was coming to an end, my dad said I wouldn't be going back. He'd made up his mind that we would be moving to Beverly Hills. His reason being that he wanted me to go to the best school. I had just met another cool student at North Hollywood High, and of course we decided to move. I didn't have any classes with this kid, but he'd stopped me in the hall, full of all exuberance. "Do you like Mötley Crüe?" he asked.

"Yeah of course."

"I gotta introduce you to Julia," he said, excitedly proclaiming, "her dad produced all their records!"

I knew exactly who he was talking about. I'd spent years reading the liner notes to every record I ever owned. I could tell you who'd produced, mixed, engineered, mastered, where it'd been recorded, who'd written which songs, who the photographer had been, you name it. In this case I also knew Tom Werman had a daughter, because on all his records it would say *Produced by Tom Werman for Julia's Music*. Julia went to the same school—I had no idea. I didn't get the chance to meet her.

I was writing loads of songs and got the itch to put a band together. I placed a classified ad in *Music Connection*, which was, like, *the* source for finding musicians in town. To my surprise, a girl responded. I hadn't worded it looking for a female singer, but that's what I got. Lori and I hit it off. We would talk for hours, she'd sing to me over the phone; this went on for weeks before we ever met. She lived farther away, not in LA, somewhere like Sacramento or Fresno. I looked forward to her calls, her voice was so seductive for someone who was only a couple years older than me. These were the days when there was no way to instantly see a photo of someone. We finally made a plan to meet up on the Strip in front of Gazzarri's. There was a show that night I was going to review for the magazine. When I met her outside, she was stunning. Tall, blond, and gorgeous. We gave each other a hug. A couple of guys from the band Tuff gave me the nod of approval like I was some kinda pimp, as they watched on. Why the fuck didn't I ditch the show and go out with her? Oh yeah, because my dad was there. I was fifteen and didn't drive yet, plus Dad was there so he could shoot photos of the bands. She didn't see him in the crowd, so it wasn't embarrassing, but I said I had to go check this out inside and that I'd find her later. Everyone would hang out on the Strip after a gig, though I never saw her after that. A week later her mom called me after finding my number on her telephone bill. She asked if I had seen Lori, and then told me that she'd run away from home. Welcome to Hollywood.

I gotta say it was fun going to the clubs with my dad. After all, we were like a team now running the magazine. All the bands got to know him on a first-name basis as well. I could tell he was enjoying it. When these girls in their miniskirts would parade by, he would tell me, "You're in the right business." He was great at networking and somehow connected with three girls who were all aspiring to be in the music business. He thought we should hire them as contributing writers/photographers. And so we did. I'm gonna use my favorite British term here and say I fancied them, especially Michelle and Kim. We drove over to their apartment in the Valley and basically hung out, talking shop, playing tunes and whatnot. Some guys from a new band were there too. I overheard Michelle talking about a shoot she'd done for *Bare Assets*. My ears perked up. I knew that name, and it wasn't a band. Later that night, I was talking to Michelle and she was looking at me with full-on admiration in her eyes and said to me, "You're so cool," followed by, "come see my room." Hell yeah, I followed her in, thinking I was about to see some *for your eyes only* proof sheets or something.

On another occasion, Kim picked me up to go see Poison at the Long Beach Arena. She'd had a little something to drink, and what should've been a forty-minute drive took nearly two hours. We made it for the last twenty minutes of the show. I didn't care, cruising around with the radio on, talking the whole way through, was way more fun.

Soon I had my day out with Michelle. When she got to my place she was in skimpy blue shorts, the type American Apparel later made famous, the type to give me a hard-on. I was WAY overdressed, in this bright-blue suit and silver metallic dress shirt. It might've been okay for a night at the Roxbury, but not a fucking daytime barbecue. She said I looked nice. On the drive there she made a pit stop at the 7-Eleven. She smiled when she got back in the car, carrying nothing except her purse. She wasn't a smoker, so a pack of cigs wouldn't make sense. I was sure in my mind she had picked up a pack of condoms.

At the park I stepped in dog shit. The stench lingered for a while—worse when people know it's coming from *you*. It started to feel like a domino effect. I was uncomfortable, first with what I was wearing, then the smell of doodie. When we left and got closer to my pad, Michelle asked if I wanted to do anything else. "We could go back to my place," she said.

"Is Kim going to be there?" I asked.

"No, nobody's there."

I mean, c'mon, she was dropping pretty clear hints for me! I was too self-conscious. She was seven years older than me. On one hand I was convinced this would be my first time, on the other I was unsure of myself. I had no experience and let that get in the way of having a new one. You could say I literally fucked myself.

Attending Beverly Hills High School was interesting. If you've seen the movie *Less Than Zero*, not only was the opening graduation scene filmed there, but its narrative also depicts the wealthy youth I encountered there. Every other car in the parking lot at Beverly High seemed to be either a Mercedes or BMW. The occasional Porsche could also be found. The cafeteria looked like it belonged in the Beverly Center mall, neon signs and all. Still it was much easier to make friends than the last school. Ching Yuan was from Taiwan, a clean-cut type of student. Some kid was bagging on him, teasing how he'd probably never seen pussy. I sold him his first porn mag, smut peddler I was. We became fast friends after that. I think maybe I corrupted him, pretty soon he was talking about wanting to go to strip clubs. We found if we dressed up, we had a better chance of getting in. You only had to be eighteen to get in to the all-nude ones, and hardly any of the doormen gave a shit anyway, they had numbers to make.

We adapted our dressing up idea and applied it to trying our luck at bars and nightclubs. Ching Yuan rolled up in his BMW all decked out in a suit when we went to a place on Robertson that was popping.

"Pull up to the valet," I said, somehow believing it would give us better odds of getting in if the doorman saw us pull up front. Throw the confetti because we didn't get carded. Making our way to the bar, neither of us knew what to order. I blurted out the first name I could think of. Black Russian. "Make that two."

Ching Yuan took a few sips. As his drink got halfway, I could see it hit him quicker than mine. He leaned up against the wall with a look of euphoria and, stretching out his words, he exhaled, "Fuuuccccck, I love it!"

At school, I recognized Guy Oseary from a music video he'd been in for Digital Underground, which was blowing up MTV at the time. I had the inclination to ask him about it during PE with Coach Newman. Guy was a grade above me, though, and as juniors typically didn't converse with seniors, our occasional exchange of the "what's up" greeting didn't go beyond that. Today, Guy manages the careers of legends, he's an industry heavyweight. Shame that I didn't get to know him better. He seemed cool then. Still does.

Sometimes a friendship can start off on the wrong foot, as was the case with Ashley Hamilton. It was PE class and this tall, thin John Taylor look-alike had just finished his rep on the weight set. Naturally I thought he had finished when I changed the settings to my own. After I was done, he came back around and said with some attitude, "Oh, man, why'd you change that? I was using it."

"Change it back," I said, and I walked away.

When I saw him in math class I thought, *This guy again*. Back on the track field I overheard him arguing with someone. I didn't catch the whole extent of it, only the words "Yeah, well, I'm going on tour with my stepdad."

Hmm, now I knew he was a musician, so for what it was worth, I said, "Hey, man, I play too."

"Oh yeah, what do you play?" he asked.

"Guitar."

"Me too." The conversation stopped there. It was more or less an acknowledgement of each other.

Later that week, during math, I got called upon to solve an equation. I was stumped and blabbed out, "I don't know." Some of the classmates laughed.

Ashley, however, turned around to say to them, "What's so funny?" Interesting, the dude was sticking up for me. The next time we were in gym, we started to talk about music and guitars. After class, I had a spur-of-the-moment idea. I said, "Let's ditch and go to Guitar Center."

He laughed, "Right now? How're we gonna get there?"

"I have wheels."

He didn't hesitate, "All right, let's go!"

Being a newly licensed driver, I'd occasionally have permission to use the car, and I took full advantage of it when I could. My PO box for the magazine was three minutes away from school; we stopped there first. I had a shit ton of packages waiting for me when I checked my box. Ashley's eyes widened, "What's all this?"

"New releases the record labels send me."

"For what?" he asked. I told him about *Rockstar*. "That's cool." Then he asked, "You know who my stepdad is, right?" I shook my head. "Rod Stewart."

"Right on." It wasn't a way of showing off, it was a way of connecting the dots and learning of our different backgrounds. After our trip to Guitar Center, Ash and I were pretty much inseparable, we became the best of friends.

The apartment where my family lived was never conducive to having friends over; with the whole family there it would've been stressful and uncool. Thankfully I was spared this. I was at Ashley's all the time. His mom, Alana, had a great house in Brentwood that was always so chill and peaceful. There was a room by the swimming pool where we would take our guitars to play. We worked up some ideas and straightaway called in two kids from school to start rehearsing with us. Seriously, we probably played less than a handful of times before deciding to make a demo. But this wouldn't be just a four-track home recording, no way, we had to rent out a professional twenty-four-track studio in Hollywood. I made the calls and settled on Paramount Recording Studios on Santa Monica Boulevard. They had the least expensive rate. We blocked it out for the night, from 8:00 p.m. until 8:00 a.m. the next day. We hired a keyboard player but never practiced with him or gave him the songs beforehand, so that burned up a lot of time. When I had to track a solo, I kept screwing it up, especially with the pressure of the clock running. The sun was coming up and we still hadn't gotten around to laying down a vocal. It was a mess, but it was also a thrill just to be in a big studio going for it.

Rockstar Magazine was making its mark. I was getting fan mail from places as far away as Argentina and Japan. Even strange phone calls—a couple girls called and asked, "Does Ken Cooper have a scar on his chin?"

"Yes," I answered. They giggled and hung up.

There was a moment when the legendary *Creem* magazine contacted us to take a meeting. They were figuring out ways to inject new life into their spin-off title, *Creem Metal,* and had proposed that *Rockstar* be featured as an insert in upcoming issues. Maybe they'd gotten wind that they could have another Cameron Crowe on their hands. Sadly they ended up shutting down before the collaboration could transpire. Many years later, when my brother saw the movie *Almost Famous,* he yelled out, "THAT'S YOU!"

Yeah, pretty much.

It was thrilling for me to be instrumental in helping bands gain recognition, many of which secured record deals and found their faces featured on the higher order of glossy magazine covers. *Rockstar's* purpose was to spotlight the unsigned talent, yet I was able to nail down the platinum-selling artists as well. One memorable encounter was late spring of 1989, I met C.C. DeVille from Poison at the Whisky during a show for the Zeros. Typically, I would drop stacks of *Rockstar* off at the clubs on show nights. In this case, I gave him a copy backstage. Immediately he expressed his excitement, probably for the fact of seeing someone as young as I legitimately publishing his own trade paper. In his quirky Brooklyn accent he said, "This is your magazine? I'll give you an interview!" He was very specific in saying he'd call me next week at said time and date, after he got off stage, and that the band would be on tour in the Midwest. Sure enough, he kept his word. When he got on the phone, the first thing he said in his hysterical voice was, "I told you I'd give you an interview!"

More than just being a journalist, tastemaker might be another role I adopted. A&R reps from major record labels were calling me to ask about bands I had featured and if I could send them the demos I had. I sometimes thought maybe I should parlay my experience into actually getting a job at a record company or management firm, but my desire to be the recording artist always outshined any other.

After that first recording debacle with Ash at Paramount, I decided I needed to sharpen my skills. There were many recording engineers with home studios to offer their services.

It didn't have to be twenty-four-tracks, and I wouldn't need to worry about spending big bucks that I didn't have. Most of these guys were charging about fifteen dollars per hour. It was the perfect environment, there was no disconnect between the glass and mixing console, I could sit right there next to the engineer and be comfortable. It was a process that happened more instantaneously. Program the drums, plug a guitar into a processor, go direct with the bass, cut a vocal, mix, and you're done. I presented Ashley with three songs recorded this way, which got him all excited. It sounded professional.

Neither of us had a decent voice back then, both underdeveloped in that area. We knew we needed someone else to sing on these recordings. Michael Chaves worked at the Music Plus store in Beverly Hills. We brought him into the fold to play bass and handle the lead vocals. A completed demo gave us confidence; Ash was convinced we'd get a deal. Getting an appointment anywhere was not difficult. The first person we met with was John Kalodner at Geffen Records. He was the man responsible for resurrecting Aerosmith's career in the eighties. We sat in front of him at his desk. He asked a little bit about us, then put the tape in his deck and closed his eyes while listening. His head was bobbing along. Ash and I looked at each other all giddy. He passed on it, though, and that was all right, it was only our first meeting.

We needed a drummer if we were going to be a band and do it right. Ash was super connected—for a sixteen-year-old he knew tons of people. We cabbed it over to see these girls he was friends with, hashing our plan. One said she knew the perfect guy.

"Let's go meet him right now." Somehow we thought we should take a limousine there. Pulling up in a stretch, we could only wonder what John Wilmer was thinking. We liked him instantly. He had certain quirks, like constantly twirling his hair, and a characteristic voice, just a cool overall style about him. Plus, he had his own recording studio. That was a huge bonus in our book.

There was one obstacle, John was already in another band, Back Alley Sally. He was loyal to them and believed his life would be in danger if he quit them. Okay, so we'd have to share. I think he was all for our team once Ashley got Terry Bozzio interested in us. We all were fans of Terry's band Missing Persons, but being a drummer himself, John idolized him. He came down to our practice space and watched us run through our songs, agreeing afterwards to produce us.

Ash had a tape he played me of a ten-second guitar riff. He said, "Check this out, I wrote it." It was cool, like a "Walk This Way" type of riff. I asked who was playing on it, knowing Ash didn't play like Joe Perry. Shit, I didn't play like Joe Perry. I was curious. "I had my stepdad's guitarist play it," he said, adding how Stevie Salas was giving him lessons.

"Cool, let's work on it."

As the weeks went on, Ash wanted to make the new riff into a hip-hop thing and rap over it. It was a great idea and relevant to what was happening. When Terry's name came up again, Ash reasoned, "He's too rock." It might've been interesting, but our direction was changing.

The first time I met Rod Stewart, Ash casually disclosed after school, "We're going over to see my stepdad." He was working on "Vagabond Heart" at Cherokee Studios. So many of my favorite records have been recorded there. I was equally stoked to see inside the studio as I was to meet this legendary hitmaker.

Ash made it a point to tell him we had a band together. He was courteous in asking what I played. Nevertheless, we didn't take up his time, retreating instead to the live room to lounge about for awhile. Ash was thinking out loud, "How great would it be to record here?" Soon we would.

On another occurrence I recall going with Ash to drop off his younger siblings, Kimberly and Sean, at their dad's. It was the time when Rod had just started dating Rachel Hunter. I can remember him introducing the kids to her. All of us ended up going out that night. Rod drove. It was certainly kid inspired, the place of choice was Carney's, the legendary train on Sunset Boulevard that serves up hamburgers and hot dogs.

Ashley's biological father is the actor George Hamilton. A terrific guy, ever so engaging and welcoming, effortless in conversing with you. Ash divided his time between his dad and his mom. At one point George moved to a building on Maple Drive in Beverly Hills, and Ash was thrilled to tell me David Bowie was his neighbor. One day we cranked up *Ziggy Stardust* hoping to attract his attention. Nobody came knocking at the door.

Don Henley's *The End of the Innocence* was our soundtrack for that year. We both loved "Heart of the Matter." It's still one of my favorite songs. Ashley's mom was friends with Don, and when he played the LA Forum, the three of us went. One of the best shows, it was hit after hit, with no gimmicks. Backstage, just before leaving, I caught a glimpse of Jon Bon Jovi hanging out. I said to Ash, "Let's go talk to him." Ash was a bit reluctant, maybe having grown up the way he did, it was no big deal. Still I reminded him how many bands JBJ had helped to launch the careers of, adding that he would likely dig our stuff. Ash opened up to it somewhat, "Okay, you go talk to him." He smiled.

I waited for the moment when Jon would be freed up from his conversation, thinking that would be a perfect opportunity and more respectful approach. It was time to leave, however, and I wasn't in any position to hold anyone up by saying, "Wait, I didn't talk to Jon yet." If only I had, I wonder.

If I wasn't at Ashley's, Ching Yuan would call, his famous words being, "Ken, you wanna go cruise?" We'd drive up and down Sunset Boulevard, Hollywood Boulevard, all over town, it was the thing to do. Coffeehouses became our jam for a while, places like the Living Room or Bourgeois Pig. Whenever I chatted with a girl, never failed that Ching Yuan would say, "Ken, why didn't you fuck her?" He was a funny guy and was becoming very Americanized. Soon thereafter he announced to me, "Ken, start calling me Ed."

"Sure, no problem." Of all the English names to choose from, it suited him well.

The magazine was still going, but only for a little while longer. Fact was, the advertising had dried up and cost of printing became more than the return. The scene was changing, and with that my taste was expanding. LA County would soon ban flyering on the Sunset Strip, it would be considered littering and fines would be in place. Bands would no longer have the freedom of self-promotion by slapping their logo into the hands of passersby or plastering the telephone poles with their advertisements. The party in the streets was about to end, and so would *Rockstar*. But damn it was fun while it lasted. I got to experience and be part of something that was more than just a local rock scene, this was a movement, a moment in time that still fascinates those who lived it, every bit as it does those who wished they had.

On occasion I'd be able to get the car keys and drive myself to Hollywood. Every time I asked, my dad inquired, "Are you going on a date?" I soon realized this was my ticket to getting the car, I just said yes. I loved my dad's mentality, decline if it's for a joyride, but if pussy's involved: green light.

5

GRADUATE

My grades in school were falling. Obviously due to how I spent my time, resulting in less academic study. One of the subjects I was failing Literature. Giving my teacher, Mrs. Himmel, a copy of *Rockstar* saved my ass. She had me write and read to the class an essay about how I'd started the magazine. I passed her class because of this. To make up the other two classes I was behind in, I had to do an extension my senior year, which involved spending three extra hours after school for the rest of the semester so I could graduate on time. One of the elective classes I took was an easy one, Modeling. We practiced strutting the catwalk and taking photos. Only at Beverly Hills High School.

Ash and I had no appointment on the books when we got the urge to just head over to Atlantic Records. We walked up to the receptionist's desk. Ash asserted that we were there to see Paul Cooper, the president of the label. She dialed his extension, announced our presence, and up the elevator we went. He was very cool, perhaps even amused. We played him the first song from our demo. After the chorus, he stopped the tape and asked, "What can I do for you?" Ash stated we just wanted to record. Instantly, Paul picked up the phone, made a call, and got us a full two-day lockout at Cherokee Studios. He said to come back with the finished results. We were in and out of there in five minutes. Outside we practically jumped up and down, Ashley declaring,

"We're going to get signed, you know that, bro, right?!" Of course I agreed, it felt like a victory.

Now we had the task of bringing in the right producer. Ash had a hosting gig at the Italian spot Mezzaluna. I'd go to hang out on the days he was working, usually waiting for his break so we could have dinner on the house. One evening the waitress spoke of her guest at another table, who was also a musician from Vegas.

When he introduced himself as Larry Hart, I tripped out. I had been to his house as a kid, my dad was friends with his mom. I spoke about how I'd been at his house for a party and signed my name on his wall. He had a room that was decorated with signatures from everyone who'd ever visited the home. Once I reminisced about that, our connection was established. I knew his style was R&B because we had one of his recordings from way back; I eventually dug it up and played it for Ashley. Larry was a talented piano player with Elton John flair. I called Ash over to the table to meet him. Afterwards, it was decided Larry should produce us.

Knowing we needed more tunes, I went back to an eight-track studio off Melrose to do a quick acoustic/vocal recording of a new one I'd been working on, called "Promises." Ash loved it, as did Larry, who turned it into a pretty piano ballad featuring Ash doing a spoken word part in the verses. We recorded this, along with the Joe Perry-ish riff, which had transformed into a dance-rock/rap hybrid called "All Night Long." Recording at Cherokee was an absolute blast. We lived there for those forty-eight hours, never wanting to leave. The time we did take a break, Larry and Michael continued working. When we got back to the control room, Ash and I were ecstatic about what they'd laid down. Michael was a real tasteful player and he brought the Nile Rodgers funk to this track, giving it that extra flavor. No surprise when he later became John Mayer's right-hand guy and a member of Adam Cohen's band Low Millions.

I called upon my pal Jeff from the Sunset Strip band Circus to come and lay down a guitar solo. We wanted the song to evoke the same feeling as Michael Jackson's "Beat It," when you hear that lead guitar by Eddie Van Halen rip through. Jeff had a custom-made guitar that had buttons on it, which, when pressed, made different sound effects. We were all amused, but not as much as him when Ashley's dad, George, was sitting in the control room with us. After a handful of takes and mess-ups, Jeff's nerves got to him. "I got Dracula breathing down my neck," he said. A playful reference to George's 1979 film *Love at First Bite*.

There was a very cute receptionist at the studio. She would pop her head into the control room every now and then, and anytime I took a breather we'd have our chats. She had a bohemian flair matched with a vivacious personality. It was obvious we were vibing on each other. On our last day, she came in to hear the mixes. Suddenly I felt her arms wrap around me from behind while her head rested on my shoulder. *Ooh, I like this feeling*, is what was rushing through my mind. Ash took notice and later remarked, "Damn, Kenny, you gotta take her out!" *No doubt.*

Armed with a new demo we were extremely confident about, we hustled back to Atlantic and played it for Paul. "All Night Long" put a huge smile on his face, and rightfully so, it sounded polished and was infectious as any radio hit. I'm sure we fantasized about him pulling out a contract and signing us on the spot, however, he told us he would sit with it some more. Still, we believed it was in our favor. "Did you see his big ol' Kool-Aid smile?" Ash jested.

He had a saying back then, "No news is good news." We weren't going to rest on one person, though, and Ash made the most of his contacts, straight to the big guns. He affirmed we were going to see Rod's manager. The moment we got to Arnold Stiefel's office, I had a nice surprise seeing Michelle at the reception desk; she was now working for the firm. It had been over a year since we'd been in touch. While waiting in the lobby, Ash asked how I knew her, then quipped, "You don't introduce your friend?" It hadn't dawned on me as it was quick and unexpected, plus he had already taken a seat. When the assistant came to get us, Ash wanted to do the meeting by himself. "I'll just go in," he muttered. I hadn't intended to come off as shutting him out, but I assume he took it that way. Nonetheless, he apologized later for going it alone.

To say Ash had plenty of women is an understatement. Sixteen dating twenty-somethings. He constantly had a new girl, all of them beautiful. It would be silly to think he'd have a chip on his shoulder if his friend was getting attention and not him. Although back at school there was a time when he was interested in my friend Erica. He joked, "Oh I see, keeping one for yourself." Never letting up until I invited her to come out with us. I couldn't blame him. Guess he just couldn't control himself, horny bastard. God love him.

I didn't go to my senior prom. I didn't have any money, so I wasn't going to ask someone out knowing I couldn't afford it. Thankfully I did graduate on time in June 1991. I was so done with the thought of school that after the ceremony, I was all too quick to turn in my cap and gown. Everyone else was taking photos with their families and celebrating the moment. When my parents found me afterwards, they were quite upset that they hadn't gotten a photo with me in all the garb. Fuck, I didn't even care to have the yearbook. It was a few months later when my parents realized I hadn't gotten one. They wasted no time in calling the school to order a copy.

That summer Ash gifted me with a round-trip ticket to join him at his dad's vacation home in Aspen, Colorado. Upon getting situated, George, ever the gentleman, said, "Now Ken, I don't know if Ashley gave you bathroom privileges yet, but you have full access." His witty way of making sure I was comfortable. The two weeks spent there was truly a great time. A lot of bike riding and going on hikes. Some evenings were enjoyed shooting pool while Bonnie Raitt's "Luck of the Draw" played on. Of course Ash had a girl staying with him most nights, which suited me fine. I'd stay up watching MTV and playing guitar, finding myself composing ideas that were different from anything else I'd come up with before.

Once I got back to LA, the thought of college did not appeal to me, and thankfully my lack of interest wasn't met with any resistance from my parents. They were supportive of my pursuit and believed I was on the right path. By no means did this mean they could bankroll me, because there was nothing to roll with. My dad had never planned well for the future. Instead of putting money down on a property in LA, we continued living in apartments from the proceeds of the Vegas house. This would burn fast. Before long, my mom took a job as a nanny. I searched the ads and did a telemarketing stint for the *Los Angeles Times*. And my brother, he started getting high.

He actually had an entry-level job at CBS Studios but soon found his way into the LA cliché of partying more than working or going on auditions. The first few times I caught him smoking weed, I lunged at him, acting like I was about to let the fists fly, hoping that would send some sort of message to him. Wishful thinking.

After I returned from Aspen, Denisa, the receptionist from Cherokee Studios, called me. She was pursuing acting and made mention of needing to update her resume. I volunteered, "Drop it by, I'll type it up for you." Hell, I was a pro on the IBM Selectric II. I ended up typing up a dozen copies, figuring I'd save her a trip to Kinko's. On the night we made plans to go out together, I asked Dad if I could have the car, saying I had a date. This time it was legit, so one would think it would be, "Okay, son, have fun." When my dad asked with whom, I said Denisa, the girl from the recording studio.

He replied, "The Black girl?"

"Yeah, that's the one."

Then he asked, "Are you getting serious with her?"

I said, "Dad, don't worry about it." Which was my way of saying it didn't concern him. Never had I heard him talk down on race or someone's ethnicity. He wasn't prejudiced, he just had his own reservations about who he thought was best for me. Since I was a little kid, my dad would always use Christie Brinkley as the image of what to aspire to when it came to a girlfriend. "If Billy Joel can do it, so can you, you're better-looking than him," he would say. I took Denisa out, but now I was overthinking stuff in my head that I shouldn't have let influence me. In this case, the fire burned out before the flame got any higher.

Dad had no intention of starting another ad agency in Los Angeles, nor did he have the finances to do so. At almost sixty years old when we relocated, he wasn't looking to grind it out like before. He favored taking a position as director of an art gallery, to keep income coming in until another opportunity presented itself. This came later in the form of managing a residential building on Hamilton Drive, of all the streets. By now my mom was going through a serious depression.

It had consumed her so badly to the point of preventing her from speaking and from doing any activities. She was afraid to make any movements. Clutching her hands together, too scared to do anything. This continued for months, even on prescribed antidepressants.

Once she began to talk again, it was always to ask, "Did I do it right?" Questioning if she had been a good mother. I didn't know how to handle this. It's awful to say sometimes I'd raise my voice to her and yell out, "YES, NOW SNAP OUT OF IT!" I just wanted things to feel normal again and for her to be well. The reality is her depression would be a reoccurring theme for many years to come.

6

NEW YORK MINUTE

Our band went by the moniker of Soul Shaker, taken from a lyric from "Love Removal Machine" by the Cult, before we changed it to Soul Garden to fit more with the times. We never did any live gigs, instead we honed our craft in John Wilmer's studio, which he referred to as Pandora's Box. It was perfect. We worked on a lot of new songs, getting into sampling beats and finding our sound, which mixed hip-hop elements with rock. Ash and I scoffed at how John was a member of our band but still charged us for studio time. In retrospect, we were more like a songwriting/production team than an actual band that pounded the streets playing the clubs. Perhaps it made sense for John to be business minded. Still we had a laugh about it.

Renowned producer Richard Perry, whose credits included everyone from Ringo Starr to Harry Nilsson to Diana Ross to Barbra Streisand, had come to produce some tracks for us. There was also a manager at this time that we met who wanted to represent us. He spoke openly about having gone to Chabad Treatment Center and how focused he was to make things happen now that he was clean. I went to his place one night to drop off a stack of press kits. I was shocked to see the biggest mountain of coke lying on the floor. I wasn't about to call him out on it, I just made it quick and got out of there. It was quite apparent he couldn't manage himself, let alone anyone else.

By now I had recorded an album's worth of material on my own, and with the flow of songs I was writing, I had every desire to keep that going. I booked time in Wilmer's studio—I could always trust that the results would be impressive. One day Ash called over there while I was recording, not knowing that I was in the studio. John didn't think twice about it when he said, "Ken's over here making hits." His excitement for the session and how the songs were turning out was unfiltered. This rubbed Ash wrong.

He knew I had my go-to eight-track studio, because he'd been there and I'd play him stuff from time to time. That wasn't an issue, but with Wilmer and I working together, perhaps this was seen as an exclusion. Later he asked why I was over there working on stuff when we had our own project together. I had to explain, "Because it's a different style from what we do as a band."

I know this created somewhat of a divide between us, yet I couldn't stop myself from growing and exploring my own creativity. Later, when Ash got his first tattoo, a snake on his shoulder, he made the symbolism clear, "If anyone crosses me, I turn on them like a snake."

Suddenly we weren't hanging out like before. On one occasion when we did, he complained about a discomforting pain he was feeling, thinking he might have a hernia. Weeks later he called and said he just had surgery and was laid up in bed recuperating. I said, "Oh, for the hernia?"

He replied, "No, man, I just had brain surgery."

I couldn't believe it. I went over to his house and was startled to see his head all bandaged up and him halfway immobile. The repercussions of a motorcycle accident.

In the fall of 1993, I was watching *Entertainment Tonight* when a story ran about the marriage of Shannen Doherty to Ashley Hamilton. I was happy for them. Nonetheless, it was recognizable to me that not being invited was an indication our friendship had suffered some. Less than a month later, Ash called. First thing he asked was if I was sitting down. His voice building up as he hollered, "Pack your suitcase, bro, WE JUST GOT A RECORD DEAL!" I didn't know if he was pulling my leg, but he added, "I told you we would get signed!" He instructed me to meet at his mom's house the next day at 1:00 p.m., that he had my ticket and we'd be leaving from there to go to the airport. Before hanging up, he checked my level of excitement one more time, "How stoked are you, man?!"

My "*HELL YEAH!*" was met with his "*THAT'S WHAT I WANNA HEAR!*" My parents had a similar reaction when I shared the news, not sure if I was being serious at first, followed by a round of hugs and congratulations.

Upon my arrival at the house, his mom announced that everyone was already at the airport. I wasn't late. *How could this be?* I thought. She handed me the ticket, and I was now stressing myself out, hoping I wouldn't miss the flight. I got to the gate just moments before boarding began. The guys looked somewhere in between puzzled and impressed that I'd made it.

New York City in November wasn't as cold as I was expecting. I overdressed, and I wore my dad's London Fog coat regardless if I was starting to sweat underneath. Maybe I was hoping to experience a picturesque winter. Prior to this trip, I had been to New York one time before but had very few memories, since I'd been so young. This time around was like being in a different world. The company had booked us at the Chelsea, Ashley's choice because of the hotel's rock n roll history. Soon one of the guys at the studio asked me if I'd seen anything strange happening there, insinuating it was haunted.

Early in the week after a session, we had dinner at Stingy Lulu's on the Lower East Side. Ash was looking dejected; none of us had ever seen him like that before. He wasn't talking or eating. When asked what was wrong, he chalked it up to missing his wife. I don't think we saw him for the rest of the evening. On another night we went to Club USA. This blew my mind. Packed with interesting-looking characters in outlandish costumes, scantily clad dancers, neon signs and flashing lights, a huge slide like the type you'd see at a water park—all part of the décor. There was nothing else like it. This was the height of the Club Kids culture, the scene that spawned James St. James's memoir, *Disco Bloodbath*, which was later depicted in the film *Party Monster*.

Walking back to the hotel at night was a colorful experience. Drug dealers were abundant and not shy to approach people. Times Square nowhere resembled the family attraction it is today, back then it was Adultland, seedy sex shops one after the other. There was an element of danger that was alive. In the mornings, I was always the first one up. I'd use this time to grab a

cup of coffee and stroll around the neighborhood, taking in the energy and
hustle of the streets.

Shannen came to visit that second week, certainly putting Ash in an elevated
mood. Naturally he checked out of the Chelsea and the two got themselves a
nice posh room somewhere uptown. Michael was beginning to complain about
not having a per diem; it rubbed off on John, who chimed in that he could
be making money at his studio back home. I didn't care either way because I
was usually cashless and hadn't been aware daily allowances were even a thing,
so I hadn't expected one. The underlying issue was that no terms of the deal
had been discussed. Day after day this was becoming a conversation, until it
came to a boil and a band meeting was called. Michael spoke his mind, "How
come we're not getting paid?"

Ash was ticked off, "Are we a band or you wanna be a hired gun?!"

The main man from the company set it straight that they were a production
company whose purpose was to cover the recording costs and then shop the
record for a deal. John therefore brought up having "points on the record,"
as we took backing tracks from his studio to use on the NYC session. My
concern was more about how the writing credits and publishing would be
divided. The producer made a list of all our songs and then went around
the table asking who'd had a hand in the writing. Reflecting back on this, it
was petty. The stupid things that come into play with young bands. Sure it's
good to iron things out, but this wasn't the time or place for it. I met with
Ash outside afterwards, and he expressed his disappointment in how he'd
expected this from the other guys but not from me.

One morning, as daylight was coming through the curtains, I was engulfed
in this image and feeling of someone hovering over with their hands reaching
forward to strangle me. My eyes were opening, it was so vividly present. I
screamed out, "GET AWAY FROM ME, GET THE FUCK AWAY!" I woke
everyone up in the room. John asked what had happened, but no one was
fazed and they all went back to bed. Not me, I was out the door. At the studio

when I told the assistant who kept asking me if strange incidents had occurred, he too was not surprised. "I told you." he said.

More NYC nightlife was to be had. If Club USA wasn't over the top enough, Tunnel made sure it would be. People in glass cages and more outrageous costumes—one patron walked past us wearing his own handmade dildo utility belt. Crazy fun set against a techno soundscape.

We dropped in at the Whiskey Bar in the Paramount Hotel. Ash mostly kept to his corner of the bar with the studio boss, while us other three hung out on the opposite side. There was a girl smiling at me, too noticeable to ignore. I pulled up a seat next to her and remarked how her smile had drawn me in. She paid back the compliment, "With one like yours you should use it more." It was amusing to watch guys try and hit on her throughout the night; she wasn't having any of it, she came back over to me and we started making out. One more reason to love New York City. John still brought this up when I saw him over the years, "The hottest girl in the room, and Kenny got her."

After basic tracks were recorded, we flew back to LA with the understanding that recording would resume in a couple of weeks to do vocals and overdubs, which I wouldn't be needed for. Ash and I would speak intermittently; I wasn't so much in the loop after that. He did inform me, though, that he would be appearing on *The Arsenio Hall Show* to promote a movie he was in and to make sure I tuned in.

There was a part in the interview when they talked about music and Ash mentioned the band was doing a gig that weekend. I was taken aback and verbally lashed out at the TV, "Really, that's news to me." I couldn't get him on the phone, so my brother and I drove to the club the night of. I walked up with my guitar in hand and the doorman asked if I was on the list. It was kind of laughable really. *No, dipshit, I'm just carrying a guitar case for the fuck of it.* My brother didn't stand for this and said, "He's in the band," as we made our way in. I was looking at all the gear set up on stage when one of Ash's friends, whom I knew from school, came up to me all excited and wished, "Good luck!" This felt strange. I was asking around looking for Ash, and I found John and Michael. "What's up, what time are we going on at?" I asked.

"I don't know, ask Ash."

When we finally found each other, I questioned why I hadn't been given a heads-up. Ash retorted, "Oh, now you want to be in my band?" It was hurtful. All I could voice was why have John and Michael here if that was how he felt. He just shrugged it off and walked away. The next day he called and gave some excuse and said not to worry, that soon we would be on tour. We didn't speak after that for quite a long time.

7

TAKE A BITE

I went alone to see Duran Duran on New Year's Eve. As the countdown was happening to ring in the new year, they chanted, "Goodbye to '93." Yes, I thought, goodbye felt quite apropos, I was ready for a change. Without any prior discussion or contemplation, my dad announced he wanted us all to leave LA and move back to New York. Wait a sec, I wasn't sure I wanted to just ditch California. He was convinced that I would love living there and that any opportunity in LA was also to be found in New York, maybe even more so.

Personal belongings were boxed and shipped to relatives, and four plane tickets later we relocated to the East Coast. First would be Connecticut at the house that belonged to my grandmother in West Hartford. My dad had the intention to sell it and split the sale with his sister. We would stay there and get the house "market ready," in addition to waiting for an apartment in Manhattan to open up. Eventually Dad took a job with an NYC television station, in charge of new accounts and advertising. This sped up the process of settling into the city.

The apartment we moved into was tiny. It had a hotel-size mini fridge, a double-burner stove, and a bathroom so small you had to turn your legs to the right when sitting down on the toilet just to fit into the space. Basically you would be shitting sideways. Three beds could line up in a row in this studio room. I slept on an army cot that I could easily fit into the open closet space, so at least I had a bit of separation at night. It wasn't terrible, we adjusted and made the best of it. The landlord was a cool old man who didn't care that an entire family was living in what would normally be meant for one person. The upside was that it was on the best cross streets possible, 65th and Park.

Bloomingdale's was the first job I had in the city, and the first one I would get fired from. I showed up late too many times. Silly on my part, considering I lived only five streets and one block away. That's what happens when you're so close, you figure you have more time than you do. My next position was at Tower Records in Trump Plaza.

I got turned on to so much great music just from all the in-store-play promos. One day a thirteen-year-old girl came up to the counter with a stack of two dozen CDs. She said she'd like to put them on her father's account. I was about to ask, "And what's his name?" when an associate stepped in to take over. It was Ivanka.

The store was located on the lower level, with no windows to see out of. One of my favorite memories was when I finished work in the evening one day. When I got outside, the city was covered in snow. It was a whiteout. I had no idea there was a blizzard expected. The best surprise was seeing my mom waiting for me. She had walked there to make sure I'd have a safe walk home. The streetlamps reflecting on the snow made it seem like it was daytime. Truly a picturesque moment.

Nightclubbing became a regular thing for me. I was going to as many shows as possible and making friends with bands like Nancy Boy and Loveless. Don Hill's was a popular rock establishment I'd frequent. At a show of the singer Dan Reed, I headed to the dressing room to say hello, having interviewed him for the magazine before. There I met Billy Squier, whose records I had many of, seeing as how he'd been a rock n roll staple since the seventies with hits like "The Stroke," "Everybody Wants You," and countless others. I was getting wise for nights like these and carried my demo tape in my back pocket. The next day he phoned to say how much he liked what he'd heard and asked if I'd be interested in signing a publishing agreement with him.

His angle was to represent the two songs on my tape in an effort to secure placement on a movie soundtrack. *Clueless* had just scored a hit at the box office and its soundtrack was equally a big seller. I sat on the contract for a few weeks. The terms of giving up 100 percent of my publishing wasn't something I was eager to sign off on. I'd always heard stories that you didn't want to give away your publishing rights. What the hell, it was only two songs, I put the pen to paper and mailed it back to him.

Every week I'd check the musician classifieds, meeting with players here and there, but nothing was clicking. The idea to just go at it alone with a guitar had struck me. The first two shows, I used only my middle name, going by Flanagan. I wish I had a recording of that first performance. The sound man had offered to do it for ten bucks. I got up on stage with my red corduroy blazer and Gretsch guitar and it was smooth as could be.

In '96 the cover of UK paper *Melody Maker* caught my eye. A scene was emerging that claimed to revitalize the New Romantics era from the early eighties. I was fascinated with the Blitz Kids movement, which had given life to Duran Duran, Spandau Ballet, Visage, Culture Club, and bands of that era. Now young new bands were attempting to capture the spirit and make their own mark. I had to be part of this. I figured if Jimi Hendrix could move to London to be discovered, it was time for someone else from the US to do it.

When I arrived in London, I went to a synagogue, at the advice of my dad, to check the bulletin board for housing options, landing in Golders Green with an Orthodox family who rented a room to me for sixty pounds per week. They were very kind, inviting me to join in having Shabbat dinner with them, making for an even more comfortable stay. I was given a key and could come and go as I pleased. Getting back at night would be a little tricky due to the tube stations closing at midnight. The buses ran later, though sometimes it seemed like I spent an eternity waiting around for them.

The first club I went to in London was called the Cell. The DJ there spun the cool stuff like Japan and Roxy Music. He looked like a dead ringer for Nick Rhodes. I had on my suit and skinny tie, but I'd have to step it up with the makeup. I approached him and asked if he was also a musician. Sure enough he was a keyboard player and introduced himself as Joseph. I spoke of being from the States and how I wanted to put together a band in London. I got his number and picked up a BT calling card. I'd make my calls from the very English red telephone boxes. Days later, I went over to Joseph's house, bringing along my guitar. We were impressed by each other. He spoke of some other guys he thought would be interested in doing a project together.

Next time I ventured into the nighttime world, before entering the club, I pulled out an eyeliner pencil and did my eyes while staring at my reflection in a storefront window. Now I was ready.

In an effort to save money, I moved to a different house, renting a room for ten pounds less. After checking into the new home, I started my day with the cheapest breakfast on the menu, which was located inside of the tube station. I ordered a sardine sandwich, thinking the protein would sustain me. Next, I headed to Camden Town to spend the day; there was a band playing that evening I was a fan of called My Life Story. My plan was to stay in the area until showtime, since there were always things to keep busy with like street fairs and record stores. For lunch there was a sidewalk vendor selling a big bowl of lo mein noodles for one pound. *Nice, saving more money.* At the gig, I wasn't hungry enough to order food, so I just got a pint of Guinness to stay full.

A couple of hours later, after the show, I was thinking maybe I needed something nutritious before I got back to the house. I stepped into a 7-Eleven. *Hmm, what should I get that won't break the bank?* Ah I saw it there, a half quart of milk. I drank three fourths of it and called it a night. Only the night wasn't done with me, it was just getting started. I woke up in a cold sweat and shivering. My stomach told me to fuck right off. I was in and out of the bathroom like it was a revolving door, soon as I got back in bed, I was on my feet again.

There was no way the landlady, whose room was right next to the bathroom, got any sleep that night either. In the morning I told her I was going to move back to the other house. She was relieved and even returned my money in full. That was the last time I vowed to be cheap with myself. A day later I wasn't feeling any better, I cut short my time in London for fear of dying.

8

BABY'S BLACK BERET

The *Village Voice* was the newspaper to place ads and find musicians in New York City. I circled one ad that grabbed my attention as I scoured its pages in hopes of starting a band. It listed one of the musician's influences as Suede, a British band with a dramatic and exciting alternative sound that I was really into. Next to the phone number was the name, Desi. There was a singer in LA I knew of with that name. The combination had me curious. When the person answered, the voice was disguised with an Asian accent. The accent sounded put on, though I took down the address and went over there anyway. When I got to the fifth floor, the door was wide open, I knocked to make aware my arrival. A blond French girl introduced herself as Désirée. We shook hands and I seated myself at the kitchen table.

She asked me if I knew her from somewhere. "No," I said with a half-crooked smile. I asked if that was her I'd spoken with on the phone.

"Yes," she admitted. It was her way to screen the calls and find out who was serious. She played my tape on her boom box. Thirty seconds into it, she looked up at me, excitedly proclaiming, "You're going to be famous!" Those words sounded familiar, I mused. Ideas immediately came to her, asking if I'd heard of Serge Gainsbourg and Jane Birkin. She had a strong sense of aesthetic and spoke about a boy/girl presentation, how the both of us should sing. I liked the idea, as no one was doing anything with that approach. Her voice was reminiscent of Kate Bush and mixed with mine it would make a nice dynamic. Everything we spoke about was in sync. What I thought would be a quick meeting turned out to be an all-day event. We hung out together until after nightfall.

The next day, when we spoke, Desi said she'd had a dream that I wanted to kill her. I laughed. "Why would I want to do that?" I asked.

"I think I knew you in a past life, and I was unfaithful to you." She always had something peculiar to say, it was just her way. Once, she described how she'd seen me in a vision even before we met—I was dressed in a top hat, holding a cane, with a crow on my shoulder. Desi was very specific with details.

We worked on our first song together, called "Under the Rain," and booked a studio in SoHo to put it to tape. It was our first collaboration. I instinctively knew what to do for this song. Desi certainly brought her own creativity to it. She was firm on the sounds she wanted to hear in the song. The partnership was evident and the result spoke for itself. In the control room I looked over to her, convinced I was staring at the next Debbie Harry. She had a definite presence, sex appeal, and unwavering determination.

We talked in depth about our dreams and the future. It was exciting to share these desires with someone who was feeling the same.

"What kind of life do you want to have?" she asked.

"To be on top of the entertainment world," I answered.

Her eyes widened, mixing in her French, *génial,* "brilliant," she was in agreement and invariably saw the big picture. "I'd like to find new artists to help, and you can continue writing songs for other people or go solo," she remarked, adding how a man can grow old gracefully, but nobody wants to look at an old woman still shaking her "hass."

"Ass, there's no *h*," I said. It was fun to correct her.

This brought up another question of hers, "How old are you?"

"I'm twenty-two."

"No, you can't be younger than me!" she half joked. Only a two-year difference. Age would be Desi's ongoing conundrum.

Our first photo shoot was taken by her friend Michael, who worked for French *Vogue*. Desi set up a space in her apartment with décor to achieve a kitschy look, taking charge of the direction for the shoot. She did my makeup, had extra clothes on hand for me to try, and positioned me to her liking. There were some great shots that Desi turned into a collage, making our eight-by-tens feel more like a pop art piece. We now had a complete package we could send out. I reached out to my contacts. Jonathan Daniel, who was with the publishing company Fiction Songs, was the first we heard back from. "Who's Désirée Amber?" he asked. "It sounds like a porn name." Yeah, maybe that wasn't the best stage name for her. He noted that our sound wasn't like what was currently going on. In my mind I thought that was probably a good thing, maybe we were ahead of the curve.

That summer Desi and I got to know each other more, sharing stories of our different backgrounds. Her father, Paolo Ambrosetti, had wanted his daughter to follow in his footsteps as an architect. She'd studied in Rome but dropped out in her last year of university because the music in her head was overtaking her. He disapproved, not surprisingly, and this put a divide between them. Strangely, Desi would tell me I looked like her father. She had dreamed of America since childhood, watching *Dick Clark's New Year's Rockin' Eve* on TV. When she moved out of her father's house, she moved to New York City.

One of her jobs early on was dancing at Club USA. I wondered if we had both been there at the same moment in time. She also spoke of being a hostess at various bistros that paid her under the table. Earning money off the books still continued to be her source of income. When I talked about my time in London, she asked if I'd go back there to live, without suggesting this be our plan or anything like that, it was just a hypothetical. "Absolutely," I said. Unknown to us then, it was more around the corner than not.

Through my PR contacts, I had scored a pair of tickets for the Cure at Radio City Music Hall on the day of the show and invited Desi. She sighed, I hadn't given her enough notice. True, I had pondered too much over it. Even though there were moments when it felt like something more was developing between us, neither of us was vocal about it. For us to see a local band at a club, that was no problem, but a Cure concert could be too sentimental.

We saw a band later called the Impotent Sea Snakes. I hadn't heard of them before, yet their New York Dolls image made it clear what they could only sound like. However, the Dolls might have been a little too polished for what we were about to witness. The band was half undressed and took the stage with dildos in their hands, spraying the audience from these X-rated pistols. Desi was disgusted. "You like this shit?" she questioned.

I had to laugh. I summed it up as "shock rock." I like theatrics, but this was a joke. Desi was convinced if people paid money for garbage, we could surely inspire an audience with real songs and our classy style.

Before long, Desi would tell me that she couldn't live in New York illegally any longer. She raised the question if I would join her in Paris, saying from there we could go on to London. There was nothing to think about, I told her I was in. Desi would leave at the end of the week, so we got together the night leading up to her departure. She had one request, that we would not turn around to look at each other once we said goodbye, reasoning that she didn't want it to be like a dramatic soap opera. We gave each other a hug. I turned around, she was true to her word.

The evening of her going away, when I got home from work, I checked my voicemail, "You have four new messages." They were all from Desi. Message number one was a snippet of the opening lines to "Unforgettable" by Nat King Cole. Message number two was "Creep" from Radiohead, starting with the part about being like an angel and ending with "so fucking special." Message number three was Cheap Trick's intro verse to "I Want You to Want Me." The fourth was her own personal greeting. Her voice never sounded more smooth and dreamy. "Hi, Ken, it's me, Désirée. I just want to say before I leave that I'm thinking of you. I hope you will join me soon, and, I love you." I smiled. Her feelings echoed mine. It was confirmation.

Desi wrote a lot of letters to me while back in Paris, her drawings decorated the contents. A simple note felt significant. It would have to suffice for now.

My plan was to keep working so I could pay for the flight and have enough cash reserved for when I was there.

It was December, the day after Christmas, when I arrived. From the airport I took a bus to Porte Maillot, where Desi casually greeted me with the cheek-to-cheek French tradition. She had told me before that she didn't like berets, but she was wearing one that day. It looked good on her. Paris was easy to love. There was beauty everywhere, in the buildings, the streets, the people. Being limited in the language only made it more appealing to me.

Desi arranged for us to stay the first night at her Aunt Marie's apartment, it was nice and big, and we'd have our own room. Her cousin Cécile was there to welcome us, she had a kind of bohemian artsy vibe, very friendly and near the same age as us. We all converged in the kitchen for a coffee. They were obviously talking about me and getting paranoid about whether I understood anything.

Night was upon us by now. "You must be tired," Desi said. We retreated to our room and tried to get some rest. Both of us tossing and turning in the sheets, fully aware of each other's energy, though not responding to it. An hour must've passed. I said to myself, *If something's going to happen then give me a sign,* hoping the universe was listening. Exactly at that moment I felt Desi's hand on my shoulder. I reached over to her and she positioned herself on top. Her kisses like warm milk. There was no time for sleep.

In the morning, there was no need to verbalize any definition of our relationship. It was obvious to us we were partners in every sense of the word. That afternoon Desi introduced me to her grandmother, whom we would stay with for a few days. If Desi and her cousin Cécile wondered if I understood French, her grandmother was convinced that I did. She would have these long conversations with me at the dining table, and I would nod my head in reaction to whatever she was saying. That would fuel her even more, she'd react and continue talking to me. It was fun. Desi would still be puzzled and ask if I understood what she was saying. When I'd say no, she would laugh and say her grandmother was crazy.

Her grandparents had raised Desi and her sister, Coraline, for some time when their mom and dad divorced. Desi spoke highly of her grandfather and said how it was a shame he wasn't alive anymore, that he would've loved me, and how he appreciated artists. He'd had his own magazine enterprise that was very successful in France. A connection between us.

Later that day her grandmother gifted me a sweater that had belonged to him. Desi was taken aback by the act of kindness, saying her grandmother never would've done that with just anyone.

For the evening plans, we'd be joining Desi's childhood friend Vanessa, who was gathering with friends for dinner. The restaurant was modern chic, or "show-off" according to Desi, not really her thing, she didn't care for what was considered trendy. I tried foie gras for the first time that evening. I'm the rare breed that grew up loving liver and pâté, so needless to say, foie was perfect. Shamefully I couldn't finish it. I was still adjusting to the jet lag, so my sense of appetite was still off.

With New Year's Eve approaching, all of Desi's extended family in France would be assembling at her grandparents' estate in the countryside, which her cousin Fabien was executor of. The house was actually a castle, I lost track of how many rooms it had, but there were more than twenty family members staying for the holiday and everyone had their own privacy without any concern. There was a separate triplex that was built in more recent years on the same lot; this is where the party was held and eventually where Desi and I resided for the rest of our stay. We played our demo in between records during the NYE festivities. By now everyone was so curious to hear what Desi and this young American sounded like. It was absolute fun to watch them dance along to our music.

The next couple of mornings after, I was confused as to why the family was eating oysters for breakfast, this seemed too early to start the day this way. Desi laughed, we were waking up in the afternoon, it was lunchtime already. Practically all of the family wondered if we were boyfriend/girlfriend. Now I understood what those paranoid discussions with her cousin had been all about. Desi denied it for a number of reasons that made sense to her. She didn't want to give them the satisfaction of knowing, nor did she want them passing judgment and thinking the only reason she was playing music was because of her boyfriend. Desi believed they were against her, she felt they thought of her as the crazy one. She would often say, "All they want is my death."

Having an entire part of the property to ourselves made it seem like the outside world didn't exist. We stayed inside day and night. The entertainment room had a stereo with a vast record collection. Desi educated me on Serge Gainsbourg, and I found some English titles to share. Genesis's…*And Then There Were Three* was among the bunch. I repeatedly played "Follow You, Follow Me," it was an appropriate message for our mood. There was a gem we discovered together in that collection that neither of us had heard before. It was a record by Donovan, the song "Celeste." We were stunned by its magical beauty and true poetry. We played it over and over again. It became our song.

When we weren't listening to music, we spent our time in front of the fireplace writing songs. An album's worth of material was born in those weeks in the countryside. In many ways we were expressing through song what we wanted to say to each other. "No walls between us / take these arms to hold you" spoke of strength in love. "If all of this is wasted / will there be just hatred" touched on the fear of it not working out.

There were no TVs, and they were not missed. When we wanted to relax, we took long baths together. That time was a luxury, but I eventually got antsy. One night, while we were preparing a pasta dinner, however my words came out, the gist of it was questioning how long we'd be staying there before going to London. I wanted to leave. Desi grabbed a handful of dishes, crashing them to the ground before storming out. My restlessness got the best of me. When I found her in the bedroom, I vented about only eating once a day and why we had to wait so late every night to have a meal. Back then she could live on coffee and cigarettes. For me, hunger + cabin fever = not a good combo. It was our first quarrel.

We spent another week in the countryside. During that time, a trip to the market was in order, so we caught a ride into town with her cousin. Desi made light of it by saying I was like the little bird that needed to be fed. She was happy, though, to get out for a while as well. We took a brief stroll to overlook the green hills before getting back to the house.

In the kitchen, while waiting for the water to boil on the stove, we were embracing and lip-locked, having a nice little make out, when Fabien burst in through the doors. Desi screamed, I laughed, he was shocked. Three different reactions. I said something ridiculous like, "She was trying to strangle me."

He retorted, "I'll strangle you!"

It was comedy. And now the secret was out.

In Paris, some time before we left for London, we had her grandmother's apartment to ourselves and were just lounging about when another secret was about to come to the surface. As she pulled out a document, Desi said, "I have something important to show you." I was imagining the worst. She stayed quiet as I read to myself. It was a police report from New York, she had been arrested for working illegally as a masseuse. I knew what that could be classified as. My mind raced, I was completely bothered by it, upset really. I asked if she had been tested. She broke down crying, saying that she wasn't a prostitute, but confessed that she'd complied when clients had doubled down for a hand job. She was ashamed, although she made it clear that she didn't want to keep any secrets between us and was telling me this to be truthful about why she had to come back to France.

By way of Eurostar, we took the train to London. All the great music we loved, we were now on our way to being part of the scene. As the customs cards were handed out, for Occupation I wrote down Musician, projecting it onto the future. When we deboarded and walked through customs, I was stopped.

"Musician?"

"Yes."

"Do you have your working papers?"

"No, it's a hobby," I said, quickly trying to spin this around.

"Where's your return ticket?" I didn't have the answers the agent wanted to hear. "Who are you traveling with?"

They put us in a holding room for more questioning while they went through our belongings. The agent found Desi's NYC arrest report, "What's this?" he asked like the cat that had caught the mouse.

"It's none of your business," Desi snidely remarked. The guy was all too pleased to refuse my entry.

There was one train heading back to Paris that night, and we were on it. It was a real letdown, both of us dejected, we snuggled up to one another to combat the terrible feeling. Being a European citizen, Desi could've continued on to London, except our hearts were with each other now. We would figure it out together.

Desi was relieved she had come clean about the New York incident. If she hadn't and that had been my first time learning about it, who knows what reaction might've followed. I likely wouldn't have trusted her. Despite this setback, we didn't give up on our aspirations of being in London. To spare the exhausting details here, ultimately I cleared up my passport circumstance with the British embassy.

The earliest mention of marriage commenced in those initial weeks in Paris. "Do you want to marry me?" Desi asked. This wasn't a proposal, it was a solution. I'd have the right to live with my European wife in the UK, or anywhere in Europe for that matter. Standing in the way was my own idea of what I thought a wedding should look like. Exchanging vows for the sake of "together forever" had more meaning to me than just a rhyme. Desi, on the other hand, didn't care for fairy-tale nonsense. We had something to achieve, and if we were in love, then why worry about it fitting the perfect image.

Since we'd be in Paris for the foreseeable time, Desi thought of some people to reach out to. She had a friend named Taxi who was an actress on French soap operas and had some connections in music. One person Desi ended up calling was from the band Telephone. I didn't know them. In France, however, they were considered rock stars. We went over to the house of guitarist Louis

Bertignac. Desi didn't translate any of the conversation, and the guy wasn't speaking any English.

"Naked (The Beautiful Truth)" was Desi's favorite song of mine, and the first one that I ever played for her back in New York. Naturally, this was the song she wanted him to listen to. We must've been there for roughly an hour, and I wasn't getting a read on whether his reaction was positive or not. When we left his house, I asked, "So, how'd it go?"

Desi replied, "Oh my god, this guy is such an asshole. You didn't see the jealousy in his eyes?" She added, "He had hatred for you," and said how he'd bragged, "All I need to do is take these three chords, change it around, and I have my own song." I agreed with Desi and asked how to say *asshole* in French. Desi ceaselessly would tell me I was the next David Bowie. Saying that in front of other people could be lunatic. I don't know if that had happened with Louis Bertignac, but it was becoming evident to us that when we were together, our energy propelled people to either greatly dislike us or totally appreciate us. There was no middle.

The good of being together outweighed all the disappointments. We had fun despite the bullshit. Desi showed me her favorite parts of Paris, we went to Montmartre, to the cinema, to the flea markets. She had the idea of dressing me up in a fur coat and found a cool grey suede with a faux-fur collar that she treated me to.

When we passed by astrology books for sale when browsing in bookstores, Desi was all about them and read up on the meaning of our birthdates. She said I was "born to be a heartbreaker" and would "find great rewards in the arts." The description she read for herself in one noted her as being born on the day of the sacrifice. She couldn't stand the thought of having to compromise her dreams or give up a part of herself to benefit someone else. I insisted she shouldn't take it at face value. It was a good laugh, though, how this made her so furious.

Another place Desi took me to was Café de Flore. She insisted we order the hot chocolate. It was so thick and strong, I seriously got a buzz off of it. One of Desi's quirks was to ask who she looked like. It wasn't superficial, it was more about trying to gauge how someone else might see her, or if she saw herself the same way. When someone walked passed us she'd say, "Does she look like me?" If I said no, she would respond, "No, she does, she looks like me." Or she'd ask, "Who do I look like, then?"

"Uma Thurman," I'd answer.

"Oh I love her, okay, that makes me happy," she'd reply.

Her way of seeing things was unique. "Don't you think some people look like monsters?" she asked, observing their features. "Look at this guy, he's grotesque. Some people have strange faces. Sometimes I see myself like that."

"But a minute ago you thought you looked like someone attractive."

She would say, "I know, you must think I'm crazy." The best was to see her pull her face back with her hands, convinced that she needed a face lift.

At the end of February, my funds were close to being depleted. I'd arranged to fly back to New York, taking any odd job, so that I could feel a little more stable upon returning abroad. I don't know why we didn't take a taxi to the station, we opted to walk from her grandmother's to where I needed to catch the bus. I had a full-size suitcase and my guitar in its hard case. They were both the same weight. Desi carried the guitar for me, otherwise I would've been walking like a snail. Now with one hand free, we had the speed of turtles. A good lesson for light packing ever after. With another goodbye staring at us, we told ourselves it wouldn't be long. Within a month and some change, I was back in Paris again.

When I was away, Desi and her friend Taxi went to a concert for the band Suede. Taxi was friends with the singer, Brett Anderson, who managed to get them both into the aftershow party. Desi gave Brett our demo, then met one of the band's inner circle. She spoke of our plans to go to London, and the guy offered to set her up somewhere when we got there. Desi didn't waste time, she went ahead to London to try and secure something ahead of schedule. When she met with him in London, the guy brought her to an apartment and, upon entering, he kicked someone else out, telling them to pack their shit and go. It was clear to Desi this was a place people used for squatting.

He asked her on the spot, "So, do you want the room?" She answered that she would have to discuss it with me. He wasn't going to wait, however, and demanded a yes or no right then and there. Ultimately, she went back to Paris, knowing I was soon to return.

Desi continued to make progress and, once I was back, introduced me to JP, a musician in Paris with a modest studio set up in his home. After completing a session with him, we were armed with more material, which gave Desi and me a push to try and establish interest for ourselves in the French market. We were there so why not try and utilize that. It could be interesting, a Parisian and an American. In the course of several weeks, we met with more people. One was A&R at a reputable label who encouraged us to sing some of our songs in French. Desi, however, was somewhat reluctant since she wanted to be established in English, for the sake of appealing to a broader audience.

A local producer also became involved for a while. At first he set up an appointment with a songwriter who wanted us to record one of her songs, a track called "Kurt Cobain." Another reason Desi disliked the French mentality, she saw this as a way for them to cash in on an American icon, with no merit to the connection. We sat through it as a courtesy. What garbage. No way we would stoop to such a thing. The song itself had no hook, no melody. We made it clear to the producer that we wrote our own material, and if he thought this shit we'd just heard was better, *au revoir, connard*. See, my French vocabulary was improving.

Without knowing how long we'd be in France for, we bounced around from place to place. Most of the time at Desi's grandmother's, especially when she traveled to her countryside estate. Otherwise, Aunt Marie would graciously host us. This time around we also spent a couple of weeks at Desi's mom's house in Senlis while she was on vacation with her husband. I found Senlis to be really charming, more like a village with cobblestone streets. Our days were spent listening to Pink Floyd's *The Wall*, making songs, and fucking. Desi was horrified one night when we'd left the French shutters open, and a peeping tom stood right in front of the window watching us. He must've thought he was in Pigalle for a moment.

Once back in Paris, the marriage discussion was reintroduced. I wrestled with the thought of getting married for any objective other than love. At any rate, I would need my birth certificate and called home to have it sent in case. When I said what it was for, there wasn't any resistance, as long as I felt it was the right decision, my parents were surprisingly cool about it. Soon as the FedEx envelope arrived, we were off to the *mairie*.

Here's the kicker. When I'd passed through customs at Charles de Gaulle Airport, they hadn't stamped my passport. There was no physical record of my entrance into the country without it. To apply for a marriage license, the *mairie* informed us that I would need to have this. "Okay, let's go to the airport then." We spoke to a number of personnel at CDG, yet the answer was the same, that they couldn't stamp it now without my original point of entry. Desi laughed. "Well how do you think he got here?" They said they didn't always stamp it, depending which country one was traveling from. And next time if they didn't, I should just ask them to. Unsurprisingly, we left there dissatisfied.

Looked like we'd be getting married in New York. In the same way I had anxiety about attempting to enter London again, Desi was worried about her prior arrest and whether she'd be detained at the airport upon entering. Now I was the voice of reason. My incident had happened at customs, hers had not. It didn't make sense to me that they would have that information, and it wasn't like she was some type of wanted criminal. This put her at ease.

Before we left, I would need to do something I hadn't gotten to do on the previous go-around. Visit my relatives. Most of my cousins from my father's side of the family lived in Paris. Meeting his uncle Joseph was long overdue and also heartwarming. The man didn't speak a word of English, yet all his emotions were spoken through his eyes, and in his bear hugs. So glad Desi could translate the questions and answers. I know she enjoyed being involved and experiencing this part of family with me, much as I delighted in her being there by my side.

9

MEET THE COOPERS

Touchdown. Desi made it through customs without a sound. We were back in the city where we'd begun. Only now we would have to stay apart for a little while. It wouldn't have been the best introduction to bring Desi into this one-room apartment to meet my parents right then and there, let alone endure the uncomfortableness of staying in this already cramped environment night after night. I figured it best to shield her from this and delay it for her own good.

She stayed with Michael, the photographer from French *Vogue*, for the first night, and with another friend for a few days thereafter. We spent our days together up until we were exhausted and ready for sleep, but it was getting stressful on us both to do things this way. I arranged for us to go up to Connecticut and stay at the house in West Hartford, at least there we could have some space to ourselves.

Mom and Dad offered to drive us there, which meant Desi would meet them at the apartment just before leaving, literally outside by the car. This was my own hang-up, I was too ashamed to bring her upstairs. The place was unkempt, stuff would pile up on the floors, almost as if my parents were hoarders, no, in fact it was just like they were hoarders. Dad came out first, and I made the introductions. It seemed cordial. While Mom and Desi exchanged small talk, Dad had an open lane to say something to me as we loaded the trunk. "I hope you're not seriously thinking of getting married." I took that as a sense of him disapproving of Desi and as another way of telling me to keep my options open.

There wasn't much talk on the three-hour drive. But that wasn't unusual. As a kid, when we'd take long trips, silence or listening to the radio prevailed over chatter. It was nighttime once we got to West Hartford. In the morning we'd stock up on groceries before my parents headed back to the city. Desi had not seen supermarkets of this size before. It would become her simple pleasure.

Desi kept a journal, writing down her thoughts and lyrical ideas, or she would draw sketches of majestic-looking buildings or dresses she had in mind to design. Never at a loss for creativity. We had our instruments with us, however I don't recall any songs being born during those weeks. Connecticut was mostly downtime to chill for a moment and plot our next steps. Going into town was easy on foot, we'd take walks to the main street, where there was a record store and a Japanese restaurant. I think that's where I turned Desi on to sushi and made her a believer. Something I would proudly be known to do for many friends in years to come, giving them their first hit of hamachi.

To paint an idea for Desi of what my hometown of Las Vegas was like, we took the bus to Foxwoods. Sure she knew the casinos of Monte Carlo, but how could that stack up to Connecticut? I thought for sure she should have the all-you-can-eat experience. An hour waiting on line and she was furious, until we were seated and she discovered all the endless options. Those big American buffets certainly became another one of her delights.

Around midnight we were back in West Hartford. Buses stopped running early and the only way home was by taxi. They all lined up in a queue; we got into an unmarked car. Sliding into the back seat we noticed the driver was not alone, he had a front passenger with him. We freaked. As quick as we got in, we slid right on out. The next car seemed more trustable, until the driver asked us why we got out of the other one. Desi nudged me and whispered, "Don't give him the address." We got dropped off on the main street and walked a couple blocks with eyes in back of our heads. West Hartford at night felt just a little bit shady.

One of the perks of the house was a vintage claw-foot tub in the bathroom. This would provide much respite. It also proved to be where too much thinking could overtake any sense of tranquility. Desi would get distressed about losing time, she saw herself as being older than she was, or in a race with herself to achieve and accomplish before some time she deemed as too late.

I understood this part, as I wanted to realize dreams and attain goals while in my early twenties as well. One obstacle between us was the more marriage was discussed, the more it felt like pressure on me. The night prior to going back to NYC, we got in an argument over when this would happen, with her reminding me that she couldn't stay there legally and how we had decided in Paris that we would marry in the States. Things got so heated we ended up sleeping in separate beds. After I had fallen asleep, she woke me up very sweetly, "Are you feeling better now?" As I reached out my hand for her, I was met with a cold glass of water being poured over my face. Not the greatest feeling when you think you're about to make up.

On the drive back to NYC, my dad passed me an article that he'd clipped out of a magazine. It was about Nashville being a hot place for discovering new talent. This sounded like a great idea; despite the city's reputation for country music, maybe there was something brewing we could tap into. The next day we went to Port Authority and booked two tickets on the Greyhound. We were assigned separate seats. The woman who sat next to me noticed Desi and I were together and offered to swap seats. I told her it was okay, we were good. Still pissed from the glass of water incident.

Twenty-four hours later we checked into a cheap motel on the east side. Mainly getting around on foot, we'd cross over the Cumberland River to get to downtown, where all the honky-tonks were. To be honest, Broadway felt run-down, it was all a bit depressing really. Most of the singers playing for change on the sidewalks looked like they lived a hard life. When passing a woman with her karaoke machine, Desi said quietly, "Please, god, don't let me end up like that."

We did the same routine for a week. Get up in the morning, walk past the hookers, and make our way downtown. Picking up the *Scene* paper en route, checking the classifieds, and even visiting apartments to gauge prices should we consider staying longer. Desi definitely stood out to the locals, no one dressed like she did, with her European poise and flair. Guys would whistle at her. Once some dude yelled out, "Some guys have all the luck."

If we could get this reaction, maybe it was possible to find our niche here. We looked into staying at a Days Inn downtown; it was the complimentary breakfast that sealed it for us. We relocated there and extended our stay in Nashville for another week. At a coffeehouse somewhere off the beaten path, we found an ad on the bulletin board, some guys were seeking musicians and listed influences like Blur and other UK bands. That was the only time we saw an inkling of something other than country music might be happening in town. I'm quite sure we called. Maybe Desi tried speaking Chinese again. No one returned the call. Another number we dialed was for a recording studio advertising affordable rates.

Why not, we thought, it'd be fun to record in Nashville, plus there'd be a chance of finding out about other like-minded musicians. The owner, who was also the engineer, sounded very nice over the phone, he would even pick us up and drive us back. Southern hospitality. We booked a four-hour block and worked quickly to do three songs. While Desi was in the vocal booth, the guy turned to me to say, "She's beautiful," and asked where she was from. He thought we sounded great together and commented that our style was different from what he was used to hearing. When we wrapped and got a ride back to the hotel, he had some parting words for me, "Don't let that one get away."

It was 1997. Whatever was written in that magazine article must've been hype. We weren't feeling it. Nashville was very much a country music city. It would be a long time before things changed. The bus on the way back to New York broke down. Damned if that wasn't a metaphor for us. Desi stayed at the apartment with us this time around, all of us together now. When Dad and I went to get takeout for dinner one night, by the time we'd returned, Desi was in tears. Apparently my mom had lashed out at her. Desi said Mom had criticized her from head to toe, right down to the thigh-high boots she wore, scolding her that only whores wore clothes like that. This was an early sign that no one would be good enough for me in my parents' minds. I'd experienced this from my dad, now I was seeing it also from my mom.

Desi slept on my army cot. I tried my best to console her while wiping away her tears. She didn't deserve that. I told her I loved her and that whatever they thought wasn't going to change anything about how I felt about us. "But you don't want to marry me," she said, sobbing even more, adding that leaving the States was her only option. I promised I would join her again. We repeated the pattern of staying out all day until it was time to sleep. A couple of days later she boarded the plane, and in a matter of weeks it would be my time to mind the gap again.

I was still somewhat paranoid about traveling with my guitar again. I wanted to avoid any questions at all costs. My proposition was to have my parents come along—no one was going to question an old man carrying a guitar. Mom and Dad had no qualms about it, plus this gave them reason for a vacation, one they hadn't taken together in a long time. Also, I'm sure they figured the more they saw my intent with Desi, the better.

Once we landed and got through customs, I called Desi to let her know it was green light go. We had a nice reunion at Waterloo Station, of all places. After retreating back to our own room at the London House, we then met up with my parents for dinner at an excellent Chinese place on Paddington Street that I had remembered from my first visit. Our immediate mission going forward was to solidify an apartment. The following day we went to an agency and looked at a number of places, although without jobs we kept running into the same issue, one of us needed to be employed and show income. Time to search the adverts for people looking for a flatmate.

We met Frances, a nice woman in Blackheath who was happy to rent us a room in her home. She was young, though some years older than us. Many nights I would fix dinner. We practically lived on a diet of pasta, and by now I had perfected Desi's sauce recipe and made it my own. I'd make enough so Frances could join us. She was very amused by our love story and pursuits. Our spirit must've rubbed off on her. Sometimes we'd come home and she'd have her music turned up loud. Eventually she had dates over and we always had a laugh when we'd hear her getting railed. Desi would ask me, "Is she being loud on purpose?"

Desi quickly found a job at a retail clothing store. With the commute from Blackheath being an hour by tube, she wondered if I would meet her after work or if I'd just stay at the house. I said I'd probably wait for her in Blackheath. Riding on the train could feel like a journey with all the stops and connections. On her first day of work, I surprised her by calling out her name right as she was heading underground into the tube station. She was so happy. The thought of her working all day and then coming home alone, that wouldn't have been cool. Every day I'd go into town to meet her after work and we'd ride the train together back to Blackheath.

On her days off we'd go into London and explore. Sometimes to the movies or to record shops, and secondhand stores. She wasn't a fan of the common type of department stores that catered to her demographic. She preferred finding vintage.

One time, when we passed by a shoe store in Oxford Circus, there were boots in the window she insisted on buying for me. Black leather with a two-inch heel. I loved the extra height they gave me. So cool, I said they would look great on stage. She thought I should wear them all the time. Desi had an eye for clothes; she always wanted to style me a certain way. She convinced me to wear my hair with a fringe. Projecting what she found to be sexy on to me.

I got back in touch with Joseph, the keyboard player I'd met on my first UK trip. He was all for getting together and was excited to meet Desi and hear what we were working on. The same day we met up, we recorded a new song with him. This guy could be the perfect addition. He had great ideas. Maybe he toked the spliffs a little too much, nonetheless his contribution was tasteful. We just couldn't seem to pin him down after that.

We went to shows hoping to meet our people, each taking one side of the venue to scope out for ourselves. When we met back in the middle one particular night, I said, "I found someone cool." He looked good, though he was clearly full of himself when we started to chat. He said he was already in a band.

"What's the name?" Desi asked.

"The Prostitutes of New York," he replied. We looked at each other, barely containing our laughter.

After a month we left Blackheath and found a flat in a three-story building in Willesden Green, right on the Jubilee line directly in London. This made our commute to the West End way easier. The apartment was a small studio with a shared bathroom located on the top floor. The hot water for the bathtub was operated by coins. If either of us had to pee in the middle of the night, we pissed in a pot. Despite its primitiveness, we were content with it, regardless that the first day we settled in, I was left to wait for the electrician to come turn on our power. That's the one similarity to the US, none of the service providers ever give a set time as to when to expect them. I was waiting all day. This was the winter and it was freezing in there.

By the time Desi came home, she found me curled up in blankets in the pitch dark. Candles would have to do. The next morning someone showed up and explained all payments thereafter would need to be made at the 7-Eleven, where we'd pay and "top up our key" for electricity. It was the most bizarre system either of us had heard of.

Thankfully we had a two-top stove and could make spaghetti now. For entertainment we would have to improvise. Desi would make a run downstairs for a pack of cigarettes and ask if I would like a treat or anything from the mart.

"Yes, bring back a porn mag," I replied once. She laughed and called me a pervert, saying she would never do such a thing. She walked in later and threw a copy of *Club International* on the bed. We could make each other laugh, we got each other's sense of humor. During sex that night, she turned the pages, saying, "You wanna fuck her, fuck her good." Porn wasn't her thing but she could have fun with it.

That night we had a sudden stroke of brilliance. Upon noticing the adverts for hotlines in the back pages, we started tearing the magazine apart, clipping out ads that read "30 SECOND WANK-OFF ACTION!" It was a perfect caption to get someone's attention. We slapped those onto the cover of our demo tapes. Who could refuse to listen to at least thirty seconds? Some tapes we decorated with the most explicit shots we could find. We bought one of those books that had industry contact info and began to send out packages.

One of the recipients was the manager of the band the Sundays. He spoke to Desi, "I'm shocked, is that you on the cover?"

She quipped back, "If it was, would you sign us?" Perhaps it was nothing more than a guy thinking he might have an easy shot to sleep with a desperate woman who'd do anything to make it. Needless to say, nothing came from it. Maybe we were better off without a gimmick.

London was a great time for us, if only the music part of it had come together. We carried on placing ads and mailing demos. I contemplated getting a job, something like one of those simple gigs handing out flyers to passersby, maybe they paid in cash.

Not the case, even that had hoops to jump through. We were basically living off Desi's retail employment. I was grateful I could call home and have money wired to me when help was needed. On a particular day when I had time to kill before meeting Desi after work, I popped into a gentleman's club in Soho, thinking I'd order a beer and see some skin. The hostess came around a second time. I'd barely gotten to work on the first drink and she was already asking me to order my next. "It'll just be the one," I said. She pulled out a menu, telling me to read the fine print. There was some bullshit about a two-drink minimum and service fee for the girls. I interjected that I hadn't requested any girl. What was this nonsense where you didn't have a choice? She raised her voice, "PAY UP!" I took out money for the beer as she shouted at someone to come over and resolve the problem. I looked to my right and saw this huge muscleman dude and thought for sure I wasn't getting out of there without being pummeled to a bloody pulp. I threw down whatever extra pound notes were in my wallet and stormed the hell out of there.

Sometimes Desi and I would speak in gibberish to each other, making up a language of our own. She would invent words, like *litaro* was added on to almost anything—sushilitaro, wafflelitaro, answer the phonelitaro. What its origin was I have no idea, it didn't matter, it was just how we spoke to each other. Every other day she had a new nickname for me. She would call me Ti Ti, and so I named her Tu Tu. I gave her the name the Little, and I became Dolittle. Then it was Carmelitu, the Cat, the Lizard, and more than I could keep track of. No shortage of lunacy.

We were utterly silly together, like the time when Desi bemoaned that a suppository she'd taken wasn't having any effect. Not surprising considering our seven-day-a-week pasta diet. I suggested an enema when I noticed a funnel in the midst of all the other kitchen supplies.

Sometimes you have to ad lib and use what's available to you. Desi frowned at this option before giving her consent. She must've really wanted to feel relief pretty damn bad to give in to my Dr. Demento idea. Tomorrow's dinner I'd use more diced tomatoes for extra fiber.

It was coming up on three months in London. That was a short time, not long enough to build a foundation on, not for us anyway. My visa was close to expiring, and I was starting to worry about being there illegally. I know we both wished things had come together faster, after all, London was where we wanted to be. These technicalities would be a burden, though. I flew back to New York while Desi stayed on until our next revelation struck.

10

THROUGH THE DESERT

Los Angeles sounded good. It had been four years since I'd left. I was reading an unofficial biography on Guns N' Roses that detailed those early years, and I started to romanticize the scene, believing that history could be made again in Hollywood. My brother had gone to live there while I was in Europe. He was promoting a nightclub with friends and said how awesome things were back in LA. Desi and I would share a two-bedroom apartment with him on Franklin Avenue.

Ever since Paris, whenever I spoke of Vegas to Desi, she fantasized about us driving there together, asking if I'd take her through the desert. She also loved the song "Horse with No Name," by America, which provided some source of inspiration for such an adventure. We'd make the trek, but not before going back to the grind.

LA had its challenges with looking for work and just getting around. I would borrow my brother's car whenever possible. Otherwise we took the bus, or, for basic needs, we were within walking distance of Mayfair Market and my old stomping grounds—the Bourgeois Pig. Anytime we shopped at Food 4 Less, we'd end up pushing a shopping cart for almost an hour back to the apartment. Missing Persons' "Walking in LA" was an appropriate theme song for us.

The usual attempts were made in search of musicians. We didn't want to play with drug addicts, but for the most part, that seemed to be the kind who responded to our ads. I called my pal Jeff, from Circus, whom I hadn't seen in years, thinking maybe he might know some people to connect us with. He invited us to meet up with him at a sushi bar next to Beverly Center. At the restaurant, he was all decked out, not at all how I remembered him. He clearly paid more attention now to projecting some sort of "supercool" image, complete with the starlet girlfriend accessory. General small talk turned into a bit of peacocking.

"What have you been up to?" I asked.

"I did a video with George Michael, haven't you seen 'Fastlove'?"

He asked Desi where she was from, then instantly mocked a French accent, laughing with his lady as if he had an audience to entertain. And this was merely three minutes after saying hello. Desi stood up and dished it right back to him. "Look at you thinking you're so self-important, but really you're just a fucking *poseur*!" Their faces dropped. She walked out. I had nothing to add to that, it was perfectly phrased. "I'm sorry I insulted your friend, but he's an asshole," said Desi. Agreed. It was actually pleasing to see Desi did not take shit from nobody.

At the apartment, there were always various characters dropping by, mostly at all hours of the night, as my brother was heavily into his party scene. Comedian Andy Dick came through a lot. You'd know when he was over because he was always obnoxiously loud. Desi and I would be sound asleep and he'd barge into our room, flicking the lights on and off while yelling, "WAKE UP, LITTLE BROTHER! WAKE UP!" Lots of girls showed up too, though typically they'd all be doing coke in Scott's room. For a while he was hooking up with porn star Tabitha Stevens. She took us out to lunch once. She seemed like a nice, unpretentious girl.

Desi would tell me if I ever cheated on her it was okay. "Just don't tell me about it," she'd say. She seemed sincere about it, that she understood men were different and that it had nothing to do with wanting to be faithful. When we had a talk about our image as a band and how to present ourselves, I told her maybe we shouldn't say we're a couple, that it would be better for people to think we were both single. I'd tease her after that by saying I was public property. She didn't like that idea too much.

From time to time, Desi would lash out at me over our circumstances, and damn, could she scream her lungs out! Sometimes she was upset with decisions I'd made or hadn't made, and sometimes upset with herself. She said I was always so balanced, while she would be struggling with her moods. After any heated argument, I'd allow space. I could keep my distance or detach from the situation altogether. It's a fine line between removing yourself and shutting the other person out though.

To her credit, Desi would always be the first one to come around and try to make things better again. Years later, she asked me how I put up with all her outbursts. I just accepted that that was how she was, and maybe that was how all women were, for that matter, I didn't have anyone else to base my assumptions on. This was the first relationship in which I lived with my other half.

We had a noisy next-door neighbor whom we would repeatedly hear through the walls. We gave him the name Rip. He was constantly burping these super-loud belches, hence the name we christened him with. We didn't actually see who this person was for quite a while, so we had an ongoing game in which anytime we saw someone in the building—when checking the mail or passing someone on the stairs—we'd look at each other and say, "That's Rip!" In due course, we finally did see him as he was opening the door to his apartment. A grizzly bear of a guy, no wonder these sounds emitted from him. Next time we heard him echo through our room, Desi yelled out, "DISGUSTING!"

He shouted back, "WHAT?!" Conversations with Rip.

If we thought the dildo band we'd seen in New York was terrible, those guys had some stiff competition. We went out to the Coconut Teazer, the band taking the stage was called Willow Wisp. Goth to the max, the unflattering kind. They brought up buckets of squid with them and began to pull them apart and chuck the pieces at the crowd. Within seconds the place smelled like the most rancid fishery you could imagine. Great way to build a fan base. Desi couldn't understand why I kept bringing her to see awful bands. It wasn't by design.

One show I wanted the both of us to go to was Cheap Trick. They were doing a night at the Roxy. Desi happened to get sick the day before and insisted I go without her. The show was great, and afterwards I fared even better. As the club emptied out, I was hanging out front to see if I recognized any friends who might've been inside.

None that I could tell, unless I considered three-quarters of KISS to be my friends. There were Gene, Paul, and Ace walking from the side door on over to the Rainbow. *Well shit, I think I'll head in too.*

Inside, I saw Tommy Thayer, who was working as their tour manager, and whom I'd sent music to before. We hadn't met previously, so I took this as an opportunity to introduce myself. "Hey! Come sit with us," he said. How gracious of him. Here I was sitting at a table with Paul Stanley one seat away from me, and Tommy being all casual and cool about it. They were digging into their pizzas, enjoying themselves. Paul motioned to Ace to grab a slice, and I was caught between one part of my brain thinking, *How am I here*, and the other part believing I should be here. Let's just get up before someone tests the latter theory.

Evidence showed the LA scene for local bands just wasn't thriving at this time, the days of old were gone. It felt like we were getting nowhere, not connecting with any of the musicians we met. Perhaps we were being too picky, we had a vision in mind and if others didn't match the criteria, then why waste time? I placed an ad representing myself as a solo artist, to see if that garnered a different set of results. I met a great guitar player. Now I had a 25 percent batting average.

As we hadn't gotten anything going within Desi's six-month passport time allotment, the inevitable was coming—she would be going back to Paris. While we still had a four track at the apartment, at least we'd write and record three new songs, this time all sung in French. This would give her something current to pitch to the French market. What else did we have going? The beauty of new songs is with them comes new hope.

A weekend in Vegas was in the cards, it was my chance to show Desi my hometown, and hers to see the desert she had imagined. She took a liking to it straightaway. The lavish hotels gave a sense of luxury, the swimming pools like paradise, nonstop action in the casinos screamed life was happening there.

But there was something disrupting her from fully enjoying it, knowing we could easily get married there and also knowing she didn't have enough money for a ticket back home. She dreaded having to ask her mom to help her out.

As we walked through Caesars Palace, the jumbo slot was vacant and right in front of us. I put a dollar in and JACKPOT! I won a couple hundred dollars like that on the first spin. Maybe Desi was Lady Luck. I gave her the winnings, she said, "I guess I'm going home then."

It was becoming routine, and dare I say the norm. It sounds crazy to say I went back to Paris, but I did just that. I joined Desi in mid-September. This was probably the most laid-back, stress-free time that we had spent together up to this point. We were able to simply enjoy our life without the added pressure we constantly put on ourselves. Sure we met with industry people again, presenting the French demos, but as this wasn't the end goal for us, we were able to approach it less critically.

Desi now had her own cute little apartment that she shared with her friend Benedicte. Most of the time Benedicte wasn't around, she had a crazy boyfriend, whom she'd stay with quite often. So usually it was just me and Desi. *Mamouna* by Bryan Ferry was our soundtrack. It was on constant repeat, pretty much the only CD in rotation. There were days we just lay on the couch listening to it, gazing out the French shutters, dreaming in unison. We celebrated my birthday together for the first time, Desi wanted to make sure she picked out a cake I would like, bringing home an amazing chocolate mousse from Fauchon. Later we went for a drive around the Champs-Élysées with Benedicte and her boyfriend, Samuel, who was revved up to take us to Queen and other nightclubs to celebrate.

The high holidays followed, with Yom Kippur falling the day after my birthday that year. Desi told me Samuel, who was also Jewish, wanted to do something special with me before the fast, just the two of us. We had dinner at a bistro. Aperitifs, hors d'oeuvres, bottles of wine. The smoked salmon platter alone was more lavish than what I'd had at my bar mitzvah. This guy just loved to order.

It was like the scene in Cheech and Chong's *Nice Dreams* when they're in the Chinese restaurant, "Gargoyle, more food!" I could barely eat another bite, and this was before the main course!

For services, all of us went to an Orthodox synagogue the day of. The temple itself was awe-inspiring. Quite a privilege to experience the holiday in Paris. Despite the separation of the men and women, I was touched to see Desi participate and be there with me. Afterwards, Samuel was all too happy to wine and dine us and break the fast with some authentic *Chinois*.

Never before had I taken any photos my previous times I'd lived in Paris. I'd packed a camera that hadn't seen one shutter of a frame until now. I was always too in the moment, caught up in the chase, no time to stop and click a single shot. And in some ways that's a beautiful thing as well, to just have the memories without a paper trail. This time however felt different. I captured the innocence while we still had it.

11

ELVIS OR A RABBI?

What I'd been waiting for was the feeling that I couldn't live without her. I could no longer stand the distance. For my own conviction I had to reach this point in order to believe in marriage. I spent a few months in Paris before returning to LA. It was depressing to be back in the Franklin apartment without Desi. I'd hear Rip and there was no one to curse at him. Some of my personal belongings were missing, like guitar pedals and a road case. I asked Scott what had happened to my stuff while I was gone. He said hazily, "I don't know, Zim Zum from Marilyn Manson was over here, maybe he took it."

I flew to Vegas to visit my parents, who were living there again now. After a few days, my dad put it in my ear, "Why not send some résumés out while you're here, see if anything comes about?" I didn't see Vegas as a place I wanted to be, although it made sense that there were a lot of work opportunities, and with nothing going on back in LA, it was a good idea. I dressed up in leather pants, my London heeled boots, vintage pink dress shirt, and tight-fitted blazer. This was my idea of fashion for hitting up the high-end couture boutiques. I walked into Versace at the Forum Shops at Caesars and was greeted by Sunil, the manager. He looked over my résumé on the spot and said he'd give me a call. For references I had given my dad's phone number, but used a different name for him so that he didn't appear to be a family member. We were in the car when Sunil called, asking a standard question, "Was he a good employee?"

Dad replied, "You'd be lucky to have him." He winked, hung up, and said to me, "You got this one." Sure enough I did.

I called Desi to share the news. She was thrilled, expressing how good of a job it was to have landed. I declared we would get married in Vegas. Understandably she was skeptical at first, but her excitement would soon overrule that. I received a phone call from her mom, Odile, who wanted to be sure I was serious this time, telling me she was coming with the family and I couldn't back out now. I reassured her I was true.

Desi arrived back in the States in December, we would celebrate the holidays again, this time in our new town. That New Year's Eve, I made my first big sale at Versace, to a couple of young dudes from Utah who just dropped some righteous bucks on jewelry. They also wanted to hang out with us for the festivities. Desi liked their wild streak, she was happy to make new friends and do something fun to bring in 1999. It was a madhouse on the Strip, no room to move, people stepping on our heels, pushing and shoving their way to get nowhere. The casinos locked the doors to avoid in-and-out traffic and to reduce the risk of trouble. Right as the countdown was coming, I nearly got trampled as some dipshit drunk was spinning around looking for a place to puke his guts out. People were forcing their way through to get out of his way. Three... two... one... and then it happened, chunks flew right on my back. Now people sure cleared the hell away. Immediately I took my jacket and flipped it inside out—it was my only blazer and I needed it for work.

Desi was in agreement that we call it a night and head home. With all the streets closed off, we walked the entire way. Our place was downtown, near Fremont Street, at a building owned by Mr. Mintz, a friend of my father's. It had been convenient to move into since it came furnished, and I wouldn't need a credit check or deposit. My parents also resided in one of the neighboring units.

The question for our wedding was if we should just go into one of those twenty-four-hour chapels. I knew there was a drive-through where Elvis could be the master of ceremonies. Desi was fine with city hall, though both our parents wanted something more meaningful than that. It was decided we'd have it at a temple and Rabbi Hecht, who was a friend of the family, would marry us. We set it up for late January 1999.

Naturally some preparations had to be made beforehand. One of which was my parents felt I needed a prenup. For what? I didn't have an asset to my name. There was property, however, forty acres of land in Utah that my brother and I would inherit, which they were concerned about protecting. Desi didn't really care, whatever would speed up the process. I met with an attorney, who advised that I add intellectual property in the agreement as well. It was a bit ridiculous adding song titles to the list; regardless, I supplied him with this, and Desi did the same.

At the suggestion of my father, we went to see Mordecai at the Jewelers for the wedding rings. In the early seventies, when my dad was advertising director for the Dunes Hotel, he was constantly approached by business entrepreneurs who would vie for his involvement to help secure them a retail space inside the hotel. One was a gentleman from Japan who offered him a fifty-fifty split if he could get him in there. Another was Mordecai. My dad had decided to help him because he was Jewish and my dad considered it to be a mitzvah. When we went to meet him at one of his many stores, we spoke of the occasion and said we just wanted simple bands, nothing flashy. What he presented us with and charged us for was an absolute embarrassment. You could find more value in a Cracker Jack box. My dad had gotten him started in this town, but I guess when some people reach a certain level, they are quick to forget their past and who helped them along the way.

My soon-to-be mother-in-law arrived with her husband, Philippe, and Desi's sister, Coraline. My brother flew in from LA to be best man. The only other people to attend the wedding outside our immediate families were Mr. Mintz and his young Filipino girlfriend. The tradition of the bride and groom not seeing each other before the ceremony was impossible to uphold. Everyone left from the apartment together, though we took separate cars. Desi looked lovely, she wore a secondhand dress that she'd reconstructed and she'd dyed her natural blond hair jet-black. I wore Versace.

It felt somewhat surreal to me, like when you're watching something unfold and realize you're the one involved in it. After the I dos, the ritual of breaking the glass followed. Rabbi Hecht placed it at my right foot so I could give it a good stomp. Maybe I was still breaking in my work shoes, but that glass did not break. I could see it on their faces, practically everyone looked at it as a bad omen. Second time was the charm.

We celebrated over sushi at Hamada, one of our favorite spots. Our families were in an uplifting mood, even Mr. Mintz was enjoying the evening and had gifted us with a toaster. Desi and I were shy of the camera, though, not one shot turned out where we look completely happy—we were, you just wouldn't know it judging by the photographs. It was a relief to not have to contemplate marriage anymore and finally be done with taking turns leaving each other. We could get on with our mission now.

After dinner, the evening was quite simple, we all went back to the apartment and gathered over a pot of tea. Our two families stayed up late getting to know each other better, while Desi spent time with her sister, speaking mostly in Italian, as they liked to do. I was first to tire, or maybe I was trying to send a signal to Desi, so I said my goodnights and retreated back to our unit. Totally cool if they wanted to carry on through the night. Falling asleep without your wife, not as cool. Never mind the glass that didn't break. Not fucking on your wedding night is the real bad luck.

In a matter of weeks I had lost my wedding band in the carpet of our apartment. It was that seventies-style multicolor shag. We probably needed a metal detector to find it. I'm too fidgety with jewelry, to this day I don't wear rings or watches, only a mezuzah necklace. If I can see it, it's coming off.

I attended my first sales meeting on a day off at 8:00 a.m. Meetings were mandatory whether you were scheduled for work or not. A time to discuss sales strategies and boost morale. I showed up wearing my London heeled boots, vintage yellow-and-black striped flare pants, and black fitted turtleneck sweater. Some of the other associates showed up in their sweats. Many confused faces. I overheard one of them ask, "Why is he all dressed up?" My boss, Sunil, didn't flinch, he said he thought I looked cool, then told the story of when I'd walked in to apply for the job, saying how I'd strolled in looking like Adam Ant and how he knew he had to hire me. Within months I was consistently one of the top three producers. It was a fun and entertaining job. We were a small staff, so it felt really close-knit and friendships formed fast.

One of my coworkers, Bernard, gave me the nickname Eagle Eye, for the fact that I could zero in on someone unassuming and convert them into a sale. If you were passive or holding out for a high roller, then you were limiting yourself. Bernard invited me and Desi over to his condo, telling us downtown wasn't a place for us to live and, as I was making good money, I should think about getting something like he had. Not bad advice, he was a nice guy and meant well. It was a shame to see him get fired for taking a lunch break and not returning that day. He couldn't wait to cash his check and spend the rest of his shift in the casino. A couple of employees fell victim to the same thing. Growing up in Vegas, I'd never had an interest in gambling, and being back in Sin City of legal age now, it still wasn't my jam. In due time, though, I would find what was.

There were many perks that came with the job. On an afternoon when I clocked in for my mid shift, Sunil was hustling to put together an entire collection from A to Z and pulled me aside to help. "Grab the rolling racks, we gotta move quick, you're coming with me."

In the car I asked, "What's up, where are we taking all this?"

He smiled, "We're going to see Elton John."

Right on! Sunil always did cool things like that to include me, knowing I was the music guy and could appreciate. We set up the rolling racks in Elton's dressing room, displaying everything so it was easy for him to see in its entirety without having to sort through. The way he shopped was fascinating to watch, walking from rack to rack and pointing at the keepers, "I'll take that. I have that already. I'll take that." Less than two minutes and done. *Sign here, please.* Better than that was now we would get comped for the shows anytime he was back in Vegas.

The most excited I got while on the job was when Steven Tyler walked in. I was near the entrance when he rolled through. I immediately called out his name as we slapped hands together. "Steven Tyler, I'm going to see you tonight!"

I said. I had tickets for the Aerosmith show later that evening. He went right over to the women's rack and put on a shiny gold metallic blazer. I told him we had that same jacket in a men's. "No, this fits me good," he remarked. Of course, what was I thinking, it was Steven fuckin' Tyler, the definition of cool.

Desi appreciated that story. She was always pulling clothes out of her closet for me to try on, ever since the beginning. "You have a thin build, skinny people should wear something that's cut for their body," she'd say. Totally logical, when something looks good, who cares what gender it's marketed to? Mix it up, rock it with confidence.

Our earliest musical outing in Vegas was performing just the two of us with guitar and vocals. Desi didn't want us to be like a folk act, though at this stage we could at least book ourselves somewhere and be active. The place was a coffeehouse, similar to the Bourgeois Pig, with a dark-lit vibe. We played a few songs together and then Desi introduced me to do a few on my own. We received a good reaction from people, and both of us were happy to sing again in front of an audience finally. Maybe we should have done this from the start. Though, we had tried it once in New York at a restaurant. It was a disaster. Probably why we were dead set on having a complete band.

The fact was we'd been pursuing our project for three years, with missed attempts and only demos to show for it. This led me to become more vocal about wanting to put together a band of my own. I felt I owed it to myself to follow through on this. I was writing a lot of songs with a different vibe from what we were doing together. Eventually Desi warmed up to understanding my desire to do something separate. On the flipside, she also resented it. Ultimately she wanted to make sure I would still help her with her songs and with assembling a project of her own.

Things came together easier when I placed an ad for my band, citing groups such as Cheap Trick and Elvis Costello as an influence, blending both American rock and British style. Within weeks I met Kyle and Michael, a drummer and guitar player, respectively. Michael soon switched to bass so we could get things rolling as a power trio. It was starting to click and gel together in rehearsals. Our immediate goal would be to record three songs for a CD and start booking shows.

With marriage came filing papers with Immigration Services. It would take a year for Desi's permanent resident status to be approved. That was fine from a monetary standpoint; with my job I was financially in good shape to carry us while she wasn't working. The hard part for her was waiting for me to come home from work, especially on nights when I had rehearsals. She looked forward to those two days off I had when we could go to the movies and Buffalo Exchange to scour the racks of secondhand goods and basically just spend time together doing the things we liked to do.

In between my days off, my parents would take Desi out, either to the athletic club to go swimming or sometimes to meet me after work. Desi would vent to me that my mom was like the KGB checking up on her and voicing her opinions of how she should dress now that she was a married woman. Eccentricity was something my mom didn't get. A pair of blue pumps that I'd bought for Desi was the offender one time. Whatever she disliked, it always came down to the shoes!

After a few months of living downtown, boredom reached new heights for Desi. There was a friend I had from junior high that was still living in Vegas whom I introduced to her. Erwen's girlfriend, Tanisha, took a real liking to Desi and over time came by to pick her up while I was working. She was a shit stirrer, but Desi would confide in her before she figured this out. Tanisha involved herself where it didn't concern her and filled Desi's head with ideas that she was living like a prisoner.

Whatever the situation—living next to my parents, verbal squabbles with my mom, or not having a car of our own—Tanisha felt inclined to make it her business and used it to egg Desi on about giving me an ultimatum to move to another apartment. Another time she dropped in on Desi and demanded that she pack her things and leave with her. Desi caved. I found a note left behind. I went over to Erwen's apartment, there was no answer. Then I went to Tanisha's workplace, where she met me outside. She was fuming that I'd showed up there, saying that Desi was staying with her until I found a new apartment. I had five simple words—"Fuck you and fuck Erwen," I retorted. This hot-tempered woman had the audacity to put her hands on me and shoved at me. Crazy bitch.

Desi would call me at work asking if I'd found a place for us yet. A week went by before I signed the lease at a new community. We met up a time or two before that, booking ourselves for the night at the Stardust. When I got the keys to the apartment, I told Desi it wasn't set up yet. The bed and furniture I'd ordered weren't scheduled to be delivered for a few days, so there was truth to that. But I took pleasure in just being alone. I'd sleep on the floor, it didn't matter. I could've said, "Come now, the place is empty, let's just be together," but peace of mind and solace from the whole ordeal somehow seemed more rewarding.

Desi greatly enjoyed living at this resort-style community. She felt we had our privacy now. She could swim and take sun while I was at work. Easy access to the Strip also meant she could join me for lunch anytime. With delight she would make sandwiches for me to take and leave notes or caricatures of herself she had drawn in the brown bag. When I forgot to grab my lunch on the way out, she showed up at work just to hand deliver it to me. It was precious. Desi could be very sweet. For the most part, things were good for us in that first year at our new place.

I'd give her silly assignments to see if she'd remember by the time I got home. "When I walk in the door, I want to find you wearing a chador." I'd walk in and she'd be wrapped up in a bedsheet with just her eyes peeking through. "When I come home, be naked on the bed and ready to make love." I walked in. "Ken, are you alone?" she called out, fearing I had forgotten and might be with someone. Sure enough, she'd remembered. Our way to keep things fun and exciting.

The band I assembled as a three piece had fallen apart before it even got off the ground. Michael was in a car wreck that left him in pretty bad shape, and Kyle had a change of heart in the direction of music he wanted to play. Finding other players came easy, although there was no unity, it looked like we'd all been plucked out of four different bands. The ace in the deck was a young guy barely twenty years old. I had found Abraham Millet's business card on a music store bulletin board and called him to do a gig I had booked. After the show, Abe told me that I had really good songs but that I should get rid of everyone else. He was confident he could bring in some other guys he knew would fit the bill. I liked his initiative and personality. Abe was cut from the same cloth as me.

Trevor Mayfield was the super hyper drummer, good-looking with long hair and an appetite for rock n roll. A powerhouse on his kit. I thought of him as a mini Tommy Lee.

Rounded out by Jacob Chidester, at eighteen he was the youngest of the bunch, but he could play guitar as masterfully as any of his heroes twice his age. He was the most reserved of all of us. The camaraderie we shared was everything I'd been looking for in a band. The feeling of brotherhood, like all the bands I'd grown up being inspired by, we had it. We instantly became a gang.

As much as I loved the band image, I decided to represent us by using my name, like how Lenny Kravitz is a solo artist, yet the players in his band are completely recognizable in their own right. Plus, band names were the norm. I wanted to stick out from the rest. Eventually I adapted a tagline when we performed live, I'd introduce the guys as the Internationals. Kind of like my Heartbreakers or the Imposters.

There was something really appealing to me about having younger guys in the band. I felt as if I was their mentor. I could influence them, or corrupt them, depending how you looked at it. Trevor had a love for red wine, so if we were rehearsing at Abe's house, I'd always show up with two bottles of Louis Jadot. It was important for me to project a certain image to them, they looked up to me, and I liked being the leader. Before a gig I'd take them to the secondhand store to find something cool they could wear. I was proud to see Jacob approve of my choice for him of a black see-through knit top, though under any other circumstances he'd never wear such a thing. He referred to it as "the boobie shirt."

At one of our early gigs, all of my crew from Versace came down to show support. Afterwards, a couple of them came back to find us in the dressing room, pronouncing excitedly that they'd just met my wife and saying how cool she was. All my guys in the band turned to me and said, "You're married? Desi's your wife?" This was part of the image I was trying to uphold, subscribing to a self-made theory that it was better if people believed I was unattached.

I think for me in this case it was that I didn't want my young mates to view my marriage as something that could slow us down. The fact that it didn't change their perception either way proved it was an unnecessary worry I'd given way too much thought to.

Our after-show ritual was to go out for sushi and sake. Easily the damage could rack up to be a few hundo, a tab I didn't mind splurging on one bit; it was one way to show my appreciation. Desi enjoyed coming to the gigs, she also loved being social with everyone. When the guys wanted to party longer, she understood this as a way for me to bond with my band and was okay with me staying out later with them, calling it a "boys' night out." However, over time these nights out would become a problem.

I'd forbidden Desi from seeing Tanisha when we moved from downtown. She respected that, though I imagine it was lonesome to be in a strange city not working and not having friends to get together with. When her mom and brother, Nico, came to visit and stay with us, that was a breath of fresh air for us both. They would spend days at the pool and go around to the hotels and shops and be like tourists. There was a water park on the Strip called Wet'n'Wild that I used to frequent in my elementary years, and now I was showing Nico, who was the same age I'd been back then, the same experience. Right as we entered the park, I said, "Follow me," and took him up to the tallest slide, a seventy-six-foot drop. He did it like a champ but called me crazy afterwards. Tackle the big one first, anything that follows after will be a piece of cake.

Desi continued placing ads for musicians and made one of her striking collages to use as an advertisement that we posted in the music stores. Eager to meet people, she invited the first responder over to the apartment. This guy seemed low-key. He played acoustic guitar, throwing out some of his ideas as Desi played keyboard. He was more introspective than talkative. Desi put on CDs of other artists she drew inspiration from. He was entranced with Peter Murphy's *Deep* record and sat there listening to it in its entirety. Hours went by.

We looked at each other like, *What do we have to do to get this guy to leave?* I powered the CD player off, and we began to tidy up around the place. He asked very soft-spokenly, "Is there a reason why we're stopping?" Dude didn't even get the hint. Once he left, Desi lamented, "Why do I always get the freaks?"

Vegas was becoming interesting, although residencies for pop performers were still years away, it was noticeable that every artist made it a destination on their tour. We saw Bryan Ferry on his *As Time Goes By* stint, even ABC managed to do a date at the Joint in the Hard Rock Hotel. No better place for their singer, Martin Fry, to wear a gold lamé suit than Las Vegas.

When Elton John returned with Billy Joel for a night at the MGM, his people hooked up third-row seats for the Versace team. My bosses were the kindest people to work for, those tickets got handed down to me. After I had gotten the business card for Elton's manager, I didn't hesitate to send him my CD. One more rejection letter to add to the pile.

I took advantage of any opportunity if the moment presented itself, and there were a lot that arose with that job, apart from when it became a spectacle if a certain VIP entered the boutique, naturally that wouldn't be the time and place. Mike Tyson was a regular. Security would have to stand outside as we locked the doors for crowd control reasons. He always drew the largest horde of spectators. A powerful presence with a down-to-earth nature. He was super nice to work with. On one occasion I was off work and passed through to pick up my check, sporting my beige suede jacket. The champ was there and gave props, telling me, "You look good." Getting a compliment from Iron Mike was pretty damn cool.

Another unforgettable night was when Dennis Rodman showed up with an entourage. He had two bottles of Cristal in his hands and plopped them down on the counter, gesturing that they were an offering for me to accept. When I declined, he took back possession.

A moment later, I walked over to the cash wrap to look up an item. We were standing eight feet apart when he shouted, "CATCH!" The bottle was flying in midair. For someone who fumbled the ball in every single sport, here was my shining moment to not be an ass and save the store thousands of dollars from buying a new computer system shorted out by champagne.

HE SCORES! Dennis came over to shake my hand and have a laugh. Now I kept it, two bottles was my prize. Head of security said to me with a sigh of relief, "I'm so glad you caught that." I opened a bottle to share with my coworkers, we polished it off before the night was through. I should have saved the second one for my bosses. Instead, I called Trevor and told him what was awaiting for our next rehearsal.

Fun wasn't just happening in the store. On my dinner breaks I was becoming a regular at Spago and one of the other fine dining spots in the Forum. When you sit at the counter because it's quicker, you become friends with the bartender. When that happens, you drink because it's social, and then you're having dinner and a glass of wine sounds nice. When repours are comped and break time is only an hour, you're working the rest of the shift with an exhilarating buzz. At closing time, you're entertaining suggestions from coworkers to go out for a drink afterwards, so you give in. If you're married, you're pissing off your wife, who's been waiting for you all day.

It's one thing to hang out with your bandmates and do what's associated with the rock n roll lifestyle. It's another if party time is happening with coworkers too and it all just bleeds together. This was starting to be the case with me. It wasn't the taste of alcohol I craved, it was the nightlife. Drinking was what I had to do to catch the thrill. And in Vegas it seemed having one without the other was not an option.

Desi bought me a present, my first cell phone. Six inches of digital technology. Now she could worry less and be able to reach me on those late nights to ask what the fuck I was doing staying out. When it got bad, she would suspect I was having an affair. I wasn't such a good husband to be away from her like I was. Even though I loved Desi beyond words, I didn't have any idea of what our marriage should look like. The concept for us was off-center right from the day we discussed it in Paris. We were the unconventional. Oddly, Desi would feel more like a housewife than I would a husband.

It was a great day when Desi received her permanent residence card. After several months of waiting, she was elated to have this new sense of independence, along with the ability to work and earn an income. Having a job could occupy her thoughts, it kept her busy and was rewarding to have somewhere to get up and go to. A boutique in the Venetian hired her to sell masquerade masks à la *Eyes Wide Shut*. If we both worked a late shift, I'd join her so we could walk home together, sometimes grabbing a midnight snack along the way. At first we were good about coordinating our days off together, for as long as our schedules would allow.

12

KNIFE IN MY SIDE

Desi constantly composed ideas and melodies on her keyboard. Her creativity was like a faucet that kept flowing. When she struck something she really liked, she'd ask me what I thought of it. Although collaborating with her had taken a back seat for me once I focused on my own project, I never stopped encouraging her. Maybe it was a form of tough love for me to put the brakes on us working together, when really I wanted to see her grow as a writer and not have to rely on me all the time to finish what she'd started. If only I had communicated that reason to her, instead of leaving it to be interpreted in a way not intended. Still, she wasn't seeking an exercise, what she enjoyed was the collaborative process and having a partner to complete her.

I remember Desi telling me she'd spoken with a guitar player whom she'd played pieces of music to over the phone. A way to gauge interest instead of meeting right off the bat and to weed through the weirdos. Dave Keuning seemed harmless, much like an average Joe. He didn't have a musician vibe about him. Plain and undistinctive. Desi could work with that, she was most excited that he liked everything she played for him. They'd rehearse in our apartment, quite often I'd find him over when I came home from working the morning shift.

Pretty Ugly was a club in Hollywood my band got booked at. It would be our first out-of-state show and hopefully a way to expand our presence. I rented an eight-passenger minivan, disassembling all but one bench to fit all our gear. Our buddy Josh came along for the adventure and so did the party favors. I think it was Trevor who dabbled in a bit of coke for the full experience. None for me meant more for them. The plan when we got to LA would be to hit up Melrose and promote by passing out flyers to the pretty girls walking by, then book a couple hours at a rehearsal space to run through the set.

Coincidentally, the studio we rented was operated by Jeff from Circus. Last time we'd seen each other, he had received a verbal lashing from Desi. When he saw me, he asked if I was still with "that bird."

"Yeah, we're married." He responded by saying how he would've left someone like that. Poor dude, still scarred by the wrath of Desi.

Our LA debut, complete with a broken string seconds into the first song. For me, those types of hiccups are irrelevant, what mattered was if I felt I performed well. Was it entertaining? Did I connect? Technical details I couldn't be bothered with. After a show, other burning questions took precedent. "Kenward, where are we going to eat at?" That was the usual discussion of importance in this band. We were in LA, of course I knew a spot that would blow their minds. I took the guys to Yamashiro, a Japanese restaurant next to a private magicians' club called Magic Castle, nestled in the Hollywood Hills. Sushi and sake overlooking the lights and panoramic view of the city. Yes, please.

We checked into a hotel on Highland and Franklin, and since my bandmates hadn't scored any women, I picked up an *LA Xpress* paper to review their options for them. For those who don't know, *LA Xpress* was equivalent to the New York paper *Screw*. If you don't know what type of reading material was in *Screw*, you're not paying any attention to the title. I made some calls to get the going rate. The boys were gonna have to arm wrestle for it, 'cause I would only be opening my wallet for one. On second thought, maybe there was something on the menu for the whole family.

"Hi, we don't wanna fuck, how much would it be for just a dildo show?"

The voice on the other end replied, "Excuse me? How many of you are there?"

"There's five of us, miss."

"Um you want me to come to your hotel room at 3:00 a.m. and give five of you a dildo show?"

"Yeah, how much are we talking?"

"Um, I'm sorry, that won't be happening. Call someone else."

Somehow at this hour, Trevor had the urge to do rudiments on his drum pad. It wasn't the neighbors he needed to worry about, it was Abe. I lost count of how many warnings he was given, but Mr. Millett had about enough of all he could take while trying to get some rest. He walked up to Trevor, grabbed the sticks out of his hands, and whacked him across the back with 'em. There was no such thing as a light touch in this moment. Trevor roared, "MOTHERFUCKER!" I thought we were going to be kicked out, either for the ruckus between them or from the boisterous laughter from the rest of us. They were on a rampage, until Abe finally declared, "FUCK YOU, I'M GONNA SLEEP IN THE VAN!!" This only added to our laughing fit—why would you punish yourself by sleeping in the van? I could only imagine what being on tour with these guys would be like.

The next day all was good, at breakfast they were back to being bros again. Our plan before heading back to Vegas would entail cruising around the landmark neighborhoods and partaking in a little bit of shopping. One thing about working at Versace was it opened up a door to wanting nicer clothes. Mixing and matching something high-end with secondhand was the only affordable way. On this outing we went to Barney's. "But first I'm gonna need two of you to jump out and raise the clearance bar so we can park this beast." No sense paying for damages when there were Prada shoes to buy. When I found a pair of keepers, Trevor offered to buy them for me, reminding me that he still owed me for covering his girlfriend's abortion. We had each other's backs.

In Vegas we set out to play at least one show a month, that was the standard for most bands. There was no concern about oversaturating ourselves since it could be a fickle scene, some nights we'd see big crowds and the next could be a mellower draw, regardless of how much promotion. Still, people were coming up to us afterwards and saying we were the best show they'd ever seen.

Some guy followed us out to the parking lot at another show, exclaiming, "You got the best front man right here, you're like Alice Cooper!" Well, half my name fit. I got his meaning, it was about the showmanship. Put me in that category any day, it's a huge compliment. There was something in the air happening we could sense was slowly brewing.

More bands were sprouting up. Abe also began to moonlight in another project. One day at rehearsal he shared photos with us from a shoot he'd done with the other band. Everyone was wearing eyeshadow and lip gloss, a page right out of the Kenward Cooper book. In 1999 I put this band together when no one else in Vegas had glam style in the way I was tipping the hat to Roxy Music and Bowie. They all were in Lit and Everclear mode. In early 2000, a producer I recorded a track with named Ron Mancuso shared his premonition with me, "There's gonna be one band that's going to break big from Vegas, it could be you."

I came home one afternoon after my shift expecting to find Desi, when in walked Dave wearing swim trunks. "Hey, Ken" was about all he could muster up. Desi followed in her bikini, "Oh hi, you're back early!" As innocent as it may have been, this was my first notion of *Hmm this doesn't feel right.* If 80 percent of your body is showing skin, what percentage of the mind is going to think the wrong idea? I'm not a mathematician, but I bet it's a lot.

Trevor had gone out of state for a few months to get certified as a recording engineer. When he couldn't commit to gigs I had lined up, I'd have our buddy Josh fill in. Naturally, Josh and I were already hanging out a lot. On a particular night after we played a show, we bounced from one spot to the next in search of a good vibe. We were at Mandalay Bay for all of ten minutes when, upon leaving, I approached a striking six-foot-tall blond waiting for her valet. "You should've been at the show tonight," I said, and then I asked her where she was headed and if she wanted to come along with us. Without hesitation she asked, "Where are you going?"

Probably back to Josh's place in Henderson. "Sure, okay." Such great hosts we were, we could offer beer and porn. We sat around watching fuck films, occasionally glancing at each other like which one of us was gonna make a move. Hey, I was a married man. There were opportunities and there was my conscience. *What's your excuse, buddy?* I ended up hooking her up with Trevor and relished in hearing all about the fun they had.

I can recall in those formative months of Desi working together with

Dave, she asked me what I thought of him. I claimed he seemed soulless. She said, "That's funny, you feel the same thing as me." She described him as having dead eyes. Hard to tell if there was more she was trying to figure out or discover about him. Overall she was enjoying being productive again. They forged ahead with the idea of a cover band, something to do on the side and make money from. With all the lounges in the casinos, carving out a niche on the cover circuit could be lucrative.

Desi would later recall how, when rehearsals took place, Jamie, the other musician, seemed to have had about all he could stomach of Dave. Evidently they were both vying for Desi's attention, and Jamie made it known he was on to Dave's bullshit. It was an attempt for him to make his play before Dave could. Apparently he said, "I know exactly what you're after here, bud," and a war of words ensued, squabbling over who was going to drive her home. At this point Desi wondered to herself if Dave had other intentions she wasn't aware of and started to have her doubts about him.

Jamie had told Desi he had dreamed about her and expressed his feelings, saying he knew she was married but thought his chances with her were still good. This confused Desi, she only wanted to play music and now found herself in a situation where both guys wanted more than that. I believe she was aware of Dave's intent, though maybe she was more afraid to lose the music relationship if she did something to squash his affections before they escalated.

Desi recounted years later a time when Dave dropped her home after a rehearsal, watching her as she walked to the front door. "Will I ever get a chance with you?" he called out.

"What are you talking about?" Desi replied. "I don't know what chance you're talking about, I'm married," she said, reiterating how she thought it was just music between them.

That didn't satisfy Dave, he repeated his question.

"I have to go" was all she could say.

I had my suspicions, yet I was living a dual existence, mostly veering on the side of my own escapism. In terms of affection, girls I didn't even know were dropping by the store and handing me their phone numbers.

It was there if I wanted it. And I wanted one, a stunning black-haired, blue-eyed beauty from Budapest. Ironically, she was married, funny how that goes. Monica was her name, she worked at another boutique on the other side of the Forum. We'd take turns visiting each other on breaks. Nothing was ever gonna happen. She was in the same boat as Desi, with the exception of skating closer to jeopardizing her marriage. I wrote a song about her called "If's & Maybe's" that summed up the feelings of being in a relationship and having the temptation to be with someone else. Writing can be therapeutic, I could release those feelings through words and music and be done with it. I left the lyrics exposed and Desi found them, confronting me about who this bitch was, as she so delicately put it. Oddly, they'd met when I took Desi to Immigration Services. Monica had been there for her own appointment.

Towards the end of our apartment lease, something else was on the verge of expiring: my band. Abe had a talk with me about his desire to put his own band together. If anyone understood this yearning, it was me. I respected him for being up front and telling me. He was a great songwriter in his own right. The hardest part would be that he wanted to take Trevor and Jacob with him. How could I argue, he'd brought us all together in the first place. To Trevor's credit, he was the only one who said he'd still play in my band.

Without my bros to hang out with, I filled the void by going out with my coworkers. And as Desi was occupied with work and rehearsals, if I knew she wasn't going to be home for a while, then that was more incentive for me to stay out. A few of us from work met up at the Hard Rock, it wasn't intended to be a crazy night, apart from someone ordering tequila shots, something that I never drank, let alone three of 'em. It quickly turned into the most shitty night. I was completely hammered, which was a first for me. One of those sequences where it happens in threes. Blink an eye and my friend is holding me up, blink again I'm in a taxi, next thing I know I'm at my front door and Desi answers. She was rightfully pissed off at me, "What the hell are you doing to yourself?!" she scolded. My friend Sidney from work calmly said, "No no no, don't do that to him, he just had too much to drink, take it easy on him." She listened. I remember she placed a large bowl next to me, asking if I needed to puke. When I did, she had her hand on my back, helping to put me at ease. She emptied it out, cleaning up the mess that was me. Next came the cold shower. She took care of me.

I know Desi spoke out about how this going out and drinking was happening too often. However, I don't think she felt empowered to advise me or that whatever words she could say would be useful. And whether I'd be receptive to it was another question mark altogether.

I did make a plea for saying we should move to Los Angeles again. A desperate attempt to save us from the inevitable, fearing we were falling apart. "I don't want to move to LA. I'm not giving up everything I'm trying to build here to start all over again. We lived there before and it didn't work." She was clear where she stood. I figured the more I spoke about it, maybe she'd see I was serious about it. "I'll go myself," I said.

"Where am I going to live if you move away to LA?" she retorted. All I did was dig myself more into a hole. She mentioned she'd have to ask Dave about becoming roommates. My new mistake.

I overheard their phone conversation, "Guess what, Ken's moving to LA, do you want to get a place together?" It sounded more like excitement for this outcome than a last resort. What was he going to say, no I don't want to? It fell right into his lap. At this point it was too far gone to change the course, even though I stayed in Vegas. Desi said Dave had given up his apartment and she wasn't going to back out of her word. We ended up moving into a bigger unit within the same complex, a two-bedroom/two-bathroom on the second level. On one hand I rationalized how you don't bring another person into a married couple's home to share living quarters, there goes all sense of privacy. On the other hand, if anything suspicious was going on, I would be able to tell and see it with my own eyes.

If I had reason not to approve of him before, seeing his CD collection sealed the deal. He had the worst taste, stuff like Crash Test Dummies and other forgettable honorees. He wasn't even familiar with David Bowie. Desi would enlighten him. In fairness, it wasn't totally uncomfortable at first having him around. With all of our different schedules, no one was treading in each other's space too much.

I started a record with Ron Mancuso, a former recording artist with Epic and Atlantic Records who came recommended to me by Jonathan Daniel years before he founded Crush Music management company. Lez Warner from the Cult flew in from New York to do the drum tracks. On another day, I received a call from producer/A&R man Julian Raymond checking to see how the recording was coming along. I'd initially reached out to him to make it known that I was working with Ron, since they'd been in a band together called Bang Bang. Ron was impressed that Julian had phoned. They hadn't spoken in years, now I was reconnecting them right there.

Ron got overly excited after the call, saying this was gonna be good, he was convinced we had a direct shot at Julian picking up our record for Hollywood Records, where he was head of A&R. Instead of continuing to work and make more progress that day, Ron said, "I think we're good," stopping the session only an hour in.

I accepted a show at one of the local clubs, even though I didn't have a band anymore, I figured it was best to stay active, and if I couldn't assemble additional guys then at least I could play the show acoustically. Trevor was down to do it, though, so we might as well find a bass player and make it a trio. Desi made the suggestion, "Why don't you ask Dave? I'm sure he'd like to do it." I gave him a cassette of songs to learn and he got on board. I remember him badly wanting us to do a cover of the Cars' "Let's Go." We rehearsed at the same studio I'd been going to. Dave liked playing in front of the mirror there, I noticed him checking out his posturing.

At the club the night of, there were a couple of under-twenty-one girls hanging out by the loading dock who wanted to come inside to watch the show. "Just grab some things to carry in and then find yourself a seat," I said. Ten minutes before going on, the club manager ran up to me all threatening, "PACK UP YOUR GEAR! YOU'RE NOT PLAYING TONIGHT!"

"Why?" I asked.

"I am not losing my liquor license because you're being a dumbass trying to sneak underage girls in here!" He was right to call me out. No sushi celebration that night.

A few months into living in the upgraded apartment, Desi was at work when a phone call came through on the landline. I answered and, not recognizing the voice although it sounded foreign, I figured it was for Desi, until the man asked, "Dave?" *That's odd,* I thought. I handed the phone to Dave. He was also confused. It was Desi's father. I had never spoken with Paolo before, although he knew me as the husband of his eldest daughter. I wondered how the fuck he knew Dave's name and had not assumed he was speaking to me.

It was another sign something was up. When I brought it up to Desi that night, her reaction was ghostly, "I wonder what the hell my sister's been telling my father," she said. Yeah, that made two of us.

As I spent more time at the apartment, since I wasn't going out as frequently, now it appeared that all Desi's free time was consumed by hanging out with Dave on the balcony, either working on songs or just shooting the breeze. I'd be in the bedroom playing or listening to music, sometimes playing the same sad songs over and over on repeat, appropriate for my mood. Desi would check on me. "I won't be too long," she'd say. Or when I'd show my face she'd wave through the glass and indicate she was wrapping it up. I got frustrated once and opened the sliding door after waiting for her, "Are you coming to bed?" I grumbled.

It's not like we stopped showing love to each other or put a halt to doing anything extracurricular. We were still intimate and could also enjoy the simpler moments of going out together. Sometimes I would second-guess our bond when it seemed we were not in sync. Such as at the movies, when a trailer for M. Night Shyamalan's new thriller *Unbreakable* showed on the screen. Desi looked over to me and said, "Are you unbreakable?" I could sense the game and answered, "Yes." She snarled back, "I bet I can break you." It felt like a backhanded slap in the face, as did the times she expressed serious intent of wanting to be a stripper or resuming her friendship with Tanisha. I wondered where these ideas where stemming from.

We got a little hiatus from Dave when he traveled home to visit his parents in Iowa. I had just sat down at the computer, when I noticed Desi hadn't logged out of her email. Right there in front of me was her inbox full of half a dozen emails from Dave, all with affectionate subject headings like "I miss you so much!" and "I love you." It wasn't a shock, more a confirmation of what I already suspected. I printed out the page and calmly handed it to Desi as she smoked a cigarette on the balcony. "What's this?" I asked.

"Oh my god," she said shamefully while placing her hands over her face.

I told her I was out of there and began gathering my clothes, not having thought it through or sure of what I was intending to do exactly. She jumped on my back and cried, "Don't leave me!" Old and new resentments came to a boil. Abandonment, neglect. We argued until we could both simmer down. She denied anything had happened yet between them physically. I wasn't buying it. A guy doesn't send love letters if nothing supports those feelings, unless he's a goddamn psycho, and on that the verdict was still out.

The morning after I felt a turning point, standing firm on what needed to happen next. I told Desi we were going to get back to us. I planned to give Dave the boot and send him packing, reasoning that with him out of the picture we could reclaim our focus and do our project again. She was in agreement and apologetic that she'd mixed it up by placing what she wanted for us onto him. It was a classic stab for me to try whatever I could to avoid losing her.

Once Dave got back in town, I confronted him in the apartment while Desi was at work. "Hey, Ken, Desi said you wanted to talk to me," he uttered.

"I know what's going on," I said.

He recomposed himself, and with a hint of defense in his voice he questioned, "What, what's going on?"

"You're trying to come in between Desi and me, and that's not gonna happen. I want you out of here."

"Fine, I'll move out," he replied.

I asked Ron to put aside the recordings we were doing so we could track three songs with Desi. Unaware of my situation, he declined, not wanting to break up the momentum as we were already at the halfway mark. It probably wouldn't have done us any good, Desi had a change of heart regardless of the outcome, taking a stand that she believed in the songs she was working on with Dave and wanted to continue collaborating with him.

She had already given her heart to him, she just couldn't admit it to me. She said I needed to trust her, and with him being out of the apartment now,

I shouldn't worry. I gave in. If I hadn't, that could easily have driven a wedge between us too. It was a double-edged sword.

My friend Sidney from work was over at our apartment when Dave was coming to pick Desi up to go to rehearsal one day. He helped carry Desi's keyboard downstairs. When Sidney walked back inside, he said to me, "Ken, I know this isn't any of my business, but I could see in his eyes this wasn't someone just thinking he's going to rehearse, he looked like someone who's picking up his girlfriend to go on a date." I couldn't disagree with Sidney, I knew he was right. He said to me if something was going to happen, it was going to happen.

That night when she got back, I started to undress her. "I'm dirty, let me take a shower," she said. My interpretation was not, *Oh she must be sweaty from rehearsing*, even though that would have been a logical result from playing in those small boxy rooms. I was convinced I knew exactly what *dirty* implied. But that didn't change my mind in taking off all her clothes. She was too clever not to know that if she stopped me, I would know something was not right.

Later that month, I had ten minutes until closing time, when a girl I had met at one of the music venues dropped by my work unannounced to say hello. She was carrying with her a pack of sushi and said, "I don't know if you had dinner yet, but I brought you something." It was a sweet gesture, she knew what I liked, and I thanked her, then she asked what I was doing after work. I hadn't committed to anything. She said, "Well, I'll be around." When she walked out, my buddy Terrance, who was closing with me, was in awe. "You're married and you have hot women like that bringing you dinner? You are such a PIMP!" He carried on, "Dude, what are you doing, you're just gonna let her walk away?" The thought had crossed my mind. I said, "You're right." I left and caught up to her. Tracy was like a Playboy pinup come to life, a petite Barbie doll. The first time we met she told me I looked like I'd stepped out of *Velvet Goldmine*. I couldn't ignore someone who paid such a cool compliment.

The one thing about having an affair, it might sound weird to say, for me, it made me appreciate my wife that much more. The differences are evident, especially when you're looking for the person you love in someone else. The connection was missing, the feeling of intimacy wasn't natural, the touch was not the same. It was trading skin for the fuck of it.

Tracy told me years later that she stalked me after our encounter. One night I was getting a ride home from work, and she and some friends followed in their car and parked by my building. When my coworker pulled into a spot, they were parked right beside us and ducked down in their seats. She had heard I was married and wanted to find out for herself. It was chance that Sidney was with me that night, as we walked into his apartment instead of mine. Mission aborted.

One day, I was working the later shift and had it on my mind to call Desi once I got to the job. We had gotten out of sync with calling each other when we were on different schedules. This particular day I had the urge to check in with her. There was a quiver in her voice, like she was catching her breath or on the verge of crying.

We always felt each other's energy, that's not some new age mumbo jumbo bullshit, just fact. I could sense something was wrong. When we said goodbye and our I love yous, I seriously had the feeling that I should go over to the apartment right then and there to see if everything was all right. Always go with that first instinct. I pushed it aside, convincing myself I was probably overreacting.

After work I got a ride from my coworker friends Courtney and Michelle. I invited them upstairs since they wanted to say hello to Desi. As I walked in, things immediately looked different, bare and empty, furniture was missing. The place was practically cleared out. I went into the bedroom, checked the closet, and all her clothes were gone except for one dress she had handmade.

I panicked, then dashed into the second bedroom, where Dave used to stay. Nothing stashed away there. I could see Courtney and Michelle clamoring around the cupboard shelf. They instantly backed away when I approached.

There was a handwritten note from Desi that they were reading. I skimmed it, folded it into my pocket, and said, "Let's go."

I needed a moment to process this and preferred not to be alone. We went to a brewery a couple blocks away and joined the rest of the crew. I pulled Sidney aside and spilled to him what had just gone down. He'd seen it coming and summed it up with a Russian proverb, "Everything in life other than shit is piss."

I called it an early night. Staying out late, which was part of why I was in this mess, was the last thing I wanted to be doing now. I went back to the empty apartment and tried to sleep it off. It was the worst and longest night. There was no rest. Every hour on the hour I would check the clock, wishing for the daylight and praying for the strength to get through this.

I went into work that morning. I must've been moping around making zero effort, all caught on camera. Sunil called me into the office. Angie, the owner, who was my other boss, said, "Look at this guy, what's wrong with him?" I broke down. There was no keeping it hidden, especially from these two wonderful people, who were so compassionate and good to me. They asked if I needed time off, paid vacation—whatever it was, they were ready to lift me up. Basically I started to go into work early every day. I practically worked a double shift for months straight because it got me out of my funk of dwelling on the situation.

A week went by before I told my parents the news. I wasn't in the mood for any sort of conversation that would breed I told you sos. Eventually I broke the lease and moved in with them for a short while. It would've been horrible to stay in the apartment that carried so much sorrow. Desi called just as I was moving my things out. She mentioned her plan was to move to Chicago. The call only resulted in a shouting match between us.

Upon returning from a lunch break one day, I was given a message that someone had been looking for me and they'd stop by again. On the second attempt this person approached me and asked, "Are you Kenward Flanagan Cooper?"

"Yes."

"You've been served." Desi had gone through with filing for divorce. If uncontested, it would be approved with no hassle. In a matter of weeks it was official. I did something I'm not proud to say after this happened, I went to the Immigration department to file a complaint against her. They had me put it in writing. My words weren't pleasant, but I wasn't doing this to get at her, it was because I didn't want it to be easy for him. You don't involve yourself with a married woman without consequences.

A decade and a half passed before Desi and I could talk openly about these events in our life without the bitterness. Dave played to her weaknesses, claiming he would never let her down, that I wasn't there every night and he was, professing how he wanted to marry her and be with her forever, playing music and touring the world together. Everything she wanted to hear, he sold her a fairy tale, and she'd bought into it.

How you gonna live with all your guilt?

How you gonna go against the will?

You did a swan dive with clipped wings.

When will you admit to everything?

These lyrics are from a song I wrote called "Swandive," which ended up on my first solo record. It was a way to ask the questions of Desi, as much as it was asking myself. We'd lied to each other, to ourselves, and kept secrets. Forgive or forget?

Music was lifting me up in this moment, as it always had. Not only my own, but whatever I was gravitating towards listening to. *All That You Can't Leave Behind* from U2 was an important record for me during this time. It's gratifying when a lyric speaks directly to you, leaving you with the belief it was intended for you. And there were many songs on the record that provided this feeling. It gave me strength.

The best remedy for me after divorce finalized was to surround myself with my band of brothers. Trevor was the first of my friends to reach out and say I didn't need that shit. There was no pity, these guys simply had my back. Naturally our time hanging out led to playing shows again. But first there was the mountain song. Abe or Josh had a Jeep for a quick minute, which we took out into the desert for some off-roading, until we ended up getting stuck in a ditch. While they were figuring out how they were going to get it out, I ventured off up to the mountaintop. I started to uncontrollably yell my face off. "YOU FUCKING BITCH! FUCK YOU! GODDAMN WHORE!" I could hear Jacob down below with much concern asking what I was doing. It was pure release. Like therapy to just let it all out at the top of my lungs. I would highly recommend it.

Desi made attempts to email me. Once a month I received another message from her. I never read any of them. I couldn't imagine what it would change, nor did I want to open myself up to going down that road. I had a sense of freedom that I welcomed, those random encounters I could have with someone and enjoy without it concerning anyone else.

Girls from work wanted to hook up. I went out for sushi with a former coworker; midway through salmon roe she said we should have sex. Easy like that. It wasn't always fulfilling though. After the divorce, my dick decided when it was going to work and when it wasn't, the fucking pecker didn't give me any say in who it was going to cooperate with. I was not in control.

Valentine's Day 2001 is when I heard Desi's voice again. I was on my way to dinner with Courtney when my phone rang. She vehemently told me not to answer it, thinking it was a calculated move on Desi's part to call me on Cupid's holiday. It's probably why I answered, knowing Desi didn't care for such commercial celebrations—this was a girl who slept through the Fourth of July every single year. It felt like it was time to talk. She was sobbing on the other end about how sorry she was for leaving and that she just wanted to come back now.

After four months, Dave had gotten cold feet. Desi described him as Dr. Jekyll and Mr. Hyde, having no sense of himself. But he must've known the shit he put her in, after making his declaration of promising to marry her if she divorced me. She recounted being horrified when he said, "I am just like Ken, I want to do my own thing!" If that wasn't enough to taunt, perhaps telling her he wanted more experience with women would solidify it.

Soon after Valentine's Day, Desi called again to tell me she and Dave, still together, were back in Vegas. I wondered why she didn't stay in Chicago, and what on earth did they have in Vegas to come back to. Unless Desi was imagining us being a couple again. When we met up, I believe I shied away from her embrace. I wasn't going to be all open arms and a mouthful of kisses like some after-school special on the Lifetime movie channel. The hurt was still raw, despite my having done a fair job of powering through it.

I drove us to Sunset Park, a place from my childhood where I used to spend my summers. Maybe I was trying to find some form of innocence. The first thing I insisted on needing to happen was that she stop living with Dave. There was no way she could expect me to see her if she wasn't on her own. In the car things heated into an argument. I floored the accelerator and raced to the red light as Desi screamed. Anything to break the tension.

I found her a Budget Suites weekly rental so that she could break free from Dave. I didn't believe she could live under the same roof as him without them having sex. She attested that they weren't and that the romantic relationship was over between them. I passed by him on the day I went to visit her at the Budget Suites, sure enough he had just been with her.

You gotta be kidding me. I threw my hands up in the air at him and said, "WHAT'S UP, MAN?" full of attitude.

"Yeah, what is up?" he retorted. If either of us were the brawling type, this might've been fun.

My bosses offered to rehire Desi at one of their boutiques, they were always so caring. The job would give her a source of income for a little while, until her resident card expired due to our divorce. Until then, I moved her to yet another more affordable weekly, located off the Strip and closer to her work. I know she hoped we could have our own place again and asked why we couldn't just live together. For me, though, it wasn't so easy with these feelings of betrayal still lingering.

Another great offer from my bosses was to send me on vacation. Terrance was making plans for his first out-of-country experience and they thought I'd make a great tour guide. Angie insisted getting away would serve me well, and I wasn't about to turn down paid time off. I also wasn't going just to play chaperone. I used the time to my advantage and set up a recording session in advance with Jake Shillingford, a superb talent from the UK band My Life Story.

I remember reading an interview in *NME* where Jake was quoted saying he would challenge anyone to a songwriting contest. I related to this ballsy statement, I loved his confidence and swagger. We hadn't met, but when I contacted him with the proposal of working together, he was both gracious and authoritative. My holy grail was to have a string arrangement featured on one of the songs. Not only did Jake recommended a wonderful arranger, Aaron Cahill, he also loaned me the string players from My Life Story and would conduct the quartet for the London session. A magical experience to hear orchestration come together on this ballad, titled "Handle with Care," which I had written about the turmoil of my relationship with Desi and the aftermath of divorce.

In a month's time Desi told me she was pregnant. At first she played it off that it could be mine, though later confessed that she wasn't sure as she was still seeing Dave. She contemplated keeping it, but without being totally sure whose it was, terminating the pregnancy weighed more as the reasonable decision. Desi asked Dave to help pay for it, and he expressed zero interest, couldn't give a shit. I covered the fees and drove her to the appointment. It was awful to watch her walk out from the clinic after the procedure, her steps were in slow motion. There used to be a photo booth in one of the casino arcades that would morph two people together to produce an image of what their child would look like. Desi always wanted to do this with me, but I never gave in. I was superstitious about having a predetermined or artificially generated photo to live up to. Sad to never know if the baby she was carrying was mine. Even more wild to think that baby would be twenty years old today.

I could imagine it was uncomfortable and depressing for Desi to be on the verge of being in the country illegally again. I'm sure living in a weekly didn't lift her spirits either. She spoke about having a new start together if I were to remarry her. It made me loathe the situation even more, because it hadn't had to come to this. But this was our reality once Dave entered the picture, and once the nightlife became my lover. We forgot how to communicate, we lost our way.

The abortion was yet another sign of how things felt grim. Trust had been broken, I couldn't think how remarrying was the answer to our problems. Regardless, I'd stay over with Desi at least three times a week. One night she did a striptease for me, complete with wig, costume, and dimmed lights. She confessed that she'd given it a try at one of the topless clubs before leaving for Chicago. Hard to tell if the lap dance was to entice me or if she felt she had been a sexual object for the past several months. I couldn't be sure, I only know she expressed the feeling that she had been used in more ways than one by Dave. Maybe this provided reason for acting out.

When we went to a limited engagement for the film *Hedwig and the Angry Inch*, the scenes when Hedwig becomes Tommy's mentor and then Tommy becomes a rock star by stealing Hedwig's ideas hit the both of us right in the gut. As if we instantly feared or knew this was going to happen to us. It's not something we welcomed, it would be crazy to say we manifested it. When we left the theater, though we loved the film, somehow it was unavoidable to think we'd foreseen on the screen what was about to happen in our lives, and this sickened us.

I helped Desi with her new ideas and put a batch of songs together with her. She was channeling true emotions, the hurt, sadness, and expectations. Right in the moment, bringing her experiences into sound and vision. I was proud and excited to see this growth in her and to put on my producer hat. We recorded these songs with Trevor in his newly constructed home studio. In writing this, I listened to the recordings again, after nearly twenty years sealed up in a box. It's a tragedy these songs weren't released. Beautiful melodies, interesting arrangements, a uniqueness of its own.

When the attacks on September 11 happened, Vegas quickly became a ghost town. I can imagine this being true everywhere. I paid Desi a visit, feeling sorry she was alone while chaos loomed. The realization of being on her own in a difficult time must've registered as well for her. An all-too-familiar scene of having to leave the country again was just around the corner. Before she left, it's no surprise to say we talked seriously about joining each other in Europe, as if we were ready for another go-around.

I drove Desi to the airport and walked her to the TSA line. With the post 9/11 security restrictions in place, this was as far as I could go. Now we had our movie moment with a long hug and kiss goodbye. I watched her until she was no longer in view. I had no idea that this would be the beginning of a new set of changes for us. A couple of years passed before we would see each other again.

13

SALT IN THE WOUND

I can recall checking the *Vegas Weekly* classified ads, it's one of those things you do when you come to the end of the back pages, just can't help but look. There was a listing from a singer seeking musicians into Oasis, the Smiths, etc. I had no reason to call, I already had a band. Dave answered.

In late 2000, while prospecting musicians for her project, Desi had met a girl who ran in the same circles as us. Her name was similar to that of Desi's sister. We'd met in passing at various shows. At one point she tried to recruit both Trevor and Jacob from my band to team up with Brandon Flowers, who was forming this new band that would eventually achieve worldwide success.

The next time I heard anything about his band was from another musician Desi had played with, who went by the name of Dell Star. He walked into my work one day to say hello and told me he was playing with this singer Brandon, whom he really liked, and that Dave was also in the band. *Damn it, that guy's still in Vegas*, I thought to myself. With Desi gone, what the hell was he hanging around my town for? Dell meant no harm by informing me, he was a soft-spoken, nice guy who simply wanted to belong and be part of something. He was the fifth member of their band but sadly didn't make the cut.

I continued playing shows, and in 2001 we did a benefit gig at the Hard Rock to benefit the firefighters of 9/11. The local FM rock station KOMP sponsored it. They were on the scene blasting my tune "You and What Army?"

a song that features the lyrics "I'm not a soldier / but I am a cavalier." Three years later, "I'm not a soldier" wound up in a Killers song. Go figure.

Now that wouldn't be the only time I raised an eyebrow. Anytime people heard my song "The Movies," they would say to me how the intro reminded them of the Killers "Mr. Brightside." There is a similarity, albeit not blatant enough for me to sick the dogs on 'em.

But if we're getting technical, my copyright predates their Hot Fuss sound recording, it's there in the public record. Maybe the riff did inspire them, maybe it didn't. Who knows, who cares?

Wanting to lay down the guitar and have my hands free on stage, I added a second guitarist to the lineup, Aaron Archer. Yet another player who claimed he could've, might've, should've been playing in Dave's shoes, having been approached early on to join their band.

Aaron, with his appetite for being up for anything, was a perfect addition to my cast of characters. Perhaps that hunger took things just a little too far when him and Abe thought they could borrow the name "the Toxic Twins" from Steven Tyler and Joe Perry and adapt it to themselves without any repercussions, and I'm not talking trademarks here. Track marks might be more in the ballpark.

Abe had an attraction to the dark road that so many of his favorite musicians traveled. He liked to romanticize drugs and gloat about taking Oxy and how heroin was in his future. My brother, Scott, was using, sometimes he'd come to our shows and if there wasn't an after-party, he'd make one. It was with Scott that Abe got his first chase of the dragon. Users love company. It was something I dreaded seeing happen to Abe, particularly knowing he had so much to offer.

The album that I'd been recording with Ron spun into a series of delays as sessions repeatedly got cancelled. *How many times can someone call out sick*, I wondered. Funny when he chalked it up as some old hamburger from the Bang Bang days still lingering in his system. Rumors spread about junk, just not the fast food kind. I would've been understanding had I known, considering too many people close to me were ordering that same happy meal. It was a frustrating experience trying to get a record made. This wasn't *Hysteria* we were making, yet it still took almost a year to complete.

I had started dating a new girl, Cortney, whom I'd met at the Champagne Lounge after work one night. I walked in and wouldn't have known I was in the middle of a crowded room when I took one look at her. I just had to slide up next to her. Our first date I took her to see the French film *Amélie*. Perhaps trying to impress her that I was so "cultured" with my arthouse cinema picks. I forget whom I got a joint from, but I went into the restroom after the movie ended and burned one.

I'd never been a smoker of any kind, though I was willing to do whatever I needed to loosen the fuck up. Only then, while driving back to her house, I was getting paranoid that I reeked in the car. She laughed, "You should've told me, I would've smoked it with you!" I needed to think ahead for our second date, since I didn't have my own place for us to go back to. My pal Sidney understood the life of bachelor needs, to the point he handed me the keys to his apartment while he stayed elsewhere. Cortney had no idea.

After this routine a couple of times, I rented a unit in the LV Country Club, best that I just get my own pad. Even with this, and the monthly gigs with a great band, a good job, and everything that was going well for me in Vegas, I was getting the itch for something else. Fuck if I can't stay still in one place for long enough. I had an unquenchable thirst for New York. Again. You would think people probably wanted to flee the city after September 11, here I was wanting to move back there. It wasn't just a longing for NYC, I'd had my ups and downs following the divorce and figured another change would do me good. There was a moment I was cleaning house, just getting rid of inventory. I hear this is common. I filled up several large trash bags of stuff that no longer seemed important. Magazine collections, memorabilia, photographs and negatives, press kits, stuff I look back on now and think it'd be great to have. What was important was Desi, but I guess in some way she'd been discarded too.

❖

With Desi being back in Paris, sometimes there were gaps in our communication. In these times, I avoided playing certain music if it carried a personal sentimental attachment. Bryan Ferry's *Mamouna* record was such and it had been a long time since I'd played it. I said to myself, *If I play this, I know I'm going to hear from Desi.* Sure enough, I could've bet money on it, hours later she called me. We could channel each other like that.

Another time, I was in a deep sleep, dreaming we were on the telephone talking but had gotten disconnected. In the dream she was calling me back and I heard the phone ringing, at the exact same moment in real time my phone was ringing and I awoke to answer it. It was Desi on the other end. Right there is a definition of true connection.

There were still things to keep busy with before making any final relocation plans. I released my debut record, *Theme for a New Aesthetic*, on CD in December 2001. Trevor and I ventured into the early morning hours to plaster the city with promotional posters. With him in the driver's seat, I darted out of the car with a staple gun in hand to cover the electric poles up and down the UNLV area and wherever there were music establishments. Abe and I drove out to LA to do the same.

After midnight was our witching hour. We hit all the POST NO BILLS and posted anyway. If there were movie posters, then there were going to be Kenward posters too. We went to Aaron's Records on Highland and covered their parking lot wall. The cops showed up, flashing their lights on us. Abe became paranoid since he had scored earlier in the day and had his stash right in my glove box. The officer asked what we were doing, I said just putting up posters for our record that the store was carrying, holding one up for him to see. "Is that you?" he asked.

"Yep, that's me."

He cracked a smile, "Okay, good luck." And on his way he went.

On another occasion, I was out all night with Abe and Josh going from club to club. Our last call was at Drai's at the Barbary Coast, it was 5:00 a.m. when we got the brilliantly stupid idea to drive to LA. I'd call out of work in a few hours, no big deal.

When you've been drinking and the sun is starting to come up, go the fuck home and sleep. Not this time. We didn't even make it to the state line. Let's just say Josh's car was not high performance. As soon as I accelerated, I felt the car wobble, my effort to correct it only made it less controllable. The front right side clipped the tail end of a semitruck as it was passing us.

We did a complete 360 from one side of the highway road to the other and watched cars dodge us in those quick few seconds. The driver of the semi pulled off to the side to stop and got out. He asked us if we were all right. "Yeah, just go!" I answered. Worried that the cops would show up and who knows what I would've blown into the breathalyzer. Maybe moving to NYC and not needing a car was a pretty great idea after all.

My brother got word there was a party for *Maxim* magazine happening at the Rio. It would be me, Scott, and Abe, and a set of balls, since we had no invitation. Once we found its location, it was over the wall we went. There's a great thrill in having no time to overthink your options. Eight feet of brick, climb it, and act like you know exactly where you're going. This led us right through the Palazzo Villas.

We entered through someone's private suite, which had its outside doors open, just a guy and his girl having a drink, looking surprised and yet unbothered by our entrance. At the front was another door that dropped us right where we intended to be, in the heart of the action. I met a girl from Sweden whom I struck up an instant friendship with. She had friends back in Stockholm who were recording artists and one who was A&R at Warner Music.

My brother had been telling me about Stockholm for years, saying I was wasting my time going to London, that Sweden was where the music scene was at. After meeting Kiki, I was now more inclined to see this for myself.

With a CD to my credit, it made sense to explore as many possibilities for it that I could. If this meant focusing on Europe, I was game to do it now that I had product. This became more apparent to me when Tower Records in Vegas stocked it. It was a downer to come back a month later and see only one unit had sold, even with placement visibility. It led me to believe there still might be a more supportive scene somewhere other than my hometown.

The Strokes came through town to play the House of Blues. The room was packed. I wondered where all these people were coming from. Not the regular faces I'd see at the local clubs. I had a copy of *NME* from several months ago that featured them on the cover, I remembered Desi showing it to Dave. She loved how they looked, young Italian NYC boys, skinny jeans and jackets. I could see her setting this as an example. When the show ended, I spotted Dave in the crowd with his new bandmates and his transformed image. He was wearing a jean jacket like a sixth member of the Strokes and had dyed his hair blond. Unquestionably Desi's influence had taken its course.

My restlessness dictated it was time to get on the move. I arranged to fly directly from Vegas to Europe. The plan would be to spend time networking abroad and take as many meetings as possible. I put in my notice at work. Sunil had tears in his eyes when I broke the news. He said he'd dreaded the day he would hear those words from me. I needed to make a new start, and after getting divorced, the feeling of staying was none too pleasing anymore. Like the Big Country song goes, "You can't stay here with every single hope you had shattered."

Some of my Versace crew pitched in for a send-off party for me. I had booked a double suite at the Luxor for an all-nighter with my friends from work, my band of brothers, and whoever wanted to party.

The television in the suite came equipped with a device that would levitate the set from out of the console table, like on a hydraulic system. Our friend Delight rode the TV up and down like a freakin' amusement park ride. The other thrill seeker present that night was cocaine. Sidney had his own code name for it. He'd make a call asking for a "white refrigerator" to be delivered. I wondered how it was, if his phone was tapped, he thought scheduling delivery for an appliance late at night didn't make him sound any more sketchy. You'd always know when he was doing a little too much of the stuff, saliva started to cake up around the corners of his mouth. Cringeable when someone had to tell him, "Hey, man, you got some shit right here," pointing to the side of their lips.

Daylight came and I would soon be on my way. I left the room keys with whoever was crashed out and said they should just leave by checkout time. The fact that I didn't get billed an extra night tells me everything worked out okay. Cortney drove me to the airport that day. She hadn't shown up to the party, but making sure I get the hell out of town, that she could do. Truth is, if our relationship had turned into something more, I know I would've stayed in Vegas. I was infatuated with her, but my headspace was a head case, and our chemistry suffered because of it. Months later she came to visit me in New York that November, and I won't forget when she told me that I needed to be in a relationship not with her but with someone like Madonna. I think she was suggesting that I'd be better off with someone with a larger-than-life personality. Perhaps she even saw me as being on par with such.

When I arrived in London, I flew right on over to Sweden, where my new friend Kiki from the *Maxim* party greeted me and got me situated. I hadn't set up any accommodations ahead of time, so getting a hotel was the day's first priority. She brought me to the Crowne Plaza and spoke for me in her native tongue, scoring me an incredible deal by saying I was a very known musician in the USA. I stayed there for two weeks, but for a four-star hotel, it didn't even make a dent in my budget.

I fell in love with Stockholm, it checked all my boxes: great balance between old and new, condensed city feel, lovely people, amazing food—how could I argue with herring and roe—and of course an incredible music scene.

I'd turn the TV on in the morning and watch music videos. The Ark was one of the bands I found exciting. They had seventies glam rock appeal, with a great singer and wonderful tunes. Also noticeable in Sweden was the music production, everything I was hearing was impactful and so on point creatively.

Prior to my visit, I had sent Kiki copies of my CD, and true to her word, she'd set something up for me once I was in town. She made dinner plans for us to meet with her friend Lili, an A&R rep at Warner who had taken interest in the record. Before the night came to an end, Lili had penciled me in for an appointment that week to meet with her again at the label's office. This was starting to feel good.

Every night was worth going out and having fun. The Stureplan in the city center was the hotspot area, lined with clubs, bars, and restaurants, with a great nightlife. Usually that's where I'd be, if I wasn't joining Kiki and her boyfriend, I'd be exploring it on my own. It was a trip to order food if the menu was only in Swedish. Most of the time I wouldn't ask what it was, I would just point and get the luck of the draw. Whatever it was, I'd be satisfied. One night, after one drink too many, I shared a taxi with a lovely lady. Despite my offer to raid the minibar in my room, she carried on her way. That's all right, there was Swedish erotica on the TV channels. I passed out naked with the volume on the TV cranked up. I can only imagine the explicit noise the guests next door had to awake to in the morning hours thanks to me. When my eyes opened in the morning, the TV was off and my underwear was on backwards. I wondered if guest services had paid me a visit in the middle of my sleep and had a joke at my expense.

Lili discussed the possibilities of having my record released on the Scandinavian market. The one thing riding on it would be to get everyone else at the company on board with it. She was all for it, though a little more time would be required. I stayed an extra week hoping she'd have an answer by then.

A new band from the States was playing at a venue called Berns. I figured I'd go and give support to my fellow Americans on their first European tour. The White Stripes had the Swedes in the palm of their hands that night. They were fun to watch, even if I couldn't help but think their boy/girl image and speculation if Jack and Meg were married or brother and sister was similar to the approach Desi and I had conjured up for ourselves years prior. It seemed after this, everywhere you looked there was a group doing the boy/girl duo thing.

While I was in Sweden I was checking my emails at a local internet café and writing to Desi, as we still talked about getting together in Paris or London. It seemed she was getting a bit wishy-washy, unable to commit now that I was in Europe. One message read it was too late for us, and another would say she needed some time alone. At the end of the second week, she finally came clean and told me she was no longer in Europe, that she had gone back to Chicago to be with a new partner now, a musician she had met the first time around when she was there with Dave. Evidently this new guy,

Damian, had invited them over to his place back when. As he noticed the disconnect between Desi and Dave, he spoke in French and told her if she had a problem with this guy that he would help her. Several months later, she took him up on the offer.

Thinking I was this close to her and we would be seeing each other, and then hearing her tell me this, well, it hurt. I felt I'd been lied to again. In some ways I suppose she did us both a service, it was what was needed to put an end to this traveling road show. My best escape in this moment seemed like a place full of debauchery. I booked a flight to Amsterdam and spent the next couple of days practicing hedonism.

After following up with Lili and learning Warner would not be pursuing a release, it was time to get back in my New York groove. There was one thing that always felt good after being in Europe, that was being able to come back home to NYC. Nowhere else I lived gave me this same feeling, New York has that magic.

Here's a shocker, while abroad, my parents took into account the fact that I would not be returning to Vegas. So, what did they do? They packed up and moved back East as well. As annoying as I found it, it was their way. They just couldn't stand to be far from either me or my brother. Sometimes they'd alternate between the two of us. I understand it better now, if they had friends in their life maybe it would have been a different story, but that wasn't the case. Throughout my life, there was never anyone in their world that came over to spend time with them, nor did they make phone calls to friends, it simply didn't happen. We were their friends and all that they knew. I didn't complain, I accepted it for what it was. And, in an expensive city like Manhattan, their presence would alleviate the financial stress while I continued to be a struggling artist.

While my search for musicians was underway, I noticed an ad for an open-call audition at SIR Studios for an international recording star's upcoming tour. On the day of, I called the studio to try and get some more info. If it wasn't someone whose music I vibed with, then there was no point in bothering. Generally, the studio wasn't at liberty to say who the artist was, though somehow my way of asking didn't come off as being intrusive, and the guy who answered couldn't seem to give a fuck anyway in telling me it was for Enrique Iglesias.

Cool, I thought, I actually liked his song "Escape," for which Anna Kournikova made her music video debut. There were some other tunes of his that I could get into. More importantly, I could see myself having a blast on tour with this guy. I had a couple of hours before the audition to sit in the apartment and teach myself that song, as well as one of his other hits. I figured the audition would probably test if I was able to play those songs, and I was right.

I asked my parents for a ride so I could use every spare moment rehearsing. I played in the back seat until I got to the front door of the studio. I was expecting a long line, however, there was only one other guy awaiting his turn before me, and he wasn't in there for very long. Enrique's band director, Tony Bruno, was in charge of the search committee. He seemed cool, a down-to-business kinda guy.

He started off by saying, "I'm going to play this riff, and I want you to play it back to me," then he picked the intro to "Escape." I played it straight back to him. "Wow! You're the first person to get that right off the bat," he said. Yeah, thanks to my head start, but he didn't need to know that. I could see he was impressed.

"Here, try this one," as he strummed the chords of "Be With You." Nice, I was liking my chances, this was the other song I'd brushed up on. He said he was definitely putting me on the callback list and told me Enrique liked having a very rock n roll type of band. I wasn't sure if he said that because he thought I fit the part or he thought that I did not. I dressed like a musician who'd already made his money, not like one who was living on the streets. At that moment, I thought about giving him my CD, which was in my guitar case. Clearly he'd be able to tell by the cover that I was rock n roll. But I hesitated, I didn't want to come off as the guy pushing his own product. Besides, he'd already said I was on the callback list.

According to him, I'd be hearing something by the end of the week. No such luck. What I did hear was an announcement on the radio that Enrique was shooting a performance for television in Bryant Park in just a few days. I searched the internet for Tony's email and sent him a message. *Just following up, any news on scheduling callbacks?* He replied with something to the effect of it being put off. I walked over to the park on the day of the shoot and saw another guitarist up there with Enrique.

Who the fuck is this goofball? He had no vibe or presence whatsoever, and since they were using a recorded track, who could say what his playing sounded like either. Shortly after, I emailed Tony again. The update this time was that they were keeping the guy they already had. What a disappointment.

On a summer afternoon walking back to my Upper East Side apartment, I could see a tall tattoo-sleeved rocker dude at the end of the block. At first glance I thought it was Tommy Lee. As I got close enough to make out the Chrome Hearts tank he was wearing, I realized to my great surprise that it was my dear ol' buddy Ashley. Ten years of separation disappeared just like that.

The mark of a true friendship is when those gaps in between are quickly erased and suddenly you're right back where you left off, like no time at all has elapsed. I ended up practically crashing in his room at the Hôtel Plaza Athénée for as long as he was in town. He had a couple things going on that had brought him to the city. A pilot shoot for a reality show also starring his mom and dad, in addition to meetings with Sony Music. He had signed a deal with the label to release his single, a tune he'd written with Robbie Williams. Within hours we had guitars in hand, Ash suggesting that we write something for his next record.

A few days later he mentioned they'd be filming the reality show at the hotel. I figured I'd better think of something to say rather than looking clueless on camera. When I got upstairs and walked into the room, they were rolling. I went into this bit about overhearing people's conversations on the way up there. Dumb. When they stopped filming, Ash quietly said to me, "What was that? Just relax, man." He was right. Kinda embarrassing. If there's a movie scene meme to embed here, it would be Philip Seymour Hoffman in *Boogie Nights* repeating, "Idiot, I'm a fucking idiot."

❖

Ash spoke about the possibility of a tour in Europe and if that happened, then he'd be calling me to come abroad as one of his guitar players. I was hoping his single would be a smash and he'd make good on his word, but if it wasn't, I was still glad to have reconnected with my soul shaker brother. Meanwhile I still had a band of my own to put together.

Chris Davison described himself as looking like the bastard son of Andy Warhol and David Bowie. This quirky dude from upstate New York became my right-hand man, as he was always down to do a gig, no matter the circumstance. A great encourager to play acoustic sets and not rely all the time on a full band.

Some of my favorite times we played were when it was stripped down. I also found a violinist one Sunday afternoon playing for the joy of it in Central Park. *Now that could be a cool idea to add strings to the mix.* A decision that predated Arcade Fire by a couple of years.

Hailing from Hungary, Krisztina Ujhazy was a classically trained musician who was intrigued with my proposition of joining a rock band. I'd play specific melody arrangements on piano or guitar that I wanted her to duplicate on violin, which equally impressed and confused her. "How are you able to do that if you don't read or write music?" she asked. That's the myth some have about composing, it's not about charts, it's from inside, intuitively, or by trial and error of playing and going with what you feel.

The *New York Post*, which had written up my mom when she was a belly dancer, now made mention of one of my shows. I was starting to generate some decent press. My buddy Aaron Archer was a contributing writer for the *Weekly* back in Vegas and had done an interview with me about my record and relocation to NYC.

When we spoke, he said there was a new band called the Killers, who were making waves and got some sort of indie deal going for themselves in the UK. This was the first time I'd heard the name, and I remember thinking it was probably Dave's band. Soon thereafter, Desi started to reach out to me again.

We hadn't spoken since her announcement that she'd moved to Chicago. She asked me to check out her website. In her bio she mentioned her past collaborations and credited Dave from the Killers. From that moment on, I couldn't get the name of the band out of my head. It literally haunted me. I'd wake up in the morning and the first thing I'd hear was a voice in my head repeating the name. It was like a warning of what was coming.

In the spring of 2004, I'd taken a job with Hugo Boss at their SoHo boutique on Greene Street. We were a small staff with no more than four employees on hand. Jorge was a cool, flamboyant Latino guy, obsessed with fashion and with aspirations of becoming a designer. His hair was total rock star, especially when he flipped one side of it to the other, with his long bangs acting like an eye patch covering half of his face. My hair, however, at this time was in the beginning stages of receding. Music-wise we shared a lot of the same taste. Though I think he was disappointed that I didn't know Christian Death quite like he did. I always enjoyed checking out music with Jorge, he turned me on to the electroclash scene, the likes of Adult, Miss Kittin, and other stuff I still get a kick from listening to.

The manager, Luis, was a funny one. One slow day, with no walk-in traffic in sight, he must've been bored or desperate to make a sale when he grabbed a pair of corduroy pants for me from the women's rack. "Here, try these on!" When I walked out of the dressing room wearing them, he gleefully said, "You look hot!" Then he took the tag and rung me up. I gotta say they were the best-fitting pair of cords I ever owned. Luis loved his Brazilian music and jazz vocalists, but every now and again he'd come to the store with a stack of CDs and say how he'd just been record shopping. He'd put on something heavy, thinking it would appeal to me. He tried to please everyone. "Do you like Duran Duran?"

"Yeah, of course."

"Did you know their guitar player, Warren Cuccurullo, posed nude in *Playgirl*?" he asked.

"Nope, sure didn't." *Why would I care, and why would someone successful pose for that?* I thought.

"I'm gonna bring it in and show you," he said all too eagerly. Sure enough he did, and sure enough there was Warren. *What the hell is going on here, I'm looking at cock with my boss.* One day I unintentionally got back at him.

Instead of running to the Apple store down the block every time I needed to check my email, it was more convenient to use the computer in Luis's office. One day, I got spammed and couldn't resist opening the email, which promised hot-girl action. *Damn it!* The screen froze on me and there was no way to exit out of it without unplugging the system. I couldn't risk screwing that up, everything relating to the store, including batching the end-of-day sales reports, happened on this computer. So, I just left it that way and hoped by some miracle it would disappear.

The next morning, I opened the store. Luis got there a little bit later. After he'd arrived and settled into the office, he stormed out, "OH MY GOD! Why is there porn on my computer screen? Who did this? I am shocked!" It was rather a laugh seeing him take offense to this when show-and-tell time with his magazine had somehow been okay in his book. I confessed to it, and it wasn't such a big deal. Not like he was gonna fire me. At one point later on he even made light of it.

Luis hired a new guy, who had a background writing for publications like *Nylon* and the *Source*. I'm convinced Luis brought him on board just so I could have someone at work to vibe with. George "Geo" Hagan and I became quick friends, and to this day he's one of the special people in my life I call a brother. He always had a positive outlook and shared a closeness to his family. I got the sense from him that those are common ways of being in Ghana, where he grew up. For me, I could relate to his ethics. When we weren't getting people suited and booted, we'd spend every minute of the day talking about music, movies, and models. The three M's. *Mmm good.* It was hard not to, there were always photo shoots with beautiful girls taking place right out front.

"That band the Killers got signed, and I'm pissed," Trevor announced when he visited me. I tried to shrug it off by saying it was just a UK indie deal. "No, over here one of the majors got them." He had two reasons to be upset. One, he felt that could've been us. Two, he'd been asked to be in the band but had declined. When he and anyone else spoke about them, they'd say to me, "They sound eighties, you'd probably like 'em." I'd do my best to avoid hearing them. Soon, however, that would be inescapable.

My song "You and What Army?" got a makeover when I decided to rewrite the words and melody, changing it to "Paris London New York." Also I had the idea to freshen it up by giving it a disco flavor, somewhere in the realm of the KISS classic "I Was Made for Loving You" and Blur's "Boys and Girls." This became the highlight of our set when playing live. One of those instantly likeable songs people gravitated to.

Chris's buddy Paul Antonell was the owner of a beautiful studio up in Rhinebeck known as the Clubhouse. He liked the tune so much he offered us studio time to record it at no charge. I said if we could get some hotshot DJ to spin this in the clubs, or have it remixed, it would be a smash. Nobody doubted it. On my visit to Chicago to see Desi and her now husband, Damian, I played her the track. She loved it.

"We should do a French version," she said. It made perfect sense since Paris is referenced in the song. On a whim I phoned my ol' pal Chip Z'Nuff to see if he'd be down to have us at his studio. Instead he suggested I call his friend at Chicago Recording Company, "And tell him Chip sent ya!"

All we needed was a couple of hours to do a vocal. "Can you come now?" he asked. I looked at Desi and she was mouthing the word *yes*, nodding her head in agreement. One minute we were talking about it, the next we were doing it. Damian looked at us in awe. We were like two kids, excited to be going to Chicago's premiere studio. You would have thought we were about to meet the Wizard of Oz. One of Desi's best traits was her spontaneity and willingness to roll with it. On our way there she transcribed the words in French and did a great job singing without having any time to rehearse it. When we heard the playback on the big speakers in the control room, both of us turned to smile, sporting ear-to-ear grins. I knew I had to act fast to get this song circulated. I imagined we were doubling our chances with French and English versions.

The Killers record hit the shelves and blew up right out of the gate. I'd hear it blaring from car stereos, in rotation at clothing stores, there was no end to it. Everything I had envisioned for myself was now happening for them. I watched a Larry King interview with Elton John where he was asked what he listened to these days. He answered the Killers. A review I read of one of their shows in New York mentioned that David Bowie and Tony Visconti had been in attendance, checking them out. At work, as I was helping actor Tom Arnold pick out some shirts, he asked me where I was from. I said Vegas, and he responded, "Oh, that band the Killers is from there." It was a nightmare. Everywhere I turned, they were being played or talked about.

When, at my favorite neighborhood hang, the bartender put on their CD, I had to tell her the backstory and I gave her orders that whenever I was there not to play them. She abided. Desi didn't take their success any better. Although she constantly put her faith in Dave helping her now that he was established. When the Killers played in concert in Chicago, she was there to greet him outside the venue after the show.

Once they spotted each other, she said he took off running for the tour bus! Finally he relinquished and invited her up. She gave him a CD of some songs we had recorded and asked him to give it to someone or however he could help. "Yeah, okay" was about all the acknowledgement she got from that. Every so often I'd hear about her email exchanges with him. This would go on for years. I couldn't have a conversation with Desi without her bringing up Dave in one form or another.

Truth be told, what bothered me most wasn't that he had made it, it was that I hadn't yet. I knew how hard I was pushing for something to happen. Networking, meeting people, booking shows, promoting, attending events like SXSW, traveling wherever I thought I needed to be, always at the ready to give someone my music. When I put out *Theme for a New Aesthetic*, year after year I was spending anywhere from four to six grand on postage alone, sending my CDs to industry people all over the world. I was going at it harder than anyone else I knew.

There were some small victories along the way that gave a sense of validation. Like landing sync licensing placements for my songs on television networks such as CNN, ABC, and MTV. Also having Jake Shillingford from My Life Story contact me to do a string of New York City dates. He asked that I be his domestic band leader and put together a lineup, in addition to booking the shows. I enlisted Desi to play keyboard and Trevor on drums. I trusted both would do their homework and learn the set list on their own time before joining us in New York, where we'd have a week to hone in on it all together.

Desi used this trip not only for playing with a favorite of ours, but also to do community service work. If she was ever going to apply for U.S. citizenship, then she best clear up any negative strikes on her record. The arrest report from her massage days was lingering over her head still. In between our days of rehearsing, she was scheduled to clean up the parks and city streets of New York, picking up dog shit.

Our first full-on rehearsal Desi was still finding her way around the songs. Jake suggested she just ghost her way through it if she was unsure—rather than hitting wrong notes, pantomime playing the right ones. Desi took great offense to this and stormed out of the room.

I was not about to send a search party after her. The three of us continued on till she returned to try it again. Eventually it all came together rather well.

We had a great second show that was recorded and we talked about possibly releasing it. On our third and final performance, at Don Hill's, we ran into a bit of technical difficulties with equipment failure after the first song. It was up to Desi to carry the weight by accompanying Jake with only piano. I sat on the drum riser and prayed, hoping it didn't turn in to a catastrophe. God bless you, rock n roll, there were zero mistakes, though sadly the rest of the night was cut short. Looking back at the photos from that night, it looked like we were having the time of our lives. We were thrilled to have played with Jake, and he showed kind spirit to weather the kinks of my crew. "I have a keyboard player who has to clean up shit and a drummer who has to eat all the time. Fucking 'ell," he joked. I was glad to see he enjoyed it as much as us.

Amazing how different LA feels when you're just visiting. I tend to have an on-again, off-again love affair with the place. I've found it to be depressing if you're not very busy but really great if you're productive. Whereas in New York City, it's great period, no matter what your status is. Being back in LA this time around to record with producer Rick Parker, I felt like I was on the right track and in the right place.

Rick was a recipient of my mass mailings and someone whom I'd been a huge fan of ever since I was fourteen years old, when his band Lions & Ghosts made its debut. Their first record remains an all-time favorite of mine, one of those desert island discs. One thing music lovers do when we have a favorite band is we stake our claim to them. Once they become too popular, it's like everyone else is suddenly in on our best-kept secret. On one hand we want them to be huge, on the other we want to keep them all to ourselves. That's how it was for me with his band.

Lions & Ghosts should've struck gold, but even if the rest of the world didn't know about them, I was happy they were mine. The beautiful mix of string arrangements, courtesy of legendary Bowie producer Tony Visconti, with their rock n roll vibe had me sold on them.

Rick's wife, Miranda Lee Richards, advocated that Rick and I team up after a bare-bones version of a song I had written called "When Summer Turns to Fall" got her attention from my demo submission. This would be one of the songs I properly recorded with Rick's elaborate production. I'd written it about Desi. Opening with the line "Everyone has belonged to someone," it recounts our time together and finds contentment in moving on. I love how Rick was able to take a sad song and make it sound victorious.

In the fall of that year, Desi told me she was pregnant. That thing I said about contentment in moving on, never mind, it didn't exist, right out the window. It was an emotional setback. Why did I take it so hard? Because she was my first love, and all the memories of what was and could have been for us had flooded me. Late nights talking about having a family of our own after we toured the world many times over, names she had picked out, right down to the morphed image of our hypothetical child that I never wanted to step into the photo booth for. Everything we strived to achieve together I was feeling depressed about. This new change could be the bookend to our story. I had nothing against Damian, we got along fine and respected each other. I just assumed things would be forever different between me and Desi now.

With a baby on the way, I feared we would grow apart. Desi sent me emails saying not to make it hard on myself, that she was happy and she trusted I could accept this as I cared for her well-being, just as she did mine. She also explained in a way that only Desi could that she had chosen to give life and this did not make her a disabled woman.

For a week I hung my head low. I thought back to our time in the countryside of Paris when we'd had our first blow-up. Desi asked me if I knew what love was. I gave her some textbook definition. With tears in her eyes she said, "No, love is torture!" It would take me years to really understand what she meant. I was understanding it now.

When I stepped outside of the apartment, it was to walk around Central Park with my Walkman. Most people I know, when they're sad, they can't listen to sad songs. Not me, I bask in it. I burned myself a mix CD of tearjerkers and felt what I was feeling.

Nearly a month later, Desi contacted me about a night spent in the emergency room. She'd been experiencing heavy bleeding, tests revealed she was pregnant, the ultrasound showed the sac in the uterus, yet something strange was happening, there was no fetus. She was scheduled back two days later to check if possibly it was an ectopic pregnancy with the egg growing in the fallopian tube.

Now that she would no longer be giving birth anytime soon, Desi believed the higher power had other plans for her. Seeing the bigger picture or analyzing reasons is something she could obsess over. As for myself, I'd come to accept and embrace her motherhood. After learning of the complications, however, my only care was that she was healthy. Ultimately, the medical news allowed Desi to divert maternity plans and put the focus back on her music and work.

From 2003 to 2005 I had a weekly gig at WXNY TV thanks to my dad's recommendation that I should be hosting a music video program for the station. There were a number of people shooting their own shows straight out of that studio. *The Robin Byrd Show* featured strippers and porn stars, always on after midnight, providing New Yorkers with titties and bush free of charge. Max Kellerman was the other recognizable personality, honing his skills with boxing commentary before HBO Sports got hold of him.

My show was called *NYC Country*, which later became known as *Video Blender*. There was quite the audience for country music in New York City, as anyone who's seen footage of Garth playing in Central Park can attest to. I played clips from Johnny and Willie, the classics of yesteryear mixed in with the Keiths and Shanias of the day. One other thing about country music—just mentioning these artists on a first-name basis, you know exactly who I'm talking about. That doesn't always fly in the rock world.

I had callers dial in with their requests, regulars such as a mother-and-daughter team who called in every Sunday. I'd hear the girl in the background with her unmistakable city accent saying, "Ma, he's so handsome." Yep, I had fans. Cool to know I provided something for people with coat hangers for antennas to look forward to. The power of public access.

Trips to LA to record became more of a regular thing. I had Rick Parker on board to produce the next round of tunes, and he was totally up for having Desi piggyback on our session. We would do two additional songs with her on vocals, something she and I could promote as new material for our project together. My original idea was to call our band Desi's Episode, because lord knows she'd had plenty. As long as we didn't use the word "the." I didn't want us to be another "the" band. This Episode has a certain class to it, and more than one meaning. It could relate to this moment of our lives, this chapter, this adventure, this matter. I thought the connotation to television was quite cool also.

For the current age, I could see This Episode being the perfect name for a streaming service/video-on-demand company. So, for the next Netflix out there, I will kindly entertain your offers to buy my .com and .tv domains.

I rented a convertible Sebring the week of our recording session, picking Desi up from LAX airport. From there we drove right to Pacific Coast Highway with the top down—there's nothing better when driving and you enter the beach zone, seeing the awesome size of the ocean there beside you. "We have a great life," Desi said. It was hard to disagree.

The beauty around us and the excitement for the days ahead had us feeling only good vibes. One of the songs we recorded was "Paris London New York." I still believed this could be the song to open the doors for us. This would be version number three, four if you count its original form. With the polishing Rick provided, it was undeniably ready for radio.

I was still actively playing the New York scene and loving the city as much as ever. Even though I didn't have a steady girlfriend, the moments of living like some kind of playboy sure made up for it. There was a gorgeous girl from India, strikingly alluring. I met Parvinder at one of the Hugo Boss parties, she also worked in fashion. For months I tried to get her to go out, invited her to shows, dinner, drinks, you name it. One night she obliged and checked out a gig of mine at the Cutting Room. We went to some East Village dive bar afterwards, I can remember this Italian musician who was part of my circle of friends asking me for her number. Yeah right, man, dream on.

A solid year went by of trying to date Parvinder. When you've run out of suggestions and repeat the same questions, what do you do? Say what's really on your mind. Get to the goddamn point. Show some cojones. With my BlackBerry in hand, I had a simple statement to make. *You and I should fuck.* Send. Almost an immediate reply she sent back: *I was waiting for you to say that.* Cha-fuckin-ching. These days that kind of assumption can land a person in trouble. But never mind that for now, back to my Letter to *Penthouse*.

We practically started in the taxi on the way to her place. The driver kept looking back, probably cursing me, thinking, *You son of a bitch, you get a girl from my country, stick to your own kind!* Or so I imagine. A couple steps into her apartment and we were going at it on the floor. I'm not exaggerating when I say her pussy tasted like curry. Look, when you eat certain spices repetitively, it's going to come through your skin.

In the morning when I took a piss, with the stream came the burn. I got into the shower thinking a scrub down would help. Soon as I toweled off, now we got the discharge. For fuck's sake! My first and only STD.

I got back in bed, she got back on top, it wasn't gonna make any difference now. As I left, I noticed in one of the empty rooms a copy of *Screw* lying on the ground. What the hell was she doing with that? I freaked myself out thinking, *Oh shit, she's a call girl, one of those high-fashion escorts that fucks on the side to pay her rent, and now she gave me a disease.*

A visit to my primary was the first thing I set up for a good ol' urine sample and blood work. My piss indicated an infection, I was prescribed antibiotics in the meantime, but it would be a couple of days before I got the rest of the results back. The waiting part was dreadful, I basically tortured myself believing the worst. When my doc called, he gave me the great news that it was negative for the scary one. Such a relief.

A week later I texted Parvinder that I'd been thinking about her and couldn't get to sleep. She messaged back, *Oh am I keeping you from that?* A girl like her doesn't want to hear that shit. What was I thinking, I escaped death and I was so quick to dip again? The simple lesson is (A) some girls just want to fuck with no attachments and (B) wear a raincoat.

In September of 2005, I couldn't believe what I was hearing when a TV commercial came across the screen for Candie's shoes and the song playing, sung by Hilary Duff, was my song, only it didn't sound quite right!

It's like one of those dreams where you're talking to your best friend but the person looks different than usual, yet you're calling them by the same name, so obviously it must be your friend. I knew it was my song, though the feeling of having just been punched in the stomach spoke loud and clearly to me that I had been ripped off.

Instantly I got on the internet and I was able to find the info I needed in minutes. Having looked up the public copyright records for the song, it listed who the writers were, and boy was I fucking pissed to see the Madden brothers from Good Charlotte given credit. The year prior I had met one of the brothers at the Bowery Ballroom in NYC's Lower East Side.

I was passing out flyers to an upcoming gig. He looked over the one I handed to him, pointed to the picture, and asked me, "Is that you?"

"Yes," I told him.

"This looks really cool," he said, and then he introduced himself. *Interesting,* I thought, I had just read something about them starting their own imprint label through Epic Records. We exchanged emails, and he seemed all about me sending something for them to check out. A few months later I followed up and got a reply that they'd forwarded it on to one of their label people and stating how he liked the tune with all the "jet set" references, obviously "Paris London New York."

From the moment I saw the TV commercial, I didn't waste a minute. I contacted a lawyer the very next morning and got things underway. It's just really low of someone to flat out take from someone else's work without the courtesy to include the person you nicked it from. I would've jumped at the chance if they'd approached me and said, "We really love your chorus, but we're thinking of trying something else, would you be open to reworking it with us?" Without question I would've said yes. Instead, it was worth more to them, for whatever reason, to think they were above that. They'd already established themselves, maybe they didn't care, maybe the concept of paying it forward didn't register with them. There was no way I was going to allow my song to be ripped off without taking action.

Desi and I came to the conclusion that we owed it to ourselves to give our musical pursuit another go. Going to California seemed like the right move. We were still young and hungry, and neither of us wanted to say "we should've done that" ten years down the line.

Desi's husband wasn't too keen on the idea at first, but then he must've known he didn't stand a fighting chance in forbidding her. To his credit, Damian was cool to accept this and go along with it. How many spouses would be okay with allowing their significant other to move to another state with their ex? It sounds crazy, but that's what happened.

We got to LA in November 2005, just escaping the East Coast winter. Our hustle was on from day one to find an apartment, buy a car, get a job, start a band. The first call I made for a used car was the one I bought, a 1980s BMW 320i. The seller said it had belonged to his son. I got the feeling something bad had happened to the son but didn't want to pry. He was kind enough to sell it to me for two grand.

The first few apartments we applied for we were refused due to my screwed-up credit. Those leases I had broken in Vegas whispered, "It's payback, bitch." The landlord at the Sycamore Street apartment we ended up at probably had seen a lot worse, though. It was a shitty neighborhood right off of Santa Monica Boulevard. There was a free clinic on the corner. Every day the junkies and sex workers lined up outside.

Desi got hired quite quickly by Miu Miu. As for myself, I did a retail job for a couple of months before taking a position as an art consultant for a Beverly Hills art gallery. I was consistent in sales, so management didn't have any gripes with me. My approach concerned client relationships more than numbers. If that's coming from the right place, ultimately the rest follows.

I generated some good clients, including the designer Christian Audigier of Ed Hardy. I went over to his house to hang a Lichtenstein I'd sold to him. Swizz Beatz was another, who was building up his Keith Haring collection at the time.

I cared enough to do my job and do it well, but it wasn't the be-all-end-all for me, like for the other consultants. If I didn't make a sale, no prob, I was in LA to rock.

Our previous string of misfortunes in not finding the pieces to our puzzle by way of musicians was dust now. We had two bands this time around. Trevor and our pal Charles Henry would drive up from Vegas whenever we had shows booked. Charles was one of the regular guitar players in the Vegas production of Blue Man Group; for us he played bass.

Depending on his and Trevor's schedules, if they couldn't commit to a date, we had a backup band in place and wouldn't have to cancel. Both Desi and I looked at each other like we'd seen a ghost when we met Dylan, our LA sub drummer. He was a dead ringer for Dave. Completely uncanny, not like when someone reminds you of someone, no, this guy was like his identical twin brother. The way he stared at Desi, with this amorous look on his face, it was just like Dave. How could this be our luck?

There was no shortage of gigs, we were booked regularly and stayed active. Alain Whyte from Morrissey had a new band called Red Lightning, which we supported as an opening act. Also, This Episode got billing on a show with OneRepublic at the Key Club, when they were about to release their first record. We walked in while they were on and got super excited when we saw the room was packed! We were going on after them, totally forgetting that hardly anyone sticks around after the main act. The venue's fully packed five-hundred-person capacity had dwindled down to ten people by the time we took the stage, forcing us to cut short our set after just four songs, because by then we were playing to only two people, the janitor and barkeep.

Recording with Rick Parker resumed and we were now officially making our own record with him. The idea was to have a finished product to shop around to the labels and industry. Early morning before a session, Desi had an idea for us to go shopping for wigs. With my hairline receding, I had no problem standing behind that.

I used to say when I could afford a good piece like Elton John, I would gladly wear one full-time. Desi was sure a wig didn't need to cost twenty grand in order to look good. We went down to Hollywood Boulevard and I tried one on that had an angular cut reminiscent of Brett Anderson from Suede. Desi cheered me on, "Oh my god, you look so great!" It did look cool. She bought it for me, and it was forever dubbed the Brett Wig.

"Put it on!" Desi said giddily, as we showed up to the session. "I wanna eat you up!" she said with one final look-over as she adjusted it for me. *Hey, if I can get this kind of reaction, I might just wear this thing full-time.* The only downfall was once I took it off, the contrast with my real hair underneath made me look like I was a cancer patient. Not the best scenario if a girl decided to run her fingers through my wig.

"Let's see if Rick notices," Desi said. Rick was as laid-back and cool as they come. If he wasn't making rock, he'd probably be surfing or sailing his days away. Ten minutes passed before he finally asked, "Are you wearing a wig?" We died laughing. If it wasn't instantly noticeable, perhaps I might just get away with it.

A manager we were in touch with came down to check out our progress and hear the mixes. Ironically, Larry Little was a partner of the guy who was managing the Killers. He liked what we were doing and made a commitment to check us out next time we played live. When he did, his critique was that he liked my presence on stage but felt that Desi was mocking me.

For the sake of keeping her marriage intact, Desi had taken a couple of weeks to go back to Chicago to spend some time with Damian. I think he thought things were unkosher and doubted that it was strictly professional between Desi and me. Even my parents suspected we were back together. But it simply wasn't true. I won't deny we took some baths together, I can say this now that they're divorced. But even then we knew where the boundaries were.

With Desi out of town for a bit, I had time to do some things I hadn't gotten around to before. One was go on a date. The other was visit with someone from my Vegas wild days. I found out Tracy was living in LA and managing an apartment building with her future husband. I was curious to say hello and catch up, as a couple of years shy of a decade had passed between us.

There was a book in her collection I hadn't yet read by Pamela Des Barres that I commented on. "Oh you have to read it," she said, and she offered to lend it to me as long as I promised to return it. The book, she explained, had belonged to a close friend and was the only thing she had of hers after she'd died tragically in a car accident. I felt a little spooked, perhaps I shouldn't borrow it. "No, I trust you," she said. I tend to not give in to such superstitions, yet when Tracy spoke about her friend in this context, it just didn't sit well. I kept the book in the trunk of the car until the desire to read it beckoned.

Noelle was someone I had seen at the clubs time after time. We'd gotten to know each other just by being at the same place repeatedly. I learned that her husband had passed away the previous year, though I didn't know the cause. All I knew was he was a talented musician and was taken away too soon. I had struck up a friendly exchange with Noelle, I liked her, was always happy to run into her. We eventually swapped numbers and planned a night out together. I suggested dinner at Yamashiro, the Japanese spot that overlooked the city.

She mentioned it would take her an hour to get to Hollywood, so we should just meet there. I had some time to kill while getting ready, thought I'd see what beverages there were in the fridge. *Oh, hello vodka*, left over in the freezer from when the boys were in town. One shot of happy, one shot of fuck me up. I was no longer drinking like the Vegas years, so it didn't take much to get to that fuzzy place.

At Yamashiro, I did what I normally do at sushi restaurants, I overordered. A large sake also was mandatory, and another for when the sushi arrived at the table. I ate a few pieces and from then on the rest of the night happened in three stages. I blinked and I was paying for the bill and staring at a lot of food left on those trays. Blinked again and we were outside waiting for valet. At this time I suggested we go to the Viper Room. Noelle was reluctant, probably because I must've looked like a madman, still she gave in. "I'll follow you," she said. Blinked again, BOOM!!

I couldn't tell you what I hit. I don't know if it was a parked car or a tree. It was on the downslope, and luckily out of the vicinity of the restaurant. Even more fortunate is that Noelle wasn't in the car, thank you above, because the front right side had caved in. Put it this way, the glove box became the passenger seat.

Noelle was calm and cool, she didn't freak out. She said we couldn't leave the car there and asked if I could drive it across the street. That meant crossing Franklin Avenue and both lanes of traffic. Well, the crash sure woke my ass up, I could certainly drive it another block. I parked it on a side street and would deal with it in the morning.

Noelle drove me home, bless her heart, and with my head pounding, all I wanted to do was hit the lights and sleep this one off. If I hadn't crashed where I did, there's no doubt I would've on one of the main streets, and that could've been horrendous. I might be telling a different story, or none at all. I got lucky. It was the last time I put myself in that kind of situation. I never heard from Noelle again, rightfully so. Maybe I gave off the impression of having a death wish, certainly not what she needed in her life, not now, not ever.

As I had the car towed to a body shop and was riding along with the truck driver, Desi called and asked how things were going. "WHAT?! Are you okay? I knew something awful was going to happen," she said, distressed. The mechanic declared the car a loss. Totaled. He said he could junk it for me at no cost. I agreed. He opened the doors, popped the trunk, and said to see if there was anything left behind before it was taken away. When I looked, there was the book I had borrowed from Tracy. Now I was convinced there was some bad mojo going on with that book. "No, nothing I need," I answered, as I left it there to be hauled off with the wreckage.

I called my parents, who were now living in Utah. Once I'd moved back to the West Coast, my brother had also followed suit, so it wasn't long before my folks packed up and left New York City. I'd urged them not to, they were on the waiting list for a new apartment that would've been theirs if they'd just hung in there a little longer. My dad had taken the liberty to write to Mayor Bloomberg about his history being a native New Yorker and his desire for better living for him and his wife in his retirement years. Whatever strings were pulled, the apartment was at 95 East Houston Street and would've been rent stabilized. I pleaded and begged them to stay. But that didn't faze them. They wanted to be close to their boys, once again, as always. I was gutted when I found out a few years later that the building opened a Whole Foods on the ground level. How perfect that would've been for two senior citizens. Anytime they needed groceries, all they'd have to do was go downstairs.

I informed them about the accident and basically asked for help. Funny to complain that my parents were always there at whatever corner I turned, although in this case it was most welcome. The used car I drove away in, thanks to them, was a nice upgrade from the previous one. Sadly, though, I didn't get to enjoy it as much as I would've liked to have. No less than a week later, I was driving with Desi on Fairfax heading toward Santa Monica Boulevard when some jackass kids slammed into us from behind as we were stopped at the light. Desi let out an earth-shattering scream; by the sound of it I didn't know whether she was hurt or just shaken up from the jolt.

I don't know where my reflex to just jump out of the car came from so suddenly, probably somewhere between adrenaline and panic mode, but in a matter of seconds I was approaching the guys. Immediately they pulled out and floored the Escalade they were driving. A classic hit-and-run.

I was informed later that the vehicle they'd been driving was reported stolen. Another hard lesson learned, always carry the uninsured motorist claim on your policy. Had I had that, the damages would've been covered. Instead, the only option was to wire shut my trunk and forget about ever needing to use it again.

We hired one of those lawyers who specialize in wrongful injury and were sent for physical therapy once a week at a luxury spa. Both of us could deal with that for a couple of months, even if we got stuck with the Russian masseuse who was intent on bringing the pain. This woman probably made it her mission to see how many people she could make wince every day. I wasn't going to play that game. An elbow to the back, digging and pressing in deeper, she only got silence in return and a thank you for her service once she finished.

My other lawyer called—this was another form of an unpleasurable massage, the Madden camp were ready to come to a settlement. Rather than taking it to court and dragging it out even more, I agreed to sign off on it. There was no upper hand for me in this deal, just had to take the money and act as if it had never happened.

My friend Jake Shillingford reasoned that I should have notified my performing rights organization about works in dispute. Perhaps a freeze on incoming royalties for the Duff title "Wake Up" would have been factored into the final settlement amount. If I'd had an attorney who specialized in entertainment law, instead of an inexpensive lawyer who didn't charge up front, I wonder if the outcome would have been different. That song ended up being the single to promote her Greatest Hits release. It spent two weeks at number one on the Billboard Top 100 chart. Exactly a week after I received the settlement money, I was walking back to the art gallery on Rodeo Drive from my lunch break when who should I pass while crossing the street? Hilary Duff and Joel Madden.

How strangely coincidental. Ironic also that Hilary shares my birth date. We made eye contact. The moment was now, if I had something to say, here it was. It crossed my mind, though I let it sail. I had their money in the bank, and they had their hands full carrying Chanel shopping bags.

Towards the summer, Desi started having mixed feelings about living in LA and being away from her husband. She was displeased that we hadn't gotten signed yet, and not only us, there were other talented bands who were part of the same scene we'd been sure would get a deal. When nothing happened for them either, Desi was convinced the industry was a joke.

On a night out for sushi, our dinner conversation turned to the broken record we'd repeated countless times. The mistakes of our past, and if I would've done this or that then, we wouldn't be in the situation we were in now. It was enough to make me leave half of my plate untouched, and for her to storm out before either of us had finished. In the car as I pulled away, Desi made the earth shatter, "YOU RUINED MY LIFE!" she screamed with all the power in her lungs of a heavy metal singer, and she followed it up with an equally piercing "I HATE YOU!" She was in tears, and I with a lump in my throat. There was nothing to say.

She would always be the first to make up. "You know I didn't mean that, I don't hate you, Dolittle." It may have taken a day to say it, but it was an apology nonetheless. Still it was clear she'd had enough of the LA pursuit. In July we had one show booked, this time in Vegas.

It wasn't intended to be our swan song gig, though in some way it was the perfect bookend to play a show together in the city where we had fallen apart. I had no hard feelings about Desi leaving. This was our footprint, one of us always walked away. She jokingly asked what her cut was from my music settlement case. I wrote her a check she could be happy with. I also made her a mix CD for her two-day excursion on the Amtrak back to Chicago. She had developed an anxiety about flying. Desi liked the scenic route anyhow. Through the desert on a train and she was gone.

I stayed in LA several more months, I was enjoying living the single life too much. I was also living a healthy life, going to the gym five days a week, getting toned. After work I would make that split-second decision: If I turned left on Crescent Heights then it was time for a workout. If I continued straight ahead I could just be home and relax and make dinner. Five times out of seven I made the left turn. It felt rewarding to make the push.

I treated myself to one big splurge from my settlement, it was the guitar I'd wanted since I was sixteen years old, a Gretsch White Falcon II double cutaway. The most gorgeous guitar ever. It's just a shame there weren't any shows lined up for me to play it. I wasn't in the mindset to put together another band at this point, or join anyone else's for that matter. I think of the friends I made along the way who have established themselves in well-known bands. Bands that have gone through their umpteenth lineup change. It never occurred to me to be the guitar player in a version of Faster Pussycat, or such and such band. Nothing wrong with that, it looks like good fun, nevertheless, I've only ever wanted to do my own thing.

I faced another crossroads at the beginning of the new year, 2007. With my parents going on a year being based in Nashville now, they were calling with attempts to entice me to move out that way. See, I'm not the only one who moves around a lot, I get it from them. My dad loved country and western ever since he was young, so that was a motivating factor for him to want to live there in Tennessee.

In his retirement he took up sculpture and wanted to focus on sculpting horses, making art to sell to all the ranchers. He always had big ideas. Though I'm pretty sure his main reason for moving to Tennessee was to lure me there.

14

TEN YEARS

For the next two months, every phone call I'd have with my dad, he would build up Nashville more. "This is where the songwriters are, you could make it big here, they don't have someone like you with your talent," he'd say. Without fail, Dad has been in my corner championing me. Since I was a teen and began recording my songs, he was my springboard, the first person I'd play anything for. The earliest song of mine he listened to, he marveled how it reminded him of Bob Dylan.

Even though the thought of being with my parents again wasn't desirable, there wasn't much keeping me in LA really. In March I booked a flight to go to Austin for SXSW, and from there I'd go on to Nashville. Tennessee felt very slow-paced. Quite honestly it didn't seem like much was different since the time I had spent there with Desi ten years earlier. *Tell me there's a decent sushi bar here.* This city had a lot of catching up to do. For those who have been to Nashville, in 2007 it did not have even the beginning of the cool factor it has going on today. The Gulch was a skeleton, not a single boutique hotel in sight, foodie culture equaled BBQ, hipsterville East Nashville was still years away from being developed. Other than the honky-tonks on Broadway, no urban-chic bars existed yet, and only a few alternative music venues could be found. Also, the job market sucked. I went from selling Warhols in Beverly

Hills to selling sunglasses at a kiosk in a suburban shopping mall in Cool Springs, which was anything but cool.

More of a reason to get out there and kick ass; the sooner I made my mark in this town, the sooner I could move out. One advantage of Nashville is the wealth of musicians and their level of talent. The players and producers alike had the reputation of spitting out record-quality demos in as little as four hours. That's how pitchable songs got done in this town.

The first musician I met had just moved from Mississippi to attend Belmont to get his degree in recording engineering. I hit it off with Breck Cooper immediately; with the same last name as me, I joked that all we needed to do was find one more Cooper and we could be like Duran Duran, where there are three Taylors, none of whom are related to each other. Breck would play bass in my band and become a great collaborator, more than that, a dear friend.

People were accessible in Nashville, if there was a songwriter or artist I thought about connecting with, I'd attend their performance and approach them afterwards. Some of the locals had a theory that you shouldn't do that. In my mind I wasn't a local, so fuck that. I was all about networking, and if this was a simple way to make an introduction, then I was going to take it.

I went right for the A-list and laid a CD in the hands of Rodney Crowell, someone whose style I appreciated and had been listening to long before moving to Music City. The next day he emailed me back with encouragement and constructive criticism. I appreciate people like him who take the time to respond. The majority with far lesser achievements you never hear a word from. I would soon find Nashville was like a tight-knit circle, not so receptive to outsiders.

I joined an organization called NSAI (Nashville Songwriters Association International), which most anyone you asked in town believed was a necessity if you wanted to have a songwriting career. I remember getting a critique back from the organization on a song I'd sent. They scrutinized my lyrics, "What did you mean by this?" It was apparent any sense of imagination or leaving something up for interpretation was not the Nashville way of storytelling. I grew up with Stevie Nicks's song "Gypsy" from Fleetwood Mac being an all-time favorite of mine. To this day I still have no idea what it's about, and I'm fine with that. It means whatever I want it to mean in that moment. This philosophy did not fly in Nashville. They wanted songs to be like three-and-a-half-minute movies, with a first, second, and third arc. Each line supporting the others.

In six months' time, I connected with a hitmaker, though it would take a year of constant reaching out before we nailed down a date to write together. Tom Hambridge was a busy man who went on to win Grammys and perform at the White House. Over the course of time we did a few collaborations. I was getting that country appeal from him, and when he had a project that called for something more pop or rock, I was glad to be the one he called on. Tom was producing a teenage girl and basically sent me a page out of her diary to take a stab at making some lyrical magic and come up with whatever type of musical composition I could marry to it. If I could put on my John Hughes hat and speak the language of youth in a song the way he connected with film, we might have something here. I made a quick demo on my laptop. It was exciting to hear they cut a real studio version of it. I hoped the best for the girl, though disappointingly it did not pan out for her. At this stage, I liked the idea of being behind the scenes. Let the young represent.

Anything that looked like an opportunity, I'd jump on it and seize the moment. I recognized manager Doc McGhee in a parking lot as I was getting out of my car. Doc handled the careers of Mötley Crüe, Bon Jovi, and KISS and had set up his main office in Nashville. Of course I approached him. He was cool and genuine, dropping the name of his A&R guy and suggesting I call the office to get in touch with him. Naturally I did. Another year would roll by before I had an in-person appointment. Nothing happens overnight. Lucky for me I have patience.

❖

One of the saltiest experiences I had was meeting Richard Marx. I'd been in touch with his manager, Wayne Isaak, who emailed me back saying he enjoyed my tracks and that he'd passed some on to Richard. I never cared much about him or his mullet, but he was cowriting with Keith Urban, and that was reason enough to pay attention. I introduced myself to him one night at the Bluebird Café and asked if he'd ever got around to playing the songs that Wayne had sent. He had this wry look and answered by saying, "Wayne would never do that."

"What do you mean, I've been in touch with him," I countered.

"He probably said that just to be nice," he lipped, as he desperately made his way to the exit.

Out of curiosity, I skimmed through the songs on his 2008 record when I saw it under the new releases. Skip, skip, skip, and then I notice a tune called "When November Falls." The title alone made me think it was close to my "When Summer Turns to Fall," which was one of the songs I had sent along to Wayne. And then I heard the intro. Let's just say he started his song in an almost identical way.

During this time of playing gigs and doing writer rounds, pitching material, writing/recording, and networking like a motherfucker, I embarked on two more projects to stir my creative juices. One, I began writing my first screenplay. Two, I started a podcast. I launched the first episode in 2008. I had people asking me, "What's a podcast?" It was new ground when *Glambone* debuted.

Now you can't bat an eyelash without seeing your brother, sister, babysitter, and favorite actor, actress, rock star, comedian, radio host, chef, sports hero hosting their own podcast. *Glambone* was another extension of what I'd done with my magazine. I featured bands from the Sunset Strip heyday, playing demo tracks and interviewing the artists and the movers and shakers. Unveiling little gems, like some of the bands' personal answering machine messages—something only a kid would think of preserving with his handheld tape recorder, as I'd done when I racked up enormous phone bills calling for press kits. I had saved those cassettes and *Glambone* resurrected them. A sort of time capsule.

I disguised my voice with a helium effect, mostly so I could remain anonymous. For ten years I did the episodes this way, before deciding to use my natural voice. Perhaps this hurt my chances of it being taken seriously, although

I was getting emails all the time from people expressing their love. There was even a new record label that cropped up that seemed to have dedicated itself to releasing demo recordings on CD of these bands. It appeared anytime I unearthed a rarity, in the following months that label would put out product from whomever I'd spotlighted. My fan base was growing, I had hundreds of Facebook followers before FB decided Glambone wasn't a real person and canceled the account. For the first few years, content was consistent with a new episode each month. As podcasts started to catch on, I'd hear about people making money from it, like loads of dough. Sign up for Google AdSense, *Sure, done.* How they were banking from it, I don't know. Maybe I needed to hire someone. I couldn't crack the code. But when you do it for the fun of it, the rest doesn't really matter. A stream of revenue would sure be nice to earn from what you enjoy doing, though. Twelve years since its debut, deep pockets or not, as far as I'm concerned, *Glambone* constituted another case of being ahead of the curve.

Ever since *Fast Times at Ridgemont High, Pretty in Pink,* **and** *Dazed and Confused,* I'd wanted to make one of my own of the high school teen film. *Fast Times* is like my *Gone with the Wind,* it's a classic. I could close my eyes and replay that movie scene by scene in my head without fail. My brother and I grew up speaking in a language of movie quotes. To this day we regurgitate dialogue, especially from that film.

My script *In Between Days* interjects some of my own high school misconduct into situations most teenagers could only wish to have play out. It's a coming of age that takes place in my hometown. This group of Vegas high schoolers receives top honors in sex, drugs, and rock n roll.

I had no expectations for it once it was completed, nor a real game plan. I thought maybe I could go the indie route and find an investor. Starting with who did I know who might be in a position to help? I dug into my old client list from art sales and began pitching it to them with a business plan I'd created containing summaries of the overview, market, distribution, taxes, and ROI opportunity. I quickly learned investing in films was considered high-risk. Especially to those who had absolutely no interest in the industry. I sent it to some friends, a couple of them actors. My buddy Trevor had a pal who was making millions from spam emails, he was buying up condos and Lamborghinis, one in every color. I flew to Vegas on a whim just to get the script in front of him. I wasn't the only one, apparently, he was getting hit up from all angles; another friend of mine had approached him about starting a record label. The guy was throwing money away. A real show-off. He sent a limo to drive me back to my hotel, a ten-dollar taxi never occurred to him. Eventually the guy blew his fortune on strip clubs and hookers—easy come, easy go.

I've been known to blow through some cash of my own, I can't blame the guy. That year I received the settlement from the car wreck that Desi and I were involved in. By this time, Desi was working as a flight attendant for Delta Air. She sure beat her fear of flying by taking it head on. I took a trip to Europe on a "buddy pass" that Desi was able to get for me and flew first class to Paris. For a moment I could pretend I could afford it. I attended my cousin's wedding and then headed to the UK.

My friend Jake Shillingford invited me to be a guest speaker on the subject of plagiarism at Brighton Institute of Modern Music. Jake had been teaching a course and used "Paris London New York" and "Wake Up" as an example in copyright infringement. His students were all on my side. Funny, the main question they wanted to know was how much I'd been paid from the settlement. Some were under the illusion that I'd struck it rich. This was hardly the case. It afforded me my Gretsch White Falcon and lots of sushi, and if I was careful, just maybe I could skate through a few more months without having to work. But who was I kidding? I booked an additional couple of trips to Barcelona and Berlin and stayed in some really nice hotels.

After leaving BIMM one day, I was walking with Jake back to his house when I was overcome by the worst urge to take a piss. I was seeing only blocks of apartment buildings along the way and started to pick up my speed. "Is everything all right" Jake asked, as I dashed into the first business with its doors open, a laundromat. This had to be a joke, I was looking in every corner for the restroom and there wasn't one. I bolted out the back door to the alley and sprinted a couple buildings down, and right there, like rays of light beaming from it, stood a toilet. Completely unexpected and out of place. It was there like something that had been discarded for trash pickup. Sometimes in life you find exactly what you're looking for.

Now if only the rest of the time life produced results as fittingly as that urinal. I was meeting many of the big players in Nashville and was relentless with my emails and phone calls. I hounded Jody Williams at BMI to put me in touch with writers. A stand-up guy he was, always took the time to reply and had other executives from his office reach out to me as well. After years of cultivating those relationships, finally in 2011 my phone started ringing. A couple of opportunities to cowrite came about. One was with a new band signed to Warner Music called HER & Kings County. They were New Yorkers who'd transplanted themselves to Nashville and leaned on the rock n roll side of country, with a funky image and great live show. I had a session with their singer, Monique. She spit out one line in the course of two hours. Eight words, nothing more, nothing less. Sometimes one line can get you there and is all that's needed to get the ball rolling. I got a song out of it and tracked the demo myself with a session singer. Now it was hurry up and wait to see if it made the cut.

For the next year I was completely in my element, my songwriting went up to a whole other level. I was confident as ever and convinced I could enter the room with any hitmaker and crush it. Quite honestly I felt I was seen as a threat. That's not to sound cocky and puff my chest out, that's just how it is. Talent will get you recognition, but when you're the unknown bringing the bulk of the ideas into a room of people who are in a higher position than you, and your ideas are the better ones, well, that doesn't exactly make you the winner. People get afraid you're going to outshine them.

Early that summer, while working my part-time job, retail for an art exhibition, it was just about closing time when a beautiful creature walked up the stairs through the gift shop. Instantly catching each other's eye, we said hello. *Buy something, anything, just so I can ring you up at the register and get a chance to talk to you.* Ah yes, a one-dollar postcard. She must've read my mind. When she brought it up to the cash wrap, I noticed this older grey-haired man waiting for her. *Damn it, she's with him,* I thought, *but fuck it, I'm still going to take my chance.*

"Did you enjoy the exhibit?"

"Yes, my dad got tickets last minute, I'm glad we came." I had assumed wrong, her date was not at all what I'd been thinking. I can't even recall what I asked after that, I just remember her writing out her Facebook handle for me to look up and find her. "There's a picture of my pussy... cat on it," she said naughtily. When she left, I was pretty sure I had just met my second wife.

Michelle could best be described as "sex on legs." She had a stance that oozed sex appeal, she could walk in high heels with more grace than a catwalk model, her presence simply turned heads. On our first date she flashed me not once, but twice. When I dropped her home and pulled out of the driveway, she waved to me with her skirt lowered below her bum. She warned me that I wouldn't be able to keep up with her in bed. Challenge accepted. Her appetite was on fire. Sex with Michelle was pornographic.

Amazing physical chemistry aside, we had more in common than we probably wanted to admit. When she asked where I lived and if we were going back to my place, I said, "Well, at the moment I'm displaced." She laughed, being in a similar situation herself, living at her father's condo. Both of us also had had the "starter marriage," as she called it, and could share our love and war stories.

We were in our thirties and having car sex. Like a couple of kids. She began to sneak me into her room once her dad was asleep, then usher me out in the morning before he awoke. He was fine with seeing me there at times during the day, though at first I wouldn't dare to overstay my welcome. And so my paychecks thereafter were expended on hotel rooms.

On a night spent in a hotel bed, candlelight flickering and Bryan Ferry's

Olympia playing, Michelle began to say "It feels like…" and before she could finish her words, I completed her sentence with "We're falling in love." Intoxicating. Remove some letters and you're left with toxic. Though that was still to come, for now we were deep in the honeymoon state.

Michelle was eager to meet my parents. Maybe because I had met her side of the family and she was paying it back with kindness, or it could be that she wanted acceptance from them since we were getting serious pretty quickly. Whatever the case, her confidence was on ten and she knew how to charm Mom and Dad. Prior to officially meeting, my dad had already caught a sneak peek of Michelle. There was a day when my folks were visiting the gardens at my workplace, and Michelle had happened to drop in as well. My dad noticed her coming into the shop, and when I caught up with my parents after my shift, Dad said wondrously, "Did you see that sexy girl with long hair walk in?"

I answered, "Yeah, that's Michelle."

"That was Michelle?! Wow!" he said. She had already gotten the approval.

She could bedazzle them further with her degree in art and design, how she'd lived abroad in Bahrain and worked for a big corporate company in Dubai. She delighted my parents. Mom said it looked like we made each other very happy. We did, but then everything's good in the beginning. Mostly we loved fucking. When cash flow for hotels ran dry, it was time to get creative. I had been going on writing sessions at BMI, and one of the perks with being affiliated with them was they had a handful of rooms in their office building available for their writers, some really nice with leather couches and stylish décor. Sometimes it was easy to reserve one on short notice if a cancellation occurred.

If the execs found out about this, I might as well have started looking at other performance rights organizations like ASCAP or SESAC, because Michelle and I turned the writers' rooms at BMI into our own personal sex den. I'd walk in carrying my guitar case and for all they knew Michelle was my singer/songwriter partner. We had access to the kitchen and upon noticing the cases of wine on hand, believe me we helped ourselves. With no locks on the doors, it was just lucky no one ever walked in on us. Usually before closing time someone from staff opened to check that the rooms were unoccupied. One room in particular was called the Fish Room, for its walls were painted like an aquarium. If a UV light shined on those walls, no doubt they would have found evidence of our activities.

In a couple of months Michelle was pregnant. We knew the night of conception it was going to happen, there was no question as we surrendered to the idea. The fact we were cash poor didn't equate, this was a love child. Michelle had just started a new job as a receptionist when she first got feelings of nausea and fatigue. After confirmation from a home pregnancy test, Michelle quit her job. This was the first sign that what lay ahead would be challenging, and that such sudden change did not fare well for her.

Within days, Michelle sank into a state of depression. She slept for two days straight without getting out from bed. That's when I learned she had run out of her Adderall, which I had no idea that she was even taking. She needed to find a new doctor who could see and evaluate her to prescribe a regular dosage. That shit was not cheap.

It was a motivational boost she needed, something to kickstart her productivity and maintain focus. She assigned me as the gatekeeper of the canister, to administer a dose when she needed it. She did not want it in her possession, evidently she could pop them like Tic Tacs, so I kept it with me. Not exactly a solution; the way she panicked, sometimes I'd drop what I was doing and scramble to bring it to her, and if I couldn't get there fast enough, she'd already be on her way to pick it up from me.

More and more I was practically staying at Michelle's the majority of the time now. Running late for work one morning, I found myself greeted by her dad. "Hi, John," I said, embarrassed, as I made my way to the front door. He just laughed. I suppose he was accustomed to seeing me there all the time. Michelle waited weeks before telling him the news, and it wasn't exactly a planned reveal.

He was coming down on her about not working, which escalated into a shouting match. She yelled at him, "I'm pregnant!" as an attempt to end the squabble. He had the best reaction any new parents-to-be could hear—"Well, WHOOPIE!" He never really warmed up to it. In the coming weeks Michelle said he wanted to have a talk with me. The main thing he said to me was, "I don't think you know what you're getting yourself into." It was hard to tell whether he was speaking about raising a kid or talking about Michelle. I took it as he knew his daughter better than I and was trying to forewarn me.

Michelle was hot and cold, sometimes she couldn't handle the thought of being a mother, and on the flip side she would talk about baby plans constantly. She came up with the perfect name if it was going to be a girl, Coco. I loved it. The consonance of Coco Cooper sounded so good. When we went for her first ultrasound appointment, we got a printout of the sonogram. Michelle wrote the name Coco on it and handed it to me, saying it was a present for my mom.

My parents liked Michelle, I would never tell them about any of the difficulties we were having, as I didn't want to invite their opinions, especially since they were happy to welcome a grandchild into their lives. When I'd announced the pregnancy, Mom and I had stayed up for hours talking about life and family. She believed having a baby was good luck and that life had gotten better for her and Dad when my brother and I were born. She was convinced that the same would hold true for Michelle and me.

Michelle talked about the physical effects pregnancy could have on her body and wondered if planning a C-section might be a possibility for her delivery, instead of worrying about being "stretched out." Certain changes were already happening, her breasts were growing, and I was not complaining. I asked when she'd start producing milk because I was going to conduct my own taste test. She joked I wasn't going to leave any for Coco.

On occasion we'd check into a hotel, particularly when Michelle couldn't stand the tension of being around her father. On one of those nights she had a complete meltdown, insisting she was incapable of going through with the pregnancy, partially blaming me, and also speaking in part of her imbalances and how this could have a devastating impact on her parental efforts. Nothing helped. She pleaded that she couldn't go through with the pregnancy and was uncompromising that an abortion was the only way out.

We had a counseling session following this, which helped for a day. The rest of the time was a roller coaster ride. With her mental state, the idea of having this baby didn't stand a chance. As I sat in the waiting room with Michelle on the day of her procedure, she turned to me and said, "Don't look at me like that."

"Like how?" I remarked.

"Like you're hoping I'm going to change my mind."

I understood her choice, though I wasn't sure how our relationship was ever going to get any better.

In December I drove my parents to New York. It was a good break to step away from one problem, yet I was stepping into another. Mom and Dad were full-on that we had to rescue my brother from the city and the bad people he was hanging around with. He was strung out again and of course they believed if we found him we could drive him back to Nashville so he could get clean. When he met us and got into the car, we were conveniently parked a block away from New York Presbyterian Hospital. Of course he threw a fit that he didn't need help and screamed his head off.

I got out to seek a medical attendant. He explained unless Scott was posing a threat to someone, there was nothing they could do, and if he was a threat, then I'd have to call the police first to report it. Sure enough I called 911 and embellished the situation. Maybe having NYPD show up was enough to get his attention. He chose to head back to Nashville with us, but I wasn't going to drive fourteen hours with him in his current state. I sat on a bench for hours until he mellowed out somewhat.

Five hours must've passed. It was 11:00 p.m. "Come on, man, this is stupid. Let's just get in the car and go," Scott said. At least everyone was tired, he could sleep it off in the car. I had enough adrenaline to go the distance, although we checked into a hotel somewhere in Virginia along the way. When we got to Nashville, the first thing Scott did when we got inside the house was raid my room for painkillers, which I'd been prescribed for a wisdom tooth extraction. I'd never bothered to take them, lucky him. After that, he got clean on his own. The advantage of not knowing anyone there, he didn't go out, basically hibernated in Nashville for several months.

While in New York those few days, I got an email from Michelle. We were on the verge of splitting up, and probably the kindest thing we could've done for each other was in fact go our separate ways. She once told me that she was no good on her own. Maybe I was away one too many days for her own liking and she felt alone. She couldn't stand loneliness, and I didn't welcome it either. I liked being in a relationship more than not being in one at this point in my life, so I clung to it, instead of breaking away from it. Still, I felt like I was walking on eggshells, being overly careful not to set her off. All that did was allow me to get too inside myself. She bemoaned that I didn't open up to her.

I wasn't trying to be smug when I told her to listen to my songs or read the things that I wrote to know me better, but she sure had a comeback for it, "I'm tired of hearing that song about your ex-wife every time I sit and watch you play!" She wasn't the first to shoot daggers at the fact that I was still friends with my ex.

For all my parents knew, Michelle had suffered a miscarriage. I'd already been guilted by them that I wasn't spending as much time with them anymore. If they knew the whole story, that would've only encouraged them to interfere. I didn't need their influence, I could already see which way this relationship was going, but damn if I didn't have a weakness for her. A few months later, my parents and Scott moved to Vegas. Michelle and I finally came to a livable solution in renting a room at her brother's house.

With only two days of work per week at my job, I had ample time on my hands. I needed another outlet. From the time I'd taken acting lessons as a kid, I believed at some point in my life I'd end up in film. I just thought I'd have a music career first and then make the transition. I had the concept for another screenplay, and not forgetting the praise and encouragement my friend Geo had given me about *In Between Days*, I pitched him the idea. Having collaborated with other writers on songs, why not on a film project, I thought. Geo and I constantly talked about movies all the time, might as well make one of our own.

I'd ride into town with Michelle and have her drop me off at a café while she went about her business. Half of the screenplay was written this way, sitting in an East Nashville coffeehouse with my laptop. I was drawing certain inspiration from my own dysfunctional relationship, other parts came from living closely with people who suffered from addiction, such as my brother. This became the basis of *Full Sleeve*. A modern tale of illicit drug smuggling, deceit, and romance. The story of a tattoo artist with a tortured past who goes on a dark journey when a client makes him a dangerous proposition.

Something peculiar was happening to me while writing *Full Sleeve*. It was fulfilling me in a way I hadn't felt in a long time, since picking up the electric guitar. I couldn't ever imagine replacing music, but the fact is, to a certain degree at that time I was falling out of love with music. The music business itself was no longer what it once had been. Those with record deals were gone if they didn't score a hit with their first single. The art of the full-length record was becoming extinct. On a personal level, the excitement of discovering new artists had dissipated. My writing sessions were scarce, and I was playing the usual writer rounds with no sense of change. The words *reinvent myself* were hanging over my head.

A change of heart also needed a call to action with Michelle. We were arguing practically every other day. It wasn't when she got so uncontrollably mad and pounded her two fists on my chest that made me realize she had issues, it was in the morning when I ate a bowl of cereal in the bedroom while she was asleep. When she started her day and saw the empty bowl still by the nightstand, she flipped the fuck out, screaming, "Oh my god, why didn't you take it to the kitchen sink?! That's disgusting!" God forbid I didn't take it immediately to wash it out. I'm not sure if the clinical term for what Michelle suffered from was obsessive-compulsive disorder or bipolar disorder, I just know it was hard to live with and I wasn't enough to help her.

I couldn't fathom buying more time with the thought that things could be different and improve between us. As summer was approaching, the only way I was going to pull the trigger was to book a ticket, instead of contemplating it. Talking it over with her would just have been a bad idea. Not talking it over was equally troublesome. When I tried to ease into it, she said tenderly, "You're going to leave me?" I had the bravado to say yes, which resulted in her getting defensive. It's shitty to say I waited until two weeks before my flight to tell her I was leaving for real. Her reaction was without drama. "When the going gets tough, the tough get going," she remarked. When more bad outweighs the good, it's time to move on.

June 1, 2012, I landed at LAX, rented a car, and headed straight to the Roxy to catch my old pals Blackboard Jungle play their reunion show, while Michael Monroe from Hanoi Rocks took stage down the street at the Whisky. What a difference a day makes. That morning I was walking away from being in a stagnant rut, and that night I was out catching thrills. When I got to Vegas the next day, I didn't have a plan, other than to spend the summer working on *Full Sleeve* and use the time to regroup. In Sin City, the latter could only mean pool parties and nightclubbing.

I was in touch with Michelle for the first couple of weeks. "Why did you leave me? You abandoned me!" she'd exclaim. Every convo ended with her shouting. Most of the time I had to hang up on her. Thankfully I was out 'n' about when these calls came through, I could return to something more peacefully distracting, except the time we spoke and she announced she had a new boyfriend. Two weeks since I'd left and she was already with someone else. I shouldn't have allowed this to bother me, but it did. It wasn't enough that I went muff diving with someone else just weeks later, that didn't ease my mind. I didn't like the feeling that I couldn't get her back now and that someone else was having his way with her.

In trying to find work, I interviewed with several of the high-end boutiques and art galleries. I've no idea what they were looking for, I was more than qualified than most, perhaps that was the problem. With zero income, I took the last bit of scratch I had and headed to LA for an interview I'd managed to line up. It's interesting how resourceful one can be when there's no plan of where to stay, just wingin' it. I had a hunch to call my pal Daniel, a cool hipster cat and restaurateur who'd acquired art from me before. I said how I'd just gotten into town, he didn't ask what for, it was just come on over, that's how chill a dude he was. Even better when I got there and he generously offered that I could crash for however long I needed.

Crash took on a literal meaning by the second week in. When I got back to the house after a job interview, Daniel and a friend were already in party mode and asked if I'd do the driving for the night. Sure I would, but I didn't have wheels out there. "We'll take my car," his friend said, sweetening the deal by adding that his brand new Porsche 911 Carrera was right outside. "That's great," I said, "if only I knew how to drive stick." I think that excited him more so, he remarked that if ever I was going to learn how, there was no better car to learn on than this.

I laughed and declined. I'm pretty sure I said it wasn't a good idea. But the guy was insistent and eager to give lessons. I looked at the car and rethought my decision, *Yeah I should know how to drive stick.* Man, what a comfortably smooth and solid ride in the driver's seat. What's the line from *Risky Business*, "there is no substitute"? In minutes I was getting the hang of it. A couple of times around the block, yeah let's take this thing down Hollywood Boulevard. I was ready. Mmm hmm. "Pull up right behind that car," he said, as I was slowing down back in front of Daniel's place. Just one small problem, he hadn't versed me on how to park a manual. "HOW DO I PARK?!" I yelled out with only milliseconds to spare before impact.

BOOM!!! Daniel was waiting outside, his jaw was on the floor. We looked at each other in disbelief, not knowing whether one of us was going to laugh or cry. The front hood had totally buckled, it had a wave that rippled straight across it. I reminded him how I hadn't wanted to do this. The guy surprisingly wasn't losing his shit, he looked at it like Spicoli estimating the damage after trashing Jefferson's car and assured me it wasn't that bad. Naturally he suggested I pay for it. That's when I allowed myself a slight chuckle. "Man, I'm broke, you're gonna have to use your insurance on this one," I said. I haven't tried driving a manual since then. If anyone wants to give me lessons, please get in touch.

I needed a job, and a paycheck, like pronto. I'd been running on empty and had exhausted my resources. Times were getting desperate. I called my friend and former boss back in Nashville to vent and catch up.

My timing couldn't have been better. Christy told me she had changed positions and her former management role was now vacant. Best of all, they hadn't started prospecting for candidates yet. With her recommendation, and her championing for me with HR, a couple of phone interviews later I was offered the job. Halle-fuckin-lujah.

Truthfully, I would've gone wherever the job opportunity took me, though I was glowing on the inside that I'd be returning to Nashville. To me this meant that I wasn't yet done with the city, that there were more impressions to make. Also, I could devise a way to try and get Michelle back into my life. Or more accurately, back in bed. After a couple of weeks resettled in Tennessee, just as I was getting ready to call it a night, I got a message from her at 11:00 p.m. asking if I'd like to meet up for a drink. I couldn't turn that down. I literally had gotten into my pj's as I was reading the text, and how quickly I was putting my street wear on again thinking it was my lucky night.

Maybe this was her way of wanting to be on good terms so that my walking away wouldn't be the last frame of us. After our nightcap followed the promise that we'd talk soon again, but this would be hit or miss. Deep down I knew better. Still I did stupid shit like buying an extra ticket to a concert just to invite her. I had great seats for Cyndi Lauper doing her first record in its entirety. Michelle texted me before showtime. She was getting ready to come join me, a few songs in and she was running late. Come on, she had to get there for "Time After Time" at least. And then came the no-show.

On another occasion she dropped off my belongings I'd left at her brother's house, some clothes and an acoustic guitar. The guitar case was lighter than normal—there was no guitar. She claimed not to know what had happened, that maybe her niece had taken it. I have my own theories that need no explaining. Why was I trying so hard to get close to her again? Oh yes, *pussy.* Some guys will lose their minds for it.

Funny enough I went to see a shrink at this time. Not because I felt I needed the counseling, but because I wanted to understand Michelle better, if that makes any sense. I thought perhaps a woman psychiatrist could drop some nuggets of wisdom onto me. I went for six weeks. She was a great listener, though she didn't really offer much in the way of deciphering what I was interested in learning. She did however ask if I would consider attending SLAA (Sex and Love Addicts Anonymous) meetings. And then went on to say how one of her clients had tried it but ended up hooking up with someone there. *Wait, what?* I had to wonder if she was trying to tell me something there. Never mind meeting a nice girl at temple, Kenward, go on and get yer dick sucked at an SLAA meeting. After the six weeks were up, she called to tell me that my insurance didn't cover the sessions. Surprisingly she added that she wasn't going to charge me at all. I think either she realized she hadn't offered me any of the answers I was searching for, or she'd enjoyed hearing about my relationship drama and that was worth the admission alone. Whatever the case, I had no out-of-pocket expense, and that was something I couldn't complain about.

In my new management role I hatched a plan to turn the back space of the museum gift store into an art gallery to spotlight local talent and sell their works. Another attempt to score points with Michelle. She was a great artist in all mediums, including sculpture, painting, and drawing. There's a drawing she made for me of the two of us making love. The style was very Daliesque. I never got possession of it. A shame she wasn't doing anything to advance herself with her gifts. Maybe this gallery idea could bring visibility to her works. At first she was interested, until she changed her mind, saying I was just doing it to try and get her back. She wasn't half wrong. I needed to stop wanting it so much. Let go, and let love come to you. Essentially this is the same philosophy I adopted for music.

15

SHINY NEW SAME OLD TOWN

Christy and her husband, Sean, kindly gave me their guest room until I got settled in again. At the time, I was also carpooling with Christy, so it made sense for me to find my own place in the same neighborhood. Apartment first, wheels second. I lucked out with a duplex in East Nashville. The owners staged it quite attractively; once I stepped inside, I immediately got a good vibe. I told them up front the place would be ideal for me because as I was on foot and I'd be within walking distance of everything I needed. They called the next day to tell me they'd liked all the candidates but the apartment was mine because they thought I would benefit from it the most. I appreciated how considerate they were.

A similar act of kindness happened when I went to a dealership and test-drove a couple of used cars. I had just gotten my tax refund and could afford to put down a grand on a VW Passat listed for just under $10K. I had a questionable credit score and hadn't established enough credit to make for the easiest transaction. I sat across from the salesman as I listened to bank after bank turn me down, a handful of different lenders all with the same outcome. He had one more on his list, basically our last hope. I could feel the conviction in his voice as he said to the person on the receiving end, "All he needs is a chance for his wings to open and he's gonna fly." True on so many levels.

I dug having my own place—driving home from work and getting into wind-down mode by cooking dinner, listening to music, reading books, and playing guitar provided such simple pleasures. I did well on my own, although after some time, not having anyone to converse with was a reality check that some companionship would be nice. Especially when I could hear my neighbors having a grand ol' shag through the bedroom walls.

Occasionally I got the odd text or call from Michelle. One time, she had locked herself out while pet sitting and asked to crash at my place. And so putting her up for the night set us on friendly terms again, but only for a moment.

We made a plan to go out for dinner together. When I picked her up she had a pit stop to make first, I don't remember what it related to, only that she needed to get there before they closed. A nice heads-up, we had ten minutes to make it on time. Needless to say I pulled in just as the doors were being locked. She threw shit at me like it was my fault, which only escalated to us bitching each other out. My parting words were "Get the fuck out and don't ever call me again." That was the tipping point. You can't fix crazy.

In the early months of 2013, Geo made some headway for our screenplay with a producer he had met while working for a fashion/lifestyle magazine. The producer, whom we'll refer to here as Chad Scoff, had read our script and contacted us to say we had a good story and he liked the grittiness of it. While he was clear that this was a first draft that could use some work, according to him it was still pitchable and easy to get a grand vision of. I took the initiative and went to New York City to meet the guy in person.

Chad had a vast knowledge of films and could talk fluidly about the business and structure of deals. He wasted no time in saying how he wanted to direct *Full Sleeve*, making it his feature film directorial debut. When he spoke about *Full Sleeve* and reference points of other films, styles, and techniques he planned to incorporate, it was easy to trust that he'd be the right person to carry out the vision. Above all, Chad was a likeable guy. Our first meeting had a certain kinship, it felt like a team had formed.

Chad suggested that if we were all in unison to move forward, he was ready to draw up an agreement back at his postproduction studio. We headed there, where his brother was editing a commercial they'd just filmed, and Chad proceeded to line up three shots of whiskey for us. We made a toast, signed the agreement, and welcomed the birth of our new career as filmmakers. When Geo and I left the studio, we hugged and congratulated each other like a couple of kids who'd just won some kind of ultimate championship. Years of our hard work and perseverance suddenly felt like they'd been all worth it in that very moment as we walked giddily down the street together. We told ourselves we could do one more drink to celebrate and popped inside a tiny bar that was near closing. We were so amped that we even told the bartender that we'd just signed a deal for our first screenplay. To hear those words come out of our own mouths confirmed it was real.

I sent the script to a friend of mine whom I wanted to attach as the lead actor. He had done a number of cool films and was already three seasons in on a popular series that was getting bigger and bigger every year. He expressed his interest and made mention of his availability as well as the months he was on lockdown filming the series. After many email exchanges, he forwarded his manager's number and said to call her if it got real. It doesn't get more legit than that. It was in our court to make the play.

Chad was all over this idea, except he stalled. Four months later I spoke to the manager myself, despite the fact that I wasn't the dealmaker in charge of making an offer. She said she'd reach out to Chad. This is when the first red flags went up; after the call, all Chad could tell us was that they'd had a good chat. No details of what the next steps were going to be in attaching her client to our project. Basically we had no financing in place to lock him in. Chad, however, would drop enough crumbs on the ground to keep Geo and I fed, not in a monetary way, but on a path that kept us going along with his blueprint, or lack thereof.

Periodically he'd tell us about an investor or group that was on board to make it happen. Two years passed before Chad suggested we update our option agreement with him. We hired an entertainment lawyer to advise us this time around. Geo and I reasoned that something must be in the works for him to want to make sure we were solid with him. Once we signed, Chad began sharing documents with us. This included the letter of terms and commitment, budget pass, and tax credit from the state of Mississippi, which was an incentive to bring the film production there to reduce costs. Also presented were various docs from companies that were either distributors or investors for *Full Sleeve*.

Some good things followed. Chad arranged my travel to NYC to do a table read and a day of brainstorming how to elevate the story even further. While the three of us were all vocal with ideas, it was always me and Geo who did the writing and completed the drafts, every word of dialogue was from our minds to those pages, despite Chad trying to talk his way into being credited as a third writer. That trip, we were also each given a check for $1,500 as a small advance on our option fee. Believe me this didn't come easy, Geo and I constantly had to remind Chad that we were past due on what the terms stated as far as payment was concerned.

Another year went by of false promises, "We're in escrow now, we can start getting offers out." Not only that, Chad would dangle more carrots in front of us that had nothing to do with *Full Sleeve*. Like the time he spoke of being a partner on the launch of a music television channel and wanted us to contribute ideas for content. Or other screenplays he was involved with, such as a series, "You guys can write an episode, it's in development with Amazon." Neither came to fruition.

After twelve months of this with no advancement on *Full Sleeve*, he still hadn't made good on paying out the remainder of our option fee. We were reaching our limit with Chad. In the fall of 2016, there was yet another producer/investor Chad claimed we would be working with who could get the film made.

I was not too pleased when I found out the guy's big claim to fame was that he'd been involved with the Bret Michaels film *A Letter from Death Row*. Not to dis it, but when you have your sights set on something more on the level of Danny Boyle and David Lynch, the bar is high. Turns out this producer was also based in Nashville. Well, if we were both in the same city, I'd just look him up and introduce myself. Wouldn't you know it, when I spoke of *Full Sleeve*, he had no clue what the hell I was talking about. That's all I needed to hear. A confirmation of what I'd already been speculating, that Chad was feeding us a load of horseshit. The next day, after Chad found out I'd spoken to the producer, Geo and I received a group text from him with his resignation. We left it at that and carried on without replying. Instead, we enlisted a lawyer to serve a formal notice of termination of our agreement to him, just to cover ourselves.

We were already sending out our deck to other production companies. By now we also had another screenplay of ours to pitch, a TV pilot for a series we'd created called *Van Nuys*. It's a story set in the late seventies into the eighties about a family whose parental figures are in the porn business. In hindsight we should have continued submitting the material ourselves and aligned with an agent to represent us, but within a couple of months Chad had emailed us an apology letter with news that some people he knew in Savannah were financing projects and had inquired about *Full Sleeve*. He pleaded how all he wanted to do was get this up, make a killer film, and get us paid.

Our rationalization was if he was coming back to us saying there were new people involved, what would be the gain for him to just string us along if it weren't true. This couldn't be a version of the Michael Douglas film *The Game* we were living. The thought of someone fucking with us for the sheer hell of it seemed unlikely, so we proceeded with him once again, with the notion that we'd have our attorney handle business communications for us. This would detach us so that we wouldn't stress over our interactions with Chad.

We were notified of a preliminary discussion regarding the option/purchase of *Full Sleeve*, which Chad and his new partners discussed with our lawyer at the time. Chad was to submit a term sheet or deal memo within a couple of days. Crickets. I think we were somewhere in between bewildered and amused by Chad at this point. There were many times we felt like cutting ties with him yet decided to let it ride. If by chance he made good on his word, then it would all be worth it. We were already four years in with this guy. It had taken *Dallas Buyers Club* ten years to get made, that was our benchmark every time another detour occurred.

Crowdfunding had become a popular alternative for raising dough, so we gave it a shot by running a campaign with a $15K goal; if we reached the full amount, we'd film a trailer as a marketing tool to further attract financiers. We ended just $14,670 shy of it. That didn't deviate us from continuing on with a casting call. Some fine talent came from our *Backstage* ad. Above all it was quite rewarding to watch actors really get into the scene and deliver a performance on the spot right in front of us. Just a shame we wouldn't be in a position to employ them.

Leading up to this moment, I was in another relationship, a three-year itch with an Australian single parent/mother of two. I became "instant Dad." The day I met Silo, I suggested with a hint of swagger that she get a sitter so I could take her out that weekend. The next day she invited me over, and in return I offered to cook dinner for her, showing up with a fillet of salmon and my culinary skills.

My first impression was that she had her shit together, or so I concluded because she had a house in her name. We see what we want to see, and we present the best version of ourselves. I introduced myself as a writer and spoke about the option on my screenplay.

The hard facts were that I was living paycheck to paycheck on a very tight budget. I told her in those get-to-know-you days that I didn't have much to offer except a heart full of love if she wanted it. She replied, "I want it." A month later Silo asked me to move in. Her girls were ages one and three when I stepped into their lives. They took to me straightaway, as I did to them. Silo and her friends marveled at how naturally I assumed the father role.

We were only a few months in when Silo decided to put her house on the market and together we bought a new home. I can appreciate a new beginning and desire to make something our own, though I had some skepticism whether this was more of a way to one-up her ex-husband by painting an image that everything was roses. She could talk shit about him, yet allow him to dictate a schedule that was convenient only for himself. This was our rub. I wasn't looking to replace him as a father figure to his girls, it just wasn't cool that he'd go weeks without seeing them and suddenly if he got back into town and had an hour to spare, then Silo became tied to that. Particularly unsettling when I had no heads-up about it. After an eight-hour work shift I would be looking forward to coming home and being together. Finding her ex hanging out or about to show up, not so much.

Eventually her hopes of having a "modern family" came to pass and we found a way to coexist. I got on with her ex-husband quite well, and Silo would be cordial with his new girlfriend. There was a mutual respect. In our first year together, Silo spoke with much intent that she was getting "baby fever" again, certain she'd have a boy this time. Only to say months later that she wasn't sure what she was thinking, that she couldn't see herself going through another pregnancy at forty years old.

Sure, statistics were showing women in their forties having healthy babies, but it was her body and her right, and not for me to convince her. The decision was made and we didn't speak of it again. Deep inside it was a letdown for me, one that formed into a resentment later on. Slowly we would unravel with other things that came to the surface. Such as when my parents and Scott drove from Vegas for a visit. They had the idea of wanting to relocate back to Nashville, now that I was firmly planted and showing no signs of leaving. Without question their only reason for wanting to be there was because I was there.

With no game plan, they had high expectations that it would be a cakewalk to just find a place. This was not the case. And while Silo showed good hospitality, the pragmatic in her was not used to flying by the seat of her pants, particularly as it pertained to old folk in their late seventies and early eighties. There was a worry upon her that she might possibly be inheriting this family as in-laws. After staying with us for a few days, my parents realized Music City wasn't singing their tune. Prices had gone up and the condos they remembered from before all had waiting lists now. Nashville had become an "it town."

When I'd moved from LA to Nashville, there'd been no Gulch. The Station Inn venue had long been on 12th Avenue South, and slowly an "upscale" restaurant or two opened in the neighborhood. Fascinating to watch that area transform into a trendy district of boutique hotels, luxury condos, and foodie culture. The city hadn't seen a ramen shop until 2016. It also seemed like most of the LA musicians were now ditching their digs in California and calling Nashville home. Those wise enough likely recognized they could easily cut their expenses and buy a house equal to what they'd been accustomed to for a fraction of the cost.

We started to do the Airbnb thing and rent out our finished basement on a nightly basis. Guests loved it, as it was an ideal setup, separate access around the back of the house and featuring private bedroom, living area, and bathroom. We quickly reached Superhost status. Never a bad review. Silo and I both enjoyed hosting. If the connection with our guests was mutually a great vibe, we'd often find ourselves sharing a bottle of wine and dinner with them.

Sometimes our relationship functioned best when there was company around us. We loved to entertain and loved our weekend getaways when it was just the two of us getting out of town together. Homelife aside from that was becoming routine, however, and over time less thrilling. Part of that routine was drinking, a three-hundred-dollar-a-month boxed-wine habit. Mommy wine time would start approximately an hour after the kids were home from school. Mine would begin practically as soon as I walked in the door from work. I'd pour myself a glass and join her in the Florida room. The thing about the box is you lose count of how many glasses you've had because it's so damn easy to constantly keep on repour before running empty.

And if it wasn't a pinot or cabernet, there'd be a martini waiting for me in the fridge by the time I came home. We liked our manhattans too. This went on continuously for two years. There were times I said to myself, *I'm drinking just to keep up with her.* I was getting tired of it, especially when any argument we had seemed to have stemmed from too much booze. Once, as Silo was putting the girls to bed, she was watching me pack my car up with practically everything I owned as I left for the night. I was somewhere in between wanting out and wanting to make a point. Something had to change.

I said to her one night that I was taking a break from the drinking. I stopped in an instant, I'd had enough. The next time an argument erupted, it was plain to see how one-sided it was. I uttered, "I know why you're coming at me like this," as I reached for the bottles and boxes. "This is the reason." And I drained every last drop of alcohol into the sink.

Not long after that, Silo said I had given her a wakeup call. She announced she'd made a decision to enter AA and follow through with the 12 Steps program. I fully supported her decision. If it meant taking care of the girls while Mommy was at a meeting, *done*. When she asked me to sit in on one with her, I was there. For the most part we were cool, but to think AA was going to fix everything between us would be stretching it far. We still had bumps in the road.

That year, 2016, was also the year my parents moved back to Nashville. I pleaded with them not to come, arguing how they'd just been there a year before and had seen how difficult it was to find a place. "You're barely paying nothing in Vegas, why do you want to move again and pay more than what's feasible?" Maybe part of it was boredom and restlessness, the other was the feeling of wanting to live close to me again, particularly in their old age. Another reason or excuse my dad used was that my brother was gambling every day in Vegas, and they had to break away from that. These phone calls went on for a couple of months and ended the same way, with me shouting, "DON'T COME!" I feared them being in the same city would be a strain on me and an interference to my homelife.

I planned ahead of time and set them up in a townhouse in Murfreesboro, about forty minutes outside of Nashville. There was no sense in waiting until they got to town, as last time they'd intended to move here had proved to be uneventful. I had to take the reins so at least they could be situated upon arrival.

Silo was warm and inviting towards them, often she'd ask me to have them over to join us for brunch or dinner. Table etiquette was a lost art in my family, they were used to their ways—if a plate was in front of them, they'd just dig in. I can still see the horror on Silo's face; she was accustomed to saying a prayer at the dining table before meals. I get the "setting an example for your children" part, nevertheless it was refreshing to skip over that every once in a while. My parents enjoyed visiting, though Mom and Dad never really expressed what they thought of Silo. I imagine it was odd for them to see me in a fatherly role with a family they didn't know. Eventually after some time, my mom would tell me I should find someone young enough to have a child of my own with. My brother weighed in on it as well, putting it more bluntly by saying, "You gotta leave this bitch, stop wasting your time with someone else's kids." I wouldn't say they deliberately set out to sabotage me, but they could be very opinionated to the point where I don't know if they ever took into account what my feelings might have been, because they were never asked or discussed.

Silo and I were complete opposites. She would think systematically, and I more creatively. Our tastes were different, our goals weren't the same. Sometimes these qualities bring you together, and sometimes they're the decisive factor that keep you apart. For all my affection for her and the two girls, there was an unsatisfying feeling enveloping me. I tried to convince myself I was good, presenting an image on the outside that we were solid. Silo once said to me, "I need to know that this is enough for you." For anyone simple it likely would be. We had a fantastic house, a mix of midcentury and ranch, the type of house you come home to and feel rich in.

I had the love of three under one roof. Still not enough. I told Silo that until I achieved everything I'd set out to accomplish, there was going to be an empty, unfulfilled part of me. A harsh truth that probably put up another red flag. Regardless, for the past two years she would ask when I was going to put a ring on her finger. She knew of my creative drive from day one, never did it take away from my commitment to love and show her that she was cared for. Still, she resented that our goals weren't aligned. "What if you don't get to make your movie?"

"I'll find a way." I understood her wanting me to be content, but to just settle as we were was not an option I was ever going to be satisfied with.

One of my outlets for escape was hitting up all the local record shops on the weekends. Vinyl fanatics are a funny bunch, flipping through the bins becomes a kind of sport, mastering the technique of how fast you can flip through each title. You start to recognize the same people, and nothing pisses you off more than when someone walks up next to you and parks his ass to flip through the next stack before you do. If I didn't score at the shops, then I'd troll online and get my LPs off eBay or Discogs. It was habit-forming, just like when I was a kid. Silo was not too pleased. "You don't even have a turntable," she'd say. That was beside the point, the fun was the hunt. Bitching over money and how I spent part of the surplus was not a flattering look on her. Just as working only to pay bills was a surefire way for me to become miserable.

What started as a simple "We're a little short this month" from my family turned out to be a regular thing. I was being asked by my parents every other week to somehow help them financially. Mom, Dad, and Scott alternating calls, so it wasn't recurrently the same one on the phone doing the asking. The rent, the electric bill, the car payment, all on steady rotation. It pissed me off that it fell on me. My brother made no effort to get a job, but then that had been his story since always. I soon got my side hustle on.

While earning extra had become essential, truth be told, I also welcomed a break from the monotony at home. Ubering around town doing the rideshare thing essentially gave me time for myself. A way to clear my mind. Just get in the car and drive, and make a lil bit of scratch doing it.

It kinda became addictive. Driving people throughout the city and seeing how excited they were to be in Nashville gave me a different perspective on where I lived. It allowed me to see this place in a new way that I could appreciate. I discovered cool haunts and restaurants by way of my passengers, making mental notes to check things out at a later time. Silo benefited from this on our date nights, one of the ways I tried to make up for lost time. I recognized I was gone quite a lot. Leaving a gift of perfume on her night table or a card to say I love you were nice gestures at first to compensate for my absence, but after a few months of getting home after midnight while she was fast asleep, this wasn't helping our relationship any.

I felt like I was doing a juggling act, trying to take care of multiple things, whether that was helping my parents out, spending time with Silo and the girls, or catching up with friends. I was also steadfast in making time for music again. After a couple of years of not writing any new songs, or barely picking up the guitar to play, for my own well-being it was a necessity I return to it. I hated the feeling of being stale, of having forgotten how to play parts of my own songs, of not having any inspiration or intuition when I turned to my instruments. In a way I had let myself down.

When I work on music, it's a personal process I like to be alone with. I typically lock myself up in a room. I get peeved if there are interruptions. Silo was respectful of this. She also had the idea of turning one of the bedrooms into my music room, which I was thrilled to do. On one occasion she brought me up a cup of tea and sat in to have a listen. I was running through an old song of mine, one with metaphoric and imaginative lyrics. Silo didn't really have any sort of reaction to it. If anything, maybe she was perplexed.

I hiccupped a slight chuckle, and somewhere in between a statement and a question I delicately said, "You don't get it." With the same matched tone, she unashamedly replied, "No, I don't." And that's all right, it wasn't validation I sought. The facts were, beyond a few shared interests we just didn't get each other.

In the fall of that year, my cousin Eric invited the family to his daughter's wedding, offering to take care of hotel accommodations if we could make our way to New Jersey. Scott offered to do the fourteen-hour drive, and everyone was happy to go, except for me. He'd already put the guilt trip on me that I only visited Mom and Dad once a week and when would we all have the chance to be together like this and see the rest of the family if not now. Not to mention they'd started to muse over the idea of leaving Nashville once their lease was up. The thought of a long road trip, stuck in a car for more than half the day, having to endure discussions I didn't want to have, left me leaning on the side of not going.

On the day of the trip, when they called to say they were leaving and asked if I was coming with them, I could feel their sadness when I declined. I used the excuse of having too much work to do. Once I knew they were on their way, I started having second thoughts. If I got a last-minute deal on a flight, perhaps I could just meet them there. Suddenly the trip sounded better to me: fly into NYC, spend the night in the city, take the bus to Jersey in the morning. I suppose I prefer doing things on my own terms.

It had been over twenty years since we'd last seen Aunt Jean, my dad's sister. They didn't speak so often, but when they did call each other, she would always ask to say hello to me. I remember her visiting once during my childhood. The next time we were together was when we lived in New York and drove to see her. She prepared tuna salad for us that day. I watched in amazement how the process took an hour, considering it was literally one can of tuna fish. More shocked how it was shared among six people.

As hungry as we were, funny how no one attempts to dish the last scoop. Jean was kinda kooky, I could appreciate that. She had always wanted to be an actress and loved hearing about my musical pursuits—anything related to the arts and she'd come alive. She gave me a gift that day; as she rummaged through the closet, she handed me a vintage Yves Saint Laurent double-breasted velvet blazer that had once belonged to my cousin. It fit me perfectly then and still does.

At the time of the wedding in New Jersey, Jean was suffering from late-stage Alzheimer's. We'd known about this beforehand, though it didn't really prepare my dad for the moment. I was helping myself to hors d'oeuvres when my brother walked by and said, "We found Jean." My dad was in tears. Even with the time he'd tried lifting up one of our sick horses off the ground and had suffered dislocation in his back, this was the first time I'd seen him cry. Nothing hurts more than the heart.

All those years of not talking to each other and now not being able to had caught up to him. When I sat next to Jean, I held her hand, she wouldn't let go. She looked at me, clutching my hand while smiling. I'm certain she recognized me.

The following day, before the drive back to Nashville, we had breakfast with Eric. This time it was his turn to cry. To be honest, I think all of us were overwhelmed and appreciative to be together. I was glad I had decided to be there. My brother was right, the chance for us to do something like this didn't come along so often. A great memory had been made.

Oddly enough the fourteen-hour drive home was also enjoyable. It didn't hurt that I stopped in at a record shop along the way and in less than ten minutes I had amassed $200 in used records. Lightning-fast finger work. The clerk himself was taken aback, he was on the phone and cut his call short when I approached the counter. "I gotta go, this guy just brought up a stack." *Note to self: don't tell Silo.*

Sometime around the December holidays, Silo made plans to take the girls and visit friends of hers in Atlanta. She extended the invitation if I'd like to come along. Nearly three years as a couple and we had yet to do an out-of-state trip as a family.

My own family were now officially going back to California the following month. I opted out of Georgia to ensure that I spent quality time with my folks while they were still around. Perhaps the wedding in Jersey played a small part in my decision. The simpleness of inviting them over for dinner and having them stay the night was rewarding for me. Except when my mom would talk about moving back to LA and she'd say, "Come with us," with little regard that I was secure in my own home, or assuming the life I've made in Nashville was something to just drop on a dime and leave behind.

I felt a sense of relief as January rolled in and they moved. I was drained, both mentally and physically exhausted by trying to balance what seemed like a dual life, how I was with Silo and attempting to be a good son. To a certain extent, my relationship with Silo suffered as a result of them being in Nashville. I know my choices in helping my parents financially had an impact on her feeling ignored, yet I couldn't disregard my mom and dad's situation either and not help them. Despite her thinking I should be setting boundaries, I wasn't going to turn my back on my parents.

A nice break came that month when my work sent me to a buyers' convention in Atlanta. We had a great three-day stay full of hotel sex, dinner at our favorite restaurant, the Kimball House, and shopping at the Buford Highway Farmers' Market.

It felt like we were on the path to rebuilding our nest. We could enjoy each other this way, but achieving it at home was often lost on us. Maybe we were just best as part-time lovers. We had our three-year anniversary, which intriguingly fell on February 24, Desi's birthday. Four days later, Silo greeted me in the living room to say, "This isn't working," and that we needed to come to an amicable separation. She tried to soften it by asking me to give her the summer to work on herself.

There was no arguing, it was rather evident to us both that this is where it had been headed. No pack up your stuff and go; she said if I didn't move out until May, that would be fine. Although I wasn't looking to drag it out, a few weeks later I had a temporary plan.

I'd be moving out on the first of April. On second thought, I deliberately changed it to April 2, to avoid being a fool on April Fool's Day. But then it looked like my move-out date would be delayed some. I came down quite ill with influenza. In all my life I don't recall ever being sick like that. Shivers, cold sweats, muscle pain, even my testicles were aching.

Days spent in bed turned to night, I was still running a low-grade fever yet somehow feeling horny as fuck. Maybe my subconscious was speaking to me, "Hey now, you're gonna be on your own for a while, you might wanna do something here." In the morning, over coffee, Silo was all smiles. "Last night was wonderful," she remarked. It had been, but I didn't hold back in telling her that I still thought we should follow through with our plan, otherwise before we knew it we were just going to end up the same way we'd been going.

She agreed, until the next night when heavy petting resumed, "Now I'm getting confused," Silo said. The mind speaking one thing, while our body language completed its own sentence.

16

TRUST IMAGINATION

In true kid fashion, when April, the eldest of Silo's daughters, overheard us discussing our issues, she burst out, "Does that mean you're moving out?"

"Yes, it does."

"Who's gonna make my dinner?!" she said, horrified. Silo had been waiting for a more opportune time to tell them, but it unfolded as it did. A child will tell it to you straight. Like the time post move-out when Silo arranged for me to have lunch at the school because April really wanted to see me. While she ate her sandwich and cheesy crackers, I was trying to be grown-up about it and told her that Mommy and I were having some time apart right now. Suddenly the six-year-old became more like the adult, "You have to listen to me, Mommy says you're never coming back to live with us."

The first week apart was in the bag. *This is going to be fine.* By the end of the following week, I was missing the life I used to have. Silo asked that I come for dinner, provided I pick something up at the store. Perhaps everyone missed my cooking, although visiting would also allow for the girls to have an easier transition. This only gave me feelings of being homesick. Silo added again that the summer was important to have to ourselves. Maybe she was buying insurance for her own emotions by saying this, instead of just calling it what it was, *a breakup*. I suppose it's more comforting for the other person this way. Regretfully I played right in to it.

I needed some distraction to take my mind away from this. New York had always been my safe place and there was no better time than now to just book a flight and go. Unexpectedly I received a text from her while I was there, expressing pleasantries. Days later, soon as I arrived back in Nashville, she called to invite me over. A little confusing when she was saying she needed space, but then wanted me to drop by.

To take a deeper look at her disposition and mine, I sought counseling for the second time in my life. The only pickle being the sessions occurred once every other week. So, to supplement for the in-between days, I would attend Al-Anon meetings, a support group for family members of alcoholics. The beginning stages of those meetings were valuable. Some of my friends thought of it as overload, but I didn't see it as such. With all my activities, I had a full schedule and preferred going at it hard.

At times I'd find myself overthinking. *If I do this, will it result in such and such?* A therapist can help bring clarity to this type of pondering. I debated whether I should send Silo a letter, stupid shit like that. If I can give any romantics advice out there, it would be don't be a jackass and send letters after you've split up. I did. #Dumb. Soon I learned it was a form of compulsion. I'd worry about things I had no control over. I needed to let go of self-made fear that the distance created more distance. I could accept that the relationship had ended, my problem started when I thought of the good parts and then I wanted it back. I suppose I invited those feelings in. Getting beyond it all was a lot like pursuing a music career. It required unreasonable amounts of patience and emotional stability, and the ability to feel real discomfort without trying to ignore it.

Eventually, I bawled my eyes out, though it wasn't during a session. It happened through music. My own song "Move On," aptly titled, allowed me to grieve. The emotions that hit me were a culmination of being on my own and realizing how far I'd come, only to end up right back at the starting point. In some way I put on my own music to remind me of who I was.

Once I heard Desi's words "It's not over," it was like her voice was there in the song to offer reassurance that I was going to be okay. It all played too loudly on my heartstrings. At the core, I had been holding on to Silo out of fear of being alone. Worried that my middle-aged existence might have its limits. The time was now to concentrate on myself, face fear, and kick this codependence junk aside. Truthfully, embracing being alone was quite liberating. I had options.

I became ironclad in doing things that fed my soul. I took road trips, went to concerts, committed to exercise five days a week. With all I was immersing myself in, I exhausted the desire for seeing a therapist and Al-Anon meetings altogether. At first it was comforting to go around the room and share my thoughts as a way of healing. There came a point, though, where it sounded like complete regurgitation. Nothing against those who are caught up in repeating their same story, I empathize with them. For myself, gratification came from other activities. With a guitar in hand, I could articulate my feelings. At the gym I could see the results in the mirror. In more ways than one I was finding my strength again.

During this period of being on my own, I recurrently would see the number forty-four appear. It showed up everywhere and anywhere. Most particularly when I would wake up during the night—2:44 a.m., 3:44 a.m., whichever hour it was, the end numbers were the same double digits. Forty-four also happened to be a number associated with Silo and her ex. My initial thoughts of seeing this was that they were getting back together. It pissed me off, until, the more the number reappeared, I realized it couldn't be a sign for only that alone. This was more significant. I started believing as my forty-fourth birthday was approaching that this symbolized something special coming. This would continue for months after, well into the new year, a way to remind me that I was on the right path.

New York City would get a couple more visits from me in the fall. I could no longer see any benefit of staying in Nashville. With my short-term rental due to expire, it made no sense to me to renew the lease. Plus, the job I had didn't provide enough growth potential. I needed a better opportunity, more out of life than work, sleep, repeat.

I gave my resignation, put my belongings in storage, and headed East once more. Mostly to buy myself some time to figure out which city I would next call home. Being there in NYC with my *Full Sleeve* partners, I could stay on top of Chad better than I had from a distance. It seemed anytime the three of us were together, things got done to keep the project moving. One box checked for the pros of staying in New York. I crashed at my friend Eric's pad on the Upper West Side, with a welcome to stay as long as I liked, if I did the cooking and pitched in here and there. Nighttime, though, not so simple in this studio apartment. TV on too loud, too much smoking, too many visitors. One time I got back after midnight and there was some strange dude sleeping on the floor. I didn't consider myself old, but at my age I was *too old* for that shit. Too many boxes checked for the cons of not staying.

A certain souvenir I kept from 1984 resurfaced as I packed up while preparing to move, a concert T-shirt that Mick Mars from Mötley Crüe had signed for me when I met them during Ozzy Osbourne's Bark at the Moon Tour. He wrote in permanent ink, "Ken, Get Rude!" Was I doomed from my youth to always be the nice boy? Maybe Mick had a sixth sense that the eleven-year-old me would benefit more in this world if I applied some attitude. I always wanted to practice being an asshole.

Better late than never. With my new approach to building a better beast, I gave it a test run first by keeping my phone calls with my parents very curt, making sure I got my point across that I wasn't going to continue paying their bills. In California, they'd had no choice but to tighten their belts, but in Nashville, them depending on my contributions had been made out to seem like a life-or-death situation. Naturally it still agitated me when they asked if I'd be coming out West now. I didn't want to be around family dysfunction. The thought of returning to live under the same roof, even if just temporarily, was upsetting. Yet the possibilities of what else I might encounter being back in LA weighed heavy on the optimistic side.

From the East Coast I drove cross-country to the West Coast, with an overnight stay in Nashville to pick up my things from storage and load up my car. It's quite remarkable how I utilized every square inch to cram in a Vox AC30, four guitars, my entire record collection, two bust sculptures, and blankets and pillows to cover it all up. With the car totally bogged down, the engine moaned the entire trip. I prayed for the car to not crap out on me. My second overnight was in Amarillo, Texas. I got there in time for dinner to order a steak at a place famous for serving the seventy-two-ounce challenge. *Yeah, gonna need to sleep this one off.* More than forty hours of driving, I did it in three days.

California State Route 138 in the middle of the night felt like a strange ride, over many dips in the road coming into the Antelope Valley. GPS indicated I had twenty minutes to my destination, I was also getting close to empty on gas. It was mostly all desert around me. Once I approached some sense of what resembled a city, I could've sworn I'd just passed a prison or detention center. I wondered where the hell my parents had moved to. I wasn't too jazzed showing up at their door in this run-down neighborhood. My mood didn't suggest the kind of family reunion they might've been looking forward to. It was late, so I resigned myself to the couch and would face my new surroundings in the morning.

The house was a complete fixer. It's not worth mentioning the details because if you know about fixers, then you know practically everything was wrong with it. Pretty sure I drove into LA that day as fast as I could. I'd gotten to California just in time for Halloween. A good dose of going out on the eve of in Hollywood quickly had me appreciating being back on the West Coast. It was like I'd lived an entirely different life in Nashville and was now getting in touch with my roots. The only bouts of frustration came from having to hole up at my parents' house in Palmdale for the time being. I found it depressing.

A week later, though, I had a job. I'd wasted no time searching the online employment sites and jumped at the first offer, a seasonal position managing a kiosk for the holidays. I wore an apron and sold goddamn sausages. Humiliating at first, oh well, suck it up, it got me out of the house and paid my bills. Barely. I saw the first signs of my parents' boredom when they practically begged me to take them along one day on my way to work.

"You're gonna spend eight hours in a shopping mall, doing what?" I asked.

"We don't mind, it's fun for us," they said, as if this were routine. I gave in a couple of times. They sat in the food court most of the day. Employees in the mall bought them lunch because they saw these two old people hanging around for hours on end and probably thought they were homeless.

Let old acquaintance be forgot, never more appropriate than when January 2018 rolled in. I remained optimistic something good was coming, still seeing the number forty-four appear. Another job quickly came my way—from meat sticks to luxury vehicles, I did a brief stint for one month at Infiniti of Beverly Hills. I loathed all the financing terms, but taking test-drives, talking to people, consuming unlimited amounts of coffee, and having an office space to duck into throughout the day was cool. I sold a few cars, though not enough to see a commission check. Fortunately I was getting paid a base rate, except I was just breaking even. After gasoline and my car payment, I was broke.

I knew I wasn't going to last there more than the first month, which is why I took full advantage of the office space, spending many hours on the phone sending résumés out. What came next was a blessing. At the start of February I was contacted by a consultant for a King Tut exhibition, which was due to open in Los Angeles for a ten-month run and then travel to cities all over the world for the next seven years. This was a traveling management position.

I was informed the chosen candidate would be required to move to every city the exhibit toured in. When asked if this would be okay with me, I gave the purest answer without having to think about it, "Well, ever since I was a kid, I always wanted to be in a rock n roll band and tour the world, so I guess this is the next best thing." She laughed and mentioned one of the bosses I'd be reporting to used to be in an eighties hard rock band. This broke the ice for a nice, lengthy conversation. I had three phone interviews in one week. The most important call of the three I did while sitting in my car. I was on my lunch break and on the phone for nearly an hour. When the call ended, I was drenched in sweat from either the hot leather seats or nerves. After the third interview I received the offer letter and happily accepted my new position as merchandise manager with IMG.

Exciting to be part of an exhibition from the ground up. I arrived on site at the Science Center in downtown LA with twenty-one days in front of me to get retail operations set up and functioning in time for the preview gala night and grand opening. I hired my entire staff of more than forty employees and trained them all, identifying those who worked most efficiently and deciding where to assign them. A room full of different personas. Put operations aside, the main part of the job was managing all the personality types. Those first couple of weeks were nutty, there was no blueprint, it was hit the ground running and figure it out. Countless individual merchandise SKUs all housed in a complete separate building on site designated for the storage. Familiarizing myself with it all was a task in itself. Many products from Egypt had no description. They did, however, come with Egyptian dust and an ass-like musty funk. Now there was something else N95s could have been useful against.

The success of the exhibition was phenomenal. Sold out daily. Retail revenue insane. I put in fourteen-hour days, if not more, every day, because I gave such importance to it. I'd been given an opportunity to tour the world with something celebrated and historical, this further fueled me to prove to the company that they'd made the right selection in hiring me.

I approached my work with the mentality that Paris, the next city on the tour, was riding on how I performed in LA, as well as treating the store as if it were my own, because in many ways it was. I didn't want to let anyone down, most of all myself. The responsibility was mine. If I wanted something done, best to do it myself, I thought. There was never a dull moment. Multitasking like a madman. A visitor once asked me what my involvement was in the exhibit, I told them I put out fires. I didn't even have time to see the entire collection myself until five months into it. Meredith, the GM, laughed at this but could relate, both of us were beyond busy. "When we close tonight come upstairs and tour it," she said. I was able to walk through at my own pace without the crowds. Seeing it this way and in the late hours added to the experience. Magical.

After midnight is when I would usually get home. Time-wise it was an easier drive than in the morning, shaving off an hour with less traffic. The only problem was I would literally be so exhausted that my eyelids would be getting heavy. I caught myself dozing and fighting off sleep too many times to count. I'd walk into the house and immediately conk out. At best I was getting four to five hours of rest. With the awful LA traffic, I'd have to wake up at five and be out the door no later than a quarter to six, just to make it on time. From the Antelope Valley, my choice route was to take the Angeles Forest Highway. Not only did it eliminate the headache of a morning commute on the 14, it was a very scenic drive. Quite awesome really. Two lanes, one in each direction, with many winding turns and steep hills.

I found it to be a pleasant way to start the day, listening to Howard Stern and Sirius XM on the way in, while taking in the beauty around me. It also became one of the moments I appreciated having a new car. I hated the high monthly payments, but I loved how it handled the turns on this highway. I got a little too carried away once when I passed a pickup truck going a tad slow for my liking. A cop was hiding out off to the side; luckily he didn't see my illegal passing, but he nabbed me for speeding.

Minutes later I got pulled over again by a different officer. I tried to reason with him, saying, "I hope you don't write me up since the first officer already did."

He asked me for the citation. "Wait, you just got a ticket moments ago and you still didn't learn?" Good point. Two tickets in one day, within a mile apart. I must've set a new record.

That brush of trouble with the law was nothing compared to what my brother was getting into. He'd spiraled right back into the dark hole of drugs and gambling. My guess is that it had started up again once they moved back to California. I'm quite sure it was his true reason for wanting to move in the first place. He'd initiated the idea of a move in Nashville, planted the seed in my parents' mind, claiming he had a friend in LA who was offering him a job. In the words of Cheech and Chong, "What, rolling dope?"

He was racking up parking and speeding tickets and eventually had his license revoked. And he still continued driving after that, until his car got impounded. In that situation I came to his rescue only once, and I swore I wouldn't be doing it a second time. I said what was the point of getting it out when the same shit was just gonna happen again next month. I was right. And then another time after that. I meant what I said. No help from me.

Scott would harass me with a barrage of phone calls and texts while I was at work. He'd send money requests from different apps; occasionally I'd send twenty bucks just so he'd go away. I had no inclination to respond to his insults, most often I'd ignore and delete. When he turned to threats, I wouldn't bother to come back to the house until days later. There were times I slept in my car. I drove to a quiet neighborhood in Echo Park and ducked out in the back seat. Sometimes I'd get a hotel room, but as this was occurring more often, that could get costly. Better, though, to spend it on myself than contribute to his bad habits.

Thankfully, a longtime friend reached out to me when most needed. She asked, "How on earth are you driving every day to and from work, back to your parents' house, and not killing yourself?" No doubt sleep deprivation was taking its toll, as was filling up the tank every two days. "If you ever feel like you don't want to drive back, you can come stay here," she said. An offer I couldn't pass up, and only thirty minutes from downtown, I could sleep in an extra hour in the morning and conserve on gas too. Talk about luxury. After the first couple of weeks, she started leaving the key outside for me, until that became "Just keep the key." I practically moved in.

At work, many VIPs came through regularly, entertainers, influencers, and the like. None, however, generated the same excitement in public as the Egyptian archaeologist Dr. Zahi Hawass. My team and I organized a few book-signing dates for him throughout the course of the exhibition. I literally saw people running to meet him and hyperventilating. I admit I was guilty of not knowing much about Zahi prior to the job. Now, when one of my assistants came into my office to tell me, "Ken, I think Billy Idol is here," you can be sure I jumped right out of my seat and made a dash to introduce myself.

I got the green light to treat my staff to a holiday party that December. They were all too eager to find out what would be on the dinner menu, considering I'd brought Thai food to our morning staff meeting on one occasion. I got some strange looks that day. Pad Thai for breakfast, why not? It's got eggs in it, delicious. One of my crew politely asked me afterwards, "Kenward, do you think next time we can just do something traditional like coffee and bagels?" They were not shocked when I announced our Xmas party would be held at the Viper Room in Hollywood. For some, it was their first time at a rock n roll club. We had the downstairs level to ourselves, with everyone taking their turn at playing DJ. The catered cuisine for the evening: Thai food.

Later in the month I flew to Paris and London in preparation for the French exhibition. First thing the Paris team asked me was how my French lessons were coming along. I thought to myself how I'd had every opportunity when I was in my twenties to really learn it. Unquestionably I'd be hiring a bilingual assistant and be able to cruise by, but damn knowing French would've been handy now.

The bulk of my days I was in meetings, either at the IMG offices or at Grande Halle de la Villette, the massive cultural center where the exhibit would be held in France. The evenings were my time to take advantage of being in Paris again and let loose. I took a rideshare and asked to just be dropped off in Pigalle. The driver gave me a tip for the night as we parted, "Go to Lulu White, you'll like." I happened to walk in on someone's holiday party. An open bar and a quartet playing Dixieland music. I spent the evening drinking with two American girls who were living abroad studying in Paris. Already making friends for when I would return a couple months later.

I'd get back to the hotel in the a.m. hours, trying my best to be as light on my feet up several flights of stairs, until I intersected with my colleague Meredith at the midway point. We'd laugh out loud in passing, the fact that neither of us could sleep. There was one solution that solved our problem, go back outside for another round. If I didn't have good resting habits before, they certainly weren't improving on this trip.

Europe had me feeling I'd reached a level in my life of security. The past roadblocks I'd hit along the way to get here seemed miniscule. I had the next seven years mapped out in front of me, and they involved living in some of my favorite European cities, as well as Australia and Japan. Like my buddy Tommy Black said to me, "You're going on a world tour with Tutankhamun. King Tut is your band."

January 13, 2019, we wrapped up the LA whirlwind. The day was like one nonstop run back and forth from storage to the store, we couldn't keep merchandise on the shelves, people were buying it up as fast as we set it down. My staff wanted to stay till the very end, even those whose shift had ended, they hung around until the last guest left. In the ten months I'd been in this job, some employees had quit, some I'd had to fire, and some who were least likely to go the distance had ended up pulling through in the end. I was gonna miss this crew, so many laughs were had. When I look back at photos from this time, I see myself healthy and happy, because despite the long hours and hard work, it was so much fun. When something is going good, it reflects outward. That night, as I was celebrating with Meredith our LA victory, my boss, Andy, sent an email congratulating us on the final numbers and how successful the entire run had been. All the more reason to keep the champagne flowing.

Everything was falling into place, until it fell apart. With less than a month to go before leaving for Paris, I received an email from my boss. It was one of those instances where just by reading the text you can feel the tone of it. "We need to talk. Call me when you wake up." I was already awake at 6:00 a.m. when my phone had dinged. I immediately walked out and got into my car to make the call. Something about cars, I always feel it's the best way to cut out all the noise around and talk in privacy.

Basically my position was in limbo. Which didn't make a whole lot of sense considering the sales for LA were through the roof, my visa had been approved, and I was dealing with a Parisian real estate agency in finalizing my living arrangements abroad. The gist of it was that word was coming from the upper heads in the London office that it would be more cost-effective to hire a retail manager locally in each city. This would eliminate salary, full-time health coverage, and accommodation expenses. Final word whether I would be onboard or not would come in a couple of days.

I drove to Vegas to clear my mind and step away from it all. If it was good news, then I'd be in Vegas to enjoy myself. If it was bad news, then I'd be in Vegas to enjoy myself. I got the call as I was walking through the Fashion Show mall. It was unanimous, I got screwed. The best compliment I received on the job came when one of my bosses asked the GM, "How's Kenward as a manager?" To which she replied, "All you have to do is watch him with his staff, they love him." In the big picture, none of that matters, though, nor does how hard you work your ass off. You hope it translates, and sometimes it does, but in the end the almighty dollar wins.

17

BLANK CANVAS

Time was in front of me, with nowhere to report to, just a clean slate ahead. I started a new project called Soft Open and released "My Favorite Records," a song I'd written before leaving Nashville and later recorded with my main music man, Rick Parker. This was a special session, as I had a surprise in store for Rick. I would be teaming him up with his ol' bandmate from Lions & Ghosts, guitarist Michael Lockwood. They hadn't worked together since 1989's EMI record *Wild Garden* and hadn't seen each other in decades. For me I was equally excited having them both on my track, as I was at the prospect of knowing this might result in them doing a future project together. I'm quite sure I volunteered to play second guitar if they ever decided to do a Lions & Ghosts reunion. Hey, the music fan in me still salivates over this kinda stuff.

The video for the song probably wouldn't exist without the help of my dear pal Charlie Overbey. I knew Charlie from my *Rockstar Magazine* days, when he had a band called Big Bang Babies. I'd become friendly with a lot of bands during that time, but Charlie and his bandmates had become bros. We'd hang, hit up the sushi bars together and the many after parties, I even guitar teched for their guitarist Keri Kelli at a number of their gigs. Back then, Charlie would also sing background vocals on my demos; my teenage voice at the time benefitted from a bit of gruff in the mix.

These days when he wasn't making his own records, he and his lady, Vanessa, ran a vintage clothing shop called Honeywood Vintage, which was also home to his other business, Lone Hawk Hats. When I proposed the idea for the shoot and said how I wanted to transform his shop into a record store, he chuckled, "I don't see how, but be my guest!" Having Charlie play himself as the shop owner couldn't have been more perfect. I love the scene where we interact, him looking real agitated as I try to purchase all the records in the shop. If you haven't seen it yet, go YouTube it!

The day after the shoot, I put my guitars back into the storage unit I'd been renting since the summer of 2018. Guitars don't deserve to be locked up, they deserve to be played. I had no other option, though, after I'd gotten a text message from Scott while I was working. It read: *Don't be mad, but I had to pawn your amp.* I walked out of the building, fuming over the phone, *YOU BETTER BE FUCKING JOKING!* I think that was the only time I left early from work. I got to the house and packed my car with everything else that was valuable to me and potentially valuable to him. No way I was going to take the chance of my guitars ending up in pawn.

At the end of March on a beautiful spring day, I went to retrieve an acoustic from the unit to take with me to the beach. This became my way of making time to play, the sound of the waves and six strings. Just a few days later, when I brought the guitar back to storage, I opened the lock and lifted the gate, only to find it had been ripped off. The victim of theft. All four of my other guitars had been stolen. At first I thought I'd gone crazy, like I was second-guessing where I could've placed them in this tiny five-by-seven box, knowing full well I'd left them in the same corner I always kept them.

Pissed would be an understatement. That saying that goes how you wouldn't wish bad on your worst enemy is rubbish, I was cursing the living shit out of these pricks. When the police arrived, an officer said this location had had many incidents and since there were no cameras on any of the floors, his assumption was that it was likely an inside job. He added how they'd come in from above, peering into each unit and going shopping. To add salt to the wound, my mom had given me two pieces of her own jewelry to hold on to, to ensure they wouldn't get pawned. Well, I'd stashed them away in what I considered to be a safe place, a guitar case. The other thing I unfortunately kept in the cases were the certificates to the guitars. Regretfully, I never wrote down the serial numbers or kept photos of them either.

With the feeling of what else could I do now, I sent emails to all the local news stations, hoping to get the word out. NBC responded and covered my story on the evening edition. I was thankful for all my friends who reposted tweets as well. Sadly, after a few months, not a single lead had arisen. None of the database searches of pawnshops matched the description of my instruments. The management at the storage facility was utterly useless. They said they'd comply with supplying LAPD with the video footage that captured the entrance and elevators, as long as it was requested by the police department, which it was. Then management claimed they didn't have a hard drive with enough space to download onto. I knew very well from my own management experience having to use surveillance cameras that this wasn't the case. So I bought a brand-new hard drive for them to use. Next, after weeks had gone by, they claimed they had technical issues trying to download the footage. Sure they did. Complete bullshit.

I'd wake up in the middle of the night with anxiety from this. I blamed my brother for pawning my amp, which had led me to put my things in storage. That wasn't cool of me, though, it wasn't him that did this. I thought if I had gone to Paris, I would've been in Europe for a year and never would have known what had happened. The thieves probably would've gone back and emptied out the entire space. My record collection, artwork, everything else I had in there could have easily disappeared. The insurance claim I had on the unit basically covered one and a half guitars. The kicker was that my dad's vintage Gibson L-50 that he'd handed down to me was among the stolen guitars. I always thought that would be the one item I'd have of his to celebrate his memory when he left planet Earth.

I'm quite certain I hit up every guitar shop from LA to San Diego in search of my guitars. The Gibson and two Gretsch hollow bodies—the White Falcon

II and 1993 Anniversary model. The Anniversary model I'd played at practically every gig, written countless of songs on. At least both these Gretsches are forever immortalized in the "My Favorite Records" video.

One of the owners I talked to at a guitar shop kind of put it in perspective when he said, "At the end of the day it's all just a piece of wood. Just be glad they didn't hit you over the head for your gear." After some time, I found a deeper meaning, that maybe this was the higher power's way of saying, *I gave you a gift and you're not doing enough with it, therefore I can take it away.* From then on I began to make a conscious effort to not only play more, but to also align myself with other musicians and put forth a new project.

"When you sell a house you can buy as many guitars as you like." That's what my buddy Jimmy Thrill told me. A fellow rocker who'd taken his swagger from the stage to the brokerage and dominated. Jimmy would be instrumental in steering me into real estate. When I'd relocated to LA most recently, we'd first chatted about it late night at a diner. Me being in the situation I was in, Jimmy witnessed as I only ate half of my BLT and wrapped the other half to take away so I could have something to eat in the morning. He must've thought to himself, *I gotta help Kenward out.* "I will be your mentor," he said. That spoke volumes to me. A year later, when the IMG job was officially over, we had the conversation again. I appreciated his vote of confidence in me and willingness to guide me along the way. Turns out real estate is a lot like rock n roll, same hustle, different game.

Back on the home front, nothing had changed. Palmdale seemed to have a distressing effect on me no matter what good was going on in my life. Of course I was still dealing with my brother's old routine, which only added to the heart rending. Any time he was around, the same demands for money would ensue. One day, I'd just finished making dinner and sat down to eat with my mom and dad when he walked in from who knows where, bullishly asking for gas money. I must've repeated my denial of his demand a few times before I snapped, "QUIT FUCKING ASKING ME, I'M NOT GIVING

YOU A DAMN CENT!" No way I was going to enable an addict. Tough love, or tough shit. He then lunged at me like a demon.

Imagine being in your midforties and fighting with your near-fifty-year-old brother, and your two senior citizen parents trying to referee. I grabbed a vase from the table; I initially wanted to hit him over the head with it, but instead it got smashed to the ground. The next couple of weeks I stayed away. Whenever I returned, I'd pick my parents up along with the dog and would tell them to grab their overnight bag. Anywhere just to get them out of the house and change up the scenery. Sometimes I felt like going as far away as possible. Once we drove up Highway 1 until we reached San Francisco. Scott would later ask, "Why do you keep leaving me alone here?" For me the answer was simple, no one wanted to be around someone who was using, especially someone who'd been doing it for thirty years.

I was losing my tolerance for bullshit. The other long dragged-out drama I was dealing with was Chad Scoff. He had been making trips into LA quite regularly during the past year. Now he was talking about how he was a major player in the cannabis business. We met up while he was in town and still the convo about *Full Sleeve* was front and center. He spoke of a video-on-demand company we'd be partnering with, yada yada yada, and how they needed to see the terms we had in place with him before they could move forward. Same old runaround. He was trying to get us to sign a new agreement with him, which we simply would not do. It was enough of this nonsense. The last exchange we had with him was in December 2019, in which I stated we would not be entering into any other contract unless it included our option fee payment. Needless to say, we never heard from him again.

There's a great proverb that goes, "You can't open new doors with old keys." Sometimes I think I've ignored that theory and gone straight to trying to jimmy doors open with a credit card. I keep looking for a way in, it's a refusal to give up. "If you stay strong, something good will come along." Words to remind myself of. Quite fitting considering I wrote them with Michael Lockwood, whom I'd first reached out to in 2002. Seventeen years later we'd finally started to collaborate. Only time decides when it's time.

One of the factors I appreciate about working in real estate is how integral cultivating relationships is. A contact I make today doesn't necessarily equal instant transaction, but how I nurture that is what counts. Six months after my official start in real estate, I landed my first listing. For all my bickering about Palmdale, wouldn't you know that's where the client's property happened to be. That's irony with a nice toothy grin, or just the way of the world, I suppose. I find it interesting how this all happened during a pandemic. It makes me think of the exhibition, had I been in Europe with King Tut, ultimately that job would have been derailed. Sometimes when our heart breaks. we get so focused on the hurt, rather than wanting to acknowledge how it very well may be for the better. I'm grateful I chose an occupation that has kept me active and in a role I absolutely get amped about inhabiting.

I watched my mom at eighty-one years old squinting her eyes while trying to thread a needle. She didn't ask for help, neither did she give up. After ten minutes she got it. Determination is something I must've inherited from her. Stubbornness, maybe that's something that comes with old age. Mom avoids doctor visits, and Dad refuses to drink water and complains about having to take his heart meds. During lockdown he caught a bronchial infection, how that's possible I've no idea, as he never left the house. It got bad, to the point where his oxygen level dropped and he had difficulty breathing. When the paramedics came, we dreaded him needing to go to the hospital, especially with the amount of Covid cases being reported. All of us worried this would be the last time we'd see him.

The worst part was when he was admitted and knowing that we wouldn't be able to visit him because of restrictions. We constantly called for an update, day and night at all hours. Amazing how the nurses and attendants were always so courteous and able to put him on the phone for us. He was under sedation to keep him calm. For the most part he thought he was in a hotel room. Every time we talked, he would ask when we were coming to get him, not quite remembering why he was in there to begin with.

I jumped to conclusions, fearing he might forget who we were and thinking maybe they were sedating him for too long. The day after he was admitted, I got up at 5:00 a.m. and drove to the hospital. That early in the morning, there was no guard at the entrance. I triple masked and walked right in. I could've made a beeline to the elevator, but a split-second decision detoured me when I saw how full the waiting room was; I'd be crossing the danger zone. In that moment of hesitation, an attendant made sure to show me the way out. When I got home, I found myself doing something I hadn't done since my bar mitzvah, I put on a kippah and tallit and prayed. A promise to the universe that if he made it through this, I would see to it that I carried on praying this way every Saturday when I woke up. So far I've made good on my word.

Dad was in there for three days. Once his vitals reached normal levels again, he was discharged. He would be under hospice care at the house now. The report stated he had about 30 percent heart functionality left, in addition to dementia. When he settled back home, he marveled how great it was to be back in this house again. Despite how we'd all criticized the house before, at this moment, he was absolutely right. By this time, Scott had passed the one-year mark of staying clean. He'd taken up the hobby of home improvement and watching the *Property Brothers*. With a fresh coat of paint he'd slapped on throughout the house, along with installing some simple fixtures, he'd actually made the house more livable.

The pandemic put things into perspective. It taught us how to appreciate what we do have. We have each other. In my adult life I've moved around with my family being in my shadow. I wanted desperately to live away from them in LA, and what happened, for the safety of not traveling back and forth from one place to the other, I ended up being with them more than ever. I keep telling myself it's just temporary. For the most part it's not so bad. Mom keeps me laughing, even though at times it feels like I'm living in a crazy house. She found a photo of my dad from 1959, he was pictured with two children. My mom acted startled. While staring at it, she said, "Look at that, he had another family."

She's taken up talking to the TV. Whenever CNN is on, she's convinced they can see her. Sanjay Gupta is her favorite. With Dad on hospice care, we brought another TV into the bedroom to make it easier for him. This upset Mom, she got angry and exclaimed, "Now they're gonna see where I sleep and shit!" Dad raised his voice and rebutted, "They can't see you!" This goes on practically every day.

"Growing old sucks," Dad said. Seeing him hunched over, walking slow like a turtle, losing his hearing, losing his appetite, yeah I saw what he meant. In a couple of years I will turn fifty, and I'm okay with saying that. The strange thing about age is, I could be watching a movie from thirty years ago and still see myself as younger than the actors on screen, even though I'm way older today than whatever age they're portraying in the film. It must be a trick of the mind. I don't believe age is a detriment, you're never too old to rock. The proof is right there with the Stones, McCartney, and countless other veteran acts still going strong while younger audiences keep on discovering their music.

After a three-year gap of not speaking with Desi, just like always, whenever her memory comes back to visit me and books an extended stay in my brain, I know we're about to communicate again. It's something telepathic I can sense, I'm quite certain it's mutual. I was wrong, however, in thinking that our conversations would always drift back to the past. We often talk about our families and present-day activities. Not a single word about the past. Maybe I'm the one haunted by it. Sometimes I still can't believe the way my life has turned out, that it hasn't added up (yet) to how I envisioned it.

When I was a kid, up into my twenties, you couldn't convince me that I'd be doing anything other than playing to arenas full of Kenward Cooper fans. When I moved to Nashville in my thirties, I thought for sure I'd land a publishing deal and be among the Music City songwriters getting my songs placed and cut. I networked like life depended on it, I got in on sessions with viable talent and persisted to get in front of industry people to hear my songs.

How long do you persist before throwing up two middle fingers? It's like a hand grabs me by the collar as I'm moving ahead and tugs me to the back of the line. Yet, I persevere. But it's still heartbreaking, thirty-two years after I was in my first record company meetings, to think that I still haven't gotten my shot. I wanted it 24/7, 365 days, year after year. I believed the arts to be my calling. It wasn't supposed to happen this way. Onward and upward, though, right? I worked with a girl who once told me the way she remembered my name was because it reminded her of the phrase *onward and upward*, and *Kenward* should be the next word that follows. So, onward and upward I go. There are songs left to be sung and movies still to be made.

I have various music projects I'm working on, one of which Desi and I have begun collaborating on remotely. It excites us to talk about putting out a new product, without stressing out every day about how we've gotta get signed. These days, self-financing and self-promotion is the norm. The true spirit of independence is more prevalent than ever. When I think about it, I've taken the DIY route as far back as when I was that kid who started his first fanzine. I don't pretend that the business model hasn't changed, or that consumer commitment to music isn't fleeting, that's all beside the point. The same philosophy still holds true in that I do it because I love it and on account of it being in my DNA. No matter the result. At this stage, whether I'm in front of the camera, or behind the scenes, or in no scene at all, it doesn't change a thing, as long as I keep creating. I never gave thought to having a Plan B, and still don't. Real estate is work, rock n roll is life.

AFTERWORD

As my business started to happen and I had three deals closing, my dad passed on through to the other side. I don't usually take much stock in my zodiac sign, but this must be what it is to be a Libra. Life throwing things all at once, see how it balances out. The night before Dad's exit, he came into my room to tell me about the gun he was leaving to me, which was already in my possession. Just a few nights before, while I was out of town for the night, Dad had woken up in the morning hours holding the gun, waving it around, thinking that someone had broken into the house. Later he told me he'd had a bad dream. Once it was put away, Mom had made sure to retrieve it and stash it away.

The gun had been in the house ever since I was a kid. He'd had a few over the years, this one was the lone survivor. That night he sat down next to me I told him not to worry, that I had it now and it was in safekeeping. There was something about the safety clip he wanted to discuss, but I assured him I was aware of it. Before he went to bed, he came back into my room to give me the gun's registration card from 1978 and said he was glad that I had it. I wouldn't have thought this would be our last conversation. I can only wonder if he had the sense that it might be. It's quite symbolic, maybe his way of saying, *Protect yourself,* or, *Now you have the power. Whatever you set out to achieve in life, go out with guns blazing.*

Some believe in the force of numbers, their patterns and energy. Dad's departure happened on May 12, 2021. When we lived in Nashville, Dad had plots reserved through the VA at the Middle Tennessee State Veterans Cemetery. Just a couple of years before, he'd left the documents for me to hold on to. After his passing, when I had to retrieve these papers, Scott broke down upon discovering the VA document was dated May 12, 2016. I could see the brilliance in it, expressing how it was all connected. Five years from the date. Five also representing the month of May.

The first night without Dad, I drifted in and out of sleep. Each time I awakened, I wondered why he hadn't come to me in a dream yet. After hours of anxiety, once I finally gave into the desire to grab my phone to look at the time, hoping it was closer to morning than midnight, the glow staring back at me read 4:44.

ABOUT THE AUTHOR

Kenward Cooper is a man of many passions. Music will always be number one. He's been a ghostwriter on a hit song and has licensed his music for television. With an urge to tell stories in another creative form, he immersed himself in the craft of writing screenplays. *Rock N Roll Will Only Break Your Heart* is another extension of his writing and his first book.

kenwardcooper.com
IG: @glam_bone

The sixteen-song *Rock N Roll Will Only Break Your Heart* companion recording is available in the metaverse as a free stream at audius.co/glambone. Scan the QR code for details.

Lightning Source UK Ltd.
Milton Keynes UK
UKHW010645090223
416681UK00006B/1382